D1044213

To the memory of my husband
H. Warren Dunham

Contents

Introduction to enlarged and updated edition

> ... in Stalin's time, when three people
> were afraid to get together under one
> roof.... —Aleksandr Solzhenitsyn,
> *The Gulag Archipelago*

Stalin loved applause, and it was bestowed on him lavishly. In the *Gulag*, Solzhenitsyn describes a district party conference at which everyone rose to applaud the great leader. The applause continued for ten minutes and still no one could risk being the first to stop applauding. Finally, the director of a paper factory sat down, permitting all the others to follow suit.

That night the director was arrested. He was reminded in the process never to be the first to stop applauding. In written transcripts of such occasions the phrase "stormy applause" provides no precise data about duration, other than the occasional use of "prolonged." However, the individuals responsible for the set of records containing Stalin's speeches evidently dared not abbreviate the applause, which covers an entire side of one record.

Stormy applause bestowed on others upset Stalin. It identified a threat to his authority, which had to be supreme. The applause bestowed on Sergei Kirov at the Seventeenth Party Congress in Moscow in 1934 sealed his doom. The applause bestowed on Vsevolod Meyerhold at the First Congress of Soviet Directors in June 1939 precipitated his arrest several days later and his death by revolver in the cellar of the Lefortovo Prison in February 1940. The applause bestowed on Akhmatova when she read her poetry in Moscow in 1944 was remembered in 1946. The applause bestowed on Golda Meir when she attended the central synagogue in Moscow in 1948 also had serious repercussions.

Strangely enough, the applause bestowed on Boris Pasternak during a poetry recital at the Polytechnic Museum in Moscow on 23 February 1948 did not have serious repercussions – even though Pasternak avoided altogether the topic of the recital, "Down with the Warmongers! For a Lasting Peace and People's Democracy!" In fact, he galvanized the packed hall by reciting his prewar poetry; when he forgot the lines, members of the audience shouted them to him.

This event, in the context of Pasternak's frequent failures to cooperate with the party during the thirties, should have led to his arrest. How did he escape the camps? No one can provide a definitive answer, but some attribute his survival to the cryptic condolence that he extended on the death of Stalin's second wife, Nadezhda Allilueva, in November 1932. She had evidently dared to condemn Stalin's collectivization policies at a dinner party. His response was so violent that she left the party. The next morning she was found shot – presumably a suicide. Pasternak refused to add his signature to the standard expression of sympathy signed by thirty-three of the nation's foremost writers and published in *Literaturnaya gazeta* on 17 November 1932. Instead, he recklessly added the following curious postscript:

I share the feeling of my comrades. On the night before, I was thinking deeply and intently about Stalin in my capacity as an artist – for the first time. The next morning I read the news. I was as shaken as if I had actually been there, living and seeing.

This postscript, with its various heresies, could have spelled Pasternak's doom. Instead, in its suggestion that Pasternak had somehow been a spectral witness of the mysterious tragedy, it seems to have served as a talisman.

Stalin infused his society with fear that was intense and pervasive. Nadezhda Mandelstam recalls in her memoirs how people lay awake at night hoping not to hear the elevator. Then, if they heard it, hoping that it would not stop at their floor. And then, if it did, waiting for the knock. People trained themselves to watch what they said, even in front of their friends and their children. Children were encouraged to report heretical utterances, or, in all innocence, the children might repeat at school something they had overheard at home. The room might be bugged. The telephone might be tapped. The secret police were everywhere. Guilt was collective. Individuals who spoke too freely endangered not only themselves, but their entire families. The only bond that survived these infernal pressures was the bond between husband and wife.

Vera Dunham's seminal book *In Stalin's Time* describes the result of this process:

Ubiquitous controls over all forms of social life allowed only one kind of relationship: that of each citizen directly to the person of the dictator himself. This bondage led to the undercutting and eventual severance of connecting tissues between the citizens. Having crushed the sense of group solidarity, Stalin achieved atomization among his subjects. [p. 25]

Professor Dunham expresses the inexorable movement toward dictatorship as a transformation of pronouns, which began with the rejection of the first person singular (the condemnation of Akhmatova to silence during the twenties, the attacks on Pasternak) and the apotheosis of the first person plural (Kirillov's "We"). Following this was the shift to third person singular (masculine, with a capital letter) in the thirties, the shift to second person singular during the war, and finally the problem of finding the right pronoun during the postwar years.

Postwar Stalinism is, in fact, the core of Professor Dunham's book. The regime was searching for a model that would allow it to retract the freedoms granted during the war without losing the popular support that had accrued. The 1917 model exemplified by Kirillov's "We" was clearly obsolete. Further evidence of this fact may be found at the end of the second volume of Mikhail Sholokhov's *Quiet Don* in the eloquent speech of Anna Pogudko:

"And besides, how poisonous and petty seems any care for the achievement of one's own individual little happiness at the present time! What does it signify in comparison with the uncompassable human happiness which suffering humanity will achieve through the revolution? Isn't that so? We must be wholly absorbed into this struggle for liberation, we must ... must fuse with the collective group and forget ourselves as isolated parts." Gently, like a child in sleep, she smiled at the corners of her tender yet strong mouth, and a wavering shadow lay on her upper lip because of her smile. "You know, Ilya, I perceive the future life like a distant, distant, magically beautiful music. Just as one sometimes hears it in sleep.... Do you hear music in your sleep? It is not a separate, slender melody, but a mighty, growing, perfectly harmonized hymn. Who doesn't love beauty? I love it in all, even its smallest manifestations.... And won't life be beautiful under socialism! No more war, no more poverty or oppression, or national barriers ... nothing! How human beings have sullied, have poisoned the world! How much human misery has been poured out!" She turned passionately toward Bunchuk and sought for his hand. "Tell me, wouldn't it be sweet to die for that? Tell me! Yes? What is there to believe in, if not in that? What is one to live for? It seems to me that if I die in the struggle...." She pressed his hand to her chest so that he felt the muffled beating of her heart and, gazing up at him with a deep, darkened glance, she whispered: "and if death is not instantaneous, then the last thing I shall feel will be that triumphant, disturbingly beautiful music of the future."

In 1940, after fighting every step of the way for twelve years to keep his novel intact, Sholokhov had to begin dismantling it almost immediately. Anna's speech was extracted from the edition of the novel that appeared in 1945. Such rampant idealism and optimism were still possible when the speech was written and published in 1928, but by 1939 the Soviet Union had been racked by collectivization, famine, and the purges. Read against the background of that history, such a speech had the resonance of a cruel joke.

Speeches of this sort are delivered by Vershinin in Chekhov's *Three Sisters*:

It goes without saying that you cannot vanquish the ignorant masses around you; in the course of your life, little by little, you will have to give way and be lost in that crowd of a hundred thousand; life will stifle you, but all the same you will not disappear, you will not be without influence. After you there may appear perhaps six like you, then twelve, and so on, until finally your kind will become the majority. In two or three hundred years life on this earth will be unimaginably beautiful, wonderful. Man needs such a life, and so long as it is not here, he must foresee it, expect it, dream about it, prepare for it; and for this he will have to see and know more than his grandfather and father knew.

In volume one of the *Gulag*, Solzhenitsyn responded indignantly to the resounding discrepancy that had apparently troubled Sholokhov:

If the intellectuals in Chekhov's plays who spent all their time guessing what would happen in twenty, thirty, or forty years had been told that in forty years interrogation by torture would be practiced in Russia ... not one of Chekhov's plays would have gotten to its end because all the heroes would have gone off to insane asylums.

Chekhov died too soon to witness the revolution and its aftermath, but Boris Pasternak was twenty-seven at the time of the October Revolution. Silenced by the oppression of postwar Stalinism, Pasternak worked secretly on *Doctor Zhivago*, which he regarded as his final testament. The novel spans the time from 1903 to 1948, but it really ends with the death of Zhivago in August 1929. Chapter 16, the epilogue, shifts the narrative from the summer of 1929 to the summer of 1943. This significant elision permitted Pasternak to omit an account of that lethal decade, which made a mockery of the idealism expressed by Kirillov, Sholokhov, and Chekhov.

Still, Pasternak violated the taboo on the camp theme, which was in effect in 1955 when Pasternak finished the novel. Chapter 15 ends with this explanation of Lara's disappearance: "She must have been arrested in the street; she must have died or vanished somewhere, forgotten – a nameless number on a list which was afterward mislaid, one woman among many somewhere in the innumerable mixed or women's concentration camps in the north." Chapter 16 prolongs the forbidden theme as it proceeds under the aegis of Dudorov and Gordon, each of whom describes his own experience in the camps.

In one of the numerous nocturnes which transfigure the novel, Dudorov, speaking to his alter ego Gordon, provides a succinct but unvarnished account of the thirties:

I think that collectivization was both a mistake and a failure. Yet no one could admit that a mistake had been made. To conceal the failure, every possible kind of intimidation had to be used to make people forget how to think and judge for themselves. They had to be forced to see what didn't exist and to assert the very opposite of what their eyes told them. This accounts for the unparalleled cruelty of the Ezhov period, the promulgation of a constitution that was never meant to be heeded, and the introduction of elections that were not based on the principle of free choice.

The Nazi invasion of the Soviet Union in June 1941 introduced a new set of horrors into a country already traumatized by a decade that began with collectivization and ended with the purges. At least this enemy had the virtue of being external. Stalin was forced to declare a truce in the war that he had been waging against his own people. Dudorov speaks:

And when the war broke out, its real horrors, its real dangers, the threat of real death were a blessing compared to the inhuman reign of the lie; these dangers brought relief because they broke the spell of the dead letter.

This was felt not just by the people who were in your position, in concentration camps, but by absolutely everyone, at home and at the front. They all took a deep breath and, with rapture, with a feeling of genuine happiness, they hurled themselves into the fearful furnace of this deadly liberating struggle.

At the very end of the novel, the time has shifted once again – from 1943 to the late forties. This time, in place of dialogue, Pasternak simply reports the thoughts of Gordon and Dudorov as they reflect on what has happened since the war:

Although victory had not brought the enlightenment and freedom that were expected at the end of the war, nevertheless a hint of freedom was in the air throughout the postwar years, constituting their only historical content.

The last part of the sentence is hard to understand, but the first part is certainly true. Stalin, wanting to make his people forget the gaping wounds that he had inflicted during the previous decade, called upon them to draw inspiration and fortitude from the heroes of their history, which no longer began in October 1917. Seeing that religion might have other uses than as an opiate, Stalin put aside the campaign against religion, which he had pursued during the twenties and thirties. Realizing the importance of enlisting the country's writers, he loosened the bonds of censorship.

After the pivotal victory at Stalingrad in January 1943 people began to think about the continuation and expansion of the greater freedom which they had been granted during the war and for which they had paid such a high price. They were, at least implicitly, encouraged to think that such would be their reward; those hopes were cruelly dashed. Within months after the end of the war, Stalin began mobilizing the weary population for what he saw as the new threat posed by capitalism. In his speech of 9 February 1946 he declared that "as long as capitalism exists there will be wars and the Soviet Union must be prepared." Mobilization required new Five-Year Plans to raise production; it also required reassertion of controls over the intelligentsia. As Professor Dunham says:

The first postwar decade, stringent and punitive, saw a wholesale assault on the intelligentsia, in which even the physical scientists came under attack, however much the country needed them. Although middlebrow fiction glossed over abrasive issues, the varnish was thin, especially in regard to stubborn scientists. In the entire social structure, only these scientists clung, at a terrible price, to a vestige of corporate cohesiveness.   [pp. 210-211]

To make sure that writers understood that they must once again toe the line, the Central Committee published on 14 August 1946 an edict condemning two literary magazines, *Zvezda* (Star) and *Leningrad,* for having published the work of Mikhail Zoshchenko and Anna Akhmatova. Both writers were expelled from the Writers' Union. The editor of *Zvezda* was fired, and *Leningrad* was shut down.

The Central Committee action against Akhmatova and Zoshchenko set the stage for the last repressive period of Stalin's rule. It was followed by an ever-widening series of attacks on institutions, groups, and individuals, including the theater repertory (too many foreign plays), contemporary music (Shostakovich in particular), and films (part two of Eisenstein's film *Ivan the Terrible* was denounced for its faulty conception of Ivan and withheld from circulation; part one, tainted by this accusation, was withdrawn from circulation).

Akhmatova had been put in jeopardy by an incident that occurred in May 1944 when she was returning to Leningrad from her wartime refuge in Tashkent. She stopped briefly in Moscow to recite her poetry to a large audience at the Polytechnic Museum. The audience evidently rose to its feet when she came out on stage. According to Nadezhda Mandelstam, Andrei Zhdanov reported this to Stalin, who supposedly asked, "Who organized this standing ovation?" Zhdanov evidently took advantage of the event to discredit his archrival, Georgy Malenkov, who had approved the publication of her new book.

The action against Akhmatova and Zoshchenko in 1946 was supervised by Zhdanov, party chief of Leningrad and primary overseer of cultural affairs for the party. Zhdanov died in August 1948. Within six months of his death a campaign against his followers took place, which came to be known as the Leningrad Case. At the instigation of Malenkov, who thus regained the prestige that he had lost over the Akhmatova debacle, all the leading Leningrad officials associated with Zhdanov were arrested and shot. It should be noted that both Akhmatova and Zoshchenko were writers indelibly associated with the city of Leningrad. The campaign against them, like the Leningrad Case, reflected Stalin's continued hatred and suspicion of the city. The University of Leningrad until recently bore Zhdanov's name, but it seems increasingly curious to honor in this way a man associated primarily with the persecution of intellectuals. The name of the city, too, is being reconsidered.

The repression took place under the rubric of anti-Westernism. It began with Stalin's aforementioned fear that the West would take advantage of the Soviet Union's weakened state. It affected writers and artists who were allegedly not putting their individual shoulders to the collective wheel (not only Akhmatova and Zoshchenko, but Pasternak, Shostakovich, Prokofiev, Eisenstein). It led to the closing of the State Museum of Modern Western Art in 1948. It spread beyond artists and writers to philosophers, economists, historians, geographers, architects, linguists, physiologists, and biologists.

Soviet work in genetics was set back by decades when the Central Committee gave its backing to the theories of Trofim Lysenko, who believed that acquired characteristics could be transmitted. Viewing "servility before the West" as a crime made it possible to dismiss Mendel's theories about genes. Stalin hoped that Lysenko's work would eliminate the chronic shortfalls in agriculture. Those biologists who held other views were liquidated. Stalin had better luck with his decision, also in 1948, to put the renowned Soviet physicist Igor Tamm in charge of a team, including Andrei Sakharov, to create a hydrogen bomb.

During the late forties another term of opprobrium made its appearance – "rootless cosmopolites" – which was reserved especially for those critics who detected any sort of Western influence in Russian or Soviet writers. Many critics were condemned for this crime; public recantations were obtained. This category was soon specifically applied to Jews. In January 1948 the great actor Solomon Michoels was killed by the secret police in a staged car accident. The Jewish State Theater in Moscow, which he directed, was closed.

Pressure against Jews intensified in the fall of 1948 when Golda Meir arrived to assume office as head of the Israeli delegation to the Soviet Union. Her appearance at Moscow's central synagogue on Rosh Hashanah was hailed by tens of thousands of Jews, awakening Jewish consciousness not only in Moscow but in the provinces. The "standing ovations" accorded to Golda Meir, like the one that had been accorded to Akhmatova a few years before, exposed a heresy that needed to be stamped out. The vastly increased number of applications for emigration were summarily rejected and those who persisted were arrested. In 1949 the last Yiddish newspaper was closed.

In 1952 dozens of Jewish intellectuals were arrested and shot. The stage was thus set for the "Jewish Doctors' Plot," which was described in January 1953 as a scheme by several doctors, most of them Jewish, to poison various prominent Soviet leaders. Supposedly, Zhdanov himself had died in this way. This plot was evidently the first step in Stalin's plan to whip up anti-Semitism, which would then have been used as a pretext to round up all Jews and send them to Siberia. This scheme was aborted by Stalin's death in March 1953. Within a few weeks it was announced that the confessions had been obtained by illegal means and that the whole plot was a fabrication.

This abbreviated account by no means includes all the repressions that took place during postwar Stalinism. The population in the camps swelled as hundreds of thousands of refugees and soldiers captured by the Nazis were forcibly returned by the Allies to the Soviet Union, where most of them were promptly sent to Soviet camps. The year 1949 witnessed not only the Leningrad Case and the beginning of the period known as the black years of Soviet Jewry, but also massive deportations from the Baltic countries – the hundreds of thousands of people who were resisting the imposition of collectivization.

Under the circumstances, it is hard to accept Pasternak's characterization of postwar Stalinism as a time when "a hint of freedom was in the air, constituting its only historical content." He expressed himself more fully in a note published by Olga Ivinskaya in her memoirs:

The tragic and harrowing wartime period was a *living* one and, in this sense, a free and blissful restoration of a feeling of community with everyone else. But when, after the magnanimity of Providence had expressed itself in victory – even one bought at such a cost – and history had proved so generous, there was a return to the brutality and chicanery of the darkest and most imbecilic prewar years, I experienced for the second time (since 1936) a feeling of shocked revulsion against the established order of things – now even stronger and more categorical than the first time.

Apart from the events already discussed, Pasternak suffered personally from the brutalities of this period. In the wake of the spearhead attacks on Akhmatova and Zoshchenko he was criticized by Aleksandr Fadeev, head of the Writers' Union, for the continuing inappropriate individualism of his work. Pasternak was particularly vulnerable during this period not only because of his Jewish origins but because of his passionate devotion to Western culture. Finally, it should not be forgotten that Olga Ivinskaya, the model for Lara, was arrested in 1949 and kept in the camps until after Stalin's death.

Under the circumstances, it is easy to fall into a monolithic conception of postwar Stalinism: the cruel dictator and his prostrate people. Vera Dunham has demonstrated the folly of assuming that everything about the era can be explained by the totalitarian model. As she says:

In Stalin's time – and even in Stalin's worst times – the regime was supported by more than simple terror, a truism still overlooked from time to time. The system did possess regenerative powers, and it was capable of responding to the pressures of postwar reconstruction. Accommodation and settlement were being used at the same time that millions suffered because of Stalin's paranoia. Despite the spread of terror, the dictatorship had to decide whether to honor wartime promises to the people – some stated, but most implicit. The risky alternative was to tear up the wartime treaty with the people. The regime chose instead a long-term middle course, and this course was that it modified its wartime treaty with *all* the people in favor of a new treaty with *some* of the people.   [p. 13]

After the war, Stalin insisted on the restoration of the third person singular with a capital letter, but he was willing to allow the first person singular as well. The regime continued to neglect the peasant, and it continued to persecute the intelligentsia. Building on the groundwork that was already being laid during the thirties, it discarded the claims of the once-hallowed worker and turned to the middleclass (*meshchanstvo*).

In her profound analysis of the features specific to this phenomenon, so different in its origins and functions from the meanings associated with the English term, Professor Dunham has made a major contribution to our understanding of Stalinism and its legacy. She shows that the Bolsheviks, in spite of all their efforts, never succeeded in eliminating altogether pre-revolutionary meshchanstvo:

It is astounding that the prerevolutionary vestiges of meshchanstvo lasted not only through the twenties, but also through the thirties and the forties, through a quarter of a century, marked for the entire population by constant pressure, terror, and disaster. Through collectivization and concentration camps, through industrialization and purges, what and who was left untouched? And then came war. Traditional antediluvian meshchanstvo ought not to have lasted, it would seem, through all that bears the name of Stalinism. Yet it did; for one crucial circumstance supported the resilience of old meshchanstvo. The men of power were kin to it, the new bureaucrat and the stakhanovite, the new army officer and the new professional. They were all *meshchane*, pulled up from the bottom of society.   [p. 131]

Building upon this vestigial stratum, Stalin began during the thirties to create a new privileged class, a new bureaucracy, which owed its allegiance only to him. That class replaced the establishment which Lenin had built and which Stalin destroyed in the purges. It acquired its privileges by its willingness to help Stalin achieve his goal of making the Soviet Union into a superpower.

Meshchanstvo was willing to offer its support in exchange for material rewards: housing, consumer goods, luxuries, and leisure time. The engineer replaced the worker as the party favorite. The partnership between the manager and the party official became preeminent. A contract was tacitly drawn up between the party and the middle class. Professor Dunham calls that contract the Big Deal. The deal had to be tacit because the party had to continue paying lip service to its old slogans.

Vera Dunham shows that the evidence to support her thesis is to be found not in the canonized literature of the time, but in the popular literature. By minutely and expertly examining hundreds of novels, plays, and poems, she shows how the revolutionary shibboleths were supplanted: in particular, the tacit endorsement of the move from public concerns to private concerns, seen in the pronoun shift from "we" to "I," in the shift from the collective to the family, from self-sacrifice to self-gratification, from proletarian austerity to middleclass comfort, from egalitarianism to social stratification. In literature this shift is reflected in the abandonment of such paraphernalia as "leather jackets, black tobacco, straight bobbed hair, bisexual boots, and barren dormitories" for pink lampshades, telltale brooches, geraniums, and canaries.

This literature is riddled with information, not all of it intended. It must be decoded. By studying the deployment of the characters, their utterances and silences, the objects with which they share their space, and the reader response to them, as well as the critical response, Professor Dunham looks behind the official slogans to draw conclusions about the values that the regime was, in fact, propagating during the period of postwar Stalinism:

The early postwar years were unhappy even for compliant writers. Official policy toward them was harsh, although they said for the most part what the regime wanted. Their compliance becomes eloquent when they succeed in obeying directives but show strain in doing so. Their default also becomes revealing when, once in a while, they cannot help deviating involuntarily from the regime's demands, and commit "errors." Whatever they do, they inform by indirection. It may seem strange that pedestrian, uninspired fiction hides anything below its surface, but it does.   [p. 29]

The foundation for this peculiar situation is the Russian tradition of veneration for the writer and the word. On that foundation the party erected the doctrines of socialist realism, which instituted a censorship not only proscriptive but prescriptive. Under conditions of extreme repression, literature offered not only guidance but the chance to participate in the social process, if only by writing letters to the editor.

In a speech made at the Third Congress of Writers in May 1959 Nikita Khrushchev shed some light on the party's view of the literary process:

The reader trusts a book which he knows to have been written by a professional author. You know of the respect for writers, for fiction, for the printed word, which the Party has inculcated in our people. This is why a literary production, even one containing serious ideological errors, may be mistaken by a section of the readers for the real thing, something to be trusted and used as a guide in life and in struggle. Judge for yourselves how harmful this literary spoilage may be to Soviet people and communist construction.

Lurking in this set of sentences is a patent falsehood – the idea that respect for the written word was inculcated by the party. Actually, this idea took root in the early nineteenth century. Here, as in so many ways, the standard was set by Pushkin – his struggle to salvage his integrity when the repressive actions of Alexander I and, in particular, of Nicholas I, made his life a nightmare. From that time forward, Pushkin became an icon for other Russian writers.

Throughout their history the Russian people had little or no voice in the selection and conduct of their rulers. In their frustration they turned to the Russian writer as someone who would understand and who would articulate their deepest aspirations. This bond was reinforced during the 1840s when the critic Vissarion Belinsky succeeded in establishing the principle that Russian writers have, in fact, a civic obligation: to write about the defects of their society in the hope and expectation that this exposure would permit such defects to be discussed and corrected. The great Russian writers who wrote in the literary ambiance created by Belinsky – Turgenev, Dostoevsky, and Tolstoy – accepted this notion of civic obligation without a tremor. The label given to this prose was "critical realism."

Knowing the people's deep respect for the writer and the power of the word in Russian society, the Bolsheviks realized from the outset that they had to harness this power. Lenin installed the censorship apparatus within months after the October Revolution, but it was not harshly used during the twenties because the party was not yet strong enough to enforce such controls. By 1929, however, Stalin had defeated his most threatening rivals, Trotsky and Bukharin. The period of relatively relaxed controls known as NEP (New Economic Policy) was terminated. The process of establishing centralized control began with the First Five-Year Plan and the collectivization of agriculture.

The stage was set for the imposition of controls on literature in the fall of 1929 when the Marxist critics launched vicious attacks on Evgeny Zamyatin and Boris Pilnyak for works of theirs that had been published abroad. In April 1932 the various writers' organizations were disbanded and the Writers' Union was created as a single organization for all writers. In August 1934 writers attended the First All-USSR Writers' Congress, at which the party promulgated the doctrines of socialist realism.

As the congress proceeded, it became clear that socialist realism entailed retention of the writer's civic obligation, but the nature of that obligation was drastically redefined. Writers were told that they were being relieved of the obligation to discern and expose the defects of their society. That would be the party's prerogative. The party would decide what those defects were and whether they should be exposed.

The new assignment given to writers was quite different – to describe only the positive features of their society. Writers had to be oriented to the people and to the party. Books were supposed to supply models which could guide the people to the communist ideal. Since literature had to contain messages that were accessible, the language had to be easy to understand. Prose (and poetry) had to be transparent so that the message would not be obscured. Proust and Joyce were explicitly rejected as models. The party would not tolerate experimentation. *Critical* realism thus gave way to *socialist* realism. The new adjective was euphemistically vague. Its lethal implications became more clear with the passage of time. Those implications appear in something that Nadezhda Mandelstam says about her husband:

In choosing his manner of death, Mandelstam was counting on one remarkable feature of our leaders: their boundless, almost superstitious respect for poetry. "Why do you complain?" Mandelstam used to ask. "Poetry is respected only in this country – people are killed for it. There's no place where more people are killed for it."

Solzhenitsyn makes the same point in a passage from his novel *The First Circle*, though the generalization is too large. It applies to the Russian situation, but not to the American. Innokenty Volodin says "a great writer is, so to speak, a second government. That's why no regime anywhere has ever loved its great writers, only its minor ones" (p. 358).

The difference between the role of the American writer and the role of the Soviet writer was succinctly expressed by Philip Roth in the *New York Times* (11 May 1981) after he returned from a visit to Eastern Europe:

I was struck by what happens to a celebrated writer there and what happens to a celebrated writer here. The differences from my point of view were almost comically vivid: in my situation, everything goes and nothing matters; in their situation, nothing goes and everything matters.

With the advent of socialist realism, writers were directed to write works on certain themes and to treat certain themes in certain ways. Thus when collectivization was encountering resistance in 1930, writers were exhorted to produce works showing the benefits. Mikhail Sholokhov put aside his work on *The Quiet Don* to carry out this directive. At the beginning of the war, writers were instructed to write works about Ivan the Terrible, showing him in a more positive light than had hitherto been the case, because Stalin wanted to encourage comparisons between Ivan and himself along the lines of the need to take harsh measures sometimes for the good of the country.

During the period of postwar Stalinism, literature, more than ever, served as a vital source of transmission to the population. As Professor Dunham says:

After the war, there was neither bread nor circuses. There were no cafes for bohemian youth, nor beaches, spas, or travel for the majority. In the gray postwar setting, reading took on new importance, partly because there was nothing else. But reading was more than a leisure activity. To a vast number of Soviet citizens, reading meant not only being *au courant*, it meant participation. It offered the reader a chance to check his own questions about postwar adjustments against the paradigms of current social issues he found in fiction. These projections directed his groping, and clarified his own quite varied aspirations by helping him understand what the system wanted of him and what he wanted of the system.   [p. 26]

Even with all the best intentions in the world, this system never worked perfectly. Eisenstein was doing his best to follow the directive in making his film about Ivan the Terrible, but he was not able to override his own artistic instincts. Sometimes it seems perfectly clear to a writer who is the hero and who is the villain in a given work, but the reader response may point to an entirely different alignment. This was the problem even in the 1860s with Ivan Turgenev's Bazarov (*Fathers and Sons*), as it was in the 1920s with Yury Olesha's Kavalerov (*Envy*), and in the 1940s with Konstantin Simonov's Kondrashov (*Smoke of the Fatherland*).

Sometimes a writer has followed the directive exactly, but by the time the work is ready to be considered or ready to be published, a new directive has come out and the work falls short. Pasternak felt that the fall of 1956 was the right time to submit his manuscript of *Doctor Zhivago* to *Novyi mir*, but as consideration of the manuscript got under way, the Hungarian Revolution occurred and controls over writers were tightened. Eventually the manuscript was rejected.

Much has changed since Gorbachev took office in March 1985. Informal discussion groups have been legalized. The monopoly of the Communist Party has been broken. Real elections have taken place. Censorship has been drastically reduced. Writers once forbidden are being published so furiously that young Soviet writers claim that they are being crowded out. Writers as heretical as Zamyatin and Nabokov are being published. More than a million copies of *Doctor Zhivago* have been published. After being rejected by the editors of *Novyi mir* in 1956, it was published by them thirty-two years later.

It took a while for the ban on Solzhenitsyn to be lifted. It looked as if his condemnation of Lenin in *Gulag Archipelago* and in his novel *Lenin in Zurich* would put him beyond the pale. In March 1987, for example, the rumor that *Cancer Ward* would soon be published was vigorously denied by Gennadi Gerasimov, who said that Solzhenitsyn is "too strong in political opposition to us." Then in July 1989 it was announced that the Writers' Union had revoked what it described as his wrongful expulsion from the organization in 1969. Excerpts from the *Gulag Archipelago* were published in *Novyi Mir* in 1989 and plans have been announced to publish his collected works in seven volumes this year.

Glavlit, the chief administrative body responsible for the ideological correctness of everything in print, continues to exist, but its chief, Vladimir Boldyrev, claims to have reduced the list of forbidden topics by half. The primary categories now enforced include the use of the press "to undermine the established socialist system in the U.S.S.R., to propagandize war, to preach racial or national hatred, to damage the country's security interests, defense capability, or public order, or to threaten public morality and health."

Apart from the fact that Soviets now have, for the first time, the opportunity to express themselves through elections, there is growing evidence, assembled by Anthony Olcott, that the fabled addiction of the Soviet citizen to books can no longer be taken for granted. More and more Soviet citizens appear to be spending their leisure time going to films, watching television, and going to discotheques. Interest in the nineteenth-century classics seems to be declining. Those wishing to read are now more inclined to choose historical romances, detective novels, or science fiction. In short, the new opportunities to participate in the political process and a growing demand for entertainment appear to have already weakened the Soviet reader's reliance on literature.

Dunham detected the early signs of these tendencies many years ago:

An evaluation of present-day Soviet writing along these lines, however, would not make as much sense. From the standpoint of the present regime and of the people, comparable materials have undergone some change in their mediating function. Even if the regime's view of the printed word as "creative" or "administrative" remains the same, there have been fluctuations in the use of controls since Stalin's death. The readership of middlebrow fiction is likely to have diminished. Soviet society has changed from being impoverished to being semi-affluent. Leisure has taken other forms, more satisfactory for the average literate person. A new divide has been erected between middlebrow and highbrow literature and writers have been splintered more than before, as have the readers, into feuding groups. And in some quarters the need for truth seems to outbid the craving for hope.   [p. 255]

The principles enunciated by Professor Dunham in her extraordinary book continue to provide essential insights into the nature of Stalinism and the techniques by which it evolved to meet changing conditions. In particular, she shows how after the war, a growing middleclass, consisting of engineers, managers, and administrators, extracted concessions from Stalin in return for its cooperation, which was crucial to the reconstruction of the country. The more relaxed controls which followed the death of Stalin permitted further entrenchment and expansion of this middleclass and the beginnings of the process by which the horrors of Stalinism could at last be exposed.

Anyone who became familiar with Professor Dunham's book when it first appeared in 1976 was equipped to understand the appearance of Gorbachev – that he did not materialize out of a population totally prostrate and monolithic. Dunham's analytic framework clarifies Gorbachev's need to meet the increasingly strident demands of that middleclass – no longer for the jellied sturgeons and creamed partridges that were available under Brezhnev, but for basic foods and medicines – meat, bread, sugar, and antihistamines – to say nothing of apartments and relief from ecological catastrophe.

Proceeding from her uncanny intuition about literature, Professor Dunham has shown how the simplest objects and events, occurring in certain matrixes and clusters, can be telltale. As the political system continues to evolve, Soviet prose and poetry will continue to be a rich source of information about incipient social change and about the reactions of the population to the changes that are taking place. Since this unique book first appeared in 1976, it has had a major impact on the study of the Soviet Union. It will always be indispensable to those who study Stalin and his successors.

RICHARD SHELDON

Preface

The subject of this book is the relationship between the Soviet regime and the Soviet middleclass citizen. In the course of my argument I often call this relationship the "Big Deal."Although its inception goes back to the thirties, the period under examination lies between the end of the Second World War and Stalin's death. Reconciling the demands of the regime and the aspirations of the middle class, this new relationship causes a lack of fit between its purpose and traditional official tenets. Although it is not discussed openly in Soviet society, this and other peculiarities of the society's embourgeoisement can be gathered by implication from popular literature.

If lasting poetry and prose had been examined, the source material would have lain altogether outside the regime's set of values. That is why I have chosen evidence largely concordant with official views on Soviet goals. This literature is didactic and unimaginative, the perishable output of safe writers. It comes from a hideous period, one in which sponsored literature functioned much as the regime wanted it to. I have avoided the freedom and prophecy of true literature and have turned to establishmentarian chronicles because it is only here that inadvertent testimony to the accommodation between private and public spheres in a large segment of Soviet society can be found.

In no way, therefore, is this a book on the aesthetics of Soviet literature. Nor does it recount, step by step, the literary development of a past era. Least of all does it aim to be a kremlinological analysis of stalinist power politics. Rather, a homogeneous body of popular tales is used to give a view of a singular type of blending of divergent interests.

As background, the impact of the war is rendered in broad outline in Part I, followed by an explanation of the mode of reading the chosen source. Middleclass objects and aspirations are ferreted out in Part II, the panoramic portion of the book. Part III, the closest knit, depicts the workshop of the "Big Deal." In the last Part, I ask why the large-scale accommodation between the regime and the Soviet middle class has not been the breakthrough it could have been.

Note of thanks

I have been collecting and discarding materials for this book for a long time – too long, perhaps.

The Russian Institute of Columbia University in the academic year of 1966–67 and part of 1968 gave me a chance to think and to work. I am grateful for the assistance I found there. Alexander Dallin made me feel at home as I have not felt elsewhere in academic places. I also thank Marshall Shulman for his support.

My debt to George Fischer is great. His unwavering interest and concern, the extraordinary generosity with which he gave his time and shared with me his thinking, helped me to put the first version together. Without him I could not have done it.

Wayne State University's administration and my department there gallantly relieved me of teaching duties in the spring of 1974. This helped in the home stretch.

Discussions over the years with Seweryn Bialer, responding to his wise and erudite judgment and to the force of his view of Soviet matters turned into an intellectual experience more important to me than the completion of this book.

Seymour Slive, my brother, stood by me in dark days and was a spirited, if not uncritical early reader.

Jerry Hough, of his own free will, plowed twice through much longer earlier versions and made valuable suggestions. I also thank Robert Maguire for his encouragement.

Ben Salzano, Carly Rogers, Toby Trister, and Nicole Loux have contributed at various times in holding the text together. Their young interest in the work sustained my aging determination.

VERA S. DUNHAM

Introduction to first edition

Much recent Soviet scholarship has focused upon the 1920s and the early 1930s rather than upon the high stalinist period. This era was described in detail in the flowering of Western scholarship of the late 1940s and early 1950s, and the quality of the literature then produced – coupled with the failure to open new sources – has discouraged scholars who might have been tempted to restudy the period. Indeed, the literature was so rich and voluminous that it is generally not even read today. For many younger students of the Soviet Union and for the vast majority of specialists on comparative government, all that has remained of the last decade of Stalin's regime have been the generalizations embodied in the totalitarian model and in the comparative textbooks. The consequences, both for Soviet studies and for social science, have been unfortunate.

Happily, signs are beginning to appear that the neglect of the post-Purge years of the Stalin era may be coming to an end. Vera Dunham's study will be a landmark in the effort to understand that period. To be sure, this book is not so much a revisionist return to the period as a continuation – a bringing to fruition – of work that was begun in that period itself. Long ago Vera Dunham introduced me to many of the novels and stories discussed here, and, as the bibliography and footnotes of my own book testify, they – and she – have had a major impact on the way I have seen the Soviet administrative system.

In this book, however, Professor Dunham goes beyond her previous work to raise important theoretical questions. She argues that middle-brow fiction provides insight not only into the details of Soviet life, but also into the essence of the relationship of the regime to the citizenry. She maintains that the regime made a "Big Deal," an alliance, with the rapidly growing managerial-professional "middle class" (really the upper stratum of society); so that any simple conception of a political leadership totally opposed to society, or of a political leadership determined to create a new Soviet man at all costs, requires serious modification.

Whatever one thinks of the nature of the literary evidence that she uses to document her argument – and I find it convincing – Professor Dunham's questions are undoubtedly the correct ones. She is surely right in her basic contention that Stalin's use of coercion is not sufficient to explain the survival of the regime during the vicissitudes of World War II and the reconstruction period As many rulers have discovered when their armies dissolved, force and coercion are not abstractions; they require the use of real people – people with their own interests and values – and they do not function automatically.

One might suggest that the "Big Deal" really originated in the 1930s rather than in the 1940s, and that its ratification in middlebrow literature lagged behind its actual enactment. (Given the evidence of recent years about the possibility of guerrilla and terrorist action by dissatisfied peasants, and the difficulty of suppressing it, it is difficult to explain collectivization without referring to the possibility of personal advancement for the ambitious and the talented, and to accommodation by the regime to many of their values.) Yet the original date of Stalin's "bet on the strong" is not important for an understanding of the last third of Stalin's rule; what is crucial is that this "Big Deal" was part of the system of high totalitarianism.

Professor Dunham is, of course, a specialist on literature rather than a social scientist using fashionable methodologies and styles. Some no doubt would have preferred her to quantify her data or use social science jargon in posing and "testing" her hypotheses. If she had done so, however, this book would not have been nearly so enjoyable. And – if the truth be known – it would not have made the contribution to Soviet studies that it does. In theory, coding and other sophisticated techniques of content analysis permit scientific rigor; in practice, they usually destroy both the reader's sense of the reality of the situation, and the possibility of verification by anyone who does not want to replicate the whole study.

The great advantage and strength of *In Stalin's Time* is precisely that it is descriptive as well as analytical. Professor Dunham has the instinct of a novelist, and she is not content simply to argue and document her case. Rather, she constructs a mosaic of Soviet society – a mosaic containing not only the worthy, but also those whom, as she says, bolshevism never reached. No one can read the array of material in this book without a concrete sense that Soviet citizens of the late 1940s were real people. They loved, they wept, they worked, they coveted, they schemed, they laughed. As Professor Dunham reports, they also read fiction, they argued about fictional characters and the questions of morality these characters represented, and they debated these questions in the press.

These are simple points, but what is simple and what is theoretically important depends, first and foremost, upon the nature of theory. As one reads this book, it should not be forgotten that the postwar years being discussed are those which others have often analyzed in terms of a total "atomization" of society – of a sense of aloneness so profound that the people were deprived of normal societal ties, even of the opportunity to develop a sense of self. Unless the evidence of this book is totally dismissed, such images become quite untenable (except perhaps in abstract philosophical terms that may apply to all industrial societies), and our basic image of Stalin society is changed in a fundamental way.

The strength of this book may also be its misfortune. It is the product of a unique set of talents and interests, and could not have been written had not its author been willing to work between the academic disciplines of literature and sociology. The danger is that the book will remain unique. Younger scholars – trained more firmly within the framework of a single discipline and more fearful of challenging its methodological traditions – may be more reluctant to use Professor Dunham's sources and method to illuminate the evolution of Soviet society in the recent past and in the future. Indeed, they may be so thoroughly socialized (one is tempted to say indoctrinated) that the thought may not even enter their mind.

Hopefully, *In Stalin's Time* will do more than redirect our attention to our basic assumptions about the Stalin period; hopefully it will also demonstrate to others that a variety of methodologies can be fruitful in theoretical terms. Hopefully there will even be political scientists who will ask themselves: how many of the innumerable quantitative studies of Central Committee members or regional party first secretaries further the theoretical development both of Soviet studies and of political science to the extent that this "unscientific" book does? Hopefully, there will be readers who will be willing to dare in the way that Vera Dunham has. If so, we will have reason to hope that the useful path to the development of theory that she has blazed will not become closed, and that there will be further studies of like nature, which will have a similar impact upon our understanding of the Soviet Union and political development in general.

JERRY F. HOUGH

Soviet novels explain both Soviet life
and Soviet novels.

Alexander Gerschenkron

Part One

Finding the Big Deal

1. The Big Deal

It did not crumble

Victorious in the Second World War, Soviet leaders were able to prevent the surfacing of overt conflicts in Soviet society. Nevertheless, there were latent conflicts. One such serious issue is a central concern of this book: it is the potential conflict about postwar rewards. Without reference to the war itself, however, one cannot begin to examine either the nature of this conflict or the way in which it seems to have been prophylactically resolved from above.

The assault of the German armies on the unprepared Soviet Union was so sudden and devastating that the system might well have crumbled altogether. But it did not. Stalin's wartime dictatorship, more absolute than before or after; the mobilization of mammoth economic resources by draconic labor laws; the vastness of the country and the enormous size of its human resources; the "Napoleonic" frost; the contribution of the Allies to the Soviet war effort and their stake in it – all these enmeshed into a formidable bulwark. Moral factors must be considered as well. Love of country, old and new (that is, a residual national cohesiveness in the older people and Soviet patriotism among the young); the Russian military tradition and its Soviet version, created by the war; anger, pride, despair, compassion blending into a new social solidarity; the bestiality and stupidity of the Nazis; the perplexing balance between the system's reprisals against disaffection, slackness, fatigue on the one hand and the wartime concessions made to the people on the other – these are the forces that worked in an intricate pattern to support the system.

Even when the occupied borderlands seemed lost, the core remained solid and Soviet society held together. There was sizable defection among minorities. Unquestionably, in Odessa the Rumanians were greeted with flowers by some Soviet citizens. Yet the inhabitants of Leningrad behaved heroically during two years of siege, and the way they lived and died said much for the morale of the nation as a whole.

The mechanisms of survival called forth by the war enhanced the system's ability to face its postwar difficulties. And Stalin, the victor, profited in a particularly dizzying manner. Victory gave him *carte blanche* and legitimated his rule as nothing had previously done, which in turn brought new hardships. The twenty million dead spoke from their mass graves for the maimed and bereaved, for an adequate acknowledgment of the people's sacrifice. While praising verbosely national heroism, Soviet leaders were less clear on the matter of rewards.

Potential conflict between the people and the regime was nothing new. But, by 1944, its social base had widened. The people knew who had won the war and how. Defeat was averted by mass exertion. So when, now in the name of peace, Stalin continued to make harsh demands of the citizens, they were resisted as they had not been during the war. And one new protagonist on the social scene proved hard to handle, the returning front-line soldier. Stalin's savagery, however, met this challenge like any other. In the early postwar years a policy of stepped-up coercion, intimidation, terror and the proliferation of concentration camps proved effective tools of control. Yet it is unlikely that these alone explain how the system managed to maintain itself. For these controls were merely negative, doing nothing to attain the goals of the system, doing nothing to satisfy popular hopes, aroused during the war, for a building of better lives. Other controls – positive controls – had to be made operative for, if next to Stalin's throne there stood Beria, Malenkov stood close by as well. Thus new policies came to be adopted, and these were policies of mediation, of concession, of internal alliances, of conflict resolution. One such major alliance during the period from the end of the war to Stalin's death will be examined in this book. I call it the "Big Deal."

A tacit concordat was formed by the Soviet leadership with the resilient middle class. This middle class had managed to increase the ground won in the thirties and, at the close of the war, had come into its own. "Middle class" can have different meanings. It can indicate a statistical entity in the stratification of the society by income, wealth, or occupation. In a society with a dichotomous and extreme class division, it can identify a stratum between these two antagonistic extremes. But it can also be applied to an attachment to specific values, to a way of life which partly crosscuts differences of position, of occupation and of income and which is, therefore, somewhat amorphous and difficult to anchor in any one sharply defined social group. It is this last meaning that the term middle class has here. Symbolically, in a somewhat perverse way, it expresses the embourgeoisement of Soviet manners, values, and attitudes. These are not confined to one demographic statistical zone. Their very diffusion, their wide resonance and appeal became a strong social force, and in it stalinism found its firm anchorage.

Despite the perils of imposing terms from the language of one culture on another, I want to suggest that the Soviet middle class does consist of many Soviet Babbitts and organization men, as well as of white-collar and mid-culture men and women. They are the solid citizens in positions and style of life below the top officials and the cultural elite, yet above the world of plain clerks and factory workers, of farm laborers and sales girls. This middle class did not weaken in the period of national devastation. On the contrary, it managed to add to the gains it had made in the thirties as a result of the country's modernization.

Two seemingly contradictory processes must be taken into account. One impeded modernization, the other worked in its favor. The wartime fatigue of the people, the devastation of the country, the infinite strain on the economy had seriously disrupted the prewar economic pace and its goals. The leadership had been forced to put a premium on skill, on productivity, on performance, instead of on political adroitness and ideological orthodoxy and, just as in the military, where the bungling mustachioed civil-war heroes were replaced by up-to-date professionals (the Zhukovs and Rokossovskys), so too in the civilian sphere the need for a new legion of productive engineers, organizers, administrators, and managers became pressing. The middle class was there to furnish it. And the very need for this class consolidated its base, encouraged its proliferation, and insured further modernization. Without the enormous middle class this would have been impossible.

This indicates the story I will try to tell. It is one of settlement and of realignment of the effective forces within the system itself.

The Front

By a procedure astounding even in wartime, a play entitled *The Front* was published in *Pravda* serially from August 24 through 27 in the critical year 1942. The playwright, Alexander Korneichuk, intimated at the time to a Western correspondent that the plot had been suggested to him by Stalin.[1] The play was staged with the best actors of the venerable Moscow Art Theater. It was an event. Stupefied at first, the critics subsequently broke out in raptures and the discussion of the play became fervent. This was understandable, for it tackled head on the foremost issue of the day, on which the survival of the country depended. Heralding the most important change of policy, the play dramatized the struggle between the obsolete military elite and the young professional technicians of modern warfare.

Surrounded by sycophants with sobriquets such as Noisy, Silent, Well-Mannered, as if transplanted from a morality play, a commander by the name of Ivan Gorlov continues to throw drunken supper parties in his quarters during the first weeks of the war. Wine flows, regardless of the advancing Nazi tanks. This civil-war hero and his dilettante intelligence outfit bungle the defense miserably. His own braggadocio and the abject flattery of his cronies prevent him having any inkling of the disaster he courts. He refuses to listen to his brilliant subordinate, the real hero of the play, the young Major General Ognev (Fire). He insults and denigrates

him, seeing this new type of trained specialist as a mere upstart. Basking
in his revolutionary memories, he considers personal courage as the only
thing that counts:

"I have learned how to wage war in battle, not in academies. I am not a theoreti-
cian but an old war horse... What matters is a commander's soul. If it is brave,
courageous, stubborn, then one needs to fear no one... I am not used to sitting
behind a desk and breaking my head over maps. War is not an academy. The most
important thing is to look for the enemy. Strike him there where you find him...
Unfortunately, some of my generals have not as yet grasped this simple truth.
These bookish strategists of mine babble about the science of war. Time and again
I must straighten out their brains."[2]

Needless to say, Major General Fire averts disaster precisely because he
is a "bookish strategist" who studies maps, weaponry, people, and the
enemy's tactics. He succeeds among other means through insubordination. He secures good intelligence. He learns to anticipate the enemy's
moves. In the nick of time, he takes the initiative into his own hands and
simply disobeys the nonsensical orders of his superior. The Kremlin, it
turns out, stands by the new professional; and that is the point.

To make the drama more poignant, Gorlov's own brother opposes him
vehemently. He is a powerful industrialist with high connections, in
charge of a military aircraft plant. After a swift visit to the front, where he
personally examines enemy planes, this modern manager hastens back to
Moscow to denounce his own brother. So, the old-fashioned general cannot rely even on his family. Even his son, a young lieutenant, turns away
from him in disgust. This conflict shows how, during the catastrophic
phase of the war, the urgent need for specialists was understood on both
military and industrial fronts. The powerful modernizing brother delivers
an indictment against all pompous ignoramuses. His words are heard
sympathetically by another highly placed personage, a political emissary
of the War Council. They deplore together not only military incompetence but the harm done to the national economy already in the thirties by
the obsolete revolutionary leadership. Stalin had liquidated it thoroughly
enough before the war, for more than one reason. Of course, the purges of
the thirties are not mentioned, but the modern manager certainly remembers the harsh treatment meted out to the earlier bunglers, and applauds
it.

"Don't you remember how it was in industry? At first in many plants and trusts
the old, honored, authoritative comrades established themselves as managers.
They boasted of their calloused hands, their loud voices, their strong words. But
technology they did not know and did not want to know. They did not know how
to manage a plant. At each step, they chattered about their proletarian origin.
And they did not want to learn. They did not want to enlarge their old knowledge
through new experience. And what came of it? The plants went from bad to
worse because posts were held by these "authoritative" and vain ignoramuses.
Had the Central Committee not veered about completely, had it not appointed
engineers, technicians, knowledgeable people to head the enterprises, the workers

would inevitably have said: 'To hell with your aging authoritarians. They don't know how to manage.' That's a fact. No matter how the ignoramuses screamed, no one supported them. The people want and demand only competent and intelligent leaders."   [p. 130]

He recommends short shrift now too for all obsolete obstructionists. To the surprise of no one but the hero – who, as such, has of course to be modest – the play, representing as it does the conflict between Red and expert, blind courage and competence, domestic cant and professionalism, closes with an order from the High Command that the old bungler be replaced by the young professional.[3]

Stalin's wartime rule had been a combination of permissiveness with drastic punitive measures or, rather, it introduced some permissive elements into a basically draconic practice. This came about neither arbitrarily nor accidentally but was implicit in the effort to fight on. Because of the country's catastrophic lack of preparedness at the outbreak of war, Stalin had been forced to realign priorities. Controls, essential to the war, were tightened. By the same token, this meant letting go of whatever seemed nonessential. Ideology and its correct exercise could neither manufacture tanks nor line an officer's battle jacket with fur. Some aspects of the ideological superstructure were downplayed, much was shelved, and propaganda underwent a change. This is one way of explaining why controls over writers in the first phase of the war relaxed at the same time that workers were being shot for turning out faulty screws.

Wartime dictatorship, with its summary courts and merciless labor laws, aimed at total mobilization. The new propaganda, curtailing the glorias to the party and shifting toward different appeals such as brotherhood, patriotism, and even primary loyalties, contributed to the same goals of total mobilization. Writers responded to this new assignment of making it clear to the people that they were fighting for themselves and not for the party, that once more this was a great national war, that the native soil and not Stalin's dictatorship was at stake. Russian history, with its travails and ancient glory, called on all of its heirs to defend Mother Russia; the marxist-leninist-stalinist dogma was blending with the larger national purpose. Immediately after the war this amalgam was to breed significant ambiguities.

In this initial phase of the war, however, and whatever the regime's reasons were for relaxing controls over literature, the war poets cast the overwhelming theme of patriotism in a populist mold. A military ethic was glorified which implied an awestruck, almost trembling reverence before the image of the martyred people, of the peasant. For example, one poem, among innumerable similar war lyrics, lingers on in the memory of the Soviet reader, not so much for its excellence as for its confessional thrust. A representative of the urban *jeunesse dorée*, having turned soldier and having been witness of the initial catastrophic retreat, admits that the stalinist social system before the war had sheltered him from contact with the life of the people.

You know the motherland, probably,
Is not the city house where I lived festively
But these villages crisscrossed by our grandfathers
And the simple crosses on their Russian graves.
I do not know about you; as for me,
It is the war that brought me together for the first time
With the longing for travel from village to village,
With the tear of a widow, with a woman's song.

As the army moves eastward in the summer of 1941, leaving the populace to its fate, the poet recalls the exhausted peasant women "furtively wiping their tears" and "whispering" to the retreating soldiers: "God be with you."

It seems behind every Russian fence,
With the cross of their hands protecting the living,
Our forefathers gather to pray, as an ancient commune,
For their grandsons who do not believe in god.[4]

So the poet foretold the proper military posture when the tide of war was to turn:

When you enter your town
And women meet you,
Holding their children high
Over their heads turned gray;
Even if you are a hero,
Don't be proud. This day
On entering the town you do not
Deserve gratitude from them,
But only forgiveness.
The only thing you have done
Is to pay the frightful debt
Which you contracted that year
When your retreating batallion
Gave them away to slavery.[5]

While wartime permissiveness was still in effect, hardships at the front gave birth to the folk hero. Not, tellingly, from the High Command, he could only be found in the humble garb of the simplest of soldiers.

You can't do without tobacco
From one bombing to the next.
Just as much you need a byword,
Some good saying and, of course,
You can't do without my Tyorkin,
Vasya Tyorkin, my dear hero.
He takes the same grim road,
As two hundred years ago
When he was armed with a firelock,
Russia's hard worker, Russian soldier.[6]

Throughout the saga of the soldier's survival, certain small but important hints disengage him from the system. With terse irony, the poet summarizes the retreat and the counteroffensive thus:

> Duty stands divided as of yore.
> Soldiers surrender cities.
> Generals reconquer them. [p. 203]

The theme of grief reigned uncontested. Even the theme of dogged survival was superseded. A soldier muses as he puts his uniform in mothballs:

> But how can I part
> With the days of war?
> How can I ever get rid of them?
> What's to be done? A soldier's
> Huge memory
> Does not fit into a trunk.[7]

Inevitably there grew up a nostalgia for the tragic years of the siege, so close and already so remote:

> My wartime youth is with me always.
> There are those years from which you cannot be severed,
> There are those roads from which you cannot derout.[8]

And at the same time a guilt for having survived surfaced, sometimes obsessive, sometimes bordering on paranoia:

> Soldiers avenge. I am a soldier.
> If to that end I have survived,
> I must be off, I must,
> The dead are watching me.[9]

Personal treasons, defined quite differently than in stalinist courts, began to be measured as intolerable in absolute terms. Loyalty to the martyrdom of the people, defying articulation, lost itself at times in a stupor. The Leningrad ordeal came to mean the revelation of the Eucharist:

> I am frozen into your unrepeatable ice.
> I am nailed to your vision.[10]

For a while Stalin was able to project an image of himself befitting the apocalypse. Acting like the Savior of 1812, like Marshal Kutuzov, he managed to reach the people. If, for example, the national purpose could be enhanced by the crowning of the Patriarch of the Russian Orthodox Church, an ecclesiastical throne abolished by Peter I, then this too could be – and was – carried out with appropriate pomp and circumstance. In the media there began the glorification not only of the leadership but of Everyman as well: of the small people, of old teachers, or rural doctors, of churchgoing grandmothers, poor peasants and mere children. Between them they undercut an extremely important character: the party official, the model of virtue and wisdom who somehow had retreated backstage.

One persona, however, took second place to none. Inspiring the refurbished ideal of national self-defense, leading one and all, there soared above all the figure of the "father of nations." The figure stayed aloft.

> Keeping his great watch alone, unrelieved,
> Stalin raises his eyes from his work
> And looks at our labor with a fatherly smile
> Like a tested soldier at his soldier sons.[11]

Stalin could do more than that, especially in anticipating victory:

> When Stalin will glance over the land
> From border to border
> The paradise we had lost
> Will rise anew like a garden.[12]

Here we see too that the order to forget and to look forward was already being prepared by Zhdanov,[13] yet it will not do to close with happy vignettes of the beatific dictator, for other tocsins started tolling at the end of the war. The front was turning inward. For example, the important but fleeting image of a malcontent veteran balances the hagiographic gratitude of soldiers to their fatherly generalissimo. Griefstricken, bitter, or frozen in a stupor, the veteran needed rest and a chance to sort things out. Instead, he was pressured.

One such young lieutenant, on demobilization from the army, withdraws rather than let himself be recycled at once into a workhorse on a collective farm. An eager party organizer, pointedly a demobilized colonel himself, hunts him out in his hiding place. The two have never met before. While the colonel hobbles on a crude artificial limb, nothing of a physical nature seems to have crippled the lieutenant at the front, all of which helps point up his temerity.

"Who is there?" shouted the lieutenant from behind the door.
   "May I?" asked the colonel as he entered.
   "Why not? Try it," an unfriendly voice was heard from inside. "Well, well, it's you, comrade. What is it?"
   "May I sit down?"
   "Why not? Sit down. Only, you know, I don't play any real role around here..."
   "I already know that you don't play any role here and that is very bad. You *should* play a role. Where did you fight?"

The lieutenant does not like the question and turns more abrasive:

"This trick, you know, will not succeed with me. I have a great deal of experience with demagogues such as you."

The colonel does finally get his answer though:

"Where the command placed me, that's where I did my fighting. And I am not obliged to answer to anyone. Why should I go around and tell everybody? You don't know the articles of war too well, comrade colonel... I was busy selling out to the enemies of the fatherland. What? You don't like that? Well, I did not fight. I am not wounded. I am simply sick. And there is no point in studying me, comrade colonel. And I have no big decorations either. That's the way it is. But my conscience is clear."[14]

But not every officer's conscience was clear even among heroes. One combat general is gripped by doubts, most interesting since, like General Fire, he is presented as a model of military stalinism. He has power. He feels responsible for the soldiers who died under his command. He is troubled about the foremost social issues at the dawn of peace. And he says so, even if in a convoluted manner. Unlike General Fire who frets about strategy, this one frets over the moral issue of rewards.

Generals do not readily hallucinate in popular novels. This commander, however, darting about the front, falls ill. Fever induces him to confront his super ego in the disguise of a beloved schoolteacher who had been killed in their native town just before the general managed to liberate it on his victorious westward march. As they face each other, suspended in the hallucinatory void, "A great question could be read in the silence of the old man." The general does not have to guess what it is. He knows, and, astonishingly, he lets the teacher pronounce the word *reward:*

"How will history repay the unredeemable human suffering caused by war? What will be the reward to the toil of our contemporaries dressed in army coats now torn by death?"

The general gropes uneasily for an answer.

He knew that the old man would not be content with a long-winded account of material benefactions or with an enumeration of paragraphs in a program not entirely fulfilled.

And he becomes defensive as he engages in oratory about the impending global progress of man and the ever-rising glory of *homo Sovieticus,* crediting both to Stalin. His unflappable nocturnal adversary daringly counters the litany to Stalin with the words "I have heard this before." He indicts the grandiose visions of a remote future for being an evasion: "To search for friends in the future is the doom of loneliness." And pertinent to the issue of rewards here and now, he tersely suggests: "The price must correspond to the merchandise."[15]

Postwar challenge

By reshuffling priorities, Stalin achieved his goals during the war. But after the war he had to face the terrible devastation of the land. The last resources had been used up. Literally nothing was left. Minorities were showing signs of disaffection. Repatriates had to be reintegrated. The whole social order was in disarray. The population was exhausted.

During the war the party itself, moreover, had undergone a disturbing change. An unprecedented increase in the military and peasant elements[16] had taken place within the party's ranks and those were the very elements that had saved the country. Mass admission of the military at the front had effectively enacted the policy of national unification. New members had been inducted on the ground of valor in combat rather than for service in the bureaucracy. This alone made party membership less a reflection of the official establishment than before and made it insufficiently reliable for postwar reconstruction. Stalin had, of course, needed massive popular support during the critical phase of the war. But with victory assured, he needed to reaffirm the primacy of his civilian and political bureaucracy, because mutual distrust between the people and the regime could not be drowned by the trumpet blasts of official patriotism.

But conflicts divided the citizenry also. There grew, for instance, a wearisome, if muted, quarrel between those who had risked their lives at the front and those who were allegedly safe in the rear. The hungry workers – to say nothing of the legions involved in forced labor – did not always approve of the privileged, army officers or officials. The cleavage between the haves and the have-nots had grown wider during the war. Lateral social stresses also became pervasive. Husbands asked some account for the years of separation from their wives, and wives, who at thirty had turned into old women, asked the same of their husbands. War casualties left so many widows, orphans, and spinsters behind that the entire population mourned. The sorrow of women marks Soviet life to this day.

Even wartime patriotism left explosive residues. Among the Russians, nationalism tended to move into chauvinism, stimulating in turn the underground separatism of minorities. Other developments, which had been useful for the war effort, now became disruptive. The dogged partisan movement in occupied territories, which had at first been wooed by the regime, later became difficult to handle after its anarchical tendencies surfaced.

Many centrifugal impulses accompanied the dislocation of the population both eastward and westward. Contact with the West created unforeseen difficulties. Defection took place in numbers that could not be disregarded. Those civilians and soldiers who had seen the West, who had come in contact with other norms, had to be repatriated. This, however, is a euphemism. They were liquidated or quarantined. Those who were permitted some modicum of normal existence were watched. In another category, some intellectuals now craved contact with their Western counterparts, as did Soviet Jews and Armenians and Ukrainians, citizens with kinsfolk outside Soviet borders. The main point of it all is that it was difficult to batten down the hatches that had been opened for the waging of a war in which the Soviet Union had to cooperate with allies. And if the Orthodox Church had lent staunch support, its usefulness after the war had become dubious. For the revival of religion pulled people away from the established norms.

Some obstreporous elements, then, took hold in the population. They derived from divided loyalties; from social differentiation; and, increasingly, from what the rulers considered heresy. They took hold by default and by the tear and pull of human experience *in extremis*. In the transition from war to peace, when so much seemed possible, popular hopes of democratization of the system ran deep. In part, these hopes went back to the dissident intelligentsia's revulsion against stalinism. But a different consequence of war also pulled in the same direction. Corruption of mores, from the elite to the poor, contributed not only to an alarming growth of crime. It also helped the spread of antiauthoritarian attitudes.

The bereaved and exhausted population was prone to disaffection. Pauperization reached tragic proportions. And at the base of it all, the war-torn family showed strain. The regime rightly feared dissent. The fear was immediate and it triggered draconian measures that swelled the size of the concentration camp population.

But the regime's need for support, on the other hand, had all the features of a long-range problem. So the regime faced those two problems differently. Decisions made to prevent dissent had little in common with the steps taken to seek new popular support.

The immediate problem of popular discontent brought the short-term response: the repair and use of its coercive powers. The challenge of social and economic betterment, however, brought forth the regime's long-term response, which was to search for new and reliable allies in the population.

In Stalin's time – and even in Stalin's worst times – the regime was supported by more than simple terror, a truism still overlooked from time to time. The system did possess regenerative powers, and it was capable of responding to the pressures of postwar reconstruction. Accommodation and settlement were being used at the same time that millions suffered because of Stalin's paranoia. Despite the spread of terror, the dictatorship had to decide whether to honor wartime promises to the people – some stated, but most implicit. The risky alternative was to tear up the wartime treaty with the people. The regime chose instead a long-term middle course, and this course was that it modified its wartime treaty with *all* the people in favor of a new treaty with *some* of the people.

Soviet political leadership had chosen and nurtured certain allies in the past. It had relied in those earlier days on the workers. It had appealed, too, to the intelligentsia. But this time it looked for a new force, sturdy and pliable. And it was the middle class which offered itself as the best possible partner in the rebuilding of the country. The middle class had the great advantage of being "our own people": totally stalinist, born out of Stalin's push for the industrialization, reeducation, and bureaucratization of the country, flesh of the flesh of Stalin's revolutions from above in the thirties, and ready to fill the vacuum created by Stalin's Great Purge and by the liquidation of the leninist generation of activists.

So it was with the middle class that the regime entered a concordat. This particular response to the long-term challenge of reconstruction – this particular social accommodation – I call the beginnings of the postwar

Big Deal. On the surface it is true that neither big nor small accommodations with any part of the population seemed probable. This was, after all, the very time when Stalin was at the height of his prestige, determined to make his power in postwar Russia secure, and when he had all the means to do it. The pressure on the population as a result of Stalin's determination had a leveling effect. No one was safe. Still, the coercive maintenance mechanism of the regime was only one of its key devices. More positively, it also sought a stabilizing accommodation with middleclass values. Thus in an inconspicuous, ingenuous, and natural way the Big Deal was concluded.

One can see this rapprochement in part as a calculated policy of the stalinist dictatorship. But the policy grew out of spontaneous, cumulative processes where the development of the new Soviet middle class was paralleled by the transformation of the Soviet political regime from a revolutionary bolshevik force into an essentially conservative establishment, intent on preserving the status quo. This dual process brought closer together the preferences and aspirations of the political establishment and those of the middle class. It made the establishment's appeal to middleclass hopes and sensitivities a reflection not only of the manipulative policies of the regime but also of its own preferences and values. Given the staggering size of the job to be done, the old mystique of the collective lost its popular appeal and its economic usefulness. What was now urgently needed was a wide range of individually hardworking and individually committed citizens.

The war had rapidly accelerated social change. Class differentiation had become more palpable, if only because the survival rate differed. In wartime conditions, naturally, the military structure reflected new class distinctions more strikingly than the civilian one. The infantry soldier, still wrapping his feet in the primordial strips of cloth and craving homegrown tobacco to be rolled in a shred of newspaper, had to be dazzled by the accoutrements and deportment of his refurbished commanders. The gap between the various classes of the classless society was symbolized by the newly introduced sumptuousness of the gold and velvet trim, the épaulettes, and insignia of rank and distinction of the new comrade generals and marshals, and the generalissimo himself.[17]

The average citizen, too, had changed. Demands on the system, as with the rapidly advancing wartime official, expressed awareness of a newly acquired status. It seemed that those citizens' commitment to the system could now best be made secure through the ties of a mutual agreement, a bargain that would give both sides the most important things they wanted. The nature of that special agreement had already been worked out by Stalin in the thirties, when he had discredited the egalitarian myth by attacking the concept of "leveling" (*uravnilovka*); by masterminding the movement of stakhanovism – that takeover by the competitive eager beavers, hated by their coworkers for their individualistic effort and individual reward. It made citizens believe that in Stalin's country they were not invited to work for themselves, for their self-interest, even for their own selfish good.

The relationship between what I call the Big Deal and the thirties lent solid strength to the transaction. But what was new in this accommodation was as important as its roots in the past. The fact that, for example, the worker was now excluded was central and strikingly new. The offer of partnership markedly shifted toward the professional groups. A new support of the system was being built with a new partner on a new basis of mutual satisfaction – a new tacit alliance between the regime and the middleclass ethos.

Of course, such an alliance was not an easy matter. Nor was it one for unabashed public display. The pressing of claims took special forms. Because Soviet society is ideology laden, it must be constantly asserted that all is just and well at all times. This makes public disclosure of significant change difficult. Also, by definition, no one can make competitive and discordant claims, nor can opposing value systems be said to exist. Throughout those years, while it strengthened its bonds with the middle class, the regime paid lip service to other themes and values. Because of the potency of its centralized, unitary, public mythology, the ruling group itself acted out this ambiguity. It did so most conspicuously in its language, for the new accommodation required the use of old language. So whatever really took place continued to be expressed in old clichés. No wonder, then, that the Big Deal called for much manipulation of the doctrine. The regime had two objectives; to obscure the Big Deal in its form, and to induce a conversion of official public values in substance.

Conversion of public values

Historians now generally agree about the reasons for the collapse of the tsarist autocracy. The old regime had, among other things, failed to enter into a mutually rewarding alliance with the young Russian bourgeoisie. The financial support given to radical underground parties by merchant millionaires was symptomatic of their own dramatic shortsightedness; but also showed the unimaginative arrogance of the declining monarchy. One can now say that where Nicholas II failed, Stalin succeeded.

The comparison points to a key difference. The ruling nobility in tsarist Russia was a rooted class with cohesive traditions. It saw itself in the mirror of a long, fairly glorious, and consistent past. It identified with its past, and it knew what to defend. The price of its stolid self-consciousness was a singular obtuseness and rigidity, which led finally to its annihilation.

On the other hand, the Soviet party oligarchy – whatever its social blend – is not so much a class as it is an organization. In the language of nineteenth-century literature, its members are the twentieth-century *raznochintsy* – a conglomerate of people of "various ranks." The varying social origins of Lenin, Trotsky, and Stalin help make exactly this point. Sharing no common social traditions and defending no common historical patrimony, the membership of this organization has been marked not only by its fratricidal propensity but by extraordinary flexibility. This last may have been a blessing in the initial turbulent revolutionary period. With the advent of bonapartism, however, the oligarchy sought its own social base, that legitimization which comes only from identifiable social roots. Obviously, a slow, covert change had been taking place from the twenties onward. The intoxication of the revolution faded. Gradually there came the canonization of revolutionary "traditions" – a telling contradiction in terms. Stalinist dictatorship, bolstered by its self-generated traditional mythology of Great and Old Russia, looked around for sturdy class roots.

To this day the party is still not a class, despite the probable desire for that transfiguration. It is true that the Great Purges led to a radical decline of the heterogeneity of the social origins of the party leaders and militants. In the wake of this calamity, the ranks of the middle and higher leadership were filled by *arrivistes*. These mostly second-generation people rose from the komsomol, or from the industrial bureaucracy, or were recruited from technical institutes. Having made their careers and having reached positions of leadership, they deliberately disengaged themselves from their social roots. They did not consider that their social heritage provided a fitting base for their newly acquired life-style, for their wider horizons. So the upper party echelons remained unanchored, yet feeling the need for a solid base.

By uniting now, after the war, with its own indigenous middle class, the stalinist dictatorship was able finally to acquire class roots and it did this by fostering the interests it shared with the middle class. It did not, let it be noted, choose to turn to the peasant, to better his lot, to increase his social mobility, to alter significantly the institutional workings of collective agriculture. Indeed, on the contrary, experimental measures such as Khrushchev's idea of "agro-towns" of 1949, which showed some active interest in the lot of the peasant, were abrogated. Neither did the regime really turn to the mass of the workers, for labor laws remained harsh, physical mobility curtailed, wages low and housing very bad, and the educational system in its lower regions and its vocational branches impeded, rather than encouraged, the upward mobility of industrial youth by pinning adolescents to the shop. Nor did the regime choose to offer the central advantages of the Big Deal to the stakhanovites; for all their ideological affinity these people had the necessary zeal but lacked the expertise required for optimum partnership. As finally for the intelligensia, it was treated for a tragic period as little short of an internal enemy. If it was unresponsive to the claims of the peasants and workers, the regime was punitive toward the cultural intelligentsia. Wanting such diverse things as the right to privacy, on one hand, and the right to participate in a substantive reshaping of the ideological realm on the other, wanting the right to err and at the same time the right to be right, the intellectuals, in short, wanted freedom. Complex and dangerous, this did not make for stabilization of the internal status quo. That was clear enough. And the regime was simply not prepared to settle for such.

Instead, the kind of social arrangement the regime was looking for was one which was capable of producing contented citizens who, in turn, would be eager to pass on the contentment to their children. It badly needed durable and reliable support and this was defined in terms of one central social group's apolitical, instrumental commitment to the system's maintenance and growth. The regime's primary demands, beyond apolitical conformism, were loyalty to the leader, unequivocal nationalism, reliable hard work, and professionalism.

The middle class, too, craved contentment. And if the regime looked for a new and broad stabilizing base, essential to the staggering job of social and economic reconstruction, it was primarily the middle class that was ready to offer it. The possibilities of rapprochement between the regime and the middle class went deep. Primarily material values were laid on the bargaining table. But this was done neither crassly nor exclusively. The regime courted its new partner in a special way and not without sophistication. What made the Big Deal strong was the fact that it worked at more than the material level. It appealed to the partner's complex of self-interests, involving his prestige, involving his pride in his work, the satisfaction derived from his professionalism, and from his apolitical conformism.[18]

What the partners shared turned out to be more weighty than what divided them. Specifically, what did they want? The middle class wanted careers backed by material incentives – housing, consumer goods, luxuries, and leisure time. Neither the regime nor the middle class was interested in ideology or further revolutionary upheavals. Neither objected to a stratified society. Both proposed to build on the basis of what was there already. Both were interested in stabilization, normalization, and material progress. Both were interested in social mobility. The new careerism satisfied the upwardly mobile individual, who was then expected to be loyal to those who permitted him to be such. Both partners were interested in affluence; one, as an incentive to ensure that work be done; the other as reward. Above all, both were interested in security.

The advantages of the rapprochement were natural. There were, it is true, difficulties. For a start, canonized bolshevik tenets abhor everything to do with the middle class, a hatred which, dating from before 1917, had given the revolution some of its thrust. The old language of bolshevik formulae remains to this day the foundation of the legitimacy of Soviet political power and proclaims the system's public rationale and, since these bolshevik tenets could be neither explicitly abandoned nor adhered to, the Big Deal had to be accompanied by an ambivalence in the ways it was explained to the people. In the end, as we shall see, it was spelled out in a quite perplexing manner. A process of translation of one set of values into another was imperceptibly initiated and it was this manipulation which served as a solution to the ideological dilemma. Instead of *doing away* with its traditional canons, the regime simply *accommodated* them to those preferences of its new partner, the middle class.

The transformation was largely semantic; it endeavored to minimize the standard bolshevik invective against private aspirations and to make certain private values legitimate. In the end, it reflected the embourgeoisement of the entire system.

Established doctrine underwent a curious change which, though difficult and subtle, carried no risk. It introduced no new ideas and no extrinsic ideological material. Yet an ideological conversion, formidable in its implications, was nevertheless accomplished. Without it the settlement probably would not have worked.

The basis of it was that, wherever possible, private values were converted into public values. The result of this is particularly vivid if set against the model hero of earlier days. From child to pensioner, the classic prewar bolshevik heroes both supported public values and were indeed their incarnation. Selflessness, devotion to the party, asceticism, quixotic courage – these were the main virtues. Heroism other than public was inconceivable. Public commitment in those early days was pitched with unequivocal shrillness against primary loyalties and private values. The canonized martyr, the "boy-scout" Pavlik Morozov, is an example. At the age of fourteen, at the peak of the collectivization campaign in 1932, he was murdered by relatives for denouncing his own parents to the authorities. He had reported them because he thought their attempt to help some outcast kulaks subversive. Choosing the state before his parents, this archetypal Soviet youth personified the then lethal confrontation between private and public loyalties.

As against such extremism, things now mellowed. A new concept of happiness formed the bridge where fraternization took place between the private and the public. A model citizen was saddled with the moral and political obligation to be happy as a person, in his private life as well as in his job. A rich home life began to be praised; self-sacrificing, ascetic satisfactions were losing ground. No hero could now claim leadership if he denied private needs. It was no longer his business to be concerned about society as a whole and still less to be dogmatic about it. In every way, moderation was emerging as a supreme virtue. Too much selflessness was as discreditable as excess of pride. There was, though, one thing where no limits, at least in fiction, were imposed. And that was work, work, work; but it was still not to interfere with the hedonistic enjoyment of material rewards. Slowly, the paragon of the forward-striding communist took on a new form. Someone resembling a middleclass careerist replaced the revolutionary saint of the twenties and the party vigilante of the thirties. He appeared now in the form of a vigorous manager. He progressed rapidly in his career. He was content in his family life. He aspired to a private house and, perhaps, to a dacha. He drove his own private car. He was disinterested in touchy matters of ideology and higher policy.

In large part, this conversion of public values is what the Big Deal was all about.

Meshchanstvo and intelligentsia with a note on kulturnost

The term middle class, even in a broad sense, lacks substantive meaning in Russian. There is, however, a richly evocative term – *meshchanstvo* – not a synonym but a cogent relative. It denotes a style of life or a personality structure. In origin, meshchanstvo in seventeenth-century Muscovy referred to a class or estate;[19] it encompassed the lower economic bracket of urban dwellers – peddlers, servants, some artisans. One might call them burghers, except that this curious administrative classification included dislocated peasants but excluded big merchants. In any event, whatever the peculiarity of this humble urban conglomerate, the word carried no pejorative overtones at first. With the growth of the urban population, however, the word changed its meaning, and acquired a figurative one. In the late nineteenth century two connotations became current. In literary terms, meshchanstvo turned into a near equivalent of petty bourgeoisie and, in a looser usage, evolving from the snobbism of the educated few, the term became derogatory. This usage has persisted, and as a target,[20] meshchanstvo helped to stimulate the revolution. But it not only managed to survive but indeed managed, too, to overcome and flourish.

This claim may sound peculiar, given that whatever else survived 1917, the prerevolutionary middle class did not. But in due time, and through the modernization the revolution brought to a backward country, the soil was prepared for a new middle class, public in employment but private and inner-directed in its strivings. And with this development, meshchanstvo got a chance to locate itself again on a solid social base. It represents today, as it did before, a middleclass mentality that is vulgar, imitative, greedy, and ridden with prejudice. Both deficiency of spirit and the defensive mechanisms of philistinism are implicit in the term. Some equivalent can be found in the German word *Spiessbürgertum*, which also emphasizes stagnation rather than the class origin of a social group. "Petty bourgeois" is not as derogatory. The American "Babbitt," although also both aggressive and complacent, seems actually weaker than the Russian *meshchanin*.

In the Soviet world, meshchanstvo appears at every rung of the social scale. In one aspect it refers to the social climbing and careerism of the newly rich; in another to complacent vegetation. A vice admiral of the Soviet navy may be a meshchanin, and a professor may as easily be seen wallowing in meshchanstvo as a post-office clerk or party official, to say nothing of their wives. In many ways in fact, meshchanstvo is a familial and feminine affair, and its pretentiousness expresses itself in the number and size of material acquisitions, by which the newly arrived aim to impress. Fervor for possessions is a key trait. Significantly, meshchanstvo can be satisfied.

Literary descriptions of prerevolutionary meshchanstvo made it appear more stifling but less pompous than the Soviet kind. Material acquisitions weighed heavily in pre-1917 Moscow suburbia, in the kingdom of stolid semi-literate merchants – from Ostrovsky's genre picture to Blok's visionary revulsion. But they did not stand for anything beyond themselves. Goods, wares, fat-bellied chests of drawers, bank accounts, were not extolled as incentives for emulation. They were despised or admired for what they were – despised certainly by the satirists of meshchanstvo from Saltykov-Shchedrin, in the second half of the last century, to the great Zoshchenko who in the twenties left behind the record of early Soviet meshchanstvo; this disdain for meshchanstvo is a venerable tradition at least a century old. With the advent of stalinism, however, and especially during its last phase, ambivalence toward meshchanstvo became noticeable. If the great writers upheld the tradition, the servants of the establishment took on an increasingly ambiguous tone.

Meshchanstvo's natural and historical antagonist is the intelligentsia. In this study those two terms are used not so much as class or social group designations, but as cultural terms and as modal personalities.[21] Meshchanstvo, as has been shown, resists translation as a word: it is singularly focused and compact as a cliché and a derogation. By contrast, "intelligentsia" has several meanings, and lacks a focus. The official Soviet usage of the term intelligentsia was, until recently, statistical and administrative. It embraced everyone who was neither a peasant nor an industrial worker. A substantial category, it covered all persons engaged in nonmanual work, and meaningless use of the term is still common in official Soviet writings.[22]

Peter I established the foundation for social mobility, for industrialization, commerce, and urbanization. Both meshchanstvo and intelligentsia are connected with the first steps toward modernization undertaken by the administrative and social reforms of the eighteenth century. Both are urban phenomena, detached from peasant culture as well as from that of the landed gentry. And both underwent considerable changes, before the revolution of 1917 and after. What is constant is the intrinsic hostility between the meshchanin and the intellectual, shown amply in prerevolutionary literature, and spilling over into Soviet literature from its very inception.

The intelligentsia, despite its historical transmutations, is capable of remembering its past. At times, it is inclined to do so openly, causing friction with the rulers. In this respect, meshchanstvo is happily blind. It knows no past. It sprouts anew at each juncture of social stabilization. Eminently visible, it does not plot. It has nothing to conceal. It is, therefore, manageable.

Meshchanstvo does not fret except about private matters. On the contrary, effectively or not, the intelligentsia, in its old form and its new reincarnation, has always been mainly preoccupied with fretting over social wrong.[23] If it were to stop worrying, it would stop existing. It cannot be satisfied; dissatisfaction is its condition. It is true that the more, at times, it has fretted, the less capable it was of social action. Intellectually and spiritually, however, it dedicated itself to the humanist propositions that salvation was corporate, that tyranny was evil, that freedom was meaningless unless it was universal. It glorified self-sacrifice, personal purity, public service. It stubbornly dreamed of an ideal society. Idealism in this moral sense of self-sacrifice and of devotion to the cause of the enslaved and underprivileged was enacted in the relentless critique of the status quo.

There was a time when ideas were taken seriously to the extent that blood was amply and ruthlessly shed on their behalf. And the Russian intelligentsia has been responsible for violence. One might say that, tragically, commitment to ideas, incited by the tornado of utopianism, became the intelligentsia's overcommitment. The spirit of the revolution was nurtured by relentless fretting.

In Stalin's time, however, the regime has managed to divide the intelligentsia and to seduce part of it. So the intelligentsia cannot be considered a homogeneous entity, and it might be useful to try to distinguish at least its "pure" from its "impure" elements. This is to say that a special type has emerged from it, powerful and vocal. He is a hybrid *par excellence:* a meshchanin, enjoying the material privileges (and the materially underpinned pretentions) of an intellectual who has been hoisted by the regime to leadership. The comfortable life-style of the prominent Soviet *homo academicus* makes the point, as do his striving emulators. Such hybrids put the less learned and sophisticated meshchanstvo to shame, and make the intelligentsia's splintering into "pure" and "impure" palpable and painful. It is one more peril that the principled intelligentsia must endure. For, deep down in everyday life itself, these hybrids help the conversion of public values. The conversion, in turn, etiolates just those values the regime had shared in the revolutionary past with the revolutionary intelligentsia, the purest of the pure and the most foolish.

Although purist idealism had provided the supreme rationale for the revolution, the stalinist regime undertook finally to obscure it. What was done was done; the past belonged to the past. The lingering of certain prerevolutionary and, for that matter, revolutionary memories spelled trouble, and because the memory cells of the Soviet intelligentsia hold the quixotic drive toward social equity and intellectual freedom, they represented a source of conflict with the system. On the other hand, meshchanstvo is entirely free of such aspirations. It thrives viscerally on distrusting the intelligentsia and shares with the regime a dislike of people who take ideas seriously. From the thirties on, when the new middle class emerged, Soviet society has been making room for meshchanstvo; the very ambiance, the underlying mood and feel of the postwar Big Deal thus had been in gestation for some time.

The regime's shift in the public realm from the revolution to stalinism determines the curious relationship of two additional words, eminently untranslatable, *kultura* and *kulturnost*. Akin in etymology, substantively they stand at odds with each other. *Kultura* is the achievement of the intelligentsia in the sense of higher culture, a synthesis of ideas, knowledge, and memories. The other, *kulturnost*, is its alternative: a derivative, second-hand notion. Having nothing to do with a spiritual legacy, it is instead a mere program for proper conduct in public. Conforming with prescribed preferences, it blends with the aspirations of meshchanstvo. The regime, especially after the chaos of war, cared a lot about the manageable, predictable, and "proper" manners of its citizens. It also cared that conduct be impeccable, inside as well indeed as outside Soviet borders. Kulturnost was thus given a weighty foreign political responsibility. Soviet representatives, with military boots as well as diplomatic footwear polished to the highest gloss; with chests covered with sparkling decorations; with hands manicured and gloved according to etiquette; with grandiose titles, and with well-groomed and stiff entourages entered the political arena as emissaries of a Great Power. Kulturnost represents, both at home and abroad, a refurbished, victorious, conservative force in Soviet postwar life, embodying a slick decorum and a new kind of self-righteousness – stable, prudent, heavy. Its special function is to encode the proper relationship between people through their possessions and labels; between mores and artifacts, to put it more fancifully. (It might even shake the individual's grip on his possessions: for instance, a strategic abstinence from acquisitiveness for the sake of displaying "good taste"; the occasional "generous" sharing of coveted earthly goodies for the sake of show and future profit.)

Strictly and minimally, kulturnost turns into a fetish notion of how to be individually civilized. In the panoramic view of Soviet society, there is much more to it. Kulturnost, admonitory and educative, and at first denoting little more than personal hygiene, expanded into a commodious umbrella under stalinism. It began to mean more important things than clean nails, abstinence from cursing and spitting, a required minimum of good manners. It began to mean the only desirable conduct, the self-image of dignified citizens. Those alone could now be models. The notion of kulturnost had grown out of mores; in turn, it began to shape them, in accord with the regime's predilection for ponderous, monumental meshchanstvo.

The usefulness of kulturnost to the regime, which exhorted the people to implement it, was manifold. Like ideological orthodoxy, it became a device for control. As a purpose shared by both the regime and the middle class, it lent support to the relationship between them. As a prescription for proper conduct, it helped build a clearing house where middleclass ways were recommended by the regime to everybody.

The artifacts of the postwar middleclass culture must be seen through the prism of kulturnost for, after the war, it was kulturnost which helped to channel the direction of sanctioned aspirations. Most of all, kulturnost helped to bestow on material possessions attributes of dignity and of virtue.

2. The Uses of Literature

Literature and society

How could one document the broad inferences made so far? The Kremlin archives are not open, nor could one assume that stenographic minutes record formal steps to the Big Deal. What of the countless published political statements? In themselves, they could say little about such a far-reaching yet gradual and penumbral accommodation. On these issues the official language of editorials is obscure, tied to the formulae of the past, and frequently misleading.

The law, on the other hand, the most rigid official language, can indeed reveal complex social processes even in Stalin's era. The decrees on inheritance of 1943 and 1945, for instance, turned a sudden spotlight on concessions to the family, on the reaffirmation of private property, on some important incentives behind the Big Deal. However, local decrees come up sporadically and codify social change in retrospect. Its very inception, its uncertain course, its shades and gradations, the bits and pieces of its ambiguities can be gathered best from the kind of documentation this study deals with.

A commodious source of knowledge on some aspects of postwar social change lies in the enormous body of Soviet popular fiction. Distinct from the lasting and sovereign legacy of great writers and poets, this establishment fiction, which I call middlebrow fiction, offers a good deal of insight into the little-known yet decisive years immediately after the Second World War.[1] Reliance on one source is a problem. Nevertheless, I maintain that the amount that can be gleaned from middlebrow fiction justifies the risk, and that the advantages outweigh the risk.

The advantages are twofold. First, the fiction accurately reflects the values that the regime propagated after the war and, secondly, literature was assigned a peculiarly important role in the period between the end of the war and Stalin's death. At that tragic time, and in a unique way, literature stood between the regime and the people, and constituted the conversation between the two – more so then than it does today. Neither before nor after that period did literature, banal, dry and tendentious as it was, mean so much to the reader.

One could not make that claim if Soviet society did not allow some insight into, or at least some conjecture at, the nature of its mass readership. By means of systemic checks, the regime not only collects the mass reader's reactions but on occasion lets his voice be publicly heard. It is a convention to publish readers' letters. Obviously the readers' response, and the response to the response, helps the regime assess the effectiveness of the literature it sponsors. So it is possible to gain a sense of the postwar citizen's attitude toward what he was given to read. A centripetal force seems to have been at work in these early postwar years, holding the mass readership together despite its wide social diversity. The topical novel of the moment proved one of the few ways of meeting the people's need to understand their society's major workaday problems. The regime put popular fiction to just this instrumental use.

Read by party leaders, by cultural luminaries, and their wives, as well as by high-school students and housewives in small towns, and by factory and farm workers throughout the land, fiction, taken as if it were life, turned into a sort of town hall, a platform from which the system justified itself. The culling of meaning was not always uniform. What the high-school student captured from a story was likely to be different from the prime minister's fancy. The diversity of the reader's reaction, as well as its frequent compliant uniformity, makes literature an important clue in the examination of penumbral, yet palpable social issues. Fiction, no matter how dreary, was called upon to play the role of substitution, a role best explained by one distinctive consequence of Stalin's dictatorship. Ubiquitous controls over all forms of social life allowed only one kind of relationship: that of each citizen directly to the person of the dictator himself. This bondage led to the undercutting and eventual severance of connecting tissues between the citizens. Having crushed the sense of group solidarity, Stalin achieved atomization among his subjects. Public discussion was closed. Even the private forum shrank. The very arena of the family became perilous as the family itself stood embattled under internecine suspicion and fear. In these circumstances, the topical novel became an ersatz social forum. Atomization was not the only form of stupor. All social organizations, the famous "societal forces" in Soviet parlance, had also become atrophied by mandatory bureaucratization. Despite the official cant about healthy and inspiring communication, social organizations ceased to transmit preferences from the regime to the people effectively, let alone from the people to the regime. In this petrification, the novel substituted for the reader's sense of participation in the social process.

Popular fiction was entrusted with another important function. It offered to those in the lower regions of society the only possible glimpse of the life of the powerful and the privileged above them. To the populace, even a run-of-the-mill district party secretary seemed a potentate. The description of such a VIP's daily travails and especially of his loves and family pleasures and vicissitudes, with details of top-drawer kulturnost, kept the mass reader spellbound. It was exotic reading matter, fascinating in a way not readily understood in another society. It impinged on the vital interests and aspirations of the mass reader. If he identified with the characters, whether positively or negatively, if the fiction evoked his dreams or frustrations, it became more than a reflective force. It had already turned into an active one. Nor did readers react to literature only passively. They discussed these books, and so revealed their opinions about life and society. They sent letters about poems, stories and plays to the press.[2] They even argued with the critics, and entered far-reaching debates. For all the editorializing and sieving through censorship, these letters made the world of popular fiction a lively one and formed a rich commentary on social change. This active reading of popular fiction, offering the curious exercise of ersatz participation in the social process, was a unique transient phenomenon of the early postwar period.

To the regime, one value of feedback is its diversity. Whether a topical novel manages to hold the attention of the mass reader or whether it bores him to tears, it induces a reaction, negative or positive. In producing a "reverse" or "surprise" reaction, the reader may, moreover, fool those shaping his opinion by identifying not with the positive hero in a "controversial" novel, but with the villain.[3]

Feedback, then, in popular Soviet fiction both molds and reflects public opinion. How far the postwar regime made conscious use of this unique mode of information about the mood of its citizens is speculative. Common sense, however, tells us that, while positive feedback may be powerless to tell the regime of covert pressures behind the readers' mood, negative feedback offers a safety valve for social tension, and can be a device for learning possible correctives as well. One may assume that negative feedback is not lost on the regime. This reflective information serves the outside observer as well.

After the war, there was neither bread nor circuses. There were no cafes for bohemian youth, nor beaches, spas, or travel for the majority. In the gray postwar setting, reading took on new importance, partly because there was nothing else. But reading was more than a leisure activity. To a vast number of Soviet citizens, reading meant not only being *au courant*, it meant participation. It offered the reader a chance to check his own questions about postwar adjustments against the paradigms of current social issues he found in fiction. These projections directed his groping, and clarified his own quite varied aspirations by helping him understand what the system wanted of him and what he wanted of the system.

Of the rules of socialist realism, the one that prescribes the "surrealistic" beautification of reality or the application of the famous high-gloss polish (*lakirovka*), the unequivocal command that the writer should lie, was the most binding and the most useful for everyone concerned. Happy endings abounded: boys got girls; tractors got repaired; job and family conflicts got resolved. It cannot be assumed that all readers objected to these lies. Some did, no doubt. Others did not. The thrust of such fiction brought solace. And there were those who craved hope more than they craved truth.

More than before, the regime used writers as its spokesmen. It is chilling to recollect that Stalin's personal impact on literature was no figurative matter. The dictator threw himself into the foray, and meddled in the work – and therefore in the life and death of his "engineers" – by cutting and crushing, forbidding and permitting. Continually interfering, startling prominent writers with his nocturnal phone calls, he pushed them all to the brink.[4] No less chilling were Andrei Zhdanov's apoplectic convulsions, induced by writers in error – not so much his vituperations against the giants of artistic integrity, Zoshchenko and Akhmatova, but his strictures against those whom he called "their ilk," the little-known and tired poets whose quietest love lyrics showed signs of despondency in the wake of the terrible war. Scandals raged about poems called "Tart Wine," the tart and, in this case, trite lament about lost love.[5]

The catastrophically inflated importance the dictatorship attached to literature might be described as the Iskra complex. In 1900 Lenin founded his famous periodical *Iskra*, which effectively promulgated the belief – strengthened with bolshevik victories – that the main function of the printed word is *organizational*. The worship of organization grows out of the fantastic belief that political, social, and psychological problems can be solved by organization. In the making of the revolution, *Iskra* was a crucial step. The organization of Lenin's party was formed around it. The press set out to organize before the revolution, after the revolution it undertook to control.

When the Iskra complex fully matured, it underpinned the bureaucratic aspect of the ruling elite's culture, one of the essential traits of which was its obsession with formal documentation, with the magic power of the printed word, an obsession which mistakes the word for reality and attempts to transform the word into action.[6] Barrington Moore calls this complex "the charter myth of Bolshevism" and suggests that such myths "do not necessarily become milder and more tolerant as they become incorporated into a working institutional system."[7] The inalienable dark side of the charter myth is, of course, the system's obsession with repressive, terminal censorship. Anyone who doubts the Soviet dictatorship's faith in the power of the printed word need only consider the mechanism devised to protect the citizenry from the dangers of the printed word. The Soviet rulers inherited censorship from the tsarist time, but their alteration of this preventive tool into a punitive one and its subsequent adjustment to Stalin's paranoid needs has been so radical that the institution of censorship has changed in kind. The tsarist censor endeavored, not too effectively, to stamp out the actual written word that he considered subversive. The Soviet charter myth, due to its organizational and paranoid nature, extends to the basically instrumental belief that the other far more crucial word, the word not yet written, can and must be prefigured and controlled. Still, despite the ruthlessness with which the regime extinguished any spark and veracity sponsored literature might have, that literature did manage to engage the mass reader,[8] and in the first decade after the war, middlebrow fiction did stand out as a tangible social force.

Middlebrow fiction

The Soviet regime has always quarrelled with writers. It has silenced, exiled, or killed the best of them. Its dealings with literature rule out tolerance and stability. Danger is always in the air, and dissenters always in peril. Even devout servants and hacks live under constant risk too, since they face possible disfavor. The possibility of being denounced, or simply not being invited or permitted to show servility, hovers over them all the time. Ironically, the system has elevated writers to a position of social leadership. This is no contradiction, for though it has abrogated literature's sovereignty, and treated it as an extension of the political arena, the regime has also extolled it. The writer is no more offered indifference than he is freedom.

Why should middlebrow fiction be the primary means of shaping current moods and propagating long-term preferences? Why is the regime not satisfied with standard forms of mass persuasion, like schools or the daily press or formalized ideological indoctrination? The answer is that an ever-evolving body of official mythology cannot be made sufficiently palatable by standard means. The flat language of bureaucrats will not do, nor the shrill and equally uninspiring language of political exhortation. The appeal must be to the emotions, by emotional means. A play or novel may or may not succeed but, as a form of communication, literature is suited to do just that. Its personalized and symbolic treatment of life distinguishes it from other forms of propaganda.

The molding of public opinion is performed effectively if the writer can create vivid images with which the reader can identify. He can hardly do so with a series of propositions. A fictional character enacts the values the reader himself holds, aspires to, or discovers. The converse is true of those characters who repel him and whose position he opposes. This personal imitation of life cannot be achieved by a *Pravda* editorial, which has only one function and moves in only one direction, telling the people in so many words what they are supposed to think.

One other feature supports the effectiveness of poems, stories, and novels. The written word is durable. Unlike film, television, theater, it possesses the quality of a personal artifact, especially where the regime, obsessed with documentation, attempts to charge serviceable fiction with lasting responsibilities. In the less than serene relationship between the subservient writer and his masters, this very "thingness" of fiction is a mixed blessing for the writer. On the one hand, the durability of his product enhances his worth to the system. On the other, it makes the product paradoxically vulnerable and its maker subject to constant scrutiny. Soviet citizens may own books which cannot be too easily cancelled, withdrawn, confiscated. A book becomes a sturdy possession, an almost inalienable – if perilous – right.[9]

Middlebrow fiction has nothing to do with the high road of literary art. Instead, it echoes the official views of the moment. It is compliant, didactic, grey and routine. Such writings are, for all the physical durability of the printed page, the perishable and soon forgotten output of average, "safe" writers. Pasternak and Akhmatova, obviously, are not among them. All great writers stand outside the establishment, either opposing or ignoring it. They speak of themselves, of human nature, of the drama of life *sub specie aeternitatis*. For insight into transitory issues we have to gather evidence from materials within the domain of the system's values, and from myths within its establishment. Soviet middlebrow fiction moves unswervingly on these establishmentarian tracks.

The early postwar years were unhappy even for compliant writers. Official policy towards them was harsh, although they said for the most part what the regime wanted. Their compliance becomes eloquent when they succeed in obeying directives but show strain in doing so. Their default also becomes revealing when, once in a while, they cannot help deviating involuntarily from the regime's demands, and commit "errors." Whatever they do, they inform by indirection. It may seem strange that pedestrian, uninspired fiction hides anything below its surface; but it does.

What makes the products of these "engineers of human souls"[10] informative is the images of people they project. This fictional population is narrowly "current," an important point in justifying middlebrow fiction as a source for the historical chronicle. The timely aspect of a tale often makes it possible to date it with accuracy. Yet the relationship of middlebrow fiction to time and current events[11] has a paradoxical aspect. What the subservient writer observes is overlaid with distortion and mythmaking. Sponsored literature mirrors hardly anything directly. It is mainly a grimly earnest embodiment of the regime's desiderata, a repository of its myths.

Because of its prescribed purpose, the key element in a tale is not within the setting, nor tone, nor mood, nor the author's personal meditation or confession, but unmistakably the fictional hero. The message he enacts is no less standard: the fulfillment of the regime's desired values. Redundantly, Soviet jargon calls him a "positive" hero, and casts him as the ideal citizen. This means that he appears as the propagated man of the future.[12] The canon of socialist realism demands that he march upward and onward and peer assiduously into the communist tomorrow, whereas the negative character is left behind, grubbing blindly in the present. Yet, in a strange way, the hero as ideal future-bound type is conversant with both temporal realms. Directed toward the future, he is still caught up in the travails of the moment. In the didactic fiction which he inhabits, he is used like all the other elements: flattened, hammered, and buffed in order to be usable and useful. So he moves and struggles as a construct, one-dimensional and only partly illuminated. And since all middlebrow fiction is harnessed to pragmatism and yet required to make pat ideological gestures, it is likely to show fissures between its contradictory tasks. The positive hero issues from just such a fissure. He comes from the gap between the real and the ideal, his character revealing itself in confrontation not with the ideal but with real problems. And these problems provide a channel through which reality impinges.

The idealized elements of the positive hero and the "fùturistic" component in his make-up have more to do with his thoughts than with his actions. One might say that the motives for his decisions, rather than his actions, are ideal.[13] The main problem with the hero is that only some of his traits are idealized. These reveal only one dimension, the public, solid, simplistic one which makes him think futuristically while acting contemporaneously. Villains stick to the present and tend to be more convincing. Therein lies their relative freedom. Full of short-term mischief, they are debarred in any case from soaring into the future. As literary characters they seem to be doing nicely as they are. By contrast, the heroes must not only stretch themselves between the present and the future; they must not tilt in either direction too much.

The writer must handle his hero with caution. Together they must propel the good ship of active, vigorous virtue on a mixture of myth and sweat; between the futuristic rocks and those others, the solid rocks of current reality. The journey is complicated because the subservient writer is required to be both docile and effective simultaneously and in correct proportions. Writers and their heroes must accept the party's vision of the future, while being vigorously effective in the solution of all the problems on the way to the Golden Age. The combination must function with precision, for the persuasiveness of the writer's product is that which elevates it above the rest of the propagandist arsenal. The writer is of value only if his book sells. If it doesn't, he has failed. But it may not be vigorous, overambitious or explosive. The regime does not wish him to come up with either a *Bronze Horseman* or a *Cancer Ward*.

Though the writer must aim at the largest possible audience and bear on mass as well as elite opinion, the bureaucracy's mid-stratum (the run-of-the-mill meshchanstvo) can use a bit of illusion, a bit of respite. And it looks for it. Pleasure, to be sure, had better stay within bounds. But catharsis, even a bland one, goes a long way under stalinism. When a harrassed administrator recognizes in a novel the insoluble problems he struggles with day in, day out, he may find it relaxing to see them solved, fairytale fashion, in the closing chapter. Excessively happy endings might irritate more dour readers, but the how-to-do-it devotee enjoys them. Ersatz participation in the social process can sometimes be an effective tranquilizer.[14]

Middlebrow fiction links the social with the political realm. This is done by lending themes and characters from the immediate present an intense "verisimilitude"[15] and forcing them into a didactic mold. Fiction reports on the state and mood of the populace, at the same time attempting to propagate official mythology. They may be combined by edict, but the two functions conflict, since the reflective issues form the basis of a tale, but the educational ones form its superstructure.

Any leeway the subservient writer may think he has must square with the unyielding principles established by his masters, giving him an extremely narrow range of themes. That restriction does not necessarily make him limp and totally passive. On the contrary: he must have his wits about him while two processes take place. They are very different, in that he is imprisoned by one, and a more or less free agent in regard to the other. By eliminating crucial topics, the regime establishes the range of social themes fit for fictional treatment. Having selected the safe themes, it ranks them as mandatory, desirable, and permissible. The stock of taboos, however, does not remain constant from period to period. Taboos themselves are not all equally sensitive. Some remain permanently unspeakable; others do not. Liberalization expresses itself in the lifting of some taboos. But the subservient writer has nothing to do directly with this. He selects from the already preselected. In order to decide what to write about, he operates within a limited margin drawn both by official censorship and by its effective echo: self-censorship. But he does select.

Despite the drastic limitations which maim his artistic integrity, the writer, however establishmentarian, is not relieved of all decisions and alternatives. In a special way, he must contend with not one master but two: those who commission his writing and those who consume it. His product must be palatable to both. If it is not, it is obviously not effective. Yet what the regime expects the writer to write about may not be at all what the reader wishes, even within the realm of the permissible. This is where the decisions come in. In a stringent period, the expectations of the regime and the reader diverge sharply. To persevere with an appeal to both masters becomes difficult. Strangely enough, when a writer complies particularly closely with directives, he unintentionally responds to the reader whose desire it sometimes is to stand clichés on their heads. This happens when the writer "errs" by being too crudely responsive to directives or too cautious with them. His hero falls flat on his face in consequence. This makes for a lively scene once in a while. Thus dreary novels can affect the reader in more ways than one and they can thereby evoke critical debate. And, of course, on such occasions the party steps in. If the writer touches on an exposed nerve, he has to manipulate the reader. But it is not a question of *either* manipulation *or* spokesmanship but, rather, of multiservice. So, from time to time, the writer also manages to speak on behalf of the reader. The release of tension this provides, no matter how limited, helps to counteract subterranean dissent. Middlebrow fiction provides that. It is in fact a safety valve.

Other channels of guided criticism exist too. But they are specialized in that they are designed for special groups. The self-criticism of the party is on occasion a tribal blood-letting. The Writer's Union occasionally performs ritual chest-beating and even self-castration. But since the general public has no way of making open criticism, novels offer a substitute. Occasionally criticism forms a means of control when it helps the checking of the lower echelons of the huge bureaucracy. For instance, in some faraway village there might be all sorts of irregularities, bribery, conniving. Some indignant accountant, even a mere milkmaid, might have decided to speak out. He or she writes a letter to the press, or complains to a journalist, or to some itinerant writer in search of "real-life" or "grass-roots" material.[16] The complaint typically involves the incompetence or crookedness of a boss. Since the press is independent of pressure from the local bureaucracy, the milkmaid's complaint can appear under her signature in the local or central daily press, or can work its way into a filed report of a roving reporter, or can be more stylishly incorporated into a sketch (a genre highly valued by the system). One way or another, the lady's criticism finds its way to the desk of party officialdom and is taken note of. Such complaints provide the system with a corrective device. They signal flaws, failures, and wrongdoings before they get out of hand. Negative feedback seems altogether more useful to the system than positive. The part played by fiction in the sequence bears emphasis: the detection of problems, leading to their diagnosis.

Middlebrow fiction, however, could not serve this or any other extraliterary purpose if it did not have an unusual public. The Soviet reader, particularly in a period of fear and duress, reads in a special, socially relevant way. Under conditions of strain, unimaginative fiction is like a Gallup poll, because the reader reacts to it as if it were one. He is inclined to read it avidly and literally, as life and not as fiction, turning fictional characters into real ones.[17] This is not to say that this precludes reading between the lines. But the reader concentrates on issues relevant to him, to his own concerns. If, in a novel set in Novosibirsk, a tyrannical party boss is disgraced and is replaced by a more gentle, accommodating, and up-to-date soul, the reader reacts to the plot as if it had really transpired in Novosibirsk or even in his own town. He responds to myths encapsulated in fiction. I do not suggest that fictional characters whom the reader transforms into meanings appear as convincing portraits of Soviet citizens, for all their meticulously pedestrian attributes and wax-doll realism. They are synthetic constructs, means and tools at best. But they are deeply imbued with reality inasmuch as they are carriers of social issues, and they do facilitate whatever minimum social debate is permitted by making it concrete. Above all, fiction conveys the regime's desired values. And the reader eagerly deciphers the message, since it originates in the mythology that engulfs him.

So the very system makes fiction real, and it is treated as such by everyone concerned. It is, primarily, the regime's interest in it, especially the obsessive nature of the interest, that makes it so. In placing fictional characters back among the living, the reader, for his part, strengthens fiction as a social force. For his part too, the stalinist literary critic, whose task calls for dogged misreading of fiction as life, does the same. And so does the compliant writer himself.

Looking for clues

Those elements of reality which found their way into postwar tales were stringently selected by the party and molded by the writers themselves according to ideological demands and self-censorship. The tales, therefore, are heavily coded. Efficient use of these materials by an outsider consists largely of converting obscure data into clues.

To begin with, one needs to be clear as to the nature of the information one hopes to find. It has little to do with the accuracy with which the life of Soviet citizens is reflected in that fiction. Traditionally, an author's commitment to objectivity in exploring experience has been called realism. This denotes the author's preference for a maximal closeness of fit between fiction and life.[18] By any definition,[19] however, realism as literary style is not relevant to the kind of reading underlying this study because, one way or another, fiction – even if didactic, stereotyped, or fantastic – deals with reality just the same.[20] Tendentious fiction informs.[21] It does so even if manufactured according to the rules of socialist realism,[22] which prescribe the blending of peeping-Tomism with instant distortion. Stalinist middlebrow fiction does not inform in the same way as do Chekhov's stories, but it informs all the same.

Since clues vary, encroach upon each other, and hide below the surface of the narrative, one or two rather simple precepts may show how to cope with middlebrow fiction. The major themes need not be the primary interest because they are always ponderously obligatory. Fortunately, secondary materials sneak in from real life, and the clues we are interested in are to be found here. I take as an example a famous bucolic ballad (A. Nedogonov's syrupy "Flag over the Village Soviet"), the main didactic thrust of which is that the war veteran, taking up life again as a proper meshchanin, not only has no grievances to present to the regime, but also is humbly grateful for his instant nook in postwar society, and stands ready to exert himself to the limit in his new job, however lowly. Once at it, he is also to convey joy through opulence. In this particular folksy narrative, love and courtship is not the main theme but, clearly, a filler. The zealously positive veteran is shown preening himself to woo his fiancée. He departs a-courting, accurately described: clean-shaven, in uniform, wearing all his medals, with a watch "on his left wrist." Nor does he venture empty-handed.

> He secured for her a couple of brooches,
> hand made
> shoes

and for a dress,
bright polka dots.
And a seventeen-jewel
wrist watch.
For the mother-in-law
his gifts of kerchiefs
of Moscow brands
are very stunning.[23]

Something to behold, indeed. Not only polka dots but a fancy watch, a veritable obsession during the famine in consumer goods. He has brought specially ordered shoes and, as a tribute to explicitly unperturbed matriarchal mores, offerings to the prospective mother-in-law. The "couple of brooches," which rhyme with polka dots (*broshek*: *goroshek*), are pinned on the bosom of full-blown meshchanstvo. Their casual redundance is eloquent: two brooches are better than one.[24]

Taken out of a sufficiently ample context, the twin brooches would not manage to say all they do. Pinned and repinned elsewhere, in many variants, some even diamond-studded, they cease to be only vulgar or simply unlikely, but become rather desiderata of both the regime and the postwar middle class. They represent first the craved affluence and then its transfiguration into a kulturnost, which is valid and unassailable.

The smaller details of middlebrow fiction, such as the twin brooches or a fleeting nuance in the authorial tone, can seem either lively or ambiguous: they can certainly be more revelatory than the massive features. One cannot, however, skip with a basket on one's arm, as it were, through the kaleidoscopic maze of all that turgid fiction gathering fragments, details, and hints here, there, and everywhere. Quite a bit of ripping and stitching is needed to put the clues together. The details must be deciphered in their relationship to each other so that patterns emerge.[25]

For example, consider one standard theme, the large theme of the travails of the professional woman. Time and again, it is unfolded that a woman is as good as any man and that her commitment to society and to concomitant self-sacrifice is just as fervent. The subtheme – that of the professional woman's relationship to her family – is in comparison somewhat murky. And this is where the details have to be examined in relationship to each other.

As a rule, the professional woman is shown as having very little time for her family. On assignments, expeditions, and emergency calls, having of necessity shifted the center of her being to the office, shop, or construction site, in novel after novel she relies for the care of her children on grandma or on a trusted domestic. Occasionally, the conduct of a semi-abandoned child, treated in the clutter of a huge novel in passing, holds an important clue to the understanding of the strains on the postwar family. It can be more profound than the pontifications of the protagonists. And the context into which the detail is wedged is as important as the detail itself. Projected against each other, the variants of the same pattern – in this case, the mother's absenteeism – signal the covert outlines of a real social issue to which they are, as it were, attached. In one novel, a perfectly adorable child responds badly to the mother's absenteeism and becomes unruly and despondent, especially when a marital conflict ripens, aggravated by the mother's professional superiority over the father. Does this mean that the author is firmly inviting the career woman to reverse her priorities, to chase the housekeeper off the premises, and to start connubial homemaking, cozy and vital, all over again?[26] There is some hesitation about a clearcut solution here and this hesitation is especially telling if other novels, eerily similar in their large features, offer slightly different views in the unravelling of this same subtheme. Consider this touching scene. A nice boy sits decked out in holiday finery, in a room scrubbed and tidied in honor of the return of yet another heroic absentee mother. She too is a perfect, positive, hardworking professional. She has been away on a scientific mission for a long time. The boy now throws his arms around the mother's neck and implores her not to go away again. She cannot give any such promise. They have a touching talk, and she will in fact then go away again. Unlike the first case, she feels no guilt about this.[27] More crisp than the first, and more matter-of-fact, the value of this variant lies in its tone. Nothing is solved here, but more important than this is just the fact that the conflict between work and home is broached at all. In addition, the very fact that it forms a pattern, however tenuous that pattern may be, nervously flickering as it does from one novel to another, indicates that the conflict is serious, that authors must handle it cautiously and must, for the time being, avoid dogmatic solutions. One might further deduce from these and other novels that the regime continued at the time to demand the impossible of the professional woman: the utmost exertion on the job coupled with high-quality domesticity; that it was unwilling to compromise on either score; but that if it had to make a choice, it was on the verge of giving preference, albeit tacit, to home over career making.[28]

One detail may matter more than a whole tale, and the feel of a few patterns stitched from eloquent fragments may matter more than ten huge novels back to back; similarly, comparison between a few strategic clues can be illuminating. Tracing the evolution of hagiographic mini-traits is especially rewarding. Since 1917, conviviality and the sense of celebration, for instance, have always been demanded of the canonized militant virtue of the young. But where a hastily spread newspaper was mandatory for the communal breaking of bread in the workers' universities through the thirties, a change was signalled when an immaculately white cloth, if only a handkerchief, became just as mandatory with the vigorous diffusion of postwar kulturnost. Far more than an artifact and even more than a symbol of refined manners, whiteness here connects with the new hagiography and stands for the hero's shifting allegiance. Instead of ascetically straining toward the tomorrow, he now honors and beautifies the today – in correct and hygienic moderation. Where an early revolutionary amazon, committed to the meager cutlets of communal mess-halls, would not have known too well what to do in a private kitchen, her postwar successor is something of a gourmet cook, even in the wilderness. She now carries her feminine world with her, no matter how curtailed. Domestic plants had no place, literally or figuratively, in the nomadic and frantic ways of the early true believers. The postwar hero, despite the high rate of his mobility, now finds time lovingly to water a potted geranium or two.

This diachronic comparison of minutiae is one helpful device in seeking clues. Contrasting the attributes of the heroes and their foils, as well as those of fathers and sons, is another. There are signals here of the rift between the top and bottom of Soviet society; there are signs of contrasts between the provincial setting and that of the metropolis; patterns of the sexual conflict; indications of hostility between intelligentsia and meshchanstvo. These juxtapositions assist the decoding of middlebrow fiction.

Suppose we find in a novel that a party secretary busies himself with the private affairs of his parishioners. He is not cast as the central character. He will, however, act deftly as a key figure. The party secretary's main function is the dispensing of ideological nourishment. The smallest detail, therefore, attaching to his person carries significance. In one example,[29] the party secretary summons a quarreling couple to his office during working hours. He admonishes the adulterer. He gives judgment about the dispute and expects his order to be executed. He continues in this vein and throughout the novel is the very epitome of bumptious good health and of vigorous energy. In a similar novel, however, the party secretary happens to have an incurable heart disease. Rather than summoning the quarreling couple to his office, he drops in on them instead in their own house. He does not shout at them and does not give any summary judgment but drinks tea meekly, sighing all the while, and ends up even siding with the more obviously guilty partner. There are two sets of signals here: heart trouble contrasted with enviable health; the office setting with the domestic samovar; the soulless bureaucratic assault on a culprit with the more imaginative compassion for the hidden frustrations and hardships of a parishioner. This interplay of seemingly innocuous and trivial detail suggests what could neither appear in a *Pravda* editorial nor indeed in the main didactic channel of a novel. The image of the party official was being altered from that of the self-righteous bully, based on the vestiges of bolshevik-proletarian heroics, to that of the understanding father confessor.[30] An ailing heart and sallow skin now stand for kindness, the strain of compassion. Thus, long before the Thaw, the good party secretary, soothing and healing, creating comfort, and sponsoring domestic bliss, had been introduced.[31] The new hagiographic stigma of the ailing heart showed not only compassion, but also prevented the party secretary from partaking too energetically of the spreading material pleasures. As carrier of minutely scrutinized traits, new and old, he had to uphold a minimum decorum of abstinence. Nevertheless, he had to be ready to eat gratefully at the table of his flock. Heart disease was reserved for benign party secretaries. The most negative complaint, ulcers, was reserved for "crazy" members of the intelligentsia and for the more obsolete representatives of the proletariat who become emaciated and sickly in their combat against meshchanstvo.[32] Such is the pattern of politicized ailments.

Often objects speak much more eloquently than people. Indeed, a curious vitalization of objects can be seen taking place at the expense of people, who tend to be dehumanized by didactic pressures. A phantasmagoric profusion of objects came not only to form the background to the stories, but began to play an important role. The material universe of the Soviet citizen, his house, furnishings, personal possessions, acquired its own life and began to express spiritual values.

In the stories to be examined, the description of home furnishing begins to glide easily into an exegesis of family activities. An orange lampshade, scalloped and fringed, invites solicitous parents to read to their children; and that was laudable, for the family had to be strengthened. An opulent room with heavy drapes and a grand piano kept young people off the street. That was good too; upper-class youth had to be protected from the roaming riffraff. A contented professional family, cheerful, hardworking, and future-oriented, needed a number of pleasure-producing objects to maintain its high level of serenity. Conveniently, the system had granted permission either to own them or to crave for them. A hoard of objects began to mean happiness in terms of the new sophistication, the new kulturnost. A windowsill in the room of a proper meshchanin would not do without potted flowers. Their absence would have been alarming. And if one finds the primordial rubber plant in the sunlit room of combatively righteous shipyard workers, the last representatives of proletarian orthodoxy, one may be assured that the regime itself undertook to water it.[33]

These plants, pictures, and wallhangings gave previews of character, of the level of kulturnost, of the ability to provide contentment. The vast tacit task of deheroization and deproletarianizing signified that the postwar ideal was for the individual to become concerned with rounded-out, integral, domestic happiness. Objects helped this new task. From our point of view, they did even more by providing guidelines for the interpretation of character in different social settings. From the vestibule of a Leningrad surgeon to the melon patch of an old peasant, the context in which objects took up residence mattered a great deal. Authors disapproved of them or they relished them according to context.

In a certain environment, faded portraits of bearded ancestors, with a tiny bouquet of dried blossoms inserted between glass and frame, bespoke admirable traits. Ancestors, even in tsarist uniforms, and folk art, even mass-produced, fused with patriotism and showed that lower-class kulturnost was able to maintain connections with the native past. This was good and proper, although an eighteenth-century etching, even Russian but especially French – and particularly if exquisitely framed and hung in the study of a professor – spelled something else. Snobbism? Yes. Escapism? Yes. Decadence, arrogance, and indeed possibly even promiscuity too. It certainly did not denote kulturnost. A pin-up of a foreign (probably Italian) movie actress, on the other hand, might perhaps signify an approved widening of horizons, particularly on the part, for example, of a recreational director in a remote province. A cross-stitched shirt, combined with slow speech flavored with local proverbs, may have exemplified the new virtue of populism. In the person of some stubborn kolkhoz chairman, however, it could have meant parochial and recalcitrant one-man bossism. An expensive fur might confirm excellence of character in a woman in charge of a factory, but turn into an indemnity on the back of an entirely too-idle wife of a provincial potentate. A wall map of the world, especially large, brightly colored and hung above a much-used buffet, could mean very different things. It all depended on the context. At the grass roots, such a map was almost a requirement of any good person aspiring to local leadership. A provincial manager of a brick plant could not do without one. A map, a globe, a dictionary, testified to his alertness and antiparochialism. But a large-scale bureaucrat or an academic potentate in the capital, especially the latter, would be better off without one, and for an intellectual, not altogether trustworthy to begin with, demonstrations of global interest might hint at the dreaded sin of cosmopolitanism. Perhaps only in the Arctic zone were five-star cognac and perfume exempt from scrutiny. Anything went there, in any quantity, of any quality. Truly of the future, luxuries were politicized into incentives for free-frontier explorers and resettlers.

Postwar strictures pushed literature toward dishonesty and distortion, toward "glossing over" and "polishing" as we know. But we need not worry whether this affluence was real or imaginary. We shall compare neither the country fare of shepherds and shepherdesses, nor the fancy kitchen appliances in novels dealing with the privileged, nor the rooftop restaurants and vintage champagne served there with statistically reliable indices in real life. We are concerned instead with the social role these objects began to play; these ambiguous maps, brooches, portraits. Information that matters will be found in the accommodating tone – despite equivocations and ambiguities – with which the cravings of the middle class began to be treated.

Part Two

Middleclass Culture

3. Possessions

V svoi prava vstupili budni,
I nam vpered idti.
Konstantin Vanshenkin

Artifacts

In postwar novels, objects, from real estate to perfume, took on a voice of their own. They provide a material inventory of embourgeoisement, raising in a new way the touchy issue of private property. Officially, of course, orthodoxy remained committed to combating the very principle of individual acquisitiveness.

All through the twenties, the mainstream of popular literature commemorated the revolution. Stiff leather jackets, black tobacco, straight bobbed hair, bisexual boots, and barren dormitories were the proper artifacts. Material possessions were few and dwellings austere. Asceticism supported the spirit of sacrifice. And the cause – unequivocal, monolithic, and enormous – dwarfed everything with its demands. All this left no place for material cravings.

After the early romantic days, all through the thirties, and deep into the Second World War, the mainstream of literature continued to extoll the dedicated young person. But the very nature of dedication to the public good had undergone a change. Stalinism had by itself reshaped it drastically by introducing differentiated incentives. And so did the war by bringing the canons of Soviet society under stress and accelerating shifts in beliefs and aspirations.[1] Marxism-leninism waned when revolutionaries became patriots. In the past, sacrifice had demanded round-the-clock heroism. Wartime patriotic ardor, no less taxing, proved to be different. It was *emergency* heroism. Rooted now in nationalism, it was no longer committed to the destruction of meshchanstvo's private values. The social base of wartime nationalism was broad; its membership motley.

With peace came the question: what was the postwar hero to be like? Which way was he going? And what was the shape of the earthly things he was to live with? What material goods were promised to youth, on whom the system still concentrated much of its appeal?   Descriptive passages, in which objects are cataloged casually, suggest an answer. This nook in a student dormitory belongs to a girl:

Over her bed were tacked a lot of colored postcards representing views of Naples, Venice, the sea, and naked mermaids. Several brightly embroidered pillows were neatly arranged on her bed. Her small nightstand was covered with pink paper, scalloped at the edge.[2]

Pink emerged in postwar books as a favorite color, rivaled only by all shades of orange. Scalloped edges would have been as unthinkable in the interior decoration of dormitories in earlier Soviet periods as naked mermaids. Personal apparel underwent change too. Leather jackets were no more. This girl, for one,

dressed and styled her hair very much according to the latest fashion. She was a mediocre student and in general did not distinguish herself at the university in any way except for her chic clothes. Between lectures, like everybody else, she walked arm in arm with a girl friend . . . "They will wear skirts cut on the bias this season."   [p. 24]

Entering a modest room in a provincial town one gets roughly the same picture. In it there lives a bitter young war widow. She is a factory worker. Rather openly, she is searching for a new father for her boy of three. The possible prospect, a student, pays her his first visit.

He took off his overcoat and she paced the room for a long time looking for a place to hang it. The walls were covered with postcards, with portraits of movie actors, and with movie stills. There was a great number of little shelves, and on them were placed bright little embroidered doilies and inexpensive little vases in all sorts of colors, holding faded paper flowers.   [p. 16]

Described in this not quite matter-of-fact way, the sad paper flowers go together with the frustrations of the young woman longing to make life a little less gray.

The right of the average citizen to desire comfort grew into a powerful theme, and authors began to inject their own judgment. The clutter of ornate objects was linked with positive personal traits. The revised style of life, downgrading stoicism, called for *joie de vivre*.

Again, the setting is provincial. A happy family appears on the scene. The young mother holds it together cheerfully. She is a local actress. Not particularly talented, she is "olive-skinned, colorful, with red lips and nails." Her husband manages the local theater. They are the leading "cultural" team in town. They are excellent parents, and there is nothing bohemian about them. The turbulent romance they had conducted before the war was savored with zest and gossip by the whole community. People in this novel gossip with downright zeal. The wedding of the nice couple had been loudly and cheerily celebrated on the edge of town, outdoors, with a victrola and cherry cakes. Both had put their whole energy into the war. The man was gone for four years. During this time his wife worked day and night as a radio announcer, raised their child, and stood all privations without a complaint. When, after the war, the husband at last returned, their love was as good as new. They picked up with ease where they had left off, unburdened by ideological considerations or human readjustments. The husband now took up the organization of the factory club. His wife became its artistic director. A glimpse of their domestic life shows the weakness for artificial flowers. She arranges hers in old-fashioned long-necked vases. She also wears them on her evening gowns in the form of silver roses. They remind her husband of cabbages. As a war trophy he had brought home

a heap of American movie magazines. And [his wife] decorated her rooms with colored photographs of film belles with scarlet mouths and film beaux with narrow moustaches ... On an intricate series of shelves, [she] arranged a display of baby dolls with large bows, bright cologne bottles, and little seashell boxes. And tea was served under an orange lampshade in red, polka-dotted cups. In this small, gay, and bright paradise, everybody was pleased with life and discussed how good it was that work in the club was becoming well organized, and how pleasant it was that Maika was frequently bringing home good grades, and how interesting it would be to make Mitya's acquaintance when he was born next spring.[3]

The author is not critical. The word "paradise" is serious. It emphasizes the advantages of a happy home, where material objects are transformed into human warmth.

Material craving engulfed postwar society from top to bottom. Coiffures, cosmetics, perfume, clothes – the trappings of enhanced femininity – gained social significance. They, too, began to represent the new public good. In real life, however, they were no more than a hope, and it is as such that they entered fiction.

The emphasis on femininity made the classical theme of bolshevik amazons singularly obsolete. The right to discover one's own physical and psychological self gained respect as much as the right to personal happiness, privacy, and self-enhancement. Especially for young women, this turned into one of the rewards to which the regime alluded during the critical phase of war.

Here we see such a happiness-dispensing establishment through the perplexed eyes of a young peasant girl. Her family had been killed by the Germans. For the duration of the war she has been adopted by the personnel of a hospital train. On a few hours of leave, an army nurse takes her to the sort of place she has never visited before:

Fascinating things took place in the beauty shop. It had a life all of its own, resembling nothing at all she knew. In a corner behind a table sat two women. One was in a white uniform and did something by means of small clippers to the fingers of the other one.
"What is that?" asked Vaska.
"Stupid!" whispered Iya "that's manicure." In front of tall mirrors sat women

in armchairs, young and old. Their resigned faces were reflected in the mirrors. Female hairdressers, young and old, busied themselves around the women. Scissors clanged. Tufts of hair, light and dark, flew about. The eyebrows and eyelashes of a brunette, who had a submissive expression, were thickly pasted over. The hairdresser blew on hot irons and twisted the brunette's hair around them whereupon tremendous steam arose from her head. The brunette cautiously blinked with her pasted eyelashes and endured everything. In the next room real horrors took place. There sat one woman. About forty electric cords or maybe more were stretched from her head to the wall. The woman could not turn her head and only moved her eyes.

"And what's that?" asked Vaska with passionate interest.

"It's a permanent," answered Iya... The woman at the little table got up and started waving her hands. Vaska could not tear her admiring eyes away from the woman's nails, bright pink and shiny, like candy. The brunette arose also. And Vaska was astounded at her beauty. The brunette's hair was arranged in tight little sausages. Her eyelashes were coal-black and curved upwards. And her brows were of indescribable beauty – long, stretching all the way from above her nose to the temples, and so very straight, and so very neat as it can never happen in nature. Vaska suddenly felt a poignant kind of envy. She too needed such beauty.[4]

Obviously, not only the underprivileged sought new beauty, now prescribed as kulturnost. So did everybody else.

What shirt should I wear: the blue or the striped, the one with the detachable collar? Vadim thought intensely, arranging on the table his shaving kit. Of course, the blue shirt! I can never manage the detachable collar with those stupid studs...

"Well, how do I look?" he said, standing for some reason sideways at the mirror.

"Not bad. Not bad. Quite presentable."

"And how is my tie? All right?"

"And the tie is not bad. Only never button your coat all the way down." [Sergei] came up to him and unbuttoned the last button. "In a single-breasted coat only the middle button is buttoned."[5]

We shall accompany this clean-cut young man on his date. He is well connected. He will take us up the social scale. With him, we shall enter the house of a well-to-do, upper-middleclass family. One might call it aristocratic. This new setting tells us something of the large span of the Soviet middle class as it strives to blend with the Soviet aristocracy. The new setting also gives an idea of the stratification of accessories, from the lowly, faded paper flowers to live mimosa, flown in from the south. And the casual ease of this particular story is of importance. The affluence of the rich is taken for granted. The author neither approves nor disapproves. One finds no note of criticism of the ways of the privileged. That is the point: affluence has entered the fare of the mass reader.

Properly dressed and correctly buttoned, the young man hurries to pick up his date. While the mother helps the girl he is courting, he waits in the parlor.

Intently and attentively he studied this room with its delicate mauve wallpaper, an airy pink lampshade like a cloud over the table, the heavy buffet, the piano upon which was lined up a whole army of knickknacks and upon which there also lay a book in an old-fashioned marbled binding, marked with a ribbon. Vadim deciphered from a distance: Danilevsky. It's probably Albina Trofimovna who reads that, he thought. Lena did tell him that her mother read a great deal, and that she particularly loved historical novels. And for some reason Vadim was pleased that Albina Trofimovna was enthusiastic about Danilevsky, although had he found that out about his own mother, he would certainly have laughed at her. And she seemed altogether a very pleasant, well-educated woman to him, and very beautiful, much like Lena.

This genre picture includes reading matter, an upperclass interior being inconceivable without it. It happens to be an old-fashioned book. The mistress of the house is quite old fashioned herself. Mannered, genteel, fussy, she likes to read nineteenth-century novels. The young man likes her for it.

The young man does have second thoughts, however, about affluence in the distant closing chapter of the tortuous novel; but his enamored fascination here with the possessions of the rich suggests a distinction between the material universe of the higher social strata and the acquisitive yen of the middle class, plain and simple. Postwar aristocrats show an attachment to things, fortified by discrimination and by an awareness of cultural traditions. A nineteenth-century historical novel stands for something very different from a movie star pin-up. And a grand piano concertizes even when untouched. The middle class, on the other hand, has another, more unassuming aura. It shows, as everywhere else in the world, a cultural lag; it strives to emulate the makers of taste. But in Soviet life, the regime reserves the right to sponsor appropriate kulturnost in various social settings.

Meanwhile, the young man is awestruck by everything he sees in this refined *haut monde*. Lena's mother may seem a little obsolete, but her father, a renowned engineer, is not. The daughter, part throwback, part Soviet modern, enters the parlor at last.

Lena stood in front of the mirror in a long dark green dress which brought out the tender tan of her bare arms and of her open neck. She seemed taller, more svelte, more feminine.

"Vadim, quick, give me your advice! Which is better: this brooch or this necklace?" She turned to him, coquettishly leaned her head sideways, and held against her breast a large round garnet brooch. "Well, how is it? All right?"

Looking at her brooch and at her bright radiant face, Vadim said with conviction: "Beautiful, very beautiful, but the first act will have started."

"But I have been ready for ages!" exclaimed Lena, taking a bottle of perfume from her dresser and pouring some into her palm. She quickly applied it to her throat, then she poured some more and dabbed herself rapidly behind her ears.

"It stays longer behind the ears. Take note of that," she explained with businesslike seriousness. "Do you want a drop of perfume too?"   [pp. 74-5]

The young people meet the father in the entrance hall. He orders Nick, the chauffeur, to drive them to the theater. The play falls into the style of the evening.

In the last act Vadim caught on to the uncomplicated vaudeville plot of the play. Two beaux plotted predatory designs against the blonde. She suspected nothing and loved one of the villains, the one with sideburns. The fat man in narrow trousers, her father, was also blind – a funny, kindhearted person! And he loved the villains like his own children. But then everything came out into the open! The old man was ruined, his daughter seduced.   [p. 77]

This Moscow is a far cry from the blacked-out, workingclass city one is used to in war novels. It now echoes the forgotten atmosphere of the turn of the century. Seductive fragrances of pine, crème brulée, tangerines and mimosa fuse with the festive perfumes in crowded foyers of cinema palaces. And as for the traffic in the street:

The cars moved in an unending column, bumper to bumper. Out of one chocolate-colored Zis there came to them muted operetta music with voices of a duet "all pa-aa-sses, a ma-an will find his love."   [p. 157]

In this manner the Moscow of postwar reconstruction was celebrated, with new residential complexes in good neighborhoods. Elevators smelled of fresh enamel. Parquet floors were heavily waxed. Electric garbage disposal units were built into kitchen sinks. The hall lights were made in the shape of lilies. The deliberate descriptions of prosperity offered escape from the piercing lament over the tragedy of war. It also offered something that Turgenev's novels, in great demand among young readers, could not offer: the hope that the entire middle class might some day share the life-style of the few.

No wonder, then, that in such fiction students admit that they know nothing of the life of the factory workers. They meet in opulent rooms under pink lampshades. Lena's mother delights over the successful assembly of young men in her salon and exclaims:

"We have so much talent here... Seriozha writes, Garik is a musician and painter, Vadim will become a scholar... Tassia dances, Lenochka sings a little, Mak I hear is interested in checkers and Nikolai is a wrestler... In a word, we have our Olympus here, a gathering of muses. Don't you agree? We could arrange most interesting evenings, concerts. Our apartment is totally at your disposal. Please, have a good time. No one will disturb you. Father is at work from morning till night... You must learn to amuse yourselves. Isn't it possible to be gay without drinking wine?"

It is true that one of the love-struck suitors feels somewhat oppressed by the gathering of the muses. He decides to flee the Olympus with the words:

"From the very beginning I didn't like this Noah's ark. Garik from the conservatory, Marik from the observatory."   [2,p. 120]

Conservatories and observatories came to be firmly included in the inventory of the middle class, admissions considered coveted insurance policies.

The cult of education became all-absorbing. Folk humor had renamed a Moscow music school for talented children into a music school for children of "talented" parents. The talent for climbing harmonized with acquisitiveness. Home ownership surfaced and, of course, car ownership.

An old retired worker remembers the revolution as his own personal glory. An enviable proletarian past allows him that. He has sired a large brood in which workers have become engineers. Grandpa takes the upward metamorphosis in his stride and keeps himself busy. He works as a night watchman in a shipbuilding yard, tending the manager's office after working hours and becoming his confidant. Deserving and wise, he can be quite harsh in admonishing the manager who is harassed, kind, somewhat flabby. We intercept them just as the manager returns from a party meeting where he has been severely criticized. He complains that he works like a dog but

"they always beat the manager on the bald head. Always."

Grandpa is not too sympathetic, for he dislikes weakness:

"For one thing, you don't demand enough from the people. And for another, you don't live in simplicity either."

He advocates frugality, as penitence for failure, and so implies that prosperity is earned by performance. He does not think much of his friend's unwarranted self-indulgence:

"And what do you keep two government cars for? One is for your use and the other for your wife to chase to markets and shops? Is that it? And the gas for this business comes from the state, doesn't it? When Josif Vissarionovich has to be driven somewhere, even he calls up the garage first to ask how they manage with gas."

Grandpa's pettiness annoys the manager. But Grandpa remains stubborn. Though a bolshevik of early vintage, he shows understanding of privileges properly handled:

"The government car you should use only for business. As to soccer matches, you should get your own car, paid for with your own money. No one will say a word to that."[6]

This private car, issuing from Grandpa's constructive suggestion, adroitly translates into public virtue. Stalin's bureaucratization demands decorum in the consumption of privileges. Car ownership itself is being cheered; it is the owner who causes doubts.

The ownership of a house carries status in a relatively low social sphere. The environment of common citizens provides the special meaning of middleclass artifacts. We turn to the purchase of a small house involving a shock-worker in a steel plant. Dimitri has just been promoted assistant foreman. The manager gives him bonuses, acting like Fortuna. Smiling a trifle condescendingly, he holds up his horn of plenty.

"How are your living conditions?"
Dimitri became embarrassed. "I live at my uncle's. He has a small house.

Discovering that Dimitri contemplates marriage and "would have liked to ask for a room," the manager summons an assistant and orders him to provide more than a room.

"Requisition a house for [Dimitri's] disposal, prepare the papers for a contract of sale with him. He will be able to pay a ten thousand down-payment right away because he is going to receive a premium for his invention. The rest we will allow him on mortgage."

No sooner said than done. "Well, there you are – the owner of a house!" says the helpful assistant as he also "began to fill out a document for the release of furniture from the warehouse."[7]

Before the testing of the device for increasing production, the worker's living conditions were of no interest to the manager. The device worked; promotion followed, and achievement is translated into ownership of a cozy house. But if one reads carefully, this is not where the translation of valor into reward stops. Material rewards undergo further conversion into rewards of the spirit.

As a sudden homeowner, the shock-worker plunges into daydreaming about ardently desired things.

Homeowner! How the sense of this old word has changed! Homeowners in Rudnogorsk were now the best shock-workers and engineers, working people. Dimitri was impatient to go with Marina to look at their new home, but it was late. His dreams carried him along with her into their own house, their new house where they would begin their life together. For some reason he imagined that the walls still smelled of moist plaster and the shiny floors of oil paint. The windows opened into the garden. In spring they would be able to plant trees. Marina would plant flowers, the kind that grew near the house he was born in – hollyhock, stock, night beauty, petunias, aromatic nicotina. Dimitri took a deep breath as if inhaling the half-forgotten fragrance of his father's garden, the modest, little garden, raised by his mother's hands.   [p. 182]

The long-tabooed idea of private property engenders ambiguity. After the war, it became important to get around this. In this example, an adroit juxtaposition works well. The author contrasts the sinister "then" with the blissful "now" and lets it go at that. "Then" was the period, before and after the revolution, when homeowners were the enemies of the proletariat. "Now," however, the best working people aspire deservedly to homeownership themselves. This formidable shift shows the deproletarianization of the traditional spirit of the industrial worker. The goals of the collective, of class solidarity, are challenged by individual careerism. And the striving worker is rewarded not only by private property but by the spiritual accomplishment emanating from it. For now, as homeowner, he is among "the best people." In this roundabout way, embourgeoisement began to show in the emerging sanction of private property. The timeless material craving of the people was linked to the new goals of the regime.

But the regime did not sanction material possessions indiscriminately. The literature of this period recorded all sorts of dreams: the good and the bad, the moderate and the transgressive. There were the approved visions of geraniums, and there were others: improper, vulgar, overreaching. Villains are made to dream in this transgressive manner. The object now is also floral, but it does not grow in a garden. A diamond rose, cut by newly restored jewelers, it becomes an obsession, blossoming in conjured opulence. This chief engineer of a large plant is a scheming careerist, even though he is an old party member. Through denunciation and blackmail he manages to unseat his friend, the manager of the plant. Triumphantly he confides in his wife.

"And you know, a year or two will pass and maybe we will find ourselves in Moscow! Masha! Moscow always collects the best, the tried and true, the tested human forces. I might become the head of a department. That isn't bad, Masha! And after that, a vice minister! Minister! Wait, wait. We will have a private villa in the suburbs, someplace near the water reservoir. Oh Moscow, Moscow! What a city! And you, my Masha, you will dazzle everybody with your stately beauty. And at some reception, I will stand aside and admire you, you who will be surrounded by ministers and vice admirals. I close my eyes now, and I see you in a long velvet dress the color of a ripe cherry. Golden bracelets glitter on your wrists. And here, Masha, just a little above your heart, my heart, Masha, in the little channel burns a diamond rose."[8]

There rises from this passage the scent of the new vulgarity wafted from Soviet villas, vice admirals, and diamond roses. The road to them was brutal, nonideological but not inaccessible. That was the *inadvertent* moral of the play. The intended message, on the other hand, spelled out the danger of overreaching, of exaggerated greed for status. Petunias were good; diamond roses were not.

Embourgeoisement made big strides in the thirties. Stalin's notion of the prosperous life permeates his constitution of 1936. The prosperous life became the end of a noble pursuit, while the ascetic life came to be seen as leading to divorce from the people and, worse, to sectarianism. The inexorably political nature of this shift, preceding the war and gaining momentum from it, is a warning against oversimplifying the signals in the passage just quoted. Some elements of the pushy postwar villain's dream remain legitimate. There is nothing wrong with the diamond rose as a symbol of prosperity. Had it been craved for in order to dazzle colleagues and their ladies at some local jubilee, it might even have passed for kulturnost. It might have joined the petunias as a symbol of life both prosperous and esthetic. But the element in it that is not legitimate is the *upperclass* presumptuousness of the diamond rose. Much of Stalin's last frantic period was marked by planting dreams and then by undercutting them, and many were undercut indeed.[9]

The redundancy in middlebrow fiction is required. An issue, overt or covert, is repeated again and again and each variant adds a nuance, rewarding the reader's endurance. In another play, a provincial careerist, a research engineer and party member, attempts to seduce the local social lioness, the spendthrift wife of his boss. He propositions her with a flow of goal-directed flattery.

"You are magnificent in that light frock! Altogether, you do know how to dress! And how could it be otherwise? In this town, after all, you are the lady minister. Yes, Lady Minister!... You could adorn any social gathering in the capital with your presence.

He, too, trespasses into the forbidden zone of the elite, his hallucinations shrouded in a phantasmagoric haze of craved status objects. But they are perilously "cosmopolitan":

"Soon we will finish our work here. It will be a great Russian contribution to world science. I shall receive a sizable bonus. And on to Moscow... You and I, we will have a Bluthner piano, a Telefunken set, and crystal, real French crystal... So that all these things should come alive, we need the poetry of an electric push-button behind which stands the charm of the French word *comfort* and the convenience of the American word *service.*"

Oddly enough, the spoiled and idle belle cuts him down to size. What this variant adds to our insight on transgression is supplied by her self-righteousness. Knowing her place as a creature of meshchanstvo and sensing the postwar respectability of her species, she rejects the scoundrel:

"May I ask you one more intimate question?... Why are you in the party? A meshchanka is asking you that!... You are even worse than I am. I am only a meshchanka. But you are not just a meshchanin. You are a slave of possessions. You are a shell... which does not contain any pearl, but dirt."[10]

The woman defends herself here on the grounds that she is *only* a meshchanka. Gradually, however, this came to be deemed good enough.

Middleclass possessions were, thus, occasionally merely cataloged; occasionally, they were extolled; at other times, they were critically inspected. But whatever the degree of approval, the avalanche of possessions in popular books shows that middleclass desires had become a force in Soviet life.

The picture would be incomplete without the new attitude toward the hard life, want and discomfort. The regime strove for affluence. Deprivation, self-denial, even frugality underwent a deheroization. They were no longer considered romantic, nor in any way useful and came to be regarded as a nuisance, a failure, to be corrected forthwith. The war had helped to bring this problem into the open. For the regime was free to attribute material hardship to the war rather than to its own shortcomings. One dark and glum passage illustrates this new stand on physical misery.

A shellshocked demobilized officer returns home after a night of heavy drinking with a wartime comrade. The setting is not festive Moscow. It is a dreary provincial town, and the time is just after the war. The man is interesting not because he lives in a wretched tenement but because he is aware of his appalling conditions.

With difficulty he found the railing and began to climb. At the very first landing he stumbled over some wood piled up there and almost fell. He had to light a match. A big grey tomcat darted from under his feet. The staircase was steep and narrow and from it ran long corridors with an uncountable number of doors. From the outside, for some incomprehensible reason, the house was divided into a multitude of small cubicles in which people lived as if in an ant heap. From somewhere above resounded hoarse sounds of a victrola. The smell of cabbage from kegs standing in the corridors, at least one to each corridor, filled the whole house with sour stench. Darkness, stench, and humidity pressed down with a repulsive weight, increased his headache, and his head began to burst, as if compressed by powerful pincers.

Finally he reaches his own cubicle and his bed, but

the water in the corridor continued to drip, and Aleksei remembered a story about Chinese torture he read somewhere – drop after drop falls and falls on a shaven head. Only now did he understand that this could bring you to insanity. He got up and went into the corridor. Feeling his way with his hands, he reached the sink and tried to tighten the faucet. But the water stubbornly continued to drip. He lit a match. Under the sink he found some rags. With disgust he took one of them and wrapped it around the faucet. The accursed noise stopped. Trying to close the door gently, Aleksei returned to his apartment, went to the kitchen to get a drink of water. In search of a glass, he lit a remnant of a candle stuck to the edge of the table. The pale light uncovered all the destruction committed here. The ceiling had turned black with damp. In the corner from top to bottom an enormous blue rusty spot was spreading, embracing two walls. The mopped up floor was not dry yet and from it rose a penetrating cold. Aleksei cursed. Eternally, eternally it's the same thing – pipes above, pipes below, pipes around. And they keep on bursting, as if someone paid them for it, flooding the staircases with shrieks of quarreling women... The sight of the kitchen prevented Aleksei altogether from sleeping. He sat down on the edge of his bed and lit a cigarette. Now everything was even more distinctly audible. From someplace came a low, suppressed giggling. Somebody else was coughing up phlegm and spitting on the floor.[11]

The details acquire the cumulative weight of exasperation akin to the one which once drove a Raskolnikov to murder. Indirect evidence, however, must not be misused. The revolution was fought in the name of economic equity. At no time after 1917 were bursting pipes admired; if they are hated here, they were hated before. From the start, the revolution promised the majority a better life and equity in material terms. Millions lost their lives for the dream of a fair distribution of earthly goods. That is precisely what the revolutionary heroes commemorated in the earlier literary periods lived and died for. Yet they themselves were without material cravings and interpreted their high duty as the enactment of self-denial. They would not have even noticed what aggravates this edgy veteran now.

Most urban dwellers were plagued after the war by bursting water pipes. The housing problem was staggering, like all economic problems. A world of soft pink lampshades became all the more desirable. If the young would work hard for them, the regime was not only willing to promise delivery at some point, but to reshape these things into ideologically desirable goals, for from them would come contentment.

Not to desire the good life could now be interpreted as either defeatism or arrogant standoffishness. Personal asceticism was now often regarded as absence of kulturnost or, most dangerously, as something analogous to political sectarianism. And the regime dreaded this. Any such likely, or unlikely, deviationism was suppressed as "divorce from the masses," not being "in touch." But what did it mean to the rulers to be "in touch" or to be "out of touch"? This distinction helps us to understand the meaning of the Big Deal. "Touching" people no longer meant sharing, renewing, repledging the vestiges of the collectivist revolutionary ethos, even if ideological cant to that effect remained in liturgical use. "Touching" people largely meant dishing out promises for a chicken in every pot. This was the only way the rulers knew how to stay in touch with the people, and the only approach they could not disregard.

Who is against middleclass objects?

Having become more than a backdrop, consumer goods now induce central conflicts. In a play about prosperity, suggestively called *Dawn Over Moscow*, a not undeserving character cannot distinguish between legitimate material interest and the obsolete resistance to it. As a curtain raiser, a party official claims clairvoyance: "I know Soviet people well. And I see they want to live a full life." What would a party official mean now by "full life?" In the revolutionary past, it meant only one thing, service to the collective. This play shows what the promise of a full life had changed into, as it revolves around the dilemma of quality versus quantity in the textile industry and the effort to dress women in gay and beautiful clothes.

One textile plant steadily overfulfills its assignment. Its manager is a woman named Solntseva, able and energetic. But she is a kind of party member who is now under observation. Her habits were formed before the war. Because her autocratic temperament overshadows her managerial skill, she is now regarded as an old-timer, an unregenerate stalinist. That she is stubborn would not in itself be bad, for adherence to principles continued to be valued. The trouble is that she is against the newly defined "full life." It goes against the grain of this ideologue that it is to be converted into a "beautiful life."

Solntseva is hardworking, but her fabrics, alas, are described by the plant's very own party organizer like this: "The patterns are all gray, all sorts of little squares and little triangles. Where in the world do they get them from? Probably from geometry textbooks."[12] Grayness is the consequence of Solntseva's conception of her factory's goal: "To give the people sufficient mass goods, practical and inexpensive." (p. 12). But these goods literally nauseate the vice minister of the textile industry. And he exclaims to Solntseva: "You overfulfill the plan all right! But the stores are littered with the junk you produce!" (p. 150). A venerable professor of fine arts joins the critics. He explains why:

"Sometimes on the street you chance to meet what I would call a marvelous girl. But she is clad like a sparrow. That's shameful! We spend our time applying all sorts of artistic notions on canvas, but in life real beauty is wrapped up, excuse me, in a sack."   [pp. 17-18]

The new dream called for women to be dressed like princesses. The manager defends the traditional philosophy:

"Basic production requires good craftsmanship too. One plant produces luxurious passenger cars and another one produces tractors. Which is more honorable, that is the question? The limousines will roll on asphalt and the tractor will plough our dear black soil. What we need is modesty. What if everybody should want to climb into a limousine?"

She forgets that everybody does. Moreover everybody – at least in plays and novels – was now ordered to wish it.

The main attack on the old principles Solntseva represents comes from a rank-and-file woman worker. She is "advanced" because she understands the new emphasis on aesthetics:

"Judge me as you wish, but I must have my say! I remember the last day of war. When they announced on the radio that we had returned to peace, I took out of my chest my best prewar fabric, on which I had worked myself, and I burst into tears! I swear to you, such an idiot I was, I wept from happiness! Now, I though,, just see what beautiful things we will make! Our women worked hard through the war, and now we will prepare a holiday for them! Let them dress up like queens! They have deserved it! Just think what technology our country has given us! But here our manager still craves to produce underwear in orphanage patterns!"
                                                                                  [p. 141]

Led by the party organizer, the champions of the new cause proceed with a counterplan. The new fabric is to be "multicolored, beautiful . . . joyful, like a ray of the morning sun" (p. 120). It is to be adorned with "a simple, clear, noble pattern . . . like a son" (p. 133). It is to bloom "like a meadow in the spring" (p. 126). Inspired by this applied patriotism, the activists choose the "pure and transparent" design of nunnery lace. The nuns had once imitated the frost patterns of their old monastery windows (p. 136). In this somewhat roundabout way, "ancient Russian fairytale motifs" and delicate snowflakes are impressed on the goods.

All alone, Solntseva resists the reform. She refuses to work for what in her opinion is the taste of extinct prerevolutionary merchant wives (p. 151). She is wrong not only as a public figure but as a private person as well. She is a war widow and insists on remaining single though there is an acceptable suitor at hand. This man raises silver foxes in Siberia. She rejects him, though he keeps flying in from remote lands to woo her. People around are critical of her stubbornness. Once, in an enticing gesture, the suitor drapes a blue fox around her managerial shoulders with the words:

"Look, Kapa, the pride of Siberian lands!"

She does not react with gratitude.

"You are laughing at me, Anton! A woman partisan and in fur stoles! Offer it to some empty-headed girl."   [p. 143]

This hurts the suitor but she presses on by hinting that authorities are doing the wrong thing. Moreover, she boasts:

"I give the country millions of yards. Millions! Do you want me to gaze into the crystal ball over each yard of fabric? We have a national problem. We must provide clothing for the people quickly."   [p. 180]

And clearly she goes too far by adding:

"The war is over, but the guns are not silent."

Her righteous suitor cuts her down to size:

"Let guns be guns. People say we should not forget them. However, the time has come to build a new life, to fill every day with happiness. But you are viewing life from behind the windows of your office."   [p. 136]

This is a momentous reproach, dreaded in Soviet doctrine: estrangement from the collective and the party. The emphasis had shifted from public duty alone to duty enhanced by pleasure and prosperity. The objects of the promised beautiful life make up a program. Solntseva fails to grasp the political significance of the tastes of the new merchant wives.

Communists like Solntseva came to be portrayed less and less frequently in a positive light. This might be put somewhat differently. The presumption of this particular amazon bothered the regime not because she could not be redeemed. *Qua* stalinist "old-timer," she could be – and, indeed, in due time in the play's finale, was – properly straightened out. (It was the real old-timers, the revolutionary ones, who proved unredeemable.) While in error, however, this particular amazon is meddling with a touchy issue. She is resisting the shift in priorities from quantity to quality and, by logical extension, from heavy to light industry. She points inadvertently to an obfuscation designed to cover government hypocrisy. For the regime was doing one thing while saying another. It was, in fact, doing what the amazon advocated: it was arming, and it was doing so at the expense of the people's hopes. Concessions to consumer demands were made largely in plays and novels. Petunias in imaginary gardens or printed on imaginary fabrics acquired promissory significance. The regime held this bouquet in its hands as bargaining trumps.

Who wins what?

The next story – bearing the name of a lovely young woman Nastya – deals with love more than with work, and dresses figure even more prominently in it. Written in 1945, its setting is pauperized and devastated Leningrad. The tone of the piece, though, is determinedly upbeat. Protagonists are doggedly concerned with the resumption of a full life, and a curious affluence surrounds the three main protagonists: a man, his wife, and his mistress.

An engineer is preparing himself for the arrival of his wife and children, who have been away from Leningrad during the war. The man is now happy with his mistress, in whose apartment he has lived through the siege, a bomb having hit his building and destroyed everything in it. When destiny had thrown them together during an air attack, they had confessed to each other their terror of bombs, of death. Soon thereafter Pavel had fallen critically ill and Nastya had nursed him back to life, sacrificing her own rations. They knew then that they were in love. With nostalgia, the engineer now recollects how irrationally glorious those days had been, and how heartily they had laughed together. In a wave of gratitude, the man realizes at last that he had not exactly showered his mistress with gifts. So he buys an expensive dress for her birthday, eagerly anticipating her joy over it.

Nastya did not have many clothes and it had never occurred to him to dress her up a bit. Strange, but this problem did not exist either for her or for him. He remembered how each spring and each fall his wife used to examine her wardrobe and it invariably turned out that she had nothing to wear. In haste, then, something was purchased, sewn, fitted. And thereupon unforeseen expenses were incurred. For the new suit demanded a new hat. A new hat demanded new gloves. Did Nastya have hats? Did she have gloves? He had not noticed somehow. She lived like a bird who did not need anything except sunshine.[13]

The expensive glittering silvery dress brings Nastya grief instead of pleasure. She weeps bitterly over the ill-timed present, and Pavel is at a loss. He realizes that he will soon be confronted by Zoya, his wife for the twelve years of marriage, and the three of separation. He does not know what to do, even though Nastya "understands." The day comes nearer and nearer.

He devoted his evening to fixing up the apartment. Zoya's girlfriend, alerted by Zoya's letter, showed up. She declared that a multitude of objects had to be acquired. He had not even suspected their existence. Perhaps they had never been there. Perhaps they had perished. Perhaps they were stolen. Kerosene cooker; floor brush; pressing iron; wash basin; buckets. Zoya's friend suspiciously asked where and how he had lived all this time.   [p. 384]

And the last night with his mistress is upon him. Nastya proves stoic, resigned, giving, tender. She packs all his personal belongings and gives him up. She does this rapidly, quietly, with pain and with dignity.

In due time he finds himself at the railroad station.

And suddenly he saw her in front of him exactly as she had been before – meticulously dressed, clean, with delicate lipstick on her lips and a bit of mascara on her eyelashes. And the long-limbed boy and girl standing by her side were undoubtedly his children, if only because they too, in all likelihood, had been scrubbed and dressed up just before arrival.

After some hesitation he embraces his wife, whose beauty remains undamaged by the three unspeakable years. He hugs his children. The chauffeur helps with the luggage. Zoya produces

suitcases, boxes, bundles, sacks. He was terrified by the quantity of objects. Zoya, however, solemnly allowed: "What do you think, we've brought lard, of course, and potatoes and onions and eggs and all sorts of things. Mother has been gathering stuff for us for two months."   [p. 385]

The car rapidly fills with all the belongings, so that there is only room for Zoya to ride alone with the chauffeur. The father and children go by streetcar.

Ensconced in domesticity, Zoya at once uses her feminine strategy. She wraps herself seductively in houserobes and drops playful hints as to the inevitability of confessions from him. She pretends to be serene. Once in a while, she pointedly tells him about the "'siege escapades' of some acquaintance or other, emphasizing that an intelligent wife would not pay them any attention" (p. 390). Meanwhile Nastya is transferred to another job, as is the wartime mistress of one of Pavel's highly placed colleagues. This seems to assuage Pavel's conscience. He says to himself: "everybody does it." But serenity will not come!

Zoya's self-control was full of hidden tension. In her habitual flirtatiousness and her imperious wilfulness there was something frantic. In her care, to which he had been long accustomed, a clinging purposefulness became now evident. It seemed that every cup of coffee, every pressed shirt collar was made to testify: "So you see, you are well off. You can't possibly part with all this."   [p. 389]

The strategy culminates in a lavish house-warming party. "The table was resplendently set for supper." The apartment that evening fills with important people,

dressed festively, with a din of voices, with explosions of laughter, with women's exclamations, with all that artificial commotion created by people when they feel obliged to have a good time.

Pavel tries hard to participate. He

showed his library to the men and offered them expensive cigarettes, purchased by Zoya for the occasion. He himself never smoked them. He also plied the ladies with monotonous amenities.   [p. 392]

The high point of this story might well be the description of the festive board.

Zoya called the guests to sit down. The hors d'oeuvres and the drinks were superb. Zoya calmly directed the supper's progress. She assisted the shy guests effectively. She enlisted the help of those who felt at ease. She also knew how to tactfully restrain those men who were inclined to empty their glasses and to refill them too rapidly. And she listened to the compliments paid to her cooking with an air as if the preparation of this supper party had not required infinite trouble, planning, effort, and two weeks of most stringent saving of money.   [p. 393]

One of the guests is a lovely young woman, full of charm, professional competence, and loyalty to her husband. She is good, naive, unscheming. Significantly, her admiration for the skill and active kulturnost of the hostess is boundless:

"You know how to do everything! I could not have accomplished any of this at all."

But the air of the fashionable soirée is troubled. Imprudently, Pavel's boss voices near-poetic incredulity that this elegantly appointed dwelling is the very one that had been gutted one fearsome morning by a bomb. That does it. The festive mood vanishes. In turn, and at cross-purposes, the guests comment on the marital hardships and advantages of wartime separations. The inquisitive "best" friend poisonously suggests that husbands may have been well taken care of during the siege. Pavel's boss attempts vigorously to clear the air. And it is his soothing proclamation that gives point to this tale:

"We should not spoil this good evening by mutual suspicions . . . We have all gone through hell. But it was an interesting period. And we all regret that we could not go through it together. However, who knows whether we would be alive and hale today had we had to support our families? And somehow now we don't understand each other perfectly. But we have returned to normal family life like exhausted swimmers who have reached the shore with great difficulty. Our arms presently clutch a cliff and our tongues hang out."

But instead of saving the day, this man, alas, trips up Pavel. For these words make him rhapsodize over the siege as a time that had been for some "the most lofty, the most beautiful in our lives." His ecstatic confession evokes a treacherous brief comment from his wife's "best" friend: "And the most sinless?" Pavel retorts with undisguised anger:

"I don't know what you are hinting at. This period may have been sinful, complex, whatever you wish to call it! But narrow measurements don't fit. When the chances of life and death are equal and, perhaps, those of death tilt the balance, puny words such as hanky-panky and sins and all the rest are inappropriate."

At this awkward moment, the imperturbable wife addresses herself to her spouse:

"Pavlusha, please, pass the pastry. And, please, pour the ladies some wine and

offer the men wine or liqueurs, whatever anyone chooses. I shall clear the table.
Let's, perhaps, put some records on."   [pp. 394-395]

In the kitchen, when the two find themselves for a moment alone, she
runs a hand through his hair and says "with her usual artificial cheerful-
ness":

"If you have a tactful wife you should be tactful yourself. Right? Keep your
tender memories to yourself. It is clear that I don't ask you about anything. You
must appreciate this, my darling!" [p. 396]

He gets drunk and plunges into self-laceration.

Why the devil had he suggested some sort of measurement to that bitch who sticks
her nose into other people's affairs? Hadn't he himself slid right down to her
narrow, philistine, petty, vicious laws of conduct? "Everybody does it." For the
sake of the family? For the sake of duty? For the sake of the children?   [p. 397]

And that very night he runs to his mistress: to stay.

Of the two women, who wins love? Who wins honor? Or, more perti-
nently, who wins approval? Who has the responsibility of representing
the rock to which the family nexus clings? Perhaps neither. The real
winner is the atmosphere, the social ambience. The postwar noncomba-
tive, very accommodating tone, sympathetically illustrates the spirit of
meshchanstvo. The calculating, manipulative strategy of the wife was
considered the norm, while the self-sacrificial vulnerability of the mistress appears colored by romanticism.

The needs of both these women coexist and overlap. It is the encroach-
ment of discordant desires that should be emphasized. It is not clear
whether the mistress, with no possessions, unburdened by nesting and
breeding, is admirable because she is new as a type, or because she is an
afterglow of a repressed and receding ideal. Nor is it clear what the
stubborn acquisitive wife represents – atavistic meshchanstvo, or a rock to
which the war-ravaged social order can cling?

The informality of a story, as against a novel or play, permits the
author to avoid mandatory resolutions. Even if the mistress acquires a
romantic halo, the wife does not come off badly. Once her kind of
meshchanstvo begins to merge with the sanctity of the family, her role
absolves her from proving herself on other scores. Her formidable social
function exempts her from being impeccably positive. So there remains a
tension in the tale. Giving and undemanding, the mistress is curiously out
of key with the milieu. She inspires the confused husband to go against
meshchanstvo. But the lovers are in a double bind, wedged between the
vestigial meshchanstvo of the wife and the systemic meshchanstvo of the
milieu which sustains the wife throughout the war, explains her make-up,
her massive luggage, and her acquisitiveness; and which manifests itself,
above all, in the matter-of-fact normalcy of the story's tone.

4. New Protagonists

Road to Life

I stand for that image of a revolutionary for whom the private is nothing in comparison with the public.[1]

So said a canonized hero of the revolutionary epoch, commemorating an entire ideology. Revolutionary literature steered the young toward the right Road to Life.[2] Truth was posited as social truth alone.

In the twenties and thirties, writers who shared the regime's views conceived man as a receptacle for external, social impulses. Society was an infinitely more valuable good than man. Collectivism was presented to the young as the highest value. All behavior was examined from the standpoint of economic and class environment. Despite the dogmatic aspect of these views, room was left for exploration. For instance, the relationship between private and public life was, indeed, considered. But though the frontier between the spheres was extensively commented on and even romanticized, the autonomy of the private, of the personal, was resolutely denied. The public was set up to rule over the private, whose subordination was justified by a streamlined, if simplistic, view of human nature. Man was the result of social impulses.

This environmental absolutism helped to sort, diagnose, and cure the problems of youth. It also led to the useful notion of cultural lag, and provided a weapon against antisocial manifestations by calling them residual byproducts of the prerevolutionary past. They were called "residues" or "birthmarks." All personal deviations from approved social norms, such as homicide or independent thought, could be seen as just such vestiges. In short, the environment in its economic and class aspects determined all problems. It was made to account for all results, the bad as well as the good.

"The family plus environment is responsible." In the thirties this casual sequence established itself firmly, and many writers illustrated it with dogged devotion. For example, young criminals in fiction were occasionally permitted a psychological twist, or tragic determinism. Here is one confessing:

"I am a thief! . . . I am a recidivist, do you hear? I have been sentenced innumerable times. It's high time they shot me " . . . He knew that his last loneliness would start right away . . . and that he would pay for his dog's life and for his death . . . for all his humiliations and for his hunger and for all the prisons and for his escapes and for his father who was a scoundrel and for his mother who was a whore, for everything, properly and fully.[3]

A scoundrel for a father and a whore for a mother; it went a long way to explain the criminal inclination of their child.

The result of impulses from without, received more or less passively, was not necessarily crime; it might be its opposite. The more common theme, in fact, was the Road to Life of the militant party activist whose heroism was motivated by revulsion against a rotten childhood.

One such hero belongs to the leather-jacket era. His jacket conceals a gun. Tense and devout, he serves in the purist ranks of the secret police. Born in degradation as a calamitous surprise to a prostitute, he spends his childhood in proximity to his mother's trade. The initial trauma is a constant ingredient in his dedication to the party. Because of his rigidity, in the end he can accept neither his own sin, which is for him the loss of sexual virginity, nor the party's sin. He sees this in the advent of the NEP, the great economic compromise of the twenties, a similar loss of virginity. He commits suicide. The genetic trauma, as it were, forces him to do so: fatalism overcomes him, anchored in the private nightmare of his childhood. His public and private purism is an attempt to compensate and atone. The key to this man, open and obvious, lies in his memories:

Lidov came, not Zavalishin. After him others. At first names, then persons, then a series of them. The dark ones. The blonde ones. And the one with warts. The one who came yesterday gnashed his teeth. And next door in a dark room . . . slept little white Kolya under a quilt on top of a chest of drawers . . . They shuffled about, struggled, gulped, groaned. Shallow laughter. A sigh. A belch. Silence. He asked. Mother sobbed. Her cheeks under tears puffed up like gingerbread and he understood: keep your mouth shut. It might be that he got used to it all. But feverishly he pitied mama. He shivered under his quilt because of a greedy compassion. During the day mama would go to buy sausage in the tavern. Then he kissed the hollow in her bed, the imprint of her body.[4]

In many novels human steel was forged out of the raw material of abandoned and orphaned children, the civil war victims. They were legion. There were those who were rehabilitated by the new mother: Mother Revolution. Lack of family was as formative a mold as the wrong family.

I know neither mother nor father. I was a waif.[5] A beggar, I slept under fences. I starved and I had no shelter. It was a dog's life. Nothing like yours, you sissies and mama's boys. But then came Soviet power. And Red Army men picked me up. As a whole detachment, they adopted me. They gave me shoes, gave me clothes, and taught me how to read. But the most important thing, they gave me a human understanding. Through them I have become a bolshevik and I'll remain one till my death. I know what the struggle is all about: it is for us, for us paupers, for the power of the workers.[6]

Out of the condemnation of the family and of the "unfamily," out of the final funeral of the old world there were born the revolutionary heroes, the promethean men, the canonized champions of the Vita Nuova. They were to be revered for a long time. Determinism notwithstanding, they articulated the grandeur of their own power as did one famous hero of the turbulent early twenties. Fearless and selfless, he leads a doomed guerilla detachment. While lost with his small unit in the wilderness of Siberia, he meditates on his faith in social change.

And Levinson was agitated because the deepest and most important matters preoccupied him. In the overcoming of all this misery and poverty lay the basic meaning of his own life. There would be no Levinson, but some other person, if there did not burn in him a desire, not comparable with any other need, for a new, fine, strong, generous human being. But how could one even talk of a new, generous human being while uncountable millions were forced to live such a primitive and pitiful, such an unspeakably shabby life?... And he tried to remember himself in childhood, in early youth. But this was difficult for him. The experiences of recent years, when he had become known to everyone as Levinson who was the leader, were too deeply and solidly ingrained and had become too important to him.

A true hero such as this was predetermined by circumstance, environment, and the ethos of the revolution. Much as there was for a man in the vanguard to think about, he steered clear of introspection most of the time. Yet:

The only thing he managed to remember was an old family photograph with a puny Jewish boy on it with large naive eyes and wearing a black jacket. He was staring with a surprising, unchildish determination at that spot from where, he was told at the time, a beautiful little bird was supposed to fly out. But the bird did not fly out at all. And he remembered now that he almost burst into tears with disappointment. He had to have many more such disappointments before he became finally convinced that "that's not the way things ever turn out!" And when he had become really convinced of it, he understood what incalculable harm was inflicted on people by those little birds which were supposed to fly out of somewhere and which many people await all their lives in vain. No, he had no need of them any longer. He had crushed in himself mercilessly this inactive, sweet longing for them. He had crushed everything in himself that he had inherited from those damaged generations, raised on false tales about beautiful little birds! "To perceive everything the way it is in order to change that which is and to bring about that which ought to be" – this is the most simple and the most taxing wisdom at which Levinson had arrived... he felt the swell of extraordinary strength which raised him to unreachable heights and from this towering, earthly, human height he conquered his weaknesses, his own weak body.[7]

Faith in the one and only Road saw at the beckoning end of it the glory of a new and just society. This faith provided the certainty with which the line of demarcation was laid between the private and public spheres. If the two coexisted, they did so in abrasive hostility. The public, much like St. George, kept fervently slaying the private dragon. The model marcher was expected to cleanse himself of personal needs before stepping onto the Road. This was the orthodox mood, which prevailed well into the thirties. And such was the message of one novel of that period which stands out as a canonical version of the bolshevik ethos. It stand out as the towering document of the whole thirties period. The author immortalized himself and the epoch of heroic valor in this semiautobiographical account entitled *The Tempering of Steel* (1934). He glorified the victory of the public over the private so well that hardly any other hero had the impact of his Korchagin.

The novel, as the title implies, deals with a man of steel, an ideal communist. His success has to do with one fact. Unlike his predecessors of the chaotic twenties, he is a man without psychological complexities. A cruel and humiliating prerevolutionary childhood gives him all the hatred necessary for a dedicated service to the revolution. As an adolescent, he goes off to take part in the civil war. The civil war leaves him with a cracked skull and a severely damaged spine, but his spirit is intact. A steellike resilience helps him to recover. At seventeen he becomes a tested communist. In the end, his struggle with death equals his devotion to the cause.

He insisted on unrelaxing effort, and craved the most dangerous assignments either in the Red army or among civilian reconstruction workers. His will to remain in the fighting ranks caused him a spectacular struggle with adversity. Before he was thirty he became paralyzed and lost his sight. And yet this living corpse stayed active. With superhuman discipline, always conscious that self-pity would destroy him, he overcame his own tragedy. He forced himself to become a student of a Red university by correspondence. Later he gathered all his inner resources to become a writer. So he continued to be a paragon of communist service. In his time such giving precluded any kind of taking. Self-sacrificial service to the collective makes vivid the comparison between the kind of heroism required in his era and that of the postwar period. His sacrifice is instructive not so much because he served the collective well but because he lived according to the dominant virtue of his time. The highest then was not wanting anything in return. Sacrifice became its own antithesis by turning into total satisfaction. Such a public man could take nothing in recompense, nothing at any rate resembling an ordinary material or status reward. The building of a new society was the gift he gave and the gift he received, the very same gift.

Not only can such a man afford no "private" life; it is incomprehensible to him. In his native town, there waits for him a long-suffering, understanding, truly proletarian mother. When, still very young, he returns there briefly, she tactfully puts a question to him. Is he in such a hurry to go back to Kiev because, perhaps, he has found a sweetheart there?

"I only see you, when you get hurt," his mother was saying in a gentle voice, packing into a clean bag her son's poor belongings... "Mother, I swore to myself that I wouldn't have anything to do with girls until we finish off the bourgeois in the whole world. You say it's too long too wait? No, mother dear, the bourgeois cannot hold out for long. There shall be only one republic for all people. And we shall send you – all you hardworking oldsters– to Italy. There is such a warm country on the sea. Mother, there never is any winter there. We shall settle you in bourgeois palaces and you will stretch your poor old bones in the warm sun. And we, we will take off for America to finish off the bourgeoisie there."[8]

As he had promised his mother, he does not permit himself to fall in love. He holds back, although the opportunities are numerous and women fall in love with him. When he does get married, the arrangement is ideological. Once more, it rests on his givingness. In the early stage of his incurable illness, he meets a girl raised in a stifling lower-middleclass family. She is mousy, oppressed, ideologically "unawakened." He transforms her. Korchagin could not very well have married his equal. That would have been too easy. As husband, he considers it his primary duty to start his backward companion on the Road. Only a short time later, prostrate with disease, he offers his wife a divorce, so as not to be a burden to her. Increasingly she has less and less time for him. For she is now strenuously training to become a party member. But, of course, she remains loyal. On his part, it would not occur to him to complain of his loneliness. He takes pride in his wife's new independence. It does not matter to him that she still works as a dishwasher. And the day when this humble woman at last gains admission to the party is a day of greater happiness to him than to her.

There was nothing unclear about the monolithic moral face of those early models. They were, to say the least, one-dimensional. They lived for the Public Purpose. And they themselves lacked differentiation, as myths do. In their case it was the grand myth of the implementation of the revolution. Dying, blind and paralyzed, Korchagin writes:

I still believe that I shall return into the ranks and that in the attacking columns there also will be my bayonet. I cannot not believe. I have no right to. For ten years the party and the komsomol educated me in the art of resistance and the words of our leader were meant for me: "There are no fortifications that the bolsheviks cannot take."   [p. 161]

These men were totally absorbed in fulfilling their faith. It ordained a revulsion against private values as a matter of belief, not celebration. Their attempt to understand themselves was a search without any private intent, largely even without individual psychological awareness. They made their self-analysis – as they did everything else – under the aspect of service to the collective.

Certain articles of faith became even more poignant when enacted with

the special revolutionary verve of the new woman, the liberated revolutionary woman. The weight of the patriarchal, autocratic, sex-
discriminating tradition in Russia had pressed especially harshly on women. Curiously, the revolution in its own way set up a new disparity
between the destiny of revolutionary men and women. It promised
woman what she did not have before: equality. But, in return, it set a
large and discriminatory "feminine" price for the promise. It took the
family away from the awakened woman, or it tried to do so.

We find one model heroine of days gone by in a famous novel, *Cement*.
One of its main themes is the development of the new proletarian woman.
The heroine's husband is fighting in the civil war. Meanwhile, the heroine
– Dasha Chumalova – learns from bloody experience all the viciousness of
the old forms of life. She grows to be a "conscious" bolshevik. She discovers the new revolutionary morality. In the end she becomes its embodiment.

The husband is a valiant Red soldier. On his return from the front, he
proves an equally valiant reconstruction worker. He is a man of energy,
willpower, and faith. Yet marital conflict becomes inevitable because he
craves for a home and a family. In his absence Dasha has changed a great
deal. He watches with apprehension her face "tired but tense and stern as
though she were clenching her teeth." With mounting irritation, he chal-
lenges her:

"Tell me, Dasha, how should I take all this? I have been in the army. It was
tough. I had no respite and not one minute to think about myself. And now I have
come home, to my own house, and for the first time I feel wretched. I don't sleep
at night, waiting for you. All this time you haven't slept at home. And I don't
know where you are; it's as if I have been pushed into a hole to sit with mice and
frogs. We haven't been together for three years."[9]

Her reply is forthright enough. The change in her signifies a drastic
departure from his views. And she is not about to regret the loss of her
domestic instinct. Her reply is a clear summary of what the new Soviet
woman rejects after the revolution:

"Do you want pretty flowers to curl on the windowsills and a bed piled with
down pillows? No, Gleb, in the winter I live in an unheated room . . . and I eat in
the communal kitchen. You see, I am a free Soviet citizen."   [p. 46]

As for him, apart from his atavistic longing for flowers on the windowsill,
he considers his wife not so much a free Soviet citizen as his property.
When she tells him that in the trying years of their separation, she had
known other men, he turns "blind with rage" and calls her a "dirty bitch"
who has "laid in the ditch with a lot of tramps." Controlling herself, she
replies with a mixture of sententiousness and hope in the educative power
of the revolution:

"Don't you see, you can't yet listen to me properly. You are a communist. But
you are still an animal. And you need a woman as a slave, a slave to go to bed
with. You are a good soldier. But you are a bad communist."   [p. 117]

Tainted with the past, this man also feels that it is a mother's duty to care for her child. Dasha's awakening, however, leads her to reject the family and let the state raise her child. When he finds out that Dasha has placed their little girl in a children's home, his first impulse is to retrieve her at once. The liberated woman threatens that he can do it only if he commits himself to caring for the child. Times are hard. Conditions in the children's home are nothing short of appalling. In bright daylight, the father sees the fledglings of the State claw each other for a morsel of food.

"All of them, those poor little creatures, will starve to death, Dashka. You ought all to be shot for the jobs you are doing."

Terrified, he wants to know if their own daughter is struggling for survival in the same way. Of all the quarrels between this man and woman, both pressed in different ways against the wall by the revolution, this one is the most revealing:

"And why is Nurka [the child] to be more favored than the others? She too has suffered. But if it weren't for us women, lice and disease would have devoured the children and starvation would have wiped them out."
    "Are you trying to tell me that you have saved Nurka, you and the other noisy women, by doing all this?"
    "Yes, comrade Gleb. Exactly. Just like that.   [p. 58]

The child dies, in that children's home: not only from malnutrition and disease, but from lack of maternal love. In a scene much discussed from the mid twenties on, the dying child implores the mother:

"I want to be with you – so that you never go away again and so that you should be close – and grapes – I want you and grapes."   [p. 313]

True, Dasha weeps, flings herself down on mother earth, and tears it with her nails. Yet she personifies the new morality by making herself free. She dispenses with her child, domesticity, her husband for the sake of her public duty and her part in the making of the new life. She breaks up her marriage because she cannot compromise with a man who does not fully appreciate the formidable and costly equality of the new Soviet woman.
    Remembering these famous novels of prewar periods helps to establish a perspective. They were imbued with the bolshevik spirit, and the values of which they spoke were anti-individualistic and "antifamily." This was not a comfortable code. With it went a zest for a barren home life, even a complete denial of it. In those faraway days, the style of life of the avant-garde meant more than Spartan sobriety. It was not sober; it was intoxicated by its own harshness. Like revolutionary fervor, however, flamboyant romanticism does not last. The classical heroes and heroines disappeared: not because of attrition alone, nor because at some point the regime had no more use for them. It was rather because they were an oversimplification in the first place. As literary images, they symbolized ideological propositions and not psychological complexities. In the de-

cline of revolutionary heroes, one can see the revenge of human nature on extreme didacticism.

But what happened next? How did the regime handle this decline? The handling turned out to be careful and expedient. The successful early heroes were never openly disavowed, for they were few and precious. Instead, they were relegated to history and their flamboyant romanticism was transformed into a sacred monument. So they were made both obsolete and ineffective. Their shortcomings (or rather "largecomings"), such as their cosmic revolutionary zeal, were in this way not held against them so much as held against their postwar heirs, who still held the tacitly disavowed beliefs. Much confusion was in store for those who wished to reopen the heroic Road to Life.

It was also seen to lead to a dead end, for the postulates about both the public and the private had started to corrode. The grandiose collective idea of the supremacy of the masses was undercut by the stalinist proposition that only the authorities were able to judge what was what in that sphere. Trespassers landed behind barbed wires. This did not mean that the individual was about to gain autonomy; that continued to be denied. The rulers, however, began to set up guidelines as to how certain features of the public will were to blend with certain manifestations of the individual will. A way was being worked out to close this gap, torn open by revolutionary zeal. So a new answer was found as to why the people should work for the social good. Coercive compliance was being converted into the instrumental.

When did the turning point occur? When did the rulers turn away from the legacy of the proletarian revolution? When did they undertake what amounted to an appeal to middleclass values? Two answers seem possible here. Successful stalinization of the social order, as expressed in Stalin's commentaries on his constitution, prepared the way for the ideological rise of the notion of prosperity. Stalin thus gave, in 1936, all the incentives needed for the conversion of the public into the private.[10] One could see this as no more than a program, or the initial stage of the system's embourgeoisement – embourgeoisement from above, engulfing the party first. It is therefore possible to argue that the real turning point occurred during the war, at a time of catastrophic strain when, inevitably, the pivotal social strata (on whom survival depended) managed to make their demands and expectations known. This could be seen as a demand for embourgeoisement from below.

There is no need to decide which of the turning points is more important: the fusion of goals from above and from below is what really matters. Stalinist literature itself is more indicative in the postwar period for the study of the Soviet middle class. One reason is that the memory of the revolution was still vivid in the thirties. Moreover, in that terrible period of transition, confusion, and terror, middlebrow fiction ran for cover. Nor had it yet been instructed to broach the soothing, slow, evolutionary (and hypocritical) theme of the blending of public and private purposes: not while Ezhov[11] walked the land, nor during the trials, nor during Stalin's first bloodbath. It is only the very perceptive and independent writer who would think of connecting the bloodbath with the regime's embourgeoisement and express fear and disgust. That perception added only to the list of martyrs. Obviously, middlebrow fiction does not explore much without orders. Subservient as it is, and so quite sluggish, it caught up with the large theme of Soviet middleclass preferences only after the war, only when it was told to do so, and then cautiously, judiciously, with a twist.

Pronouns in transition

Proletarian poets speak neither of "I"
Nor of the individual.
"I" for the proletarian poet
Is the same as an obscenity.[12]

Soviet youth of 1917, engaged in changing the world, reappraised pronouns. In the wake of the revolution, poems glorified the collective "We." The "I" seemed both puny and shameful. The "collective breast" had won the revolution at home and was now marching triumphantly to conquer the world. The spirit soared to messianic heights.

We are the countless, awesome legions of Labor.
We have conquered the spaces of oceans and land,
With the light of artificial suns we have lit up the cities,
Our proud souls burn with the fire of revolt.
We are possessed by turbulent, intoxicating passion,
Let them shout at us: "You are the executioners of beauty,"
In the name of our Tomorrow we shall burn Raphael,
Destroy museums, trample the flowers of art.
We have thrown off the heavy, crushing legacy,
We have rejected the myths of wisdom bled white,
Young girls in the luminous kingdom of the Future
Shall be more beautiful than the Venus of Milo . . .
Our muscles crave gigantic work,
Creative pangs seethe in our collective breast,
With miraculous honey we shall fill the comb to the brim,
For our planet we shall find a new, dazzling path.
We love life, its intoxicating wild ecstasy,
Our spirit is tempered by fierce struggle and suffering.
We are everybody, we are in everything, we are the flame and the victorious light,
We are our own Deity, and Judge, and Law.[13]

This poem, composed triumphantly in 1917 by a young proletarian, became a model. Many such "We" odes were chanted and marched to.

Pronouns denote relationships. In the loud language of revolution what gives man promethean power is his relationship to society. Actively linked to the common good, man can apotheosize his small individual destiny. He can become sovereign. But the revolutionary ardor subsided and the feel of collectivity changed. Some twenty years later – during Stalin's purges – a typical rhapsody sounded like this:

> For the sake of our happiness
> He marched through all storms.
> He carried our holy banner
> Over our enormous land.
> And fields and factories rose,
> And tribes and people responded
> To the call of the leader
> To face the final battle.
>
> From his eyes, clear and pure,
> We took courage and strength
> Like radiant water from a deep well
> On our fighting road.
> Let us, comrades, sing a song
> About the greatest general,
> The most fearless and strong,
> About Stalin let's sing a song . . .
>
> He gave us forever and ever
> Youth, glory, and power.
> He has lit the clear dawn of spring
> Over our homes.
> Let us sing, comrades, a song
> About the dearest person,
> About our sun, about the truth of nations,
> About Stalin let's sing a song.[14]

"We" poetry had become "He" poetry. The collective was no longer its own Deity and Judge and Law. It was transformed into grateful recipients of benefits bestowed by Stalin. If the collective still marched, it did so awkwardly, on its knees.[15]

The revolutionary hero was clearly in trouble. A play written in 1930 deals with a revisionist attitude toward the collective. Small wonder that the play was blacklisted during the years of terror.[16] Its setting is Stalin's war against the peasant during the agricultural revolution. A man and a woman are arguing. He is a party official sent to uncooperative villages where he must enforce grain delivery and punish resisting peasants. The woman, whom he loves, suggests that since the job of executioner goes against his nature, he should refuse it. His confessional answer, shedding light on the fear of self under fear, has a significance to this day, and not only in relation to public Soviet man.

RAEVSKY: The party uses people where it needs them.

OLGA: But people may be guided by personal considerations. They cannot be covered by the work "party." The party is people.

RAEVSKY: No.

OLGA: What is it, then?

RAEVSKY: The party is a hoop. It is an iron band which holds people together.

OLGA: Perhaps. But that band sometimes hurts. Not everybody is alike. People are not like small bushes. It's impossible to prune them and make them all even. You are different from –

RAEVSKY: I have thought about it. The band often cuts my flesh. But I cannot live without it.

OLGA: You say incomprehensible things.

RAEVSKY: It is complicated, Olga. There was never a chance to talk about it. Imagine a crowd. A standard crowd with identical people wearing ties of the same color. The crowd moves in one direction and speaks the very same measured words. I do not want to be like them. Sometimes I think with horror that every day I put on the same tie as all of them. But there is a more frightening feeling than that. Imagine, Olga, that the crowd passes by without you. And you are left behind alone with your own thoughts and doubts. And the columns keep on marching by. They repeat their words. They sing their songs. And no one turns toward you and their measured step is merciless. I cannot step out of the column, precisely because there are in me these divergent thoughts and divergent feelings. I cannot go away. I need somebody's shoulder next to mine. I need someone to order me and restrain me. I need the band which holds together the various sides of my I.

OLGA: And what if you are misled?

RAEVSKY: I will go and die with all the others. I have fought for the party. I am its soldier.[17]

The first person singular, uncovered in its weakness, eventually spells this soldier's undoing. It turns out that he takes more than he gives, for his personal needs dwarf his energy. It is also obvious that the party, then as later, had more urgent matters on its agenda than to "hold together the various sides" of an unsturdy ego. This old believer craved to remain true and ardent. But he was bothersome to stalinism, and was done away with. A more suitable believer was recruited. The revolutionary collective had marched in ecstasy toward a Utopia; but under Stalin the destination was reached. Utopia had come about and it had to be lived in. The party soldier in need of being propped up is at fault because his introvert proclivities induce him to scrutinize his own life at the end of the road. He fails not so much because he whines – anachronistically at that, while he is stalking about shooting recalcitrant peasants – but, rather because he flails about as a self-conscious person, painfully aware of his fragility. And it was against this that Stalin's purges were to be directed: to crush the searching self in the party's rank and file. The revolution required true believers. So did Stalin. The violence of both periods required them. Yet Stalin liquidated an entire generation that had answered the call. Why did they have to go under, for all their exercise of absolute discipline?

The reasons for the purges are many. Stalin's alteration in the nature of obedience helps to explain it in part. No matter how absolute revolutionary obedience had been before Stalin, it had called for consent[18] and it had been anchored in some modicum of reason. This had entered into the relationship between the party leadership and the rank and file, and had formed the basis for identification with the symbol "We." Stalin annihilated just that element of reason. The obedience he required – and obtained through terror – bypassed the brain, aiming at lower organs. Obedience turned blind, reflexive, visceral. It blended with professional, military, automatic discipline.

The metamorphosis of pronouns accompanies this shift. The revolutionary collective was made up of persons who entered it eager to give up their individual self for what seemed to be a higher, heroic group-self. Their sacrifice sprang from a conscious decision. Self-abnegation cemented the "We" experience and launched it at the heights. But the supreme symbol faltered under the pressure of stalinism. "We" turned into "He" by becoming personalized. On the shambles of "We," Stalin's personality turned into a monstrous shibboleth. And by a compensatory logic, as his personalization swelled on top, the depersonalization of the party ranks began from below. All were sucked dry. The group adhesion of bolshevik comrades disintegrated. A subservient flock was now being sorted out under a relentless vertical pressure, with the purpose of compromising relationships among equals. And even this very shrunken sense of self was dropped on each citizen from on high, as the twenty-odd years of verse- and prose-glorias to Stalin indicate. One by one, the subject fell into formation to receive His guidance and benefactions in a posture of adoration. With his survival at stake, any functionary endeavored with zeal to detach his "I" from the "They" of his peers. But it remained to be seen whether atomization could last unamended.

To the reasons why the system did not crumble under the war, one more could be added. And the shorthand of popular poetry shows that it withstood because, once more, the pronouns shifted. Consider this one war poem. Poignantly sentimental, it entered immediately into the mass culture, instantly setting a trend. It is Russia's best-known Second World War poem.

> Wait for me and I'll come back
> But wait with all your heart,
> Wait when yellow rains
> Bring gloom,
> Wait when snowstorms rage,
> Wait through summer heat,
> Wait when other men are given up
> By those who turn away,
> Wait when from afar
> Letters come no more,
> Wait when those who wait together
> Grow tired of waiting.
> Wait for me and I'll come back.
> Don't consort with those
> Who know by heart
> That time has come to forget.

Let my mother and my son
Believe that I have died,
Let my friends, grown weary,
Sit by the fireside
And drink the bitter wine
To my memory.
Wait, and do not hurry, please,
To drink with them.
Wait for me and I'll come back
Defying many deaths.
He who did not wait for me,
Let him say t'was luck.
They'll never know
Who did not wait
That in the midst of fire
It is you who saved me
Through your waiting.
Why I survived
Only you and I will know,
Simply, you knew how to wait
As no other knew.[19]

Popular "Thou" poetry gave strength to, and in turn reflected, wartime patriotism. Official poets were permitted to say what people craved for. Love poetry was ushered in too, to supplement the glorias to Stalin, to blend with them into a soothing mixture. A lyrical discovery of primary loyalties was permitted, because in apocalyptic circumstances it did not clash with Stalin-worship. Concessions were made to keep morale up in the catastrophic phase of the war. Since the revolutionary mythology of public heroism was only a dim irrelevant memory, wartime heroism found inspiration in the fortitude of individual patriots and lovers, one by one. Primary loyalties furthered national solidarity, and the appeal to basic private emotions helped the survival of Soviet society as a whole.

As tragic events succeeded each other like waves, from one phase of war to another and on to peace, over the bones of the twenty million dead, the feeble but stubborn lyrical violin responded with several leading themes. It seemed that even love between man and woman yielded to compassion for the fallen brothers. Mixed with guilt, it pressed for expression. Poets repeated again and again that war could not be forgotten no matter how hard one tried to forget; nor could sorrow for the bereaved mother and orphans. One should not even try. "Thou" poetry, mournful to begin with, turned to lament. There surfaced also a newly insistent theme, that of trust and faithfulness.

Should I be accused by my motherland,
Should foe and friend turn away from me,
I would not seek strength from metal.
You would give it to me. If only you
Would not stop believing in me.[20]

One could hardly be more explicit than that. Strength, dignity, truth, in fact, were now linked with the "Thou." One more shift in pronominal use and it was possible that the single personal "I" was about to stand alone, doing the job all by itself of holding together the divergent sides of an individuality. Curiously, grief, compassion, war as a national experience, all that had turned into lament, managed to encourage the individual stance.

But it was largely by default that the humanization of mass poetry, the rapprochement with the personal needs of a bereaved population, had come about. The government's stringent surveillance over literary output had yielded in the early war years to more urgent and more material priorities. At the end of the war, however, the entrenchment of colorous lyrics, dramatized by singular pronouns, and populated by private mourners and lovers instead of public party heroes, came under scrutiny.

The regime decided to intercept the spreading lament with a massive barrage of ideological edicts. That was one of the main purposes of zhdanovism. It undertook to cancel personal stocktaking by enforcing, once more, forward-strutting public jubilation. It began to steer the citizens away from the mass graves and on to the postwar Road to Life while also steering, in real life, newly uncountable victims into concentration camps.

As for usable literary models, however, there was little to fall back on. The collective tenets had long since corroded. And the pattern of stalinist, atomized heroism, a contradiction in terms never particularly apt for literary image making, clashed with the people's mourning. Although it was attempted by orthodox writers, the restoration of the clichés of the thirties did not work. For one thing, the pronouns balked. Too much had happened in Soviet society to permit large retroactive movements, even in middlebrow fiction. For many reasons, the first pronoun singular would not give way, so the creation of the postwar public hero became a problem. A poem about the newly required heroism illustrates the predicament. Working loudly with the henceforth tenacious personal pronouns,[21] a model veteran promises his abdication from lament.

> You think
> I'll bring to you
> My tired body.
> No,
> Don't think that.
> That's not the way
> I'll come back.
> We shall return to work,
> To puff tobacco,
> To fill the room with smoke.
> I am not seeking gratitude.
> I offer it myself,
> That's what I want.
> What I had to say to the enemy,

I have said it.
Now I want to work.
I'll cross your threshold
Not to be consoled
But to console.
That which I have done
On my way to you,
Is not a favor
But duty.
I want to work in the smithy
And sleep in bed.
I want to write verses about love.
In the windy conflagration of war
There was hardly a choice.
But it is bettter to return
With an empty sleeve
Than with an empty soul.[22]

On the brink of peace, the regime paid special attention to how the returning soldiers were to be handled. The same orthodox poet keeps repeating:

Don't pity us,
Don't invite us to rest.
We are not at all tired.
We are impatient to take off!
We need no respite,
No quietude.
Don't flatter us with the title
"War veteran."
We want to renovate
Trough labor
Our medals and honors.
The urge for difficult work
Cuts into our palm.[23]

This is a blueprint for a postwar hero, rather than a large-scale embodiment. In fact, the embodiment failed to arrive. The problems in the way were pragmatic and political, the most difficult being that the soldier's war sacrifice had to be minimized and that the regime was ambivalent about heroism anyway. Heroic on first hearing only, the loud lines just quoted are so ambiguous as to help deheroization. And the supreme truth was rebroadcast: there was only one hero. Adoration of Stalin blossomed with renewed vigor,[24] affecting positive characters to the core, and undercutting them. This strategy went into top gear, as the following typical vignette demonstrates. Amorously, just before ensnaring him, a stalinesque amazon probes the soul of a young man as positive as circumstances would allow:

[She] "Tell me, do you have a sacred dream? You know what I mean? A fantastic dream, an almost impossible one, but such that you do not wish to part with it. Do you have one?"

[He] "I do." [He meditates.] "I would like to have a talk with comrade Stalin".[25]

In another instance, the hagiography of feudalism, which had torn all lateral ties apart, reaches a peak when Stalin personally takes the hand of a deserving servant and leads him across the threshold of death, one of the rare instances when the presence of civilian death in the epoch of zhdanovite jubilation was altogether permitted.[26]

The last phase of stalinism brought forth the search for builders, not avengers, or spokesmen for a new justice for all. Work was extolled, but with a significant modification when compared with the labor the revolutionaries had craved. Instead of asceticism, the model of what became known as "greedy life" was advertised, satisfactory from a private point of view, with room for leisure, gregariousness, and the chance to write love poems.

The revolutionary "We" mood was crushed by the cult. Enforcing a break between the surviving comrades, Stalin tolerated only the direct bondage of each subject to the state, personified by him. But to those who were with him, survivors and recruits, he had promised already a thing or two before the war. Prosperity, no less, was in the offing, provided the subjects gave him all that was in them. This largely demagogic happening prefigured the wheeling and dealing after the war. The supreme victor was prepared after the war to reach down and distribute some rewards among his best subjects. This much-heralded munificence shaped the postwar hero's happiness, which, incidentally, was required of him. His giving was now to join with his taking. Even at the formulaic level, private aspirations became a prerequisite for entering the public realm. Nevertheless, the regime did not spell all this out with immediate and unequivocal clarity. It kept the new prerequisites for postwar model citizens, as well as the benefits they were to receive, shrouded in ambiguities.

Truth in trouble

The Russian word *pravda*, from old Slavic through all Slavic recensions, tantalizingly is not altogether synonymous with the cognitive sobriety of the western word "*truth.*" It connects rather with *rectus, dexter, justus*, and has a strong undercurrent of justice and due process before God.[27] The ancient moral meaning was revolutionized by nascent bolshevism into aggression. And truth as retaliatory social justice held the entire bolshevik ideological framework together. But that which was participatory or corporate in this principle began to ring hollow under Stalin's rule, and its didactic travails commenced. The war, in a way, only aggravated them. Sometimes, lightheartedness was evoked to mask slippage in meaning. A wartime elegy for an adolescent subsequently martyred by the Nazis is here made to participate in the cover-up. Here is how Zoya Kosmodemyanskaya is depicted, before her personal and national ordeal, in her prewar youthful normalcy:

Truth has become your very demeanor,
Your very drive and involuntary gesture
When you talk with adults, when you play
with children.
Like a white cloud in the sky, like
the trace of an oar
Your golden youth rushes on.
And your pioneer truth grows.
Your komsomol truth matures.
And you advance with a gait
flying forward,
The half-open secret tomorrow
inside of you
And above you, like the arch of the sky,
Shines your bolshevik truth.[28]

Truth, merry and zephyr-like, dances with the girl in pastoral mode. At the outbreak of war, instead of stalinist ideological verities, the private idyll was greatly extolled. It was politicized, and charged, like every other policy, with mobilizing all resources. The lovely pictures were, in essence, promises for the future, a glimpse towards the postwar Big Deal. In poem after poem commemorating that June 22, the Messerschmidts swooped down apocalyptically, not on the collective at work, but on a single bucolic family, basking in domestic bliss and stalinist prosperity. Just before the tocsin, a hero cuts his private grass in his private garden. The green around him sparkles with sweet peas, clover, and wild strawberries. Happiness culminates in serene domesticity:

The front garden lies under the windows,
And in the garden onions grow in rows,
All this together was his house, his home,
His cozy comfort, and his tidy life.

The hero is no hermit. On the contrary, generous hospitality enlivens his rural style. His bare feet at this moment derive sensuous pleasure from the glistening, freshly washed floors. He is relaxed, unpublic.

It's pleasant to sit down at one's own table
In a tight family circle,
And, leisurely, to eat one's bread,
And to praise the glorious day.[29]

Torn between the private and the public, Truth – with tidy rows of private onions – became unsteady, subject to thematic fission. Moreover, under looser control, writers became spontaneous enough to let several subtruths slip out. A youth falls on the battle field.

A boy lived on the edge of the town of Kolpino.
He was a dreamer. He made up stories.
They called him a liar.

He collected the gayest and the saddest of stories.
They were evoked by casual talk, by a book.
At night he dreamed that the road
Thundered, enveloped in dust.
He dreamed that the cavalry was pursued
By reddish fire through the rye fields.
And in the morning he turned to his fantasies —
Just like that.
And they accused him of lying.
This boy despised tin soldiers
And other merry war games.
But road ditches seemed to him trenches.
Such fantasy was held against him also.
He grew and became a man on this troubled unkind planet.
And when in the winter of 1941
He was killed,
I found in his officer's folder
A short letter he wrote home.
And the letter was filled with the same
Stories made up by a boy.
But I could not smile.
The corner of the gray page, tightly filled,
Was drenched in blood.
He collected many different stories.
I chose to believe him.[30]   [1945]

A child's imagination creates a truth all its own, honored by the poet who now, during the war, first pleads for his own right to distinguish truth from fantasy without supervision.

For a while, the official dogma sagged altogether under the eidetic images of suffering:

A man leaned over a body of water
And suddenly saw that his hair was gray.
The man was twenty-two years old.[31]

Such national experience stimulated an introspection which did not subside in the transition from war to peace. On the contrary, this other young person also looks at himself:

A minute hung suspended
On the thread of time
And fell. And it flattened out like
A trace on dry sand.
It cannot come back. A sand pebble,
It will now course through time.
It was a particle of my life.
I did not let it live.
I killed it this winter afternoon,
Spoiled by richly available days.
I filled the minute with nothing.

I kept no memory of it.
A tiny chink in the century,
I failed to save it.
Here hangs a new minute.
I will not give it away.[32]   [1946]

A fragment among fragments, this is the most personal. The fretting about the meaning of time implies – in the face of Soviet reality – the vulnerability of life which must be filled, individual minute by individual minute.

The old took stock, heavily, in a melancholy mood. Their sadness and stoicism emerged in personal spasms. One pensive, quietist poem caused grief to its author. The vehemence of the criticism[33] indicated that in the hazardous year of 1947 an important issue had inadvertently been stepped on, and that old beliefs, in a state of coma, were coinciding with the birthpangs of possible substitute thoughts.

People don't forgive me my errors.
That's all right. I learn to answer for myself.
News columns in morning papers
Do not promise me an easy life.
Lavish in empty promises,
Days burn out like moths in the fire.
There are no kindly signs ahead
Promising an easy life ahead.
What do I know about it?
Only what I read in poetry, perhaps.
Dry snow twirls and glistens,
Lights beckon from afar.
Heavy burden of my lot,
You end up by being feather light!
I am older now, my hair more gray,
And if I grieve, forgive me.
Let my burden turn more heavy.
To throw it off is much harder
Than to go on carrying it.[34]

Though alone, this person does not seem to need a collective to hold together the divergent sides of her ego. Hers seems to respond to an internal truth courageously: the truth is somewhat drab, but it is sturdy.

How did the regime handle this shift from the public to the private? The answer could not be a simple one. The difficulties can best be gleaned from the ambivalence toward the war hero himself. He was found sorely wanting as soon as the war ended. With his populist leanings and lyrical meditations, he took too much to lament and hand wringing, so irritating the regime. Doleful self-searching disqualified him for postwar onward-and-upward marching. And the stark fact that mourning was as personal as it was national did not help soften the new political edicts.

The regime's ambivalence toward the mythological legacy of the twenties and thirties, complicated by distrust of the returning soldier, did not make it easy, either, to work out clear directives for functional official postwar heroism. Nevertheless, guidelines were issued soon enough.

Inevitably, new ambiguities emerged with them. The postwar model was charged with keeping a balance in general and with balancing clashing traits in particular. For instance, simplicity and extraordinariness were to blend. A completely simple person, he was to be enraptured by that tidy row or two of private onions. At the same time, he was to perform inspiring deeds in the shop or field. But there too, he was to be a radiant achiever, not a brain-straining recluse. Avoiding any kind of exaggeration, his thinking, whether at home or at work, had to be undercut in favor of dreaming. Yet dreaming was not to go wild. It was to be directed to one main channel: good things.

He was to offer an alternative to the depersonalization of Stalin's subjects. What the regime now advertised was a chance for citizens to express themselves in striving for material things, leading to contentment. Just as effectively, and perhaps more importantly, the hero was to reject the lure of that other threatening alternative, a possible revival, some twenty-five years out of season, of large-scale purist public dreams – the seduction, in other words, of residual bolshevism. The regime tolerated least of all the craving for any kind of sectarianism. And it was prepared to pay the necessary price by controlling a blend of the private with the public. Public efforts were henceforth to be tempered by private aspirations. The new hero was to teach how the mixture worked. A three-page ballad with the unpromising title "The District Boss Bids Farewell" offers a good set of clues. In it a deserving industrial administrator, fully entitled to his ennobling cardiac trouble, contemplates retirement. "Somewhat stooped, somewhat tired" he knows he must give up his job because he is "stricken with severe and deep illness," and he knows just as clearly that "nothing will help him forget . . . the cement and iron ore" to which he has dedicated all his life. Stooped shoulders harmonize with his heart ailment, a demonstration that he has sacrificed himself to public duty. By inference, a deheroization takes place and in its wake the transfiguration of a value or two. Although, if needs be, he would repeat from the very beginning his "swift, hard, nomadic life," a curious discomfort stirs in his, yes, in his soul:

> There is only one thing that fills his soul with anguish,
> There is only one thing that he cannot correct.
> Beloved hands he recalls as they cared for him,
> Hurrying, full of sorrow over parting.
> Did they not bid him farewell too often?
> Were the separations not too long?

Even at home, he worked from dawn to dawn. And over his cup of tea, he buried himself in a newspaper.

Concerned with people, concerned with the Don and Volga,
It did not occur to him to think about Olga.
How many were the nights she waited.
How she blossomed under sparse tenderness.
It had seemed to him that this was a private matter.
It did not fit into projects and plans.
But meanwhile Olga Andreevna turned gray.
Perhaps, too gray. Perhaps, too early.

With equal anguish, he now feels remorse about his feelings for his children: he had neglected them. Meanwhile, though, the telling line is buried furtively in the text: "It had seemed to him that this was a private matter." It was not. He was wrong. Former prescriptions for former heroes, calling for the neglect of the family and of domestic bliss, were no longer in effect. A desired new balance was in the making. Private matters were no longer private at all. They were now subject to inspection. The heart ailment here in part means retribution. The boss has learned the lesson so well that he passes it on to the new generation. Bidding farewell to his subordinates, he confronts a young trade union representative. The young man is entirely positive. Of course, he is nervous. He expects to receive orders from the powerful superior on the proper placement of engineers. Instead, the boss astonishes him by insisting on the crumbling of the wall between the private and the public:

Quite unexpectedly for such a moment
The boss asked:
"You are married, are you not?"
And the young man stands amazed.
He stares at the boss's faded tunic.
He hears the old stern chief of the district
Say to him:
"Take care of your beloved."[35]

We now observe that tender care of wife and brood has become the new mandatory element of Truth. This timely new component, however, proved hard to tag on to the standing commitment to public exertion. The fact is that the two did not fuse very well. A model citizen pleased with himself was called upon. Obviously, he could not be smug. He was charged with seeking useful positive self-fulfillment. And the awkward problem of careerism surfaced.

Careerism as a key theme also signalled the regime's shift toward middleclass aspirations. It could not, of course, be too openly proclaimed, but it could not be denied either. This double predicament interfered with the didactic task of fiction. Its young heroes and heroines indicate this in their confusion, as we shall now see.

Young people quarrel

Becoming "somebody" was desirable. What was the proper way? How could individual social elevation be squared with traditional collectivist ideals? This remained unclear for a while. Some notions were borrowed from the private system of preferences – malleable ones, such as the efflorescence of a "rounded personality" and "personal happiness." They were then grafted on to the primary allegiance to public duty, on to public valor. Their grafting, in part because it was an afterthought, betrayed the strain of keeping up the old catechism. They solved some problems, but also created new ones.

For one thing, if the new prescript for "personal happiness" was to be understood as a franchise for career satisfaction, it also seemed to be granting a contrasting franchise: seeking happiness in apathy. Initially the limits in either direction were not clearly staked out. Unlike the earlier eras of categorical answers, this turned into a period of questions, uneasy and frequently muted.

For instance, in Yurii Trifonov's widely read *Students*, a young veteran adjusts as best he can to the postwar atmosphere. Although his function in the novel is that of a hero, tellingly, "Truth" and "Road" beckon him with not much clarity. And they become altogether obscure if he is going to share them with his girlfriend. So, he asks whether she knows where she is going:

"And what is your goal, Lena?"
  "What goal, Vadik?" she asked softly and with surprise.
  "Of your life!"

She bursts out laughing at his "loud words." Embarrassed, he turns silent for a while, for the girl, here as elsewhere, steals the show. It is she who superimposes the visceral aspect of the conflict upon its semantics.

The girl happens to take private singing lessons. The young man wants to know why she does, considering that she studies in a pedagogical institute. She answers that she does not sing for professional reasons.

"What for, then?"
  "For – " Lena turned silent for a second and then uttered with her habitual sententiousness, "a woman, Vadik, must know everything. She must know how to dress, how to be beautiful, how to sing – you understand."
  "I understand. So, it follows, that you are studying to become a woman?"
Lena looked at Vadim with silent outrage.

When her outrage subsides, she adds in a conciliatory fashion:

"How can I in two words tell you about all my plans, about my future? What's more I don't trouble my mind over such things. What for? I am only beginning to live... Students in olden days eternally argued about something. About the final goal in life, about the supreme good, about all sorts of nonsense. But you and I, why should we start these abstract arguments? I am the same kind of komsomol as you are. We have the same ideology. What can we argue about?"

Not that there is nothing to argue about. His remembrance of the war irritates the girl more than anything. It is noteworthy that only here he takes a strong stand.

"No, excuse me," said Vadik firmly. "Let me finish. At the front I learned to understand many simple things in a new way. Much deeper. And sometimes I discussed with my comrades our future life, our work, our profession. We discussed what we love, what we dream about. We even talked about our goal in life and, you know, the words were very natural and very simple and sincere. They helped us, they gave us more strength. And now – why is it that now they seem so blatant and naive?"

The girl neither knows nor cares. She dismisses the war and its truth. Thereupon, the poor fellow insists that he simply must find out how she wants to live.

"Well, how do I want to live? I want to live honestly, peacefully, well, happily." After a pause she added undecidely, "I want to participate in work."
    "Happily, in the sense of getting married happily?"
    "So what? Every woman hopes to get married happily," said Lena, immediately turning haughty, "You know, today you are terribly boring and unoriginal. You are even, forgive me, somewhat vulgar. Do you want to pick a fight?"
    "No," said Vadik, shaking his head, "I don't want to."[36]

Where his aspirations seem vague, the girl clearly hopes for a comfortable married life, accented by the songs she will sing to her husband. And she says so plainly. These hopes are carried on the crest of rising meshchanstvo. It equips her with a potent weapon: derision of the futility of the intelligentsia's posturing. The tone of the argument, however, matters more than the subject of discord. The young man's insecurity, inarticulateness, and embarrassment stand out in marked contrast to the girl's ease, even nonchalance. The language of his insecurity in itself points to the trend of deheroization among postwar young heroes.
    Failure to achieve a happy family life began to be frowned upon. This pretty, well-dressed miss with her middleclass ways was *en vogue*. Her aspirations could not be dismissed, nor had the regime any intention of dismissing them: on the contrary. Even if the young man attempts to oppose meshchanstvo by expressing correct ideals, he is shown as somehow losing all the same.
    Such quarrels filled many a novel. The scope of the problem becomes clearer if one looks at the mirror image of the dispute in another tale. In this reversed version, it is the woman who stands for public heroism; the man is not sure. The man has just been demobilized. He has been a brave soldier. We find him fatigued, drained. He needs time to take stock and rest. He craves to be left alone. It is as simple as that. And it is not that he finds himself at a loss what to do with his life. Having reached home at last fills him with ecstasy. This is to him a miracle, even if it happens to be shell-shocked Leningrad. He has found his young wife safe and sound. He loves her. He relishes a nest of his own. But her arms turn out soon enough neither warm nor soothing. In fact, whatever else she may be willing to offer, it is not shelter. She begins to throw serious accusations

at him. Her demands that he adjust his image of public valor cut him deeply. His self-defensive responses seem reasonable.

"I hope you don't think that I don't understand postwar tasks. You may rest assured that even during the war I knew perfectly well that there will be no respite and that there cannot be any. All that is elementary. But I am speaking of something else. I am speaking of that life on the very brink of which you preach and which you practice... You need some sort of super-work which takes away all one's life leaving nothing over."[37]

He obviously does have in mind her presumptuousness, strain and exaggeration. But she remains adamant and keeps nagging. At one point, he pleads with her:

"Let's be grateful for what we have. In the past they would have said, don't invite the wrath of God. Don't you think...of those without a family, without a shelter, of those who have lost their own happiness in the struggle for that of others? And we, we have found ours. Is this not enough?"

For her it is not, and she counters with a weapon that ushered in much ambiguity wherever proper postwar aspirations were debated. She accuses him of smugly reclining on his laurels. Anything but placid, she shouts:

"It's not enough, do you understand, it's not enough! What you are talking about is happiness, but it is small, dried up, as if it were in a tin can. I always wanted something bigger and I want you to get cured of your disease, of your sleepy life."   [p. 33]

Another pair in a much debated novel takes us to the countryside, which suggests less sophistication as well as less confusion in the probing which they undertake. The man in the first tale seems a mixed-up boy; the man in the second worn out by the war, but this one is vigorous and rugged and ambitious. He knows what he wants. His name is Rodion; hers Grunia. He returns a glamorous warrior. But his reception leaves something to be desired. To begin with, his wife had been erroneously notified of his death. She had drowned her sorrow in work, and became famous in agricultural work, a much photographed amazon. But now her reputation is no help to them. They do not see eye to eye. He is eager to get on, but for himself. Her dreams are cut of a different cloth, those of an impeccable party-minded heroine:

"What a wonderful life there will be in about a hundred years. It stops your breath to think what people and science will attain!"

This opening gambit of hers does not enthuse him:

"I also like to dream a bit... But I don't like my feet to leave the ground. All right, so you dream for a while. But what sense is there in it? And I think that for us... there is no point in guessing what is many years ahead. It's too far for us!... Better hang on to what is given us now in our own life! Let's not give it away to anybody! Let's enjoy it to the brim so that our heads swirl!"[38]

He had hoped that his wife would support his ambitions "for a prosperous life and his own great glory."[39] But his goals hold little attraction for her. She

rejected everything he suggested! She wanted him to drop all his plans and to follow her in her footsteps. To place himself under the command of his wife? No, she will never achieve that. [p. 50]

There is no way they can manage together, for he does not even understand her working methods. She works for the good of the state, so much so that she loses interest in the very success of her team and in her own merit badges. And he is greatly perplexed at her commitment to national productivity rather than any interest in winning a medal for herself. Immediately after his return in a nocturnal dialogue, ponderously dedicated to career aspirations (rather than to making love after years of separation), he asks for her support, promising

"Only in one year's time . . . here in this very spot you and I will each pin a Gold Star! . . . For the sake of that little star I will do anything!"

She reacts with some dismay.

"But does happiness consist really of working and living for rewards? All through the war I didn't even think of rewards. I worked without sparing myself. And didn't you do the same over there?"

He, in turn, finds her reasoning peculiar and retorts:

"Pride will move everybody these days! Everybody wants to distinguish himself and to be seen by all! Don't tell me that even now you don't think of rewards!"

He has touched a soft spot. She blushes, gets up, becomes agitated, and burns with the inner fever of true believers, exposed to new pressures. Confused, she clutches the collective dogma:

"It is so very much to be awarded the title of Hero of Labor. And if, for instance, one of us receives it, it certainly does not mean that just one person is honored but the whole team, the whole collective farm. Could one person achieve anything without the others? . . . It is exactly the same as the passing red banner which hangs in our administration, that's how it is!"

Rodion does not accept the analogy. He wants his own reward, all of it, and not without a touch of paranoia.

"Oh no! . . . The passing banner is ours today, but tomorrow it may be taken away! The little star I speak about, however, will shine for all your life, for you and no one else! And no one will take it away!"

It's her turn now. She regains her composure, sounding as stern as the revolutionary amazons of yesteryear:

"Well, all right! Suppose you are awarded a Hero's Star. And then what?
    "Then I will earn a second one!"
    "And then?"

Naturally, he hesitates. But he assembles his wits and points to the refurbished instrumental incentives: recognition, status, and envy produced in others.

"I will be known everywhere; such glory will make everybody envious! If you can't achieve that, then what's the point in putting all your strength into work, what's the point in killing yourself over it?"   [p. 103]

Ritual and reward have not yet come to a proper balance. Medals are not used to *close* an account between the regime and the striving citizen. They symbolize rather an ongoing relationship. Byzantic, they are effective devices in the promulgation of the Big Deal. The purist young woman here is indifferent to them but her stance seems hypocritical to her ambitious husband. When the accusation of hypocrisy surfaces, she must ponder whether to keep moving along her zealously orthodox path or to backtrack.

These quarrels give us one useful hint: nobody wins. In the past, that draw, that open-endedness would have been impossible. But of course, since nobody wins, nobody loses. And what is becoming clearer is the nature of the groping itself: the search for the self more than for The Road and Truth.

It is remarkable that this gray and undistinguished fiction managed to convey that even young lovers ceased to communicate too well. The guiding principles to close debate seemed in disrepair. Youth was confronted with an unprecedented problem. It was expected that they make sacrifices. Even more, it was expected that they be happy. The combination of new efforts remained to be worked out.

Jaded people adjust

A look at an older couple shows that the conflict does not disappear with age nor with language which says one thing and means another. A district party secretary named Dry (Sukhov) is having to contend with the illicit love affair of his second party secretary. The "second" is married. Petulantly, Comrade Dry orders his subordinate to stop the affair.

"Tell me, how long is this going to continue?"

"What?" asked [the second secretary] unsuccessfully pretending that he did not know what it was all about.

"You know very well. Your wife was here again. She cried. She threatens to write to the regional committee. Are you some sort of a low person without status? The masses must emulate you. And you, you display immoral conduct. It's high time to stop this."[40]

This interchange between two party officials captures an eidetic image of meshchanstvo mores. The wronged wife weeps, she seeks revenge through denunciation at the regional level. At the same time, Comrade Dry suggests that extramarital relations may be acceptable for lowly folk but not for someone whom the masses must emulate. The gap between language and its merely conventional meaning (what "masses?" what "immoral conduct?" what "emulation?") jumps right out from these few lines. One needs no larger context. For the ways of meshchanstvo permeate every line of the story. And Comrade Dry transforms his own fears into coercion, his own insecurity into deadly formalism.

Ordered by the boss to stop the illicit affair, the "second" replies quickly:

"I can't. Do with me what you wish. I can't."

"What kind of an approach is this? What do you mean, you can't? The situation in the district is far from brilliant even without you. All we need is that they should start working us over along this line too. Watch out! You can lose your party card for this sort of thing!" [p. 51]

The inadvertently grotesque here combines with the pathetic. Comrade Dry's philistinism becomes threatening. The cluster of terms such as "they," "working over," "along that line" show how helpless the exposed functionary is against the establishment. The forces that impinge on him are formidable, those of stalinist meshchanstvo, bureaucratized and canonized.

This genre picture contains other interesting detail. A charming girl with freckles has meanwhile been hired in Comrade Dry's office as a new clerk. The comrade's own family life is not all that it should be. He is married to a representative of arch-meshchanstvo, exploiting her position as wife of the local boss. In the oppressive provincial summer heat, Comrade Dry feels that he is falling in love with the fresh, uncontaminated, freckled office girl. All of a sudden he begins to understand his "second." In frustration, he takes a close look at his wife. Until now her abuse of privilege has not bothered him much. Instead of going shopping like everybody else, she has managers of stores deliver merchandise to the house. She sends the party office chauffeur on constant errands to the regional center. She has an employee of a dressmaking atelier come to her house for fittings. All of this is not legal. Worse, she has brought up her son to be a snooty, spoiled brat. Comrade Dry cannot explain her at all. His inability to do so connects with the fact that the "birthmark" or "residue" theory, once used declaratively, no longer explains much. But now at least the good comrade is beginning to be aware of the process involved. He meditates:

At first she somehow developed a greediness for material affluence. And now that she has attained it, she has developed, God knows why, a need to boast about material success way out of proportion to reality. Doesn't she know that I cannot permit the district committee car to be commandeered for some silly sewing supplies? How has she come to be like that? [p. 53]

That is just the point. Meanwhile, the marital conflict takes on the age-old form. Over the dinner table, in the presence of their small son, two people shout at cross-purposes. The good comrade engages in rhetoric. And the wife fights back. With singular expressiveness, gray everyday language, interspersed with cant, opens up sorry horizons beyond these three sitting under one dining room lamp.

"Tell me one thing. Are you a Soviet person or are you not?"

"Eat your borsch."

"We have discussed this question with you repeatedly," he continued, "and I thought you had arrived at appropriate conclusions."

"Conclusions, conclusions!" his wife exploded. "Stuff is being carried to the Evdokimovs every week. And here on account of some miserable two meters of fabric for Petya, I must listen to a long lecture. You don't pay any attention to your son. Are you his father or what?"   [p. 54]

The "second" must be punished because his love-life is in disarray. The wife of the "first," however, gets away with a great deal more. But she also bears herself self-righteously. You can steamroller a small person, but the hard power of the bosses spreads to their wives and makes corruption. Mouthed by those centaurs, half leaders of the masses and half somnolent philistines, ideological tenets lose all meaning and turn into menacing clichés.

The ending is not without a twist, not without a human note. Comrade Dry turns out to be not so dry after all. He seeks a way out in resignation. To remove temptation from his uninspiring path, he requests the transfer of the freckled office girl. Moreover, he even manages to caress his wife's hair after years of marital estrangement. This startles her. He accompanies this gesture of compassion with muted Chekhovian words:

"Well, what are you looking at me like that for? Let's go on living."

Shame awakens in him for having used nothing but clichés in his attempts to solve personal problems in a party way. In the end, this impotent, mediocre party official does manage to take a look at himself.

5. Status

The ways of a scoundrel

Just as concepts of truth and notions of right and wrong began to wobble, so the theme of careerism showed how hard it was to distinguish between healthy and unhealthy aspirations. Under Stalin, education provided the key channel for social mobility. The regime sponsored careerism because it needed technocrats and bureaucrats. And the middle class wanted to be needed in that way. But to earn good marks for proper career making, one had to watch one's step. Unobtrusive conduct was mandatory. A story about a pushy veteran points to the pitfalls created by the greater scope for personal ambition. A friend chides our protagonist:

"You measure everybody with your own yardstick. In every person you see only what is in yourself: self-interest, greed and a drive to arrange your life comfortably with whatever means and at whatever price. It doesn't even occur to you that people might act from other motives!... There's nothing you can be accused of. You haven't done anything really dastardly or illegal. You were always one third scoundrel and two thirds heel...You want to live easily, comfortably, profitably. You are satisfied in everything with substitutes such as half-sincere feelings, easy love, ersatz friendship. They are less bothersome. You love only one thing passionately. You cultivate only one thing properly, with zealous and selfless energy, sparing neither time nor effort. You love yourself. And you care for your own future."[1]

The accused, named Palavin, is a veteran in his twenties, demobilized as an officer. He is now studying at the Pedagogical Institute in Moscow. An extremely active komsomol member, he applies for party membership. He comes from an urban professional background. A stylish dresser, he cultivates his good looks as well as his swift progress.

Difficulties, except for the usual ones connected with examinations, did not exist for him. He adjusted to student life at once with astonishing freedom and ease. He got acquainted with his fellow students in no time. He managed to impress his professors favorably. And with girl students he behaved with nonchalant camaraderie. He was a trifle condescending to them.   [10, p. 69]

Conquest of women is part of the plan which calls for all-round prowess. As he moves from group to group, he knows when to talk about sport, when to tell tall military tales, when to discuss problems in linguistics "authoritatively," when to smile, when to joke, and when to offer a cigarette. All this is part of what he repeatedly calls "getting ahead and becoming somebody."[2]

Nice people admire him and vie for his attention. Rewards materialize as soon as his reputation as a brilliant student spreads. He makes the pages of the student journal. He gets a research paper published. He wins a coveted scholarship. He is elected sole delegate to an intracollegiate komsomol convention. All this is achieved by scheming, effective and transparent. He secures a leading position in the literary club by ridiculing other student members. A rapid and sardonic speaker, he pushes the less articulate to the wall. He gains prominence in the komsomol by denouncing others. He plays a winning game by siding with the faculty against some student groups. And he finally acquires a potent faculty sponsor by the old and tested method of flattery. The professor helps him to obtain the prestigious scholarship. And the relationship turns into a friendship, quite intimate. An aesthete both in his scholarship and his personal habits, the professor is a bachelor, with a taste for the finer things in life, such as ballet and the fine arts in general. The piquant ambiance surrounding the professor enchants Palavin. He basks in the role of disciple, up to a point.

The relationship breaks up abruptly when controversy ensnarls the professor. Palavin's antennae work well. He knows whom to drop, whom to denounce and when. The professor gets into trouble. His new book is attacked for formalism. Some of his own students denounce him. With Palavin's help, he is fired from the institute. It is the language of this polished scoundrel, casual and vulgar, which warrants attention. With disdain, he calls his mentor now "that unfortunate fellow," going under and so "blowing his last bubbles." He refers sarcastically to a phone call he had received from the poor man.

"He asks me to write my opinion about this work in our scientific literary circle. He wants me to write it down as a memo so that he can show it wherever they have it in mind to give him a real licking. He wants to take it to some institute or to the ministry, I am not sure which. In a word, he wants me to cook up some sort of defense for him and collect a few signatures. How do you like that? It seems to me the old man is so scared, he is out of his mind. What an idea! Of course, I told him I couldn't do it. I said that I was ill and couldn't leave the house. He understood. He apologized. So long. Good-bye. That's all. Silly old man!"
                                                                      [11, p. 114]

Palavin laughs, and in a flash it all becomes very clear to the reader: the chill in the spine of the anguished professor who "understands" and "apologizes," and all the other things a scoundrel understands. And *he* understands perfectly who is going to get "a real licking" from "them" and when and how. He now works on a denunciation of the professor to be delivered in open council at the institute. As he puts it, he plans "a post mortem, as it were" because "the professor has already been thrown to the pigs"(11, p. 114).

Palavin's private life is not edifying. He has an affair with a medical student, a nice, quiet, intelligent girl. Although his mother considers the girl socially inferior, she does not oppose the relationship. The girl's mother is all in favor of it. In love with him and expecting marriage, the girl not only shares his bed but cooks for him, does his washing, and helps him in his studies. As her affection grows, his declines. He does not take her out. He avoids introducing her to his friends. She begins to realize that he is ashamed of her and had been lying to her from the beginning. What he needed was a conquest. And so, brave and decent, she decides to break with him. Nothing could please him more. To her surprise, after an interval he reappears as if nothing had happened. Charmingly insouciant, he reconquers her. The affair is resumed on his insistence. But the girl suffers because of her own weakness. He has, of course, an ulterior motive. Meanwhile, the love interest unfolds in a traditional mold. The girl thinks herself pregnant. Her mother and sister find this out and confront the culprit. He demands "proof" and refuses forced matrimony. A brawl ensues; the sister slaps his face; and it is he who stalks out in righteous indignation. The girl shudders at her family's "stupidity" and at his baseness:

"And he left as if he had been insulted, but probably very pleased, you understand – *he* was insulted! He went away to write his play, to prepare student skits, to appear at public meetings, to be witty, to debate."

Crying over her bitter memories, the wronged girl enacts the "new attitude" in this old drama. Absolving the scoundrel of old-fashioned guilt and responsibility, she insists that she feels only contempt for him. She sounds noble and firm. But her clarity abandons her as soon as she looks at the larger scene and turns her concern to public matters. She struggles to understand why the system should benefit such a person.

"But there is one thing I cannot understand . . . This man holds a scholarship, he is everywhere. He is a member of the activists, he is preparing to enter the party. He is being sent to Leningrad. He has written a novel – not altogether brilliant, perhaps, but correct. Everything in it is as it should be. But in personal life he is the most trite, most despicable egotist. I am sure he is very happy now that everything has turned out "well" for me. And he is doubly happy that I am moving to Kharkov. Never mind. I am not leaving because of him. I don't want to get even with him in any way . . . He no longer revolts me. He means nothing to me. He has gone out of my life and will never return. But I am in the komsomol . . . So I ask: did he really deserve all those distinctions? Did he deserve this outstanding scholarship? But perhaps it all hangs together, and it has to be that way. I don't know."   [11, p. 127]

What stands out is the tentative, questioning nature of the girl's belated indignation. She is not sure whether ruthless self-interest can or cannot be considered compatible with changing norms.

But Palavin is quite sure of that. The scoundrel's certainties emphasize the disarray of the virtuous. A cocky cynic, he offers his best friend the familiar bet that he will seduce his girlfriend. He believes in no one's chastity. He mocks idealists and envies the socially established. Since, however, in middlebrow fiction some sort of justice occurs as inevitably as a happy ending, Palavin is uncovered, even if rather late.

A term paper on Turgenev has been assigned in one of his courses. This happens to be the time when he presses his mistress to introduce him to her cousin, a brilliant young literary scholar writing a doctoral dissertation on Turgenev. The young scholar responds generously and helps with materials, bibliography, and outline. Unsatisfied, Palavin wants to see the dissertation itself. And the fool lends Palavin several chapters for a day. He asks Palavin, however, not to use his findings. In time he learns that Palavin's paper has been successful and he is glad. Needless to say, Palavin now carefully avoids him. Some time later, the young scholar – poor fellow – is summoned to his professor, who hands him a published collection of student articles which show that he has been plagiarized. Curiously, the harmed scholar joins hands with the harmed woman. Both equivocate about the far-reaching activities of the scoundrel and the leeway the new mores offer him.

"Yes, indeed, an adroit student outsmarted me. No, there was no direct quotation in it. The article was written on a different level. It had many original ideas. But, you understand, I find in it just precisely those little discoveries of mine that I asked Palavin not to mention. They are right here, in his text. Yes, of course, I am upset. And so is my professor."   [p. 154]

And so is everybody; but not enough. Not enough, at any rate, to punish Palavin with anything more substantial than a reprimand and then to go on to explain why plagiarism is not exactly plagiarism. After a few days of seclusion and meditation, Palavin crawls out, reformed. He asks to be readmitted into the community, and permission is granted.

Palavin is cast as a negative character and the author disapproves of him. But though he overreaches as a cynical climber, he turns out to be entirely corrigible. The criticisms directed at him sound partial, ambiguous, ineffective. And he submits willingly and reforms unaided. One might add that his evil is largely private. He does no real harm in the public realm. He deceives and uses his mistress; he drops his mentor and threatens him; he engages in a bit of plagiarism; nothing more. And, as his girl puts it, didn't his peers admire him and his superiors reward him lavishly? And wasn't the academic community, committed to the making of careers, receptive both to his type and his person? No wonder the girl becomes confused. She, for one, does not know if his strategies are not compatible with the prevailing ways. If she does not know, we at this point do not quite know either.[3]

New child rearing

Did the system want from the young the same, or roughly the same things, as middleclass parents wanted for them? The answer is difficult, for this is a matter presented in a lopsided way. Middlebrow fiction does not treat both sides of the equation with the same lucidity. It reveals parental aspirations rather directly. But the system's expectations are obscured by doubletalk. The source of the ambiguity is the one we are used to: the catechism interferes with the recording of the social process. But authorial tone and the reactions of foils toward the hopes of parents may give some sense of the problem.

The family theme began to overshadow all others. None brought the mass reader to the literary town hall with such effectiveness. Within the family domain, it was neither sex nor love nor the nexus of marital problems nor even promiscuity which most fascinated the regime and the public. What held everybody's attention was the new relationship between parents and children. It is from this special angle that the regime confronted the postwar family; from the same standpoint the common reader confronted his own most pressing needs. More than any other, the "generational" theme, linked to the issue of inherited privilege, forced into the open the issue of the perpetuation of middleclass values.

A kolkhoz carpenter returns from the war. He soon finds that he no longer has much in common with his wife. He is irritated with her and with the children. There is friction over the raising of the children. In the eyes of the father, his daughter

has started putting on tiresome airs and behaving arrogantly . . . She was learning to dance in her school club. She danced while setting out to school, she danced on her way home, she danced preparing the dinner table. She danced at home, in the yard, on the street.

The father orders her to do something useful instead. The mother defends the child.

"Dancing is a serious thing . . . She has real talent."
  "Are you preparing her to become a ballerina?"
  "And what's wrong with her becoming a ballerina?"
  "You should teach her how to mend stockings."

The father forces the girl to scrub the floor. She bursts into tears, insisting that her mother never makes her do such unpleasant things. The mother protests. She would rather do all the chores herself.

"My grandparents forced me to do everything when I was only six years old . . . So let my children live in luxury. The Soviet government gives it to them."
  "The Soviet government does not teach you to bring up children as parasites!"[4]

The mother's voice blends with other versions of parental compensatory dreams.

The same kind of motherly opinion comes from a real-life celebrity, Pasha Angelina, the much decorated tractor driver, who contributed an autobiographical sketch, a sort of postwar idyll.

With astonishing ease my Svetlana recited one of Pushkin's fairy tales from beginning to end. I always very much enjoyed listening to Svetlana when she recited poetry and when later she sat down at the grand piano and played Chopin and Tchaikovsky. I would listen and see nothing except her face and her plump little hands flying like birds over the keyboard.

The youngest daughter, pointedly named Stalinka, climbs into her mother's lap and asks:

"Mama, mama, and when I grow up like Svetlana, will I play the piano too?"
"Of course you will." I listened to Stalinka with excitement and happiness. My childhood was different: I couldn't even think of music.[5]

Staunch mothers uphold the program: "Our children should have a better life than we did" which was not new, having emerged quite prominently in the literature of the thirties. At that time it was a matter of intense debate. Makarenko, the leading pedagogue and influential designer of The Road for the New Man, took a poor view of the urban family's overprotectiveness of children.[6] He criticized it as divisive, retrogressive, and destructive. But after the war, the terms had changed, for normal parental concern was compounded by guilt for the suffering of the children in wartime.

When the war-torn family began to succumb to the strains of separation, compassion and anguish had been fortified. One portrait of a twelve-year-old boy[7] can stand for the hardships of innumerable children. The story deals with the cruel rifts the war had brought to an average family. The boy was not wounded by a bomb, nor was he too badly damaged emotionally. The thing that happened to him was that he had become an adult. He had learned to stand hunger and cold, to boil frozen potatoes, to haul water from a faraway well, to saw wood and light the stove. He had learned how to take care of his little sister. He had also learned to comfort his mother in her loneliness, anguish, unbearable overwork, and promiscuity. And so she says to the father just back from the front:

"I go to work early and come home late. And the children are alone all the time. Look, how they have grown up! They know how to do everything themselves. They have become wise before their time."

And gently and sadly she adds, "Whether it's to the good, I don't know."[8] She knows. And so does one frightened soldier just before battle in a nocturnal conversation with his comrade.

"I should think that after the war they will build a lot. All the cities will have to have statues of victory. If I live, I will dress my wife in silk. And my little girls too. I have two of them. Let them grow up in crêpe-de-chine."

"There is no point in spoiling them."
"Why shouldn't we spoil them, if we win?"⁹

Crêpe-de-chine, ballet and Chopin stood for real wishes. They meant different things from one family to another, but what they point to by joint inference was the actual harshness and grayness in the life of the average citizen. A dream of crêpe-de-chine for one's child was an outlet for frustration. What the war was doing to millions of children was an oppressive parental anguish. This made the wish for luxury all the more poignant. War orphans augmented the guilt, the frustration, and the dream.

Here is a sketch written by a teacher in a vocational school. She is reminiscing about her work with adolescents during the war. A reticent girl, an orphan, had at last brought herself to tell her about the death of her parents during the siege of Leningrad – terrible, stark deaths from starvation unbearably close to the child's shattered sensitivities. In order to survive, in order to take up a monstrously premature responsibility, the girl had frozen emotionally, turned hard. In the melancholy safety of evacuation, she recalls her dying mother's admonitions:

"When I die," she said, "please behave well. Study,¹⁰ and be more soft with people. Your character has become terribly harsh. You must be more soft, more kind."¹¹

One can imagine such maternal pleas sounding through the whole lower domain of Soviet society as it began to recover after the war.

Social mobility was possible only through the educational system and its institutions. A despairing mother would not normally couch her appeal in terms of pure learning, understanding, and knowledge. The full meaning of the imperative "study" is: "teach yourself how to use the channel open to you." This comes across in one other poignant moment of the girl's recollection: she had come upon an extraordinarily large poster on a street fence. She cursorily remembers now that at the time she had realized that the outlandish size of the lettering was necessary because people had become physically too weak to pay attention to small print.

"Industrial School No. 5 is open for admission. A worker's ration card is guaranteed to students." I read all this, go home, and say: "Mama, mama, listen to this announcement." And I tell her everything. She listens to me, listens attentively, and suddenly says: "What's the matter? Have you gone mad?" It's the first time she said such a thing to me. "What?" I said. "What are you saying? What do you mean, gone mad?" But she started to cry terribly. "Where are you going? They are artisans,¹² aren't they? What will become of you?"   [p. 67]

Even in the conditions of the Leningrad siege, this mother thinks ahead. She is in despair that her child should enter a vocational school and tries to prevent it. She wishes her child to move up, above the artisans, toward a "proper" life.

Under duress, parental ambitions came into sharp focus. And the urban family's urge for social ascent became important to national reconstruction. And the regime approved, because its rapprochement with the middle class presupposed just that thrust from below.

But compensatory dreams varied and authorial attitudes diverged according to one important variable: the family's social position. It mattered a great deal whether the fretting mother was underprivileged or whether she was already solidly ensconced in a middleclass ambiance. In seeming contradiction to the incentives now offered, there was frequent and heavy criticism of middleclass mothers accused of perverting educational goals. One extremely agitated urban lady is absorbed in the raising of her little prince. The factual account is given by the school principal, who has summoned the mother to her office. The latter arrives full of anxiety:

"What is the matter? My Igor is an excellent student. He is an obedient boy and well behaved."

The school principal does not disagree:

"Yes, your son is a good student. But there are things I don't like in him."

The tone of the mother's quick response, defensive and abrasive, leads to the heart of the conflict:

"But what is it? Dear God! My husband and I are so concerned about his development. What has my boy done? Oh, these evil influences!"

By invoking God, her husband, and evil external influences, she sets the middleclass family apart. She does so consciously and fastidiously. It is fairly clear that the school principal recognizes this apartheid for what it is and disapproves. In turn, the mother's contempt for the school signals that she wishes something better for her son and heir.

[Principal] "But the question is not at all one of evil influences. I observed him during an algebra lesson. The class could not solve it. But Igor raised his hand. He knew the solution."
    [Mother] "So you see, such a capable boy!"
    [Principal] "Yes, but you should have seen the expression on his face at that moment: triumph, haughtiness, arrogance."
    [Mother] "Naturally, the boy is pleased that he knows more than the others! Igor is so proud; he is so terribly proud! But if *that* is why you called me in, then, really, this is most strange."
    [Principal] "Your son requires special care. Success would be better assured if we could work in collaboration with you."

At this point the mother contemptuously shrugs her shoulders:

[Mother] "I can't understand the state of affairs here! Children run absolutely wild in your school! And instead of summoning the parents of hoodlums, you summon me, only because my son has looked askance at somebody or didn't smile properly. Not so long ago, I dropped in on him at school myself. The children had a free hour. In Igor's classroom there was unimaginable noise and chaos. Real bedlam. Some children were shouting for no reason at all, others were trying to stop them and to bring them to order. But my Igor was sitting quietly and reading a book. What do you want? He told me: 'There's absolutely nothing to be done with the others. So I had better read. At least that will be some use!' And the boy is right."

[Principal] "No, he is not."

The school principal has, of course, arranged for the mother to meet Igor's teacher. When the latter joins them in the office, she warmly shakes the outraged mother's hand and hastens to reassure her that the boy is an excellent student, disciplined, well read, far ahead of his years in mental capacity and appreciated by all his teachers, but:

"But don't you see, I want to say, if your son is endowed above and beyond the average, more will be asked of him. Don't you want Igor to become a real person? Of course you do! So I am signaling a danger to you. The danger lies in Igor's social passivity. He will simply have nothing to do with the other children, he is preoccupied only with himself. He stays within the shell of his exemplary behavior: 'I am good, I don't misbehave!' However, he and some of his friends could easily become the conscience of their class."

"But you can't demand this of an eleven-year-old."

"Yes, you can and must. Do you want to make your son a cold, self-loving egotist? He must feel responsibility not only for his own conduct, but for the conduct of his comrades. He is a member of a collective. And he was elected leader of a link. He was trusted."

"Oh, all these elected functions! Really, Igor should be relieved of them! All these superfluous burdens tax his health. It's enough that he studies and does not disturb class discipline. And you want to impose on the boy the functions of a pedagogue. Who should be blamed that some teachers are incapable of managing?"

"The task of the teacher does not consist only in preventing a breach of discipline. Our main task is to raise a human being! In the character of your son I see traits which, if not corrected, will interfere with his becoming a human being worthy of the epoch of communism! It's too bad that you do not want to understand me!"

And that is that. According to the school principal, who records this conversation, "They parted displeased with each other. The mother went away, on her face was an expression of hurt and estrangement." And the disappointed teacher sums it up:

"There you have a so-called cultured mother![13] Her son doesn't get poor grades, doesn't walk around with black eyes, smiles pleasantly – oh, a wonderful boy! But that under her own wing there grows a repulsive snob, a narcissist, that does not touch her."[14]

This Igor issues from a crêpe-de-chine dream. A congenital achiever, he is starting to "become somebody" in good season, by his mother's lights, if not those of the pedagogues.

Middleclass language now began to manipulate the difference between a "simple person" (*prostoi chelovek*), an "average person" (*srednii chelovek*), and a "real person" (*nastoyashchii chelovek*).[15] These terms were not merely descriptive but became value judgments, laden with emotion. Nor have they become identical in sense throughout the social structure. In the passage above, the teacher and the mother disagree. For the class-conscious mother, the words "simple" and "average" have become pejorative. Her criticism of the school is peevish. Her squeamishness about "hoodlums" and her stand against the vestiges of collective values have already affected her eleven-year-old son. The school principal and the teacher oppose this middleclass stance.

The collision is less simple than it seems. One important idiosyncrasy of stalinism can be extracted from this innocuous scene. The importance of education for the entire postwar society lies behind it. The two educators are irritated much more by the mother than by the son. Accused of no serious transgression, Igor, the little conformist, seems to be criticized for one thing only: for his mother. And this is the heart of the matter: the problem of " familiness" (*semeistvennost*), of lineage, of inheritance. As far as the boy is concerned, he will succeed on his own. Precociously, he will do all that is required and all that is opportune, and get on. But mama seems determined to make it easier for her boy. And her compensatory drive, unlike the crêpe-de-chine dream of the poor, is adjudged pernicious. She behaves badly in stressing class differences, and implying a right to exercise class privileges. She wants special treatment for her son because of the social status that he was born into. And that was transgression. Atomization meant not only that group loyalties were abrogated, but primary loyalties were closely inspected. To put it simply, if the individual was not supposed to lean on the shoulders of his comrades, he was not supposed to stand on the shoulders of his parents either. And if, in fancier words, the generational continuity of the family nexus – and most specifically of the middleclass family – was questioned, it follows that Stalin preferred every person to start from scratch, achieving everything in direct relationship to him. So the middleclass family could be a headache. Its cohesiveness and aspirations contributed to the system's stability. Yet it was also assailed because it competed with the regime in bestowing privileges that only Stalin could bestow.

It remains to be seen whether the limitations imposed on family feelings were not counterproductive. The issue obviously harbored ambiguities. For the middleclass way of life continued to be supported. The notion of work plus pleasure remained intact. The middleclass family continued to be charged with the production of affluent contentment, and it was held responsible for children who turned delinquent, rebelling against the very idea of a "good family." Nevertheless, middleclass parents were not allowed to compound their privileges into an inheritable package. One can see that this systemic paradox may have somewhat reduced the material and instrumental attractiveness of the Big Deal for the middleclass partner.

Status and love

A *grande dame*, her name can be translated as Madame Pike, stops in a kolkhoz on her way to a Caucasian resort. She has interrupted her journey to visit her brother, a painter spending his summer constructively. He is engaged in immortalizing rural faces. Besides, the charms of a milkmaid have overcome him. This upsets Madame Pike, for she has better plans for him, such as the pursuit of a Moscow ballerina. So it is urgent that she remove the innocent young man from the rural scene and get him to Sochi, a fitting location for the higher romance. The satirical tone is not ours but the playwright's.

Flirting with the kolkhoz chauffeur, Madame Pike, with her curls, pearls, and powder puffs, arrives at the house of the manager. The rural hostess is an enlightened lady peasant. As they introduce themselves to each other, Madame Pike reacts to the hostess's first name.

MADAME PIKE: Natalya, my maid's name is Natalya. And you know, she resembles you. She is also from the village, also illiterate, but nice, very nice.
HOSTESS: And does she serve you well?
MADAME PIKE: She tries hard.

Enter the daughter, the milkmaid. Madame Pike, after looking her over, invites her to sit down, disregards her name and patronymic, and calls her "honey." The girl ironically inquires about the voyage.

MADAME PIKE: Terrible trip, honey, you have no idea... They do not have an international sleeper on this line. They only have couchettes. And there, facing me, sat an unpleasant character. He stared at me all the time and hiccuped. I got so nervous. (She hiccups.) Excuse me, I am so nervous.
MILKMAID: Maybe he was nervous too?
MADAME PIKE: No. He was simply an uncultured boor.

The hostess offers refreshments, but the guest refuses.

MADAME PIKE: Oh, honey, my health is in a terrible state. My husband has called all the outstanding professors for consultation. But our medicine is still so powerless, so powerless. They can't find anything. But I am sick.

The guest thereupon is invited to convalesce in the kolkhoz.

MADAME PIKE: Unfortunately, I can't. My doctor demands that I stay a month in Sochi, and then a month in Kislovodsk.
MILKMAID: Two months in resorts?
MADAME PIKE: Yes, two months. It is so fatiguing. My husband simply does not recognize me when I come back from resorts. I usually return so emaciated. (She hiccups again.) That boor in the train simply infected me with some hiccuping virus. Yes, I am worn out. In Sochi I shall rest. I am taking Kolya with me, straight to Sochi. Kolya can't waste his time here. He is a portrait painter. Whom can he paint here? Whom? Tell me yourself.
MILKMAID: Don't we have people here? Can't he paint them?
MADAME PIKE: There are people everywhere, but during the season famous generals and decorated actors vacation in Sochi. And for a painter it is not important *how* he paints, that's formalism, but *whom* he paints. That's the most important thing.[16]

The painter, however, prefers to remain a formalist and throws his sister out, threatening to drown her.

Satire reaches its permissible limits in this model comedy. Neither wit nor anger motivate it and it goes no further than slapstick. The mixture of caricatured villainy and socialistically realistic positive characters makes no sense. Mockery of meshchanstvo in this manner reverts to meshchanstvo itself, for its ugly features are blown up here beyond what is plausible in Soviet circumstances, and made grotesque in the single figure of crazy Madame Pike, a procedure which contrives to stand socialist realism on its head. Instead of coming to grips with meshchanstvo as a widespread epidemiological phenomenon, it makes it untypical, shrinks it *ad absurdum* and so minimizes and almost denies its significance altogether. Nevertheless, one learns something.

The questions of status, social climbing, and class divisions were first introduced in just this buffo manner. Famous doctors consult over the imaginary maladies of silly women. Generals vacation with their retinues of ballerinas and portrait painters. All this says something about mores at the top. Reactionary attitudes, complacency, promiscuity help along the fierce upward scramble. The foils – the shepherds and shepherdesses disguised as kolkhoz folk — seem pitifully tasteless. Pseudo-satire treats them almost as if serfdom had not been abolished. Such mockery was not very funny.

By contrast, a love ballad, only two pages long, is both funny – if unintentionally – and pertinent. As servant, the author succeeds, unlike most, in complying perfectly with directives. He spells out to the letter the official position on the connection between love and work. By succeeding, he demonstrates that success is failure. The extraliterary purpose turns against itself. Folksiness, declarative simplicity, party-mindedness – all the elements of prosody favored by Zhdanov – conspire to turn the message into a parody. Now parodies, especially unintentional ones, are good reconnaissance tools, providing condensed information. Instead of wading through thousands of dreary pages, one can find in this particular short item nothing less than the core proposal of the Big Deal.

The ballad lends itself to reduction: boy-gets-girl-but-only-after-over-fulfillment-of-work-norm. Public exertion is rewarded in private currency. Eros is fully negotiable. The object of the hero's infatuation is a woman in a neighboring kolkhoz team. They are both foremen. She is formidable. He, alas, is not. The hero, such as he is, tells his woes himself:

> A map of the world hangs between the windows.
> In the corner stands the bookcase.
> Lysenko's portrait from the wall
> Leans over the table,
> Geraniums bloom on the window sill,
> The loudspeaker is on the wall.

I did not come to visit Tanya,
I have come for her advice.
I don't want to tell her
Anything personal today,
For in her presence as usual
I lower my eyes.
"Tell me, foreman,
What is the secret of your success?"
"What is my secret?
I don't understand you.
I don't have any secrets."
"I can't believe it!
How can it be?
Foreman, tell me the truth!
Why is your harvest
So rich this summer?"
She narrows her eyes mockingly
And she says to me:
"Michurin leads my link
In the fields.
That's quite simple.
While we work
We befriend science.
Each ear of grain
Is accounted for.
Each blade of grass
We keep track of."
"What else?"
"So you don't understand, do you?
That's the secret.
It is simple."
Somewhere a clock tick-tocks
Properly beating the measure.
And suddenly I ask,
Without hope of an answer:
"You don't love me, Tanya?
You don't love me, no?"
How I managed to say it, I don't know.
My heart simply brimmed over.
"Tell me, foreman,
Tell me, don't torture me!"
It's almost midnight.
Near the staircase
With repeats and echoes
Three accordions
Started playing.
And I heard them say
Happiness was not far away
But it knew not for whom I waited.
Lonely, I did wander

And I did not let someone sleep
And my queries were in vain
And in vain was my journey also.
There was no point
In my coming from the neighboring kolkhoz.
Komsomol foreman that I was,
I had tried in vain.
I arose and took my leave.
But no sooner did I leave –
Suddenly I hear,
She calls me back.
Be quiet, heart,
Be quiet, heart!
Listen to the voice from the window:
"Listen, lad!
In parting I must
Tell you something.
If you win in competition,
Send the matchmakers.
But if you fail,
If you lag behind
Don't come near me!"
I did not come to visit Tanya.
I have come for her advice![17]

This genre piece, packed with coordinated detail, celebrates meshchanstvo as it makes inroads into the remnants of peasant culture and splendidly renders the proper kulturnost: science and beauty; Michurin and matchmakers, Lysenko and geraniums. The towering superiority of the woman over the traditionally inept male lends the proceedings a Russian flavor. The system promises love as reward for work delivered; but if the maiden gives, it will be for reasons of her own: "Raise your status, fellow, and then . . ."[18]

Both pieces so far involve the grotesque, the second less by design than by accident of "romantic" stylization. How was social climbing handled in less contrived forms than slapstick and folk ballad?

An engineer rejects, with some torment, a female factory worker with whom he is in love. She is an embarrassment to him. He explains, on being prodded, the problem to his superior.

"You understand, she is a worker. It seems to me that it will be difficult for us to get along. Well, how can I explain it to you? I wanted somehow to raise her so that she should find out about everything, about museums, theaters, books, lectures. But I feel that she gets bored with all that."[19]

In another variant of ensnarled love and status, a shock-worker becomes quite flustered when he first meets the girl with whom he falls in love. When the business matter which brought them together is settled, he feels that:

He didn't want to break off right there his acquaintance with this girl. If only he were a chief mechanic, maybe he would have had the courage to accompany her to the administration offices. But right now he had the feeling of some sort of insecurity of which he could not rid himself in any way. Why should she be even acquainted with an assistant mechanic when she herself was an engineer?[20]

To his surprise, the girl falls in love with him too. But as time progresses:

He dreaded to appear in the eyes of Marina as an uncouth person who only knew how to press the buttons of his machine. Before the war, his school education had seemed entirely sufficient to him. He had not only achieved record after record, but he had produced a high norm, month-in, month-out. He was written of frequently in the newspapers. He was an eminent person in the plant. But now he felt that his knowledge was unsatisfactory.   [p. 159]

In spite of the class problem, they are finally about to be married. But the hero has more insight than he gives himself credit for. The young woman is not enthusiastic about becoming the life companion of an assistant mechanic, or any mechanic. In fact, she is rather sorry that she ventured out into this remote industrial area.

"At times I watch these lights down here and I try to forget that behind them there are only monotonous standard houses. When I went to school as a child, I envied the builders of Komsomolsk-on-the-Amur and dreamed that as soon as I grew up, I would go there without fail. What was I talking about? Yes, about the faraway lights. It seemed so tempting to live in tents, to clear the taiga, to build factories! But now it seems to me it is exactly like these lights burning over there. They are beautiful only from a distance. No, no, don't argue."   [p. 174]

So she makes a suggestion:

"I suggest that we go to Moscow. There you will be able to study, you will become an engineer. With your talent, you will be much more useful there than you can be here. You are a capable, talented mechanic. But it is not too late to learn. You can become an engineer, a manager of some large combine." [p. 173]

To remain a mechanic is to fall short of expectations. In this matter of status and privileges, the mechanic suddenly turns clairvoyant:

"No, Marina, don't deceive yourself. You don't want to go to Moscow because a more interesting job awaits you there. Rather, you want to live in such a way as to avoid difficulties as much as possible. And you offer me such a life. You love yourself and not me."   [pp. 174-5]

Another pattern of avoiding difficulties while acquiring status comes out in the following exchange between students:

"You are not married, I hope?" Sergei suddenly asked Vadim.
"No, No, how could I?"
"Well, that's fine," said Sergei sententiously. "You and I, brother, cannot prematurely acquire a family. It's absolutely impossible for us. Now we must start learning. Now we must start, as they say, pushing ahead to become some-body. And to do so is much easier when you are alone, unburdened."[21]

A short novel, *Finally at Home*, deals with postwar adjustments in a provincial town, quite cozy. The war did not touch it directly. Far in the hinterland, it appears sleepy – the way, one suspect, it has always been. The main enterprise is a wallpaper factory. Nothing earthshaking transpires, nothing critical is contributed to the economy. Provincial meshchanstvo blossoms unperturbed.[22] It is embodied in two middle-aged women, a widowed schoolteacher and a plain gossipy housewife, each fretting over a daughter. An army nurse, Taya, is the daughter of the first; Nina, the secretary of the local party secretary, is the daughter of the second. Both mothers are preoccupied with getting the girls married and worry about prestige. It is the relationship between the two generations that is of interest.

The housewife looks at the men in her social orbit from one point of view only, their marriageability. She is torn between the party secretary himself and the newly appointed assistant manager of the factory, a legless veteran. Looking him over, she remarks:

"Only think what good luck means! All of us, thank God, remember Zakhar. He was nothing special. Well, he was a shock-worker, entered the party, and went to war like everybody else. And now? Should the ailing factory manager die tomorrow, Zakhar becomes the first man in the outfit. In fact, he is already the first man. And watch out, he might even become a deputy. Or else they will transfer him to Moscow. It's too bad," she added casually, "that Ninochka got a job in the party committee and not in the factory. The factory's social world is more interesting."[23]

A typical postwar semantic shift transforms the former factory collective into a "social world." Its pacesetter commands admiration:

"There's a bridegroom for you. It doesn't matter that he is a cripple. Happy is the girl who is destined to marry him."

Taya, the young nurse, overhears her mother's friend and she is not pleased:

"You are a cripple yourself!" Taya thought with irritation – she had never liked this woman too well. "How can one look at such a man simply as a potential bridegroom? From such people grow generals and statesmen. And this woman says 'bridegroom!' Stupid woman."   [p. 54]

The two generations are not so very different. The young nurse understands very well what the matchmaker means, for she too sees career possibilities as a first priority. Given the shortage of men, the matchmaker keeps an eye on an elderly widower as well – just in case. This comes out in a girlish heart-to-heart talk between the two potential brides, Taya and Nina. Nina complains that her mother intrudes into her life a great deal. Of late, her mother has been pestering her to pay attention to the widower because he has his own apartment and because "a lot of good things" had been left to him by his dead wife.

"First of all, he is old, ugly, and gloomy and then, all this talk about a fur coat and dishes. Only my mother could think like that! But that's nothing! She has figured out a much better deal!"

She is ashamed to continue. Promising discretion, the nurse extricates the information that the mother is scheming to ensnare the party secretary. She can hardly believe her ears:

"But he is married!"
"Married, that's nothing! Married! He has grown children. The whole family lives heart to heart. And they are both so good to me."

The mother, it turns out, is egging the daughter on to lure this potentate away from his wife because, as she puts it,

"You will be the wife of the district party secretary. You will be the first lady of the district." [p. 65]

Husband hunting as part of social climbing, and sights set high, is a solid part of postwar meshchanstvo; it produces no drastic indignation in the girls, who are cast in the tale as thoroughly positive. Instead, a covert rivalry springs up between them, for both are interested in the legless manager, who is fortunately single. Unwilling to seduce happily married men, they are still much concerned with marriage. The nurse reports casually that her superior, a woman pediatrician, seems to get on well without being married. This is "decisively" rejected by her friend:

"Nonsense. How can you know what's in her heart? How do you know if she is happy? Of course, it's possible to live the way she does. One can live in many ways if one is a human being and not trash. But there is no great happiness in it. And let us both hope that some day good men will come along to marry you and me." [p. 66]

This tame grayish tale substantiates the effect of deheroization, the accompanying acquiescence in the strategies of meshchanstvo. For instance, the nurse clearly intends to capture the lame factory manager. This is all right because heroines must now secure their personal happiness. This can best be achieved by feminine ruse. And she proceeds. When the manager at last responds, pleased as she is with their budding romance, she is somewhat apprehensive that he " might think that she is 'scheming,' 'playing a game' with him because of some sort of 'careerist' considerations" (p. 85). The lady protests too much. And the quotation marks seem to express her coyness more than any disapproval of prevailing mores. When he kisses her for the first time on the traditionally dark staircase, she mutters all aglow:

"I wouldn't want you to think that I, because you are a manager that, in a word, I didn't get stuck in that kolkhoz on purpose to make you pick me up in your car – "
"That's all foolishness," he said. [p. 89]

Not in the least outraged, the first man of the district dismisses her fears lightly. Why not feel flattered?

The regime was anxious to move its citizens in the direction of rebuilding the family. And, in this portentous matter, no better ally could be found than the young woman craving marriage, polka-dotted tea cups, orange lampshades, and the status of the first lady of the district.

What became of the simple worker?

What became of the simple worker? What happened to his pride? Who wanted to marry him now? We turn in the same rich tale to a simple worker who sinks below his station in life instead of climbing. One way or another, to stay in one's niche, at least in fiction, had become difficult. Two brothers had gone to war. The older and solidly positive one, a deserving veteran, had lost a leg in the defense of the motherland. On demobilization, he is entrusted with the only factory in a provincial town and so becomes a powerful person in the community, "the boss of the whole outfit" as we know. We focus, however, on the younger brother, one neither as deserving nor as lucky. Instead of turning him into a hero, the war had corrupted him through the privileges he had enjoyed in the army, especially when stationed abroad. He comes back a restless, greedy show-off, clinging to the memory of exhilarating adventures which increase his bitterness against his successful brother. At a loose end, he frets, depressed.

In forty-four he had cultivated the acquaintance of an Austrian girl whose nails were painted purple. He remembered the Austrian girl frequently. He also remembered how cheaply one could buy an American watch in Germany, a tie, a cigarette lighter, and also how good the food was in the army and how happy the Latvians were when he had entered the city of Riga. And what was there here?[24]

Nothing. Only hard work and the unbecoming status of a "simple worker." No luxuries and no glory. And his irritation with his brother, who is unwilling to go out of his way to help him, grows. Was it fair?

But no! He was to remain what he was: a simple worker. And so he was rotting away with miserable pay, unknown. Could one live on such money? Well, maybe one could live. But where was he to get the money for a restaurant, for treating his acquaintances? How could he buy imported goods which had become his passion, worse than a woman's? And the point was not in the things but in the effect they produced.   [p. 79]

The disaffected young man looks around for solace. "Effective" possessions, acquired on the black market, are some consolation: a zippered jacket, copper-red shoes with rubber soles, and a loud scarf allegedly of Australian origin. All the while he longs for Moscow with its stadium, cinemas, dance halls, and girls. Feeding on dreams, he falls prey to a peroxide blonde whose occupation is dubious and connections unsavory.

She is interesting not so much for her underworld connection, a milieu seldom shown,[25] but because she offers a standpoint for utterances about the hardships of being stuck with a mere worker. There is no question

that she yearns for glamor. Her dyed hair was arranged in neat little sausages. Silver teeth glistened in her large mouth. She dressed very well and was fastidiously clean. In the summer she wore crêpe-de-chine dresses and red sandals. In wintertime, she made her appearance in a fur jacket, felt boots, and a fashionable plaid scarf.

After the war she had found a job in the local department store but soon moved to a better one in a food cooperative. She steals goods wherever she works and gets away with it. She manipulates those around her, including her new lover. He needs her because she supports his battered ego; and she can use a dapper escort. Their marginality is less striking than their cavorting on provincial Main Street.

The central point of this tale is that this young man feels degraded as a simple worker. It is not that he is stupid, the author assures us; he knows that his mistress is a black marketeer and her contacts criminal. But frustration lets him be sucked into the underworld.

In this morass no one told him that he should work harder, that he should marry [a nice girl], or that he should try to catch up with his brother. On the contrary, everybody admired his jacket, his ability to play the guitar and to empty a shot of vodka directly into his throat without touching or moving his lips... And since at the time he had some money and stood treat frequently, he felt completely at home with them.   [pp. 30-1]

He miscalculates, however. The blonde begins to denigrate him. Her underworld language, spiked with low-grade meshchanstvo, talks of the cleavage between the haves and have-nots with a lucidity legitimate citizens can seldom afford.

"Yes, of course, that's the way life always is. One person has everything, the other nothing. One has his own car, he is boss over everything. The other has no benefits, no power, no profits, nothing. He can't even treat his lady friend to a bottle of champagne!"   [p. 32]

When he is completely broke, she vilifies him in front of the gang for being too stupid to "arrange things" for himself and his friends. Someone in the entourage summarizes the prevailing philosophy:

"She is right, devil take her and her mother!... One must, dear Sir, know how to live. That's the way it is these days. And he who does not know how to live doesn't count."   [p. 80]

Materialistic craving at all levels of society, from the underworld to metropolitan salons, had undermined traditional proletarian pride. Even its official mythology was beginning to crumble. From a play called *Party Candidate*, however, one gathers that embourgeoisement was not universally accepted and that in some quarters it was resisted. The hero here is a shock-worker on the production line, teamed with another mechanic. They are given a special award for their efforts which, in the bygone era of proletarian austerity, would have been reward enough. No more. The champions are dined and wined and showered with flowers. A busybody functionary congratulates them ebulliently:

"Comrades, let us wish for our dear Kolya and our no less dear Tolya that their names resound all over the Soviet Union! Let us wish that they may become great men, that they may become ministers, deputies, laureates, that they may glorify themselves as well as our plant!"[26]

Neither the playwright[27] nor the hero accept the equation of "great" people with laureates, ministers, deputies. But everybody else in the play does, and key figures proceed toward the goals set out by the toastmaster. An aggressive female press photographer decides to assist the hero's career, thinking him incapable of taking care of himself. She also develops marital designs on him.

VENTSOVA: Tell me, what are you trying to achieve in life? What do you want to become?

NIKOLAI: What do I want to become? What do you mean? I don't want to become anything. I am a worker and I want to be a worker.

VENTSOVA: What nonsense! You are an intelligent, capable fellow. Why shouldn't you study?

NIKOLAI: I do study. My sister and I are in the fourth year of a technical school. I study by correspondence.

VENTSOVA: So, I am right then. It would be stupid for you to remain a simple worker.

Challenged, Nikolai delivers his great speech, somewhat defensive, dole-ful, off-key:

"Instead of being a simple engineer, I would much rather be an unsimple worker. I love to cut metal, I love to work with machines. Look at my hands. They are created to make things. Take work away from them and they will wither. And I don't like it when people say: "Look at Ivan. He started as a simple worker, and became somebody."[28] For me a worker is the first man in the world. Come here. Look. Everything is done with the hands of workers. And even the stars over the Kremlin were made by working people. And workers raised them on the turrets and other workers lighted them. If there were no workers, there would be no Moscow. Just think: Blacksmith Bridge, Carpenter's Street, why do they call them that? In honor of blacksmiths and carpenters, in honor of my ancestors."

[p. 19]

The hero's proletarian stance seems anachronistic in contrast with the lady photographer's heavy meshchanstvo. Why this misalliance? The photographer confesses to a friend:

"I will tell you frankly that when I first saw Nikolai, I immediately saw that this boy was indeed that most precious material out of which ministers and deputies are made in our country. Nikolai has remarkable potential, but he is too soft . . .

Think what you like about me, but I know that if he will stay with me, I'll be able to direct him and in five years I'll make a man out of him." [pp.21-2]

It is not to be. For frictions grow between them over her strategic advice for his career and her plans for an affluent life. They revolt him. After an unsuccessful visit to a fashionable rooftop spot overlooking glittering Moscow, the hero balks:

"I am tired of noisy society life. Tomorrow I return to where I started from. I will come to the end of my shift and I will go home. Drop in on me sometime if you are not afraid to be bored by a simple worker. The address is still the same. Or else marry me. My wages are decent and, when drunk, I am quite docile." [pp. 31-2]

This purism smacks of individualism. He is a throwback. This noncareerist resists the Big Deal, and it is interesting parenthetically to note that the author of this play ran into trouble with the authorities over this particular hero.

One orthodox writer in another model saga about model workers contrives to tell one story and imply another. At the first level is a paean of praise for a heroic family of workers; three generations of proletarian shipbuilders. The plot involves a great deal of sweat, strain, innovation, and laborious demonstration that not one single thing, from the welding of new battleships to the repair of old schooners, could have been achieved without these weatherbeaten rivetters and their know-how and devotion to the Soviet fleet. On another level, however, this is a tale of pure careerism. For not only is production on the docks revolutionized from rivetting to electrowelding but all the people involved are transfigured accordingly, from workers to professionals. What stays particularly muted, however, is the documenting of the forces which stimulate deproletarianization, their real consequences, and meaning.

By the end of the coy tale, the pater familias, a venerable sextagenarian foreman, deceives his family by pretending that he is fishing during his leisure hours as he used to. Little do they know. Instead, like a schoolboy, he is secretly poring over private lessons in mathematics and physics. Now why, do you think? He is toying with the idea of trying for admission to a technical college. All the young people are off, climbing the educational ladder; one son has already become an overachieving academician and another a Stalin prizewinner for the invention of a tool, and now great grandpa reads books on leninism-stalinism, and makes himself indispensible as the manager's most trusted adviser.

In counterpoint, much is hotly argued about the gratifications of being a worker. But all the defenders of calloused hands have to agree that arithmetic and physics open up greener pastures; that automatic welding beats hand-rivetting; that the former requires training, that training for upgraded jobs is better than basking in obsolete glory; that to be an engineer is better than to be a worker. Moving onward and upward, the pater familias poses, mid-book, a succinct question: "One might ask why should my children be obliged to keep on rivetting and planing? Yes, indeed, why?"

Militant proletarians stand to gain a lot by leaving low-grade skills behind, not only in terms of wages. And the future holds more. Self-respect blossoms as former common laborers take in kulturnost. The public myth of the country's progress celebrates individual achievement, and vice versa. Women, too, show how the private and the public merge. The matriarch of the clan is tireless in cooking, pickling, watering plants indoors and out; anticipating and averting friction; making large-scale domestic comfort. To a prospective daughter-in-law she explains the family's life style:

"We are workers, Zinochka, just as your papa and mama were, may they be in the kingdom of God. Our road is the same as the government's. When the government was poor, we too were poor; when the government became richer, we too took heart. Well, and now you can see for yourself. How many thousands do you think they bring in all together as a family team with their wages! If we were blatant show-offs, as some are, not only would we have grand pianos standing around, but we would have cut-glass chandeliers in every room. But we don't like display and glitter."[29]

Plural pianos, even in absentia, speak for the Big Deal.

When the youngest son gets his first wages, he brings the mother every penny. "There was pride in her eyes, and tears." And the father turns to the youngster resolutely:

"Well, Alioshka, now you are a gravedigger of capitalism! You are the lord and master of the whole earth." The next day, having obtained a coupon from the supply department, the father took him to a big general store and, pretending it was entirely out of his first wages, bought him the most expensive and the very best serge suit that could be found in the store. "A lord and master ought to dress like a lord and master. Understand?"   [1, p. 25]

A small yet pertinent problem then requires their attention. The young man in his new blue serge suit contemplates marriage. He applies for new housing. Meanwhile, because of emotional stress with his troublesome fiancée, his work norms have gone down. He fidgets uncomfortably when summoned to see the manager. With his defenses up, he thinks angrily:

"To hell with them. If they won't give it to me, it's just as well. It won't be the end of the world. I'll figure out a way. And I won't be obliged to anyone for anything. For some small room that they may come up with, they have cooked up a whole investigation! And later, if something happens, they'll start reproaching me: 'we have been taking care of you, we met your needs, and you . . .' and so forth."

Looking straight at his superiors, he tosses a challenge at them. "I don't work for rooms, comrade manager." The manager only gestures in dismay at such haughtiness. But the trade union chief's reply is right on target:

"Hold on, there. What *is* it then that you work for, friend? You don't need rooms. So, perhaps, we don't need to pay your wages either? Is that it? What a generous fellow you are! Why, to give you a room today, we had to make a revolution, sleeping on the bare ground and holding our rifles tight. And you, you wave it all aside! Some gentleman you are!"   [1, p. 67]

The young man bristles for a while, unwilling to come forth with the gratitude he thinks the older generation expects of him. He would prefer to go it alone. One friend of his seems to breach the generation gap much better. He, for one, knows what wages are for and assumes everybody else does. He provides the book with a pronouncement that could stand as its motto:

"Thousands of roubles, that's reality. If you live better, you work better. If you work better, you live better."   [2, p. 43]

6. Parasites and Builders

Key representatives of meshchanstvo are about to recapitulate here, in their own words, some of the issues introduced so far. For the sake of thematic tightness, the portraits are, with one exception, of women. Familial and feminine meshchanstvo schemes, knits, goes to market, and drinks a great deal of tea. Feminine meshchanstvo makes beds – soft ones – and seduces, gossips, quarrels, hovers over children, craves sweets. It bargains hard. It prods husbands to get on. It also gives shelter, makes comfort. And it either shirks public duty or it builds and produces for the common good. When it engages in building, it is, as a rule, unruly. For it tries to function in the system on its own terms.

Their domestic tasks and restrictions entrap women more readily in private worlds than men. So they inform us more directly about the system's ambivalence toward the private domain, its vacillation as to whether to undercut it or let it be. To keep the balance, however, and to stress that meshchanstvo is universal, one powerful male character will speak for the key type the regime was most uneasy about.

In this order, I take, first, parasites, then those who cooperate halfheartedly and, in conclusion, true achievers. In *The Day Starts in the East*, a long tale involving places that are remote even for Siberia, a creature "like a ripe melon" represents the tenacious subculture of gold prospectors. In her ample thirties, she is illiterate and believes in witchcraft. When her husband takes up with a gypsy girl, she runs into the taiga, feeling wronged. Equipped with a dead snake and other tools of black magic, she is about to effect his return to the conjugal bed. But an up-to-date hero, her own nephew, discovers her at work. He thinks her mad.

"How can you live under socialism? Among reasonable and sober people? You believe in sorcery! Shame! Shame and disgrace! Just wait! I will display you and your snake in such a way in the wall newspaper that you won't rejoice!"[1]

She turns pale, but nothing much happens except that she is removed from kitchen work in the prospecting camp. After some complaining she turns to busying herself with making preserves in which "one berry was more beautiful than the other" (7, p. 38).

Greed for gold and sex move this novel along. The team of heroes work their good deeds rather slowly, and an aura of obstinate obscurantism envelops all the natives. Everyone pursues private goals and all remain as untouched by the war as their impregnable dwellings, whose dark rooms secure their possessions. Peasant food and hard drink are shared in a Rabelaisian manner. "Most of all they drank to the health of the Russian people and separately to that of the Siberians" (5, p. 37).

Embarrassed by the separatist ways of his relatives, the emissary from Moscow attempts to rouse their dormant patriotism by suggesting that they purchase a "family tank" for the sum of one hundred thousand roubles. By making this donation to the government, they would redeem themselves. But the clan resists. Having earned considerable riches in perilous combat with nature, they are not going to give them up even if the Germans are pushing on to Stalingrad. Our heroine shouts:

"We must buy a house! ... We are fed up with living in back yard wings and dragging ourselves from flat to flat. We have a whole trunkful of honorary awards! And we have two medals also! Where should I put them? On top of the icon? Yes? We certainly will buy a house and that's all that there is to it. I want to live properly as a person should. That's how it is!"   [7, pp. 25-7]

This frontier life seems to afford "freedom from." In the cluttered postwar panorama of Soviet life, put together by cautious and compliant writers, this vignette seems fantastic and at the same time eerily real. That is to say, it is pointless to ask how this woman could have survived in Soviet society. She could and she did, both in socialist realism and in real life. Untouched by Soviet ideology a quarter of a century after the revolution,[2] ineradicable provincial self-interest serves as a background to the forthcoming portraits.

The next picture of meshchanstvo on the periphery seems even more parasitical. The story is set in the Donetz Basin during the advance of the German armies. Entire plants and enterprises are being dismantled in a frenzy. Trains evacuating the population are about to leave. The hero, an engineer, rushes home to get his wife and child. He finds her reading a book. She is an attractive woman, her last name evoking extremism: Mrs. 'All-or-Nothing' (Kraineva). Out of breath, he urges her to get ready in an hour. She reacts calmly.

"First of all, good morning ... and, secondly, I am not going anywhere."
   "What do you mean? he asked, not trusting his own ears.
   "It's very simple. I am staying here."
   "With the Germans?"
   "Why with the Germans? With Russians."
   "Well, you know, this is news to me! Didn't you yourself want to leave?"
   "And now I don't want to. Where am I supposed to go, under fire?"
   "Yes, but everybody else is leaving."
   "Oh, 'everybody' again," she said with irritation

"Listen, Ira, to the devil with your jokes," he exploded. "We might be late!"

"I am not going to be late because I am in no hurry," said Irina with the same calm. "And where are you hurrying, Sergei? You are neither a communist nor a Jew."

The words communist and Jew come out easily in their new and old ominous proximity. And she goes on, as he stares at her stupefied.

"Where are you going?" . . . and her voice seemed as new to him as that of a stranger.

"What do you mean where? To the Urals."

"And what's in the Urals? The Germans will get there too . . . Are you sure that Russia will win?"

The hero proclaims his faith in the fatherland and upholds "the dignity of Soviet man." This fails to impress her. "Condescendingly," she establishes a very important difference:

"I understand. This regime has given you a great deal. It has transformed an illiterate fellow into an engineer. But what has it given me?"

Some citizens defected in just this way. Old, ripe, smoldering grievances came out. And they turned into conscious alienation from official norms. The hero, indignant at last, defends the system's generosity:

"What! It has given us both the same thing: the right to everything. You must use this right. I have used it. I have worked hard. And you? All your life you have looked for some illusion of happiness. Until today you've visualized life as some surprise candy box. But in our society nothing is given for nothing and everything can be obtained with stubborn work."

"If one cannot find the treasure in one spot one looks for it in another."

"So, that's what you think? You want to look for it among these cannibals?"

"Who believes that the Germans are cannibals? . . . People who have given the world a Schiller, a Goethe, a Wagner, a Mendelssohn are cannibals? Ridiculous! It's the usual war propaganda."[3]

Without another word, the hero goes into the nursery and awakens his son.

Disaffection of this magnitude has to be accounted for. The author tries, but he explains only certain things. Among those he does not explain is the problem of a misalliance between a perfectly proper citizen and a potential enemy. She knows the main recompense in his world, the hoisting of a compliant achiever from the bottom of the social pile to the realm of middleclass partnership with the regime. But he seems to know nothing of her frustrations. He mistook her babbling in painting and music and her craving for Moscow for kulturnost. It was large-scale nostalgia instead, and a clue is provided to this type. In the twenties, Mrs. All-or-Nothing had been raised in the "residual," archbourgeois family of a prerevolutionary industrialist, where her mother functioned in the double capacity of housekeeper and mistress to the head of the household. The mother sacrificed herself for her child's proper upbringing. In that house there had "reigned an atmosphere of tearful memories of the past and of vague hopes for the future. The present did not exist" (p. 149). The masters managed to emigrate, leaving one son behind. He changed his name, waited for Stalin's all-forgiving constitution before making a career, and remained a glum subversive. It is he, of course, who crosses this woman's path at the outbreak of war and seduces her. Neither of them succeeds, however, under the Germans. From this shady lover she passes into the hands of a Nazi officer and from there into many more beds until she becomes a prostitute, inhumanly treated by the invaders.

During the war itself, severe stress was portrayed in fiction without too much editing. This permitted occasional side-glances at the system as a whole. The disaffected woman here clearly settles an old score. The regime, it turns out, had given nothing to this type of meshchanstvo, or not enough. The war had subjected the entire social system to so much pressure that grudges and weaknesses stood out under the test as much as human stamina. War fiction reflected this dichotomy. Although toler-ated for a while, the polarization did not harmonize with the official position on the state of the embattled nation; and the depiction of the spiritual collapse of young people, products of Soviet education, became irksome to the regime. Ideologists were hard put to explain weakness and defection among the young.

In a tale about the siege of Leningrad, a young girl disintegrates morally and turns into a little hyena. The interest here is the prophylactic failure of the system in ferreting out faulty individuals in time. What warrants attention also is the effect the little hyena has on the good people around her. She damages her entirely positive boyfriend. Both under twenty, they had been raised in puzzling proximity of each other. Neighbors since early childhood, they went to the same school. The boy's awkward love for Verochka causes him pain. She flits from ballet studios to singing lessons without taking either seriously, and inhibits the boy with her dazzling kulturnost. She is a flirt, surrounded by beaux. His jealousy is mixed with feelings of his own inferiority. "She reads and knew consider-ably more than he. Outwardly indifferent, but secretly with great re-spect, he listened to her discourses on Priestley's plays and Hemingway's novels."[4] Differences in upbringing are here signalled by the author. But rather than providing the needful explanation of how a young person goes bad, it inadvertently emphasizes the social splintering. The boy comes from a working-class home, where his parents exert a beneficial influence. As for the girl, she has been brought up by an aunt about whom nothing is said except that she removes herself conveniently in the first days of the siege leaving her niece to her fate. The girl's isolation does no honor to the celebrated youth organizations and " social forces."

The boy is called to arms as soon as war breaks out. And the girl is drafted and set to digging ditches. She discovers that she dislikes the heavy spade for ruining her hands. And so, not without guile, she be-friends a plain and trusting girl named Katya.

Katya fell in love with Verochka as sometimes plain girls fall in love with beautiful girls. And she worked for two. Katya was uneducated. But she was full of curiosity. And she liked such a division of labor . . . Verochka had money. Katya did not. And Verochka kept running to the village to buy sour cream and honey for two.   [p. 168]

The boy, his superb parents, and the humble mate digging ditches all admire the girl because they think her their social superior. But something, not accounted for, happens to her. Fending for herself and panicking at the thought of hunger, she stops sharing anything with anyone. When she exhausts her hidden supplies, she crawls out of her hideout and finds a job as a waitress. The job embarrasses her, but she can explain that an architect and a student are her co-workers "so that, God forbid, no one should get the idea that she was engaged in lowly and unbecoming work"(p. 187).

She is fired for trying to steal a packet of rice but manages to get another job in the warehouse of a factory. The manager, a sinister crook, seduces her, staging orgies with wine and wondrous foodstuffs. He also gives her a fur coat. Working now hand in glove with the petty criminal, she cheats her boyfriend's mother out of a cherished possession, a small blue wall rug, the very symbol of that model family's peacetime bliss. And then she accepts it as a special present from her lover and hangs it on her wall. It is a sad occasion when the boy returns on his first furlough. His father had been killed transporting victuals for the besieged city across Lake Ladoga. Full of grief, the boy runs to Verochka's. She feeds him; more, she gives herself to him. But, in his arms, she tells him casually that she had run into his mother a day or so before. The mother, it turns out, had died of starvation ten days earlier. When the boy finds out that she lied, he vomits.

Carry-over meshchanstvo, exemplified by the first two examples, might be considered peripheral to the main stream of Soviet life. The very question, however, of what constitutes the periphery in a society which claims to be centralized and unified, is a difficult one. A huge no-man's land in a land allegedly all accounted for is a paradox. Nor should the difference of origin among these portraits be overlooked. The marginality of the Siberian matron might be geographical; that of the out-and-out defector genetic. But what kind of marginality does the little hyena issue from? She is at the heart of society. Why has her socialization turned out so badly? War trauma alone might explain her to an outsider. But for native apologists of the system's infallibility she is a severe problem.[5]

It is curious that some types of systemic meshchanstvo elicit more justification than others. Benign parasitism circumscribed by domesticity makes little social trouble. It seems strangely normal even when caricatured. Nesting creatures do not greatly trouble anyone, provided they are absorbed in nesting. This is the major point that this portrait gallery collectively makes. If deheroization was taking place in our period, so too was "devillainization."

An idle creature, whose name, Pava, suggests a peahen, is provincial yet distinctly urban, uprooted yet cocooned. Her case says something about peacetime mores. She understands the system well, and profits from it. She is married to a mousey bookkeeper endearingly called Musiurchik, and urged by her up the promotion ladder. The children have been grotesquely christened Camelia and Landelius. Here she is, bubbling and smiling "with all her dimples" as she returns by car from a shopping spree.

"Only think! In spite of everything, how much Soviet power has given the backward provinces! What a turbulent growth of culture! What building projects!" But there and then her face dropped. "Musiurchik, I forgot to buy a little cape for Camillochka!"

A quarrel follows because the spouse sees no sense in "a stupid little cape." The peahen has the last word:

"No, just listen to him! What does a man know of the problem of how to dress children!"[6]

This version of meshchanstvo is cheerful, dimpled, and moronic. It is devoted to acquisitiveness and to the care of a precarious natural possession.

"I was really beautiful before I got married. But pregnancy spoils a woman's figure. It is terrible! It is simply an injustice. I swear! They talk so much about the beauty of a healthy body. But what beauty can there be in a child-bearing mother? Of course, children are a goal of life. That's what my Musiurchik always says." And for an instant she closed her mouth. The torrent of words ran out. She sniffed at a perfume bottle and continued thoughtfully: "No, seriously, I must take care of myself. I don't want to get old." [p. 86]

At this point, and out of the blue, the peahen dissolves in sobs, imploring the wife of a doctor for help. She needs an abortion; she confides that it is not Musiurchik's child. Legality bothers her least of all:

"Even in these times we are all forced to get around the law. It can be done in my house. I don't dare offer anything for it. But I am willing to spare neither money nor things. And [my husband] can be useful to [your husband] in return. I swear! He has such connections! Such friends!" [p. 87]

The doctor does not take the bait and, inclined toward serenity as she is, the peahen calms down. This does not mean that she does not fret over what she called her kangaroo shape. But in due time she gives birth to a healthy baby. Examining the newly born, the friend whispers that it looks like Musiurchik. A bit peeved, the peahen responds:

"Well, who should he look like? Do you really think that I am such a careless fool?"
"But you said yourself –"
"Who cares what I said! . . . I simply did not want to go through having a child again. But [your husband] turned out to be unfeeling. But I don't regret it now,

particularly since I have borne such an adorable little 'fact.'"   [p. 109]

After all, she is not a bad mother. And the nursery is immaculate: pink and cluttered, with lampshades adorned with large bows. The house is soft with a profusion of embroidered pillows. She wears heels of threatening height; shaking hands with men, she always pushes hers upward so as not to miss a gallant hand kiss. She earnestly counsels amorous affairs, preferably illicit. And, in what in the novel is called her salon, she gives what can only be called soirées. On such occasions, cakes are decorated with buttercream curlicues, and plates of them alternate with bottles of wine on the table. Spirits flow; the victrola plays, and the peahen bursts into gypsy solo dances. It is then that some guests get gloriously drunk. Two drives move the peahen – flirtation and gossip. Or rather, three drives: she also schemes to strengthen her husband's connections, preferably with party members. And the empty vodka bottles, unremoved in the old tradition, form a primordial forest of their own on this calculatingly hospitable table.

A good samaritan, she unloads gifts at the bedside of a sick friend.

"Here are some tea biscuits, some chocolate... candied fruit and candied lemons... I have sent the chauffeur especially to Ukamchan to buy sweets for the children. They are growing. They need sweets. And, generally, it is pleasant if they can have everything. Childhood happens only once in a lifetime, a golden time!... At one go Landelius ate almost a whole kilo of chocolate. I had to give him a laxative... The boy has peculiar inclinations: he breaks everything, destroys everything. But he has a strong will, I can tell you! If he doesn't want to do something, you cannot force him in any way. And Camillochka is very coquettish. She can wiggle a whole hour in front of the mirror. But she has her funny ways too. She breaks everything too. Why are they so careless with things?"

Gurgling on and on in mini-brained sovietese, she comes up with a poignant answer to her own question: "I think it's because of their contempt for private property!"(7, p. 81).

Reluctant bricklayers

Across the entire social spectrum, class differences became visible even in middlebrow fiction and the centrist stage of professionals, especially among women, holds interest.

We turn first to a prima donna, a Leningrad actress. The marital difficulties of the genteel and languorous Nelly Ivanovna[7] summarize certain developments in Soviet mores. In the twenties, she had fallen in love with a Red Army commissar.

She loved him and was afraid of him. She was impressed with his physical strength, his self-control, and strong willpower. Nelly had never met such people before. But he frightened her with his reticence and silence.

In spite of the birth of one daughter, Nelly soon became bored.

But he did not know how to amuse her. He disappeared at work for days on end and in the evening he read enormous books entirely bewildering to Nelly Ivanovna.[8]

She takes to crying frequently. But soon her stern husband is transferred to Moscow. Living headquarters are unobtainable for the family there and Nelly remains in Leningrad. Her baby grows into

an adorable child, blond, gay and bright. Nelly Ivanovna tied enormous ribbons in the child's hair and called her Bunny. [p. 17]

In the park where she took Bunny to play in the sand, she meets a matinée idol with graying temples. He brings her flowers daily and helps her to a brilliant theatrical career. He himself is on the way up as a director. She arranges for a divorce in order to marry this more compatible mate. The luxury reserved for theatrical celebrities surrounds her. She lives in a handsome apartment, frequents the best nightclubs, has the use of an automobile and chauffeur. The admiring public showers her with acclaim.

She raises her child with fervent expectations that she will become famous. When Bunny tires of ballet lessons, the mother tries to steer her early enough toward the career of a concert pianist. Nelly's world is luxuriously fenced in. The point is that when cast once as a heroic working-class girl she panics because she knows nothing about the working class. She

had never known or seen such a young woman. In the circle of her numerous friends there were none. Or maybe she had never noticed them. And she believed only very feebly that they ever existed at all. [p. 36]

Fear now piles on fear. When the war breaks out, her husband dreads that he may have to surrender his automobile. The theater is evacuated to the provinces. Nella Ivanovna takes a dim view of the new environment. Green hills and ancient churches do not enchant her. Nor can she be pleased with a small apartment, with no telephone. In addition, her husband's pessimistic speculations about the growing weakness of the Soviet armed forces depress her. The severest blow comes when her daughter abandons music and enters the service of her country as a nurse. Since the family atmosphere is tense and the young girl despises her stepfather, Nelly at first tries to be tolerant. But in the end, grasping at the last straw, she puts pressure on her straying child.

"It's time you gave up this whim."
"What whim?" Nina did not understand her mother.
"Well, this hospital of yours."
"But, mother," Nina laughed, "I don't go there for the sake of fashion." [p. 64]

The daughter goes to the front and treats Nelly's "theatrical pastime" with contempt.

When the theatre is moved to the Caucasus, the situation becomes

critical; the advancing enemy is only hours away. The matinée idol refuses to flee. With a "sneer" and "evil laughter," he insists that well-
known actors are safe anywhere and enemy occupation may not be the
worst thing that can happen. The aging Nelly is shocked, for the first
time. This belated jolt at last puts her on the right road. As she says to
herself, for sixteen years she had not known that she was married to a
"nonentity," something of a euphemism. Rapidly packing her perfume
bottles, she walks out on him.

From Tashkent she went to Samarkand. From there to Alma-Ata. But even there
she found the same old thing. Her friends played on the stage, made movies,
argued about salaries, got married, and got divorced.

The next step is her estrangement from her own milieu. Abruptly,
applause and baskets of flowers stop giving her satisfaction.

It seemed to her that for all these years she had been lying in a case and now for
the first time she saw the world around her. In comparison with the enormous
suffering she witnessed during these days, the suffering of the people, of whom
she had heretofore thought so little, her own sorrows suddenly seemed petty and
negligible.   [7-8,pp. 136-7]

She goes to the front and offers her talent to the soldiers. She is saved not
by the system but by her awakened patriotism.

The theatrical world, commodiously harboring a pretentious kind of
meshchanstvo, might be thought of as peripheral. The medical sector of
the armed forces in wartime, on the other hand, certainly cannot be called
socially marginal.

"A small, slender woman, with somewhat slanted eyes and a row of
magnificent white, even, sparkling teeth,"[9] Dr. Vetrova – literally, Dr.
Wind – is working at the onset of war in the hospital attached to a southern aviation base. A famous pilot is sent there for a cure. Dr. Wind takes it
upon herself to take care of him and to keep him entertained. "She was
particularly successful in the latter. Judging from all the evidence, she
was amusing him excellently"(p. 21).

With the enemy threatening to encircle the hospital, the staff has to be
evacuated. Dr. Wind chooses to stay behind. A month later, with the
hospital settled in a safer place, she comes rolling along in a field staff car,
wearing a handsome naval uniform, though without insignia. Her lover
has enough power to force the much-hated medical commanding officer to
take her back on his staff in spite of her insubordination. Ecstatic, and
bursting with pride, she tells the story of her miraculous escape. Two
hours before the old base had been taken by the enemy, her idol had sent a
major in a special plane to whisk her out of the encirclement and bring her
into his renowned arms. With the name of her powerful benefactor constantly on her lips, she boasts that he has given her his car for "her
personal use" and that she can drive "wherever and whenever" she
wishes (p. 22). She also declares that she prefers to live with her lover at
his base rather than at the hospital. Reminded that she may not flit about

without the commanding officer's permission, she indignantly replies that she does not "intend to obey some puny little doctor." In self-defense, the "puny little doctor" predicts that her luck cannot last. The prediction proves correct. The powerful lover takes off "for another front without so much as saying goodbye." She is forced to return to the hospital "like a beaten dog with its tail between its legs." And she now discovers that she is pregnant.

The poignant part of the story, though, is yet to come. Her superior's retaliation is his refusal to notice her. He sees to it that she gets no duties. Once in a while, he mutters ugly remarks about her. He treats her with such disdain that she fears to come under his eyes. The most telling turn of events is this:

Some people, in an effort to please the boss, began openly to insult the poor woman also. The situation became so bad that she was afraid to go alone into the staff dining room... The very same people who used literally to throw themselves forward to open the door of her car and who outdid each other in lighting matches whenever she took out a cigarette, those same people now humiliated her human dignity on every occasion. Because of her youth, she did not know that that's the way it sometimes is in life. In the period of her short bloom and of her small and fleeting power, she had taken all these signs of attention at their face value. Everybody seemed to her good, pleasant, attentive, and devoted. Now when these people had turned away from her, she did not understand them and she was afraid of them. [pp. 22-4]

Promiscuity had fed on the recklessness of front-line life, making a parasite out of a professional young woman. A casual mistress, recognized by everyone as such, she has enough power to threaten her superiors. But when she is brought down to earth, her puff of fleeting glory vanishes and she has to face the ancient merriment of vengeful philistines. Dr. Wind is vulnerable and stupid. But other types are better at survival. One, well equipped to fend for herself after the war, has the common sense and prudence which Dr. Wind lacks.

Rima had lost her husband during the war. She had served in the army herself. After her discharge she goes back to the university to work for an engineering degree. Capable, intelligent, well groomed and well dressed, she now deceives people as to her age. She uses perfume heavily. Her nails are scarlet. She flirts a great deal, though within the limits of propriety. There is a note of sadness in her appearance. She is aware that her life has not turned out as it should have. As a war memento

there remained the medal "For Merit" in the lapel of her jacket. Soon the medal was substituted by a ribbon, and then the ribbon disappeared. Rima explained casually: "It is no longer fashionable."

We value her highly. The author does not, using her merely as a foil to a pallid heroine.

Rima clings to a dingy room in the center of the city. She could live more comfortably elsewhere. But the Intourist restaurant downstairs provides her with the distant sound of jazz and she loves the glitter of the city.

She loved, for instance, to enter some beer tavern in her smart spring coat and hat, copies from the last Moscow model. It amused her to watch the waiter stare at her. A beer, a cheese sandwich, and a cigarette. On Rima's face there was an immutable calm. And from every table men hurried to offer her a light.[10]

As the expression goes, she has seen life. In the Soviet Union, as anywhere else, this means that she has known men.

Rima's practical turn of mind contrasts with the idealism of the heroine, who has divorced a man because he did not fully appreciate her professional drive. He is now about to come all the way from Siberia to see their child, upsetting the heroine no end. Rima stands by with counsel, even if a little patronizingly.

"Take it easy. At our age it is very difficult to find a man who can give complete happiness... because it is necessary to give up everything for such happiness, one's habits, predilections. One must sacrifice oneself. But we are not capable of that."

The heroine bristles, and defends love pure and deep. But Rima continues to advocate reconciliation with a man who

"is making enough money and it would be so much easier for you and the child."

She clinches her argument with the admonition that

"happiness, perfectly round like the moon, does not altogether exist."   [p. 48]

This debate runs through the novel. On one occasion the two philosophize in the shady coziness of a Russian veranda. Unwilling to strain for ideals and perfectionism, Rima's pragmatism recognizes that "everyone has flaws" and that the best thing is to take it calmly. When the driving heroine demands a detailed statement of her aims, Rima gladly answers:

"We should strive to make life easy, beautiful, gay. We should strive to abolish all these perpetual mountains which have to be overcome. We should strive to make life like a broad, surfaced boulevard on which you can walk in high-heeled shoes because it is so smooth and even."

These confessions, evoked by the peaceful setting, indicate her wistful longing for serenity and she remembers her protective father, who was a professor, her own beauty as a young girl, the promise of dawn.

"In a word, everything was wonderful, school and summer vacations in the south. I was told that I was born under a lucky star. And I myself thought that I had drawn the winning lottery ticket for a hundred thousand. And on that ticket, on top of everything else, there was written something veiled and promising, something to the effect that, dear Rimochka, you can expect enormous future happiness. Then father died, and the family disintegrated. I was married, my husband was killed, and so on and so forth. And the marvelous thing prophesied on my lottery ticket is not here at all. That's why I am disappointed . . . Everybody has a house and I have only a shaky little shack." [pp. 85-6]

The combative heroine says stodgily: "One must build one's own house." To this Rima coldly replies: "I am not a bricklayer. And then I am tired, terribly tired." Not terribly negative, and not sour either, this capable professional woman merely feels tired of the onward and upward march. Honesty supports her common sense. She is not an overachiever; the promises of adolescence have not materialized. Yet, in the face of disappointment, she does not fall apart, she merely wilts a bit. Her needs are not exorbitant, and possibly they are more compatible with the system's needs than a purist craving for full-scale social responsibility.

The "reluctant bricklayer" represents the core concern of postwar meshchanstvo. Such a person looks for a winning lottery ticket without exactly shying away from a reasonable commitment to work. Whether spoiled like the actress, pushed off-course like the gullible young doctor, or simply deflated like this widowed lady engineer, these women survive. Not heroines but key types, they do not strike us as maladjusted. They are diffident but not harried, pushy but not erratic. Nor are they sour. The longing for "sweets" overcomes them all. Some manage to maintain a balance between private cravings and public commitments. Still others convert the dream of affluence into a socially useful force. It is to such achievers that we now turn. They show how much resilience in the hard postwar world and the pursuit of material gratifications, whether in the making of homes or in providing for them, mattered to the system.

A residue to reckon with

Folk meshchanstvo appears, of course, in both feminine and masculine forms. Just as obviously, it produces zealous builders as well as parasites.

A tale about the head of a district housing administration provides a portrait of powerful builder, involved in the huge task of resurrecting the scorched wasteland of the Smolensk region. This character created a memorable controversy. Patriarchal and self-made, he is presented as negative. But the author's intention was one thing, and the final effect of the story another: the diagnosis did not convince the readers, who applauded this particular troublemaker for doing his job well and for stealing the show from his adversary, a rigid, stultified hero.

When war broke out, Kondrashov[11] volunteered, although he was above military age. On his return, he picked up where he had left off. In his fifties, a splendid physical specimen, he craves work, and is an excellent provider for the community and for his family. He knows how to meet difficulties: looks for loopholes, twists and turns, bribes, pulls and pushes, cuts corners incessantly, violates regulations. At one point, this style gets him into trouble. He is fired from the district job and demoted to the job of a mere contractor in a small town. He smolders with anger, and his contemptuous use of the pronoun "they" betrays his dissociation from the authorities, his informed alienation. The brittle, ideologically immaculate hero needles him for his unruliness. To this Kondrashov replies grouchily:

"I keep remembering how they read sermons to me there. Do they think that as a builder I will not first put up a good house for myself? They transferred me here. The first thing I did here was to build myself a house. Let them reduce me to a mere carpenter. All the same I will build the first house for myself. Nor will I beg forgiveness for it. They drive me crazy with 'moralities.' As for me, I am used to working without 'moralities'. I do my job. And I should be appreciated for what I am!"[12]

The ideologist keeps reprimanding him, but not so much for greed, as one might expect, or pushiness or antisocial behavior. Perceptively, he accuses him of pride. And Kondrashov responds with pride. He shoves under his adversary's nose his "enormous, weather-beaten hands, covered all over with callouses" to illustrate his point:

"When I work, I don't care if there is no bulldozer around, I lift the logs myself. But as to how I do it, what I give, where I take, let them not meddle. Or else I'll bite."   [p. 27]

Contrary as he is, adversity hones his initiative. He knows the source and purpose of his energy. Accused of selfishness when life is so hard for everybody else, he overturns the argument: just *because* life is hard, he, for one, must look out for himself and his family. Sure of himself, he explains his mode of operation. For instance, he has postponed completing of the town's courthouse in order to build a warehouse for meat. In exchange he wants from the local meat distributor half a cow at wholesale price for his own use. As far as he is concerned, the courthouse can wait forever. "To me the judge is a useless person." When the adversary interjects that a judge might bring him to justice for cutting too many corners, Kondrashov considers such a thing stupid and unfair. He does not intend to resell the meat for profit, but to eat it.

"I simply want people around me to live well. I want all those who depend on me to be well taken care of."

Kondrashov never hides his crudely materialist aspirations, his robust meshchanstvo. He talks back with common sense.

"No, my dear man, they will not prosecute me. I am, as you people put it, a product of the times, of the times in which we lack everything from soles to bricks. And most of all we lack people, working hands. Give me normal conditions first and then surround me with 'moralities.' Then I will be a moralist myself. I will be a saint! But when one works as I do, when there is nothing around, when in order to live and to work one has to turn and twist every day, then ask me for work but don't insist on 'moralities.' I have pawned them. Till better days."   [pp. 34-5]

Further assaults on this outsider uncover his affinity with the past, his kinship with the prerevolutionary merchant builders, the oak-strong Morozovs and the mammoth Mamontovs who emerged singleminded, individual, marked out by generosity and tyrannical caprice to build, just before the apocalypse, grandly noncorporate bourgeois fortunes. And Kondrashov puts his finger on the connection when he asks:

"So you think I am a residue of capitalism, is that it? Or, how do you put it, a birth-mark?"

Trapped into admitting that he accepts the system only with some unspoken reservations, he turns the matter into a joke:

"Well, I will be on my way in spite of my day off. I must cast my capitalistic glance over our socialist construction. I have a young foreman there whose soul is not in the right place. He might mess things up."   [p. 37]

The pompous hero happens to be Kondrashov's own brother-in-law, a party official just back from a long assignment with the Soviet purchasing commission in Washington. He returns full of hatred for the United States, a tribute to Zhdanov. Kondrashov, however, a premature and daring prophet of today's détente, is fascinated with the forbidden land and rhapsodizes over an electric razor the traveler has brought him:

"The truth of the matter is that this is real culture . . . Small things are the mirror of culture, if you want to know! You don't agree, do you?"

Not only does the hero not agree, it sends him off inveighing against "Americans who hang Negroes on lampposts" and block the sale of penicillin "to Russians because Russians are communists" and so on. But Kondrashov has forgiveness in his heart, even for Germans (in visionary anticipation of Willy Brandt's Ostpolitik), all the more heretical at the time for having lost his son at the front. His voice turning low with anxiety, he asks: "Is it true that there will be war?" The hero says yes, indeed, war is inevitable if capitalism, synonymous with fascism, continues on its imperialistic course. Kondrashov's interpolation is one of the most amazing in all the middlebrow fiction of that period:

"I am fifty-two years old . . . Three wars in one lifetime. A little too much. Too rich. I am not greedy. Two would have been enough for me."

The hero assures Kondrashov that his opinion is of no interest to anyone. And Kondrashov retorts, raising his voice:

"Well, that's just too bad. If I were asked, I would say: one system! Two systems! There have been all sorts of systems on earth. And people somehow lived, somehow they arranged themselves, somehow they managed to agree with each other. There must be no more war! It has no right to be! At no price! Because I say: our system is wonderful but when I am dead, it's not much use to me."   [p. 25]

That is precisely the point. Never mind the system. In this debate, over which a servile author seems to have lost control, an early, lonely harbinger of détente sets his truth against party truth. He skirts heresy by minimizing the system's infallibility. Is this the voice of a marginal character, of a residue, of a freak?[13] Productive in his own terms, he implies, among other things, that only those viscerally committed to exertion for the sake of the good life have any chance of salvaging the ravaged country. But for the time being, this obsolete achiever was too lonely and too self-willed.

Fighting achievers

Two women join their hardworking hands. They can hardly be seen as residual. Nor in any way marginal, they make a fit ending for this chapter. The first is very young, the second more than mature. Both are characterized by independence, one a productive farmhand, the other an efficient kolkhoz chairman. The kinship between them shows how raw vigor is tempered by common sense.[14]

Frossia, a spunky kolkhoz girl, is portrayed — although not without important reservations[15] – as a generally positive character. She makes her appearance in a splash of color.

Her blouse was green. The beads around her neck were red. And her skirt was blue. It seemed appropriate for her eyes to be different: one yellow, the other blue.[16]

Loud and wild, she does everything well. She is especially good at hawking goods – cottage cheese, sour cream, and salted mushrooms – at the market.

With the passion of a gambler, Frossia bargained over every penny. Once in a while she would let a customer go and then she would lure him back. Her eyes fluttered at every client of the male sex and, not sparing her voice, she praised her wares so loud that one could hear her a kilometer away. She performed an entire show in which her grief over the stinginess of some customers alternated with haughtiness and, in turn, her haughtiness suddenly transformed itself into a startling amiability, which, however, would be immediately replaced by total unyieldingness. [6, p. 40]

Frossia's old-fashioned mother delights in the commercial prowess of the twenty-year-old. But can the school, the komsomol, the formative socialist environment?[17] Under less than vigilant guidance, the girl seems to have developed on her own.

Inclined to make large gestures, her wheeling and dealing takes a frivolous shape. Having sold her private potato crop well, she decides to buy, of all things, picture window frames, "fashionable in a certain suburban kolkhoz into which one of her girlfriends had married" (6, p. 40), with "high-quality" glass to go with them. She pays "no more and no less than a thousand roubles." The purchase turns into an excellent private investment, for she begins to sell pieces of glass in the neighborhood. The profitable trade does not last. In an erratic moment, Frossia gives all her precious stockpile away as a present to the komsomol group. This is to aid in some experiment concerning seedlings. She can barter for a penny as if she were possessed, but "she throws thousands away without blinking."(6, p. 41).

The same impulsiveness rules in the other area in which she excels. She is, after all, the sexiest girl in the village. During a meeting,

on the windowsill, next to the presidium, there sat Frossia in all her beauty. She established herself on the windowsill not because there was no room elsewhere but because it was easier from there to astound everyone present with the magnificence of her new rubber half-boots. These half-boots were aimed at everybody in general and at Andrei in particular. Frossia would not have been Frossia had she not been dreaming of bewitching the district party secretary. She had curled her bangs and painted her eyebrows. But she relied most of all on the half-boots which glistened like a mirror. So that, God forbid, they should not go unnoticed by anyone, Frossia from time to time raised her foot, twisted it either tip or heel forward, or even sidewise, and assiduously and lengthily kept checking the silvery zipper.   [5, p. 102]

With characteristic energy she puts up a fight head on when her mother's individual plot, given them for a decade's use provided it be cleared, is about to be taken away according to a new ukaz.

"That's all we needed! What is this? . . . Mother and I cleared that strip of land of all the tree stumps with our own hands. How much labor we put into it! How much sweat we shed! And we did not get it for the sake of my pretty eyes . . . how I bent my back! How much dung I carried up that slope! And now you want to take it away? Is this justice, comrade secretary?"   [5, p. 105]

And she finds herself, at every turn, in conflict with her superiors. When drought comes, she disobeys orders and stops cultivating the plot for which she is responsible as link leader because she does not believe that cultivation will do the scorched crop any good. So she highhandedly permits the girls under her command to take to the woods to pick berries.

"What do you mean? Haven't I worked since spring? Who carried more fertilizer than anybody else? My link! Who was the first in finishing supplementary feeding? My link! I worked as long as it made sense. But why should I work now?" And with eyes full of hatred she pointed to the sun, "Look, how it beats down!"   [6, p. 69]

The threat to demote her does no good, and in fact her insubordination makes good sense in view of work teams, large and small, pitched against each other at cross-purposes. She replies to an order to help irrigate a seed plot with an insolent note:

"Go and irrigate your seed plot yourself! We are not hired hands and we are not so stupid as to break our backs on plots that are not ours!"

Confronted with superiors, she stands her ground:

"Why should we cultivate and irrigate *their* rye? That's all we needed! They don't irrigate ours, do they?"

"But their plot is for seed! On their rye depends all of our next year's crop!"

"It's *theirs*! Let *them* irrigate it!"

"So, according to you, ten people must work day and night in the field while ten others are picking berries in the woods? The entire kolkhoz depends on that plot."

Laying her finger on the confusion of incentive, competition, and responsibility, she continues:

"What kind of competition is that? They want to beat us with our own hands! We do their job and our own job and they receive the first honor place on the red bulletin board! And the additional pay for a high harvest goes to them! Very smart! But you can't outsmart me! I am not so stupid!"   [6, pp. 69-70]

Frossia is inseparable from the soil she works. And she works best on her "own" plot. There is certainly an ambiguity in the word "own" when applied to kolkhoz land, but what matters too is the difference in productivity and so in reward. Both seem to increase inversely with the size of the work team. On the other hand, a team that was small enough to be effective was likely to develop an internal solidarity deemed dangerous.[18]

Frossia's importance is that, grasping some of the system's mechanics very well, she sees the stupidity and injustice in its workings. Her lack of "consciousness" or lack of cant permit her to question things. And she sees through the oppressive motives of the bosses:

"You are itching to write in your reports that you have done everything according to orders. Go ahead, write whatever you want but leave us alone. There is no point in torturing people for nothing! We slave only to please you."   [6, p. 69]

The second of these fighting achievers finds herself in a different setting. She is the chairman of a collective farm coming into existence on the banks of an almost inaccessible Siberian lake. Fertile wilderness surrounds it. Her persistent demands in pursuit of supplies make the lives of the local officials miserable. From the start they nicknamed her the Fighting Broad (Boi-Baba). The fact that she is a party member sharpens the conflict, especially since it is rumored in the district that she is involved in breaking the law. The regional prosecuting office prepares to do something about it. Under a cover, a young prosecuting attorney is sent to the troublesome farm to find out what is going on. The immediate result is unexpected. The young man seems overwhelmed by the achievements he sees. He even thinks of his own work as petty by comparison.

The new settlement is prospering. The peasants are working hard. And so is their leader, who sees herself as *primus inter pares*. Morale is high. The manager commands everybody's respect. Her vision is neither quixotic nor narrow. Her populist goal is the good life, even at a high price, not social sacrifice. And her community supports her. They agreed to sleep for three years under the open sky, having rejected the shabbiness of prescribed temporary barracks, and they have built, for perpetuity, capacious log cabins, adorned from the start with handsome traditional Siberian carving. Looking beyond her kolkhoz, she sees the growth of fishing and lumbering communities, the construction of shipyards, the building of cheese factories. Her practical sense tells her this. Party officials, on the other hand, do not know how to use already available resources. They seem incapable of noticing the abundance of fish in the local lakes. Bureaucratic stupidity always sends her into a rage. It saddens her, for instance, to feed fish meal to her pigs when so many settlers suffer from shortages. So she keeps imploring the officials to start on the building of fisheries. The answer, as persistently, is that the budget does not permit departures.

"No fisheries. No transportation. The whole region could be fed. These people are communists only in name. If it were in my power, I would throw all these good-for-nothings out of the party. I beg the party secretary and he tells me the budget won't allow it. But the budget is right here, here! . . . Your budget is in the water! You blockheads! They can't find the budget! Pull it from under your rump and you will find it all right!"[19]

It emerges, though, that this woman has used a remarkable device to keep her people happy and to procure unobtainable supplies for her community. She runs a highly profitable but illegal vodka distillery. The prosecuting office suspected as much. To make things worse, the distillery is in her own cabin. When the prosecuting attorney discovers this, she tells him the whole story. The criminal operation turns out to be somewhat peculiar since it has been voted upon by the entire community. She explains calmly:

"We passed the resolution about the distillery in an open meeting."
   "Wha-at?"
   "What, what! Sure, that's the way we did it. Of course, we didn't put the resolution in a folder and we didn't submit it to the district executive committee. But among us, we passed a vote, as it should be. And I was appointed to run the business. I am not a man and they know that I won't get drunk. And they know that all the profit will go to the community."

The prosecuting attorney suggest that she may land in jail. With undiminished composure, she replies:

"I know that. Only I was born fearless. I am not afraid of responsibility when my conscience is clear. Why does the government prohibit home-distilled spirits? Because they don't want grain to be misused. Well, we don't use any indispensible grain. We only use a bit of our own. In liquid form. And we are in no way competing with vodka because no one brings us any. Therefore, I do no harm to the government. But if they had been sending vodka here, then we should have had all sorts of saints' days, orgies, and absenteeism. Instead, I keep control myself. I supervise everything. Have you seen one single man drunk among us? That's just the point! We haven't had a single case of a man not coming to work or upsetting the norm. In the forest, in the field, in the farm, all our plans are fulfilled in good season."   [p. 224]

And so they are. Shaping her environment with beneficial results, this woman has no trouble winning the prosecuting attorney over to her side. For this very reason he is torn. The investigation of the Fighting Manager is the first assignment of his career. His training has been anchored in the proposition that there is only one truth, the party truth, and one set of values, the official public values. All of a sudden, the uneasy realization comes to him that there is no one truth. For three weeks he struggles in his office with the "multiplicity of truths" until his superior tells him he should prosecute. While so pushed, a truth, no longer customary, reveals itself to him.

He felt outraged through and through. It was as if he had received the order to slit the [Fighting Manager's] throat, to stick a knife into her from behind her back at that very moment when, suspecting nothing, she was marching calmly forward on the other side of the lake, carrying in her mighty embrace enormous harvests, houses, and heads of cheese. No, he could never respect himself again if he brought this woman down. He could not do it for anything in the world!

[p. 227]

Against the dry letter of the law, of dogma, of bureaucratic stupor, an indigenous and ingenuous leader marches on. The people lend her support. The official investigator refuses to send her to jail. He turns against the system on her behalf and closes the tale by walking out on his profession to look for something else to do with his life. The fighting achiever herself, of course, does not have to search. Her purpose blends with the fisheries, the cheese factories, the whole life of plenty, in which the private and the public converge.

7. Twin Roots of Meshchanstvo

The resilience of meshchanstvo, its thrust and spread, suggest that it cannot be dismissed as peripheral, parochial, or spurious. On the contrary, it is of central importance to Soviet life. It is not monolithic, because its origin is not solely Soviet. Having spread from two sources, the vestigial and the systemic, it currently possesses two aspects. Sometimes these are at odds with each other, but mostly they are tenaciously combined. The old and the new meshchanstvo coexist. How was it possible for the old meshchanstvo, pre- and antirevolutionary, to have survived the revolution and to have surfaced in the new social order, particularly since the revolution and the evolving goals of Soviet society were aimed at its destruction?

The revolutionary cataclysm swept through the land. The entire society was torn from its roots and catapulted into drastic change. The social order was turned upside down, and the country was drenched in blood. Millions of people were killed in the name of the new society. The postrevolutionary spasms took their toll, and the subsequent stalinist revolution was even more costly. New millions perished. The official purpose remained the same. Under Lenin, it was the destruction of all counterrevolutionary forces. Under Stalin, it was the destruction of all that stood in the way of the new society as conceived by the ruler.

After that unspeakable sacrifice, a new society came into existence, and yet meshchanstvo survived. For one thing, the citizens who passed through the gates of the new social order at its inception were dichotomized into those who embraced the ideological change and those who managed to resist and evade it. The participants differed vastly from the endurers. The former were relatively few. And this numerical weakness of the revolutionary intelligentsia and of the workers' avant-garde allowed meshchanstvo, by default, to keep its subterranean domain.

The limits of bolshevization show the gap between the idea of the power of the revolution, with its maximalist principles and cruelty, and its actual thoroughness. The continuity of the upward and onward thrust is a myth of great importance, but a myth nonetheless. The revolutionary momentum had its setbacks. NEP alone modified the goals of the upheaval. The vastness of the land put brakes on it as well: the impact of the revolution was not the same in Petrograd as in a village near Irkutsk. In a professor's study it was not the same as in a cobbler's shop, a fishing vessel, or a whorehouse. The no-man's-land seems never to have been conquered, never bolshevized. This spottiness involves cultural and social, as much as geographical, space. In a realm so huge, the forces bent on educating the people reached the periphery more slowly than economic and administrative decrees. In addition, the change between Lenin's torrent and Stalin's imperial aims worked against the primacy of the ideological transformation of the citizenry.

Despite the catechism, meshchanstvo weathered it in the enormous population of some hundred and fifty million:[1] it survived tacitly, but it survived. In some vast conclaves it even flourished; and it did good. By undergirding the family, it helped to shield the individual against the onslaught of the dictatorship, both leninist and stalinist.

It is easier to create a new political regime than to create a new man. Leadership needs a very deep commitment if it is to strive for the latter, and no such commitment was made. Stalin, specializing in genocide, did not care about man and his nature. He undertook to change society, not man. Accordingly, he launched a bureaucratic revolution, not an educational one. He did not have anything like the educational obsession of Mao Tse-Tung. He was obsessed with other matters, far more coercive, and largely organizational. He was not interested in souls but in bodies, not in what people were thinking but what they were saying and, even more, what they were doing. Consequences mattered more than causes. He was a pragmatist, involved with his subjects' reflexes, not with thought reform. So, perversely and naturally, there was some autonomy left for the populace, some human soil in which meshchanstvo, a sturdy plant, could bloom. Nor can one say that the blossoming came about solely by default. It turned to Stalin's advantage and he knew it, for he could build on something organic existing in society. The ambiguous, reactionary, and yet hugely accommodating compromise with meshchanstvo issued from the core of stalinism, making both the recruiting and the liquidating of his subjects a highly "personalized" matter, fitting Stalin's predilections.

The Noah's ark of bolshevism was, to begin with, all-inclusive, and the cravings of prerevolutionary meshchanstvo found some leeway even in the events of 1917 and their aftermath; they also managed to prepare the soil for a new meshchanstvo in contemporary Soviet life. Old meshchanstvo in fact is a survival which neither the leninist nor the stalinist reign stamped out. It is the folk meshchanstvo of the little people in its traditional aspect; the petty matriarchal, everyday dreams of pink lampshades regardless. The vacillations in the leninist process, and stalinist indifference toward educational absolutism, gave it a chance to endure. All the same, it is astounding that these prerevolutionary vestiges lasted not only through the twenties, but also through the thirties and the forties, through a quarter of a century, marked for the entire population by constant pressure, terror, and disaster. Through collectivization and concentration camps, through industrialization and purges, what and who was left untouched? And then came war. Traditional antediluvian meshchanstvo ought not to have lasted, it would seem, through all that bears the name of stalinism. Yet it did; for one crucial circumstance supported the resilience of old meshchanstvo. The men of power were kin to it, the new bureaucrat and the stakhanovite, the new army officer and the new professional. They were all *meshchane*, pulled up from the bottom of society.

Soviet meshchanstvo does not grow from a single root. Its second root was solidly planted under stalinism. And that is why, reinforced, meshchanstvo gained momentum. Its root in the system, unlike the vestigial one, supports a large social aim and has the means of implementing it. The stalinist drive for modernization is the goal, and the stalinist bureaucracy its instrument. The transformation of Soviet society into a military-industrial power put an end to egalitarianism. Lenin had already recognized the necessity, and Stalin did so with contempt and mockery.[2] His regime had to, and did, set up differential wage-incentives, resulting in a rapid social stratification without which that goal could not be achieved. Nor could it have been achieved without the proper response of the citizens, Stalin's working force. Their striving for material goods became an obligation and this imperative became functional. This is one way of saying that in due time the profit motif became the basis of Stalin's state capitalism. All this was done and wrapped before the war. Stakhanovism exemplifies this, and Stalin's speech to the 1935 congress of stakhanovites so testifies. His claim that "life has become better, comrades, life has become more merry"[3] is eloquent.

Something special was added to the growth of meshchanstvo in the postwar period. In the thirties some lingering excuses were still proffered as to why the collective goal could not be attained by the dedication of the true believers alone, and rationalizing excuses were made for the appeals to materialistic self-advancement and piecemeal incentives which were tactically necessary. They were said to be temporary, just as Lenin had called his NEP a transitional measure between war communism and socialism, with true communism nowhere in sight. Stalin set the coming of the millenium into a more distant future still. What marks the postwar period with its culmination in the Big Deal is that the pretenses about the temporary nature of "concessions" disappear. Meshchanstvo's aspirations unite with the goals of the regime in a stable, uninhibited, and functional way.

In order to press on with modernization, Stalin fathered a new service class, which grew into a hydrocephalic bureaucracy. In this way alone, he put an end to much of the revolution. Unlike the revolution's "founding fathers," the bureaucrats were not even good at ritualistic worship of the credo. The vision kept receding: emphasis shifted from the creation of a new society to the perpetuation of the regime. Without it being admitted, "futurism" came to a halt in the Kremlin. A pragmatic program was embarked on, smacking of meshchanstvo whatever the ideological label.

Stalin moved into the center of a huge mechanism of his own creation, and controlled it totally. His regime sponsored a proliferation of bureaucratic institutions. In turn, these required the parcelling out of limited, yet lucrative, power to the bureaucrats. With it, something else emerged, especially visible in the middle ranks: anxiety. The middling bureaucrat, wedged between the high and the low, between those on whom he depended and those who depended on him, feared to rock the precarious boat. He feared decisions, for he could neither make them nor not make them. He feared change, from within and from without. All he wanted was to hang on and to exploit his position, and its material advantages, while he could. Yet stalinism gave guarantees to no one. Instead, privileges were handed out. Revocable at any moment, they had to be paid for, when the worst came to the worst, retroactively and unconscionably. Yet the arrangement between Stalin and his servants was not unilateral. The omnipotent donor needed recipients, and the apportionment of privileges was transacted in terms of mutual accommodation and not in terms of ideological principles. The main point is that the vast bureaucratic structure gave birth to a new, systemic kind of meshchanstvo, resulting from the impact of stalinism on the mores of the middle class.

The soulless, greedy, pompous philistine, who needed Stalin and whom Stalin in turn needed, came on the scene. The regime's interaction with the people was mediated by the local chief, a middle-rung executive. It is he who imposed stalinism on the populace. But such power as he held was penetrated through and through by fear, which he transmitted in turn to the people. Fear shaped his conduct, and while not necessarily paralyzing him, it certainly made him alert and braced him in many ways against adversity. It made him stronger, up to a point, and his appetite voracious. He spoke of the clichés of "party-ness" which made him legitimate. Such a stalinist drowned ideas and ideals in bureaucratese. Bowing and scraping to superiors, dealing and wheeling with peers, oppressing those below him, he ensconced himself behind the desk of local power. This new phenomenon might well be called upper meshchanstvo. In contrast with folk meshchanstvo, this recension is institutional and establishmentarian.

So the system both inherited traditional meshchanstvo and produced its own. The former went on craving for sweets and pink lampshades. The latter craved affluence braced by power. There is no cleavage between them but, rather, cross-fertilization. The social origin and progress of the stalinist establishment bears this out. It was different from that of Lenin's men. The old party came largely from the intelligentsia and from the working class. The city had shaped the bolsheviks with its universities, Putilovsk works, freedoms, secret police, agonies, and anonymity. Stalin's men, on the other hand, were overwhelmingly peasant in origin. Their development led them from their early socialization in the village to intermediary training in small provincial towns, the main domain of old meshchanstvo. When, thereafter, they were pulled up into positions of power, they enacted a blend of the old and the new. Stalinist fiction abounds with emotional scenes in which peasant mothers, wearing humble black aprons, with their hair pulled tight into primordial knots, hands and faces weatherbeaten, visit their VIP sons. They either bask in their sons' glory or, on occasion, needle them. And the sons, having arrived, refurbish meshchanstvo from strength, as a gift to their worn-out mothers.

In the persons and vested interests of Stalin's bureaucrats, the two currents blend so well that they feed on each other. Folk meshchanstvo forms a broad base. Systemic meshchanstvo provides staying power. Together, as the twin components of middleclass culture, they not only survive but thrive.

Part Three

Partners at Work

8. Comrade Chameleon

Comrades Wholesale and Retail

In the arrangement we have described as the Big Deal, it is the local party official who becomes responsible for supervising the producing partner. The ability to inspire is essential. In novel after novel, two contrasting types of party officials – Comrade Wholesale and Comrade Retail – both fail to inspire. Their generic negative aspects are full of revealing signals. On the primary but shadowy issue of partnership in the Big Deal, what not to do is as instructive as what the model party partner ought to do.

Comrade Wholesale in our first tale here is not a bully but rather an unhappy man whose personal shortcomings illustrate the local party's problems.[1] The war has barely run its course; times are difficult and everyone is on edge. Pressured and hounded, Comrade Wholesale can hardly breathe. Stress cuts through decorum, and so he barks:

"Brother, I am not interested in your separate individual. What I am interested in are people in general. I like to generalize. I am not interested in your ideas if they are only yours."[2]

The local Crimean population is in bad shape. The refugees from devastated areas have to be taken care of, the kolkhozes must somehow be reorganized and so must every other institution. Strained to the utmost, Comrade Wholesale is being pestered by a meddlesome "humanitarian." This unexpected troublemaker is a demobilized colonel, a war amputee, who does not lend himself to easy handling. His civic courage is formidable. Instead of rest and rehabilitation, he plunges into party work. The tale emphasizes how the hero learns to help himself through selfless work. Comrade Wholesale – the foil – cannot help him nor anybody else. The size of his problems has overwhelmed him. But the troublesome hero presses an unpleasant question and an even less pleasant inference:

"What do you mean, a separate individual does not interest you? . . . You take people wholesale because there is no point in studying them retail. But that's stupid . . . Brother, it does not even smell of marxism."   [p. 18]

Comrade Wholesale detests argument, especially with ex-officers. One catches here the hostility between civilians, bogged down with their unmanageable responsibilities, and the dislocated, if bemedalled, veterans. Civilians regarded the latter as usurpers. So instead of being grateful to the colonel for volunteering his services to the local party organization, Comrade Wholesale counters with a tirade:

"Of course, it was easier for you at the front. There you had plenty of adjutants, automobiles, telephones. You only had to give orders and they were executed. Isn't that so? But here in our rear, in the devastated areas, it's sheer disaster. For instance, I could send you twenty-five miles away. But I have no automobile and I have no telephone and the mail goes only twice a week, by foot. Get it?"

Undiscouraged, the colonel exacerbates our comrade further:

"Does everybody share your mood around here? . . . Why do you convince yourself that failure is inevitable?"

Sarcastically, the comrade invites the colonel to set about infecting the people with enthusiasm. The colonel shouts back.

"Infect! Infect! What's the matter with you? Why don't you yourself infect anybody around here all this time? What are you waiting for? The people around you are infected with disbelief. They are burdened with difficulties, and you keep shoving idiotic papers under their noses."

"You are arrogant, oh, God, are you arrogant! The war has spoiled the likes of you! The war has corrupted you dogs! What the hell kind of communist are you if you have lost the habit of hard work! All you want is to give orders and to write pamphlets."

"Listen, where is your conscience! It is you, brother, who are running along behind the people shouting 'look, what a marvelous job of leading them I am doing!' People will move mountains without you. But if you lead them properly as Stalin ordains, they will even move an ocean.

Here the distance between the parallel tracks of these two party men becomes clear. The colonel accuses the comrade of carelessly wielding a power which oppresses the builders without inspiring them. Comrade Wholesale adheres to a rigid dogmatic position: organization supersedes inspiration.

"Wait a minute. Listen to me. Try to understand one thing. One can infect only through action, not through words . . . Heroism is not a natural force. It's organization. Heroes, my dear friend, are in need of nurses."   [p. 19]

His obstinacy here takes the form of the orthodox distrust of "natural forces." In the dilemma he is in, he clings to the faith in organization *from above* – without which nothing. The colonel, in turn, cannot disagree with this, and their quarrelsome accord indicates the problem of striking a proper balance between the party's two tasks of organization and inspiration; of controlling the partner in the Big Deal and trusting him. If the Big Deal wavers, it is between restraints and incentives.

If the exchange of words is turgid, Comrade Wholesale's mien informs right off:

Yellow and wrinkled, he looked sick, and uncertainty, almost anxiety, was noticeable in his eyes.

He lives with his family in one room, without heat, water, or window panes. "Terrible business!" is his standing expression. And the sequential method adopted here is interesting. The wrinkled face and neurotic personality seem to *originate* all the insuperable difficulties which, in turn, crush him.

His thoughts circled constantly round difficult – insoluble – problems which he had to solve immediately. Not waiting for him to find his way out of one impasse, the center kept piling new problems on him . . . and he understood that he had no right either to postpone them or to pile them on somebody else's shoulders. Therefore, irritation did not abandon him even in sleep. Even in his sleep, he was always cursing or fighting somebody. [p. 6]

Since a sour disposition does not help at all, Comrade Wholesale is removed from the job and it is obvious who is appointed to take his place. Yet for all his lack of bonhomie and the author's affection, he manages convincingly to vent the discontent of overworked party functionaries. He does not really obstruct the Big Deal. He simply does not help it because he has no time to grasp even what it is. And if he has little comprehension of this alliance, a typical Comrade Retail, on the other hand, does; although the special trouble of the man we consider next is that he does not particularly like the Big Deal.

If a cantankerous inability to see faces in the crowd is bad, too close an interest in people does not *per se* guarantee success. A certain kind of "retail" approach had also come under the regime's scrutiny. Here, then, is presented an oppressive specimen of a party functionary, a real bully. He comes from the working class and is proud of it. A Russian, he rules in a remote Siberian area, peopled by Asians. It is not, however, the natives but his fellow transplants who give him trouble. In turn, he troubles them. He

did not drink wine, did not play cards, did not court women and with full justification considered himself pure as crystal. So he took it for granted that everybody should fear him a little and try to please him. Everybody knew of his previous achievements, recognized by the order of the Red Banner. Nevertheless, there were many people in the district who did not like him too well.[3]

Obviously, the author's heart is not with him. Even his appearance has a sinister touch:

His self-assurance, the slow glance of his imperious and slightly bloodshot eyes, his large face, enlarged even more by his baldness, this face which turned purple when he was enraged, all this oppressed even those who were not in the least shy.

As guardian of morality, he soon finds out the personal indiscretions of citizens under his purview. The district's – and the novel's – most important personage happens to be a renowned surgeon engaged in heroic ministration to the natives. After long separation, his attractive Muscovite wife joins him to share his frontier life. But she flirts with the bachelors, so numerous in this frontier land, be they engineers or mechanics. Before summoning the temptress herself, the comrade conducts a preliminary investigation by pulling up a guilty mechanic.

"What's going on there with you people? . . . Don't you all dance around [the surgeon's wife]?" he exclaimed somewhat rudely because of his irritation with his visitor's stupidity. "All your intellectual-type tricks![4] You forget that you live in a worker's milieu! What an example! Nothing but provocation! . . . I won't let this kind of indecency go on spreading!"   [6, p. 86]

Taken aback by this meddling in his personal life, and thrown off guard, the young mechanic defends himself by insisting that he respects the woman in question very much. Comrade Retail turns on the young man with sarcasm. The young man, not able to fight back effectively because of a "disconcerting awareness" that the party secretary "had an unwritten right to interfere in such things" (6, p. 87), shrivels under the attack. This detail suggests the conflict between two prescripts for administrative conduct; ubiquitous vigilance as against the fostering of contentment. Completely insensitive to the contradiction, Comrade Retail presses on in his ire against the immorality of what he calls the intelligentsia. He summons the woman herself. When she, too, does not quite grasp his question "What's going on here with all you people?", he turns purple and screams "Stop your little girl act!" The woman keeps her composure:

"I am not acting. And by the way, what kind of tone is this? It seems to me you are forgetting who you are. Are you not the secretary of the district committee?"
    "No. You are forgetting yourself!" he shouted, "I don't like your behavior."
                                                                            [6, p. 88]

This time, however, the dislike of his behavior by the collective prevails. A special party meeting is called. It is presided over by a regional party representative. Comrade Retail looks balefully at all those who denounce him. But he banks on the stranger from the higher power. His reasons make the point. He

stared with vague hope at the energetic face, framed by a shock of grayish hair. The firmly put-together stocky frame, the unhurried movements of his good, big, clean hands, the firm gait, and the open, somewhat tired expression in his eyes, all this suddenly attracted him. "He is one of us. He is a worker!"   [6, p. 91]

This reflex of identification with the superior makes the blow harder. For the very man whom he considers a class ally announces that Comrade Retail's "estrangement" from both the party and the collective "confronts the regional committee with the necessity to draw corresponding organizational conclusions" (p. 92).

In the end he is punished for having been too meddlesome with the people under him. His kind of nosiness goes beyond meddling. It is now also seen as affecting the important but fragile balance between restraints and incentives. He has been obsessed with control and out of step with the new tolerance, even if somewhat opaque, for the craving of citizens for privacy. And for this delicate issue, he has no sense at all. Instead, he hates cloudwalkers, cardplayers, and womanchasers. The old-style adrenalin of the workers makes him detest the growing middleclass environment. He joins the many dismayed party functionaries whose adjustment to the Big Deal proved poor. But as in the case of Comrade Wholesale, it is not primarily discontent, typical of entrenched stalinists under threat, that matters. What he does is more interesting than what he is or what he thinks. His oppressive meddling with people, his attempt to shackle them, shows what a party functionary should no longer do.

Uninspiring indifference is bad enough. Tyrannical meddling turns out to be worse.

Myopia

In a play dealing with rural problems, the corruption of wartime management provides the plot. While veterans are being wedged into administrative posts, unseating their predecessors, strife fills the air. A tenacious clique system feeds on distrust, blackmail, and denunciation. Speaking for his kin – the prime victim of malfeasance – a salty peasant sums it all up with an old proverb: "When masters fight, the muzhik's head gets bashed in."[5]

The chairman of the local executive committee is both embattled and combative. Her name, Tverdova, translates as Comrade Tough. She is middle-aged, single and proud. She dislikes being pitied for her sacrifice in the war, the loss of her two sons at the front. In many years of party work, she has acquired the nickname of "ruler." That alone makes her vulnerable. She has always acted high-handedly, and has shoved several chairmen down the throats of the intimidated peasant population.

Ruling with manorial and matronly aplomb, Comrade Tough has used – and abused – her power. Now, in the postwar reshuffling of cadres, she must stand up to a new party secretary and also she must cross swords with Comrade Pure, a young woman newly entrusted with one kolkhoz. Unceremoniously, Comrade Pure attacks favoritism and accuses Comrade Tough of "soiling" herself "as a communist." Comrade Tough's response is that of a prewar official whose ego, ways, and beliefs are now suspect:

"I have been working here for twenty years! My achievements speak for me. When I was exterminating kulaks, you were just learning how to walk."

Comrade Pure's criticism of Comrade Tough's "extravagance," of, for example, her "personal" vegetable garden and her own melon patch, brings forth Comrade Tough's further defensiveness:

"Good God! Is that all they can find to accuse me of? I gave them my life, but that does not count, does it? They measure my spent strength in sacks of potatoes? But the point is that they owe me so much that their debt cannot be estimated."

The pronoun "they" is purposely vague here; there is a hint of something important, the interdependence of colleagues balancing between denunciation and the breaking of the law.[6] Everybody is in debt to everybody. And when the day of payment comes, the mutual debtors – always keepers of their brothers – do not seem to be able to settle accounts. Nor can the culprits be neatly cut out of the social fiber. Instead, entire agglomerations of citizens topple together, because the involvement in improper practices is so general. Reformers are dreaded as much as the police.

Comrade Tough is tough enough to speak out with some self-confidence against reformers:

"All of a sudden we get a new broom! Go ahead – sweep! But we have been praised for what we have done! What's there to talk about! We have done the job! Now, of course, it's easy to philosophize. After all, you are stepping into something ready made."   [pp. 32-3]

Challengers do not inhibit her in the least from lavishly celebrating her own jubilee. She invites them to the feast. Leading her guests toward the splendid table laden with spirits, homegrown turkeys, big fish from the kolkhoz ponds, and golden honey, she proudly announces that she is not the only one to savor such earthly riches. "All my faithful peasants have as much" (p. 8). The one word "faithful" is eloquent, implying strife between the faithful and unfaithful, and the advantages the former reap. On behalf of her underlings, Comrade Tough, for one, adheres to the "reap and let reap" school.

Her kind of productivity shows at her rich table as well as at her desk. In favor of turkeys and fish and honey, she opposes speculative dreaming. The distant tomorrow interests her very little. And this is the myopia that will bring her down. Still, for the time being, she holds her own fairly well in the inevitable confrontation with the new party secretary. He engages her in debate about short-term and long-term goals, proposing in high-flown language the theory that preoccupation with the future means progress. She rejects the "futurist" invitation:

"Well said, but nothing to do with us. Our future here is to fulfill the harvest plan. That's the limit of our dreams."

And she goes deeper into the ever-present and ever-evaded problem of postwar rewards that one would have thought permissible in a character as yet, before her metamorphosis, among the negative:

"To dream is the easiest thing in the world! You should have worked here with us during the war. Not only did we supply the front with bread, but we achieved a thing or two on top of it. Without fanfare, without noise, but we achieved it. What's the good of all this shouting and excitement! We have had enough of it!

Everybody longs for peaceful life. After all, it's time to commence a postwar existence. The war has been over for over a year and a half. What are we waiting for?"   [p. 4]

The question sounds imprudent during the impending party purges of which the play is a reflection in the first place. Comrade Tough's impatience is used as evidence of her myopia, and is equated by her adversaries with the "glorification of banal meshchanstvo comforts" (p. 14). Yet curiously, in the long run, it is the playwright who proves myopic, for it is difficult to make short shrift of Comrade Tough. First, she champions systemic meshchanstvo, and combat with it has already become ambiguous. Secondly, her achievements stand up well to attack. So, to bring her to her knees, special casting of villains is required.

A favorite among her underlings is a shady character called Quiet. Adroit and effective, it is he who provides her with choice melons, poultry, and other delicacies. Warned about his conniving, she is not perturbed:

"But he does not dare to move a finger. If he stirs, I'll tie him up into a triple knot."   [p. 27]

Mr. Quiet, alas, gets caught and is about to stand trial for thievery. At this point it is plain to see who does what to whom as he drags his patroness to perdition with ominous panache:

"Well, if we are about to order a funeral service, it is not for me alone. I have here a precious little notebook. Everything is written in it – who got what and when! . . . O, yes! That's where I have you! You are tied up in a triple knot." [p.46]

Comrade Tough fails because of myopia. Not dishonest herself, she had been careless of detail in her short-term overachieving pragmatism. And her virtuous foil preaches:

"You were honest? In the interest of today you overlooked the most essential? In the pursuit of immediate success you forgot about the consequences? Lenin said . . . that honest opportunism is the most dangerous of all!"   [p. 47]

So a sour "wholesale" approach to the daily round is as erroneous as "retail" interference with coworkers; neither will do for a party official. Shortsighted pragmatism on behalf of the flock is better, but not as yet all that much better.

Learning is forever

Clearly, the party is involved in a lot of teaching, followed by periodic cutting-down-to-size and retraining of its deputies. A task for Sisyphus, apprenticeship is mandatory and never-ending. The proper blend of dignity and humility continues to elude the disciples. These difficulties are illustrated in this section, in the learning experience of a novice, then of a party functionary in his early boisterous prime, and finally of a model but somewhat worn-out party man.

The fate of the novice emphasizes standard inner-party workings. The government is slow to allocate funds for the reconstruction of a Black Sea harbor, damaged in the war. It expects the local administrators to draw up a plan, to be carried out entirely by the enthusiasm of the local workers. The man who is to inspire the builders is a novice: no one could be more astounded than he at the awesome assignment. A veteran, just demobilized, and an engineer by training, he had hoped to work as such in his beloved native harbor. But the city party secretary – stern, wise, gray – informs him of his appointment as the harbor's party secretary, at which the young man blushes with surprise and embarrassment.

He blunders a good deal by inspiring the wrong people in the wrong places. Of course he cannot and must not correct his errors himself: errors can only be detected and remedied from above, it is the duty of an apprentice to learn but not to understand. He learns from his master who

attended party conferences many times. He was personally acquainted with outstanding party and government leaders. Undoubtedly, he had himself learned from them to be attentive to people, to be able to grasp and analyze correctly all the manifestations of life and to discover the shoots of the new which strove toward existence in a struggle against the decaying.[7]

No wonder, he "penetrated everything" in general and "the reorganization of party training" in particular as well as his pupil's mind.

The master scolds him for everything. What is more, he is chastised for not defending himself like a man. Clearly, he is in a double bind. In succession, he is accused of narrow aims, of wrong personnel policy, of matters possibly within his scope and of those outside it, of foreign ships not holding schedule, of his legs giving out. All the while the master thunders:

"Tell me, do you read Lenin and Stalin? Or maybe you don't have time to brush up on your studies of the classics of marxism and leninism? That's just it. No wonder you are silent."

The apprentice turns white when reprimanded fiercely for the habit of saying "basically" and "generally speaking." He is reprimanded because the bark of a sapling tree in front of his office seems somewhat wrinkled and its roots are sticking out:

"Why isn't the soil cultivated under the trees? You people plant trees and then forget all about them. Or do you only want to report 'Tree planting has been performed according to plan'? Do you realize how much a hectare of planted trees costs in our part of the country? A million roubles! So you have your tree planting here!"

And he is chastised when he prepares to go to a meeting without a briefcase:

"Why are you so unburdened? Don't you carry any reports? . . . It seems to me you are not taking enough material with you."   [11, p. 54]

The moral? The story is as much about the old salt as about the greenhorn. The latter must endure with joyful rapture. But the former must endure also. The more powerful he is, the more his job splinters into incongruous components. He must uphold large visions of the future and keep guard over one neglected sapling. He must never weary, as the apprentice must never find carping either menacing or debilitating. Unto him is done what he is being trained to do to others: to control without undercutting initiative.[8]

High party officials, the licensed Big Deal partners as against the novices, are expected to juggle well the requirements of control and inspirational charisma. Even for the most mature – perhaps especially for them – this is a difficult exercise. There are two sides to it. First, success is relative. The key person cannot be successful without occasional lapses. He must periodically fail in order to submit to a dressing down. These purification rites uphold him. Remarkably, the rural party functionary is more involved in the ritual than the industrial one is, for he must be reminded that he must maintain the role of deputy instead of the more rewarding role of a local boss. Time and again, he must be shorn of his possible loyalties to one kolkhoz or to one rural district. Secondly, and this goes for the "urbanites" as well as for the "rurals," a model party partner cannot act as if he were altogether up-to-date. He must be something of a throwback. He must engage in a certain amount of ascetic posturing. He cannot himself take up the Big Deal with quite the gusto he inspires in others. If jovial, he must be lean. In the new mythology, where everybody else worth the trouble is invited to enjoy himself, the party partner must still for the sake of decorum be asked to remain "merciless to himself."

Comrade Alert, just out of apprenticeship, is a tough district party boss. He rapidly masters a number of responses that novices badly need. At first, his youthfulness made him unpopular. But:

He was serious. And because of that, traces of fatigue appeared on his broad, bright-eyed face. A thick groove like a cut between his eyebrows, shadows under his eyes, the stern line of his firmly pressed lips – all this spoke of a man who was merciless to himself and who had seen much.[9]

Since the ennobling heart disease would be premature, he must make do with severe migraines. The stern facial attributes indicate a war veteran.

The requirement to be merciless to himself is fulfilled in the way Comrade Alert arranges – or rather deranges – his personal life. Although unspecified self-sacrifice is desirable, he fails in the alchemy of converting the public into the private and vice versa. War and studies had separated him from his lovely wife. Now that she had been assigned as an agronomist to his district, he himself evicts her from their nest, long yearned-for, on the very day of her arrival. He orders her out into one of the lagging kolkhozes. To his consternation, typical of the obtuseness of heroes, he sees her cry bitterly, and consoles her not without sophistry:

"As I have already told you, all is not well yet with our party cadres here . . . You are a communist. You were born and raised in the region. Everything speaks in favor of sending you there. The only thing that speaks against it is the fact that you are my wife. But if you were not my wife, I should have sent you there. How can I act differently now? If I act differently, I deprive myself of my internal right to send other people wherever I must send them."   [5, p. 58]

Now this is a saccharine tale and one must be patient with it. Cant is informative. The story's tedious pages reveal interestingly that Comrade Alert rejects both the wholesale and retail approach and proceeds according to a stunning method of his own. He reveals this when a new manager proposes to lift a decrepit kolkhoz from its decline "by force." This enrages the good comrade:

"That's nonsense! You may reform one person 'by force' but the others will turn away from you. How will you lift your kolkhoz? All by yourself? . . . If you are dealing with an enemy, you must chase him and put him on trial. If you are dealing with our own Soviet citizen, you must take him not by force but by persuasion . . . you must kindle a fire in people, you must bring it about that they themselves turn their faces your way and follow you! That's what you must do. You must march ahead of the people, but with the people! Always!" [5, p. 23]

But in order not to march too far ahead, the leader must be clairvoyant. To that effect, Comrade Alert sends his "second" all over the place. An older man, he is not very alert. Returning from a wearisome tour of inspection, the poor fellow must account for the mood of every manager and the state of every shed and barn. He admits that when he reached the seventh kolkhoz, instead of climbing out of his car, he had summoned the manager for a chat on the road. That does it. Comrade Alert rants and raves against the accumulation of meaningless mileage, against "guest artist tours," against phoney "martyrdom" (p. 161).

With becalmed bureaucrats on one's back, moving "ahead of but with" is not easy. His tactics have a special interest. He is in a position where he has to blow alternately hot and cold. He must criticize everybody; but he must also provide special treatment for everyone, yet not so special as to lose general applicability. He must rely on select partners, yet keep them anxious.

His best partner by far is an explosive, proud, energetic veteran, obsessed with saving one pauperized kolkhoz. This manager has just managed miraculously to acquire some electric motors, yet he does not put them to use immediately. Knowing and seeing everything, Comrade Alert takes him to task, in public, for this oversight, despite the man's other achievements and although they have become extremely close in outlook, and firm friends. Publicly humiliated, the man winces as he thinks about it: "You could work yourself to death on this job, they curse you just the same! . . . And he didn't even listen to me!"

Two telling details must be added. Comrade Alert had smiled benevolently while dressing the man down. This is to personalize chastisement.

Secondly, he had explained the general reason for the attack. This is to make it prophylactic. He tackled the partner's potential deviation:

"Maybe it's simply too early to praise you, although there are things for which you deserve praise. The newspapers were right to write about you. But I am afraid that you may get complacent about it. Complacency as such is not in you yet and couldn't be, but the tendency is there!"

Though the logic is uncertain, one rule of thumb emerges: the better the partner, the more he must be watched. Nobody can be trusted. Man's character is treacherous. And from the best, only the worst can be expected.

The détente comes about in a curious fashion. While one culprit repairs to a corner to sulk, Comrade Alert turns on the next, the head mechanic of a large MTS.

"And what were you thinking about?! The district party committee has helped you people to get on your feet and from now on you must walk by yourselves! You are big boys now! Go ahead and work with the people on your own! . . . Neither the party nor the executive committee are your nurses!"   [6, p. 53]

The first partner is rebuked for complacency; the second for insecurity. The argument continuously revolves around initiative and control; responsibility and discipline; the narrow versus the large view. And unto Comrade Alert, as unto all chameleons, is done exactly as he does unto his own partners. At the regional level, his entire district shrinks to the insignificance to which he reduces one mere kolkhoz under his purview. He craves a model MTS. The regional administration turns down his request. Quite daringly, he complains to the regional party secretary, who summons him and his opponent to a showdown. He makes a fiery speech which the opponent counters with words one might by now expect:

"Construction funds are distributed among all the districts according to plan . . . Every district has its own characteristics and its own pressing needs. Comrade [Alert] lacks the ability to approach facts from a statesmanlike point of view. He is concerned only with his own district."

If that sounds familiar, the rebuttal of the rebuttal holds no surprise either. Comrade Alert insists that the party had ordered him to be concerned with just one district. Executing his orders, he sees "nothing unstatesmanlike in giving the greatest help to the weakest link." Both have a point. But the regional party secretary has a dialectic gift. He rescinds the administrative decision, bestows the necessary money on Comrade Alert, and ordains that the neighboring districts somehow subliminally profit from Comrade Alert's good luck: "The significance of the task we place before you transcends the limits of your district" (7, p. 36).

The tale might well have ended on this transcendental note. Shifting gears all the time from control to coaxing, from daily chores to large visions, from scolding to being scolded, Comrade Alert proves flexible. The one thing to grasp in all this adaptability is the importance of a party official as party *deputy*. He is not supposed to act as representative of the people, either in general or in the narrower sense of spokesmanship for a group.

The third example, a near perfect comrade, adds to the account of endless learning the somewhat doleful paragraph of final failure. This comrade is of peasant stock and bolshevik past. His eyes "which in all probability have already seen everything in their lifetime" pierce "to the very heart of any person with whom he talks." His "thoughts about himself disappeared" in his militant youth because they "merged into the thought of his responsibility."[10] Small wonder that he suffers from heart disease, aggravated by the fact that he "generously poured out his soul from its very bottom to every chairman and to every party organizer summoned to his office" (p. 170). Great talker as he is, he does not blabber.

Words and ideas, heard and read innumerable times, after passing through his soul, came to light weighty, rounded, juicy, angry, funny, or even sly – but always genuinely his own.

In one important respect, he steers clear of acting on his own. As mediator, he does not lose sight of the origin of his franchise. He remains the regime's deputy.

It was easy for him to say at a meeting of ploughmen, "Vassia, comrade Stalin would like you to –." And the words sounded as if Stalin himself had just telephoned him, specially so that he should transmit his words to Vassia. [p. 179]

Everything about him fits. His apartment, clean but "somewhat empty," expresses "his sense of his time and his connection with the outside world" through recent issues of fat journals piled on windowsills. The office, called the "watch tower" conveys the same impression, with its three telephones and radio. The comrade uses this "to adjust his watch by the Kremlin clock" (p. 177). A portentous desk calendar speaks of his work habits. The tiny details of daily chores pertaining to human mending and tending grow on the pages for months far ahead into notations concerning large-scale projects, "perhaps, only dreams – dreams on the verge of becoming plans" (p. 180). It is true, though, that while he expertly blends daily duties with long-term dreams, a strange question does occasionally creep into his busy mind: "To whom must he answer: to the top or to the bottom?" But then, illustrating the principle of salvation through eternal discipleship, the hero turns to the fourth chapter of the canonical *History of the Communist Party of the Soviet Union.*[11] Instructing him that wherever else in the world there may be contradictions that are "antagonistic," they are not so under Stalin, the chapter brings him "the joy of the discovery of the world, the joy of knowledge" (p. 166).

At this point of his ecstatic progress in dialectics, the war breaks out and the stalinist pupil backslides a little because he finds himself torn between populist feelings and the responses of a deputy. The war becomes a hard test. Under stress something happens to his joyful knowledge. Recruited into the underground, he is ordered to cross the front line and to operate in his own district, now under German occupation. Making his way through woods and swamps, sinking up to his waist in snow, he recalls how he had raised the district up from poverty and how to accomplish this "he had to break many people" (p. 167). He has only one thought now: "Will they give me away or not?" While he wonders whether his attitude toward "the people" had been correct, a surprise awaits him.

The first person he meets is a kolkhoz chairman, much rewarded and decorated on the comrade's recommendation. This man "recognized him but refused to give him shelter." The second man he runs into happens to be an agronomist whom he had fired. This one, "risking the life of his family," took him into his house, fed him, gave him clothes and provisions and drove him to a secret place in the woods. On the same mission, a poor peasant woman aids and comforts him. Yet, before the war he had failed to provide her with the new house which she needed and deserved.

He felt suddenly that life was just as tangled as this virgin forest. And he seemed to himself so unwise, so much a mere novice. He had worked with people and directed them. He had thought that he knew what's what in life. Now he felt like shaking everything up and starting from scratch.   [p. 168]

This self-recrimination supports the proposition that learning is forever. But it has a special flavor of populist regret at not having done justice to those at the bottom. And that is where the comrade's scrutiny parts ways with criticism from above.

After the war he is removed from contact with peasants and reassigned to desk work only. He does not like it. He looks at the plush city office with irony and the "inky souls" around him with downright sarcasm. Curiously, the reason for his removal is clear to him. Encumbered by his populist meditation and distracted by his passion for inspirational propaganda work, he had shown a serious flaw. Despite a good grasp of the deputy role, he had proved undereducated, lacking in sufficient expertise and organizational prowess.

From his city office, the comrade looks back a great deal. Not without anxiety, he takes note of his successor. Of the new generation and climbing rapidly, the new district party secretary stands for smooth efficiency. Stylish and well trained, he serves to counterbalance the hero, who helps in this task himself by dolefully envying his successor's relaxed and efficient performance. He realizes that when he had been winning the "battle for bread," he had won by driving himself and others. Nor did he know how to give orders, rushing about feverishly, trying to do everything himself.

The Big Deal opts for organizational knowhow over nervous populist compassion and even inspiring deputy talk. It is the humble streak in this comrade which makes him aware how imperfect he is.

"If it were in my power, I would now study and study. Last year I attended courses in Moscow. I would have loved to go on and to enroll in the party institute. But they said that somebody had to do the work. No, I would study and study. I am terribly envious of [the new party secretary] and of Volodka, my son. They set off straight from the books." [p. 69]

The seraphic comrade

The spectrum of party functionaries runs from oppressors to saviors. The range from virtue to villainy, however, did not remain static between the end of war and Stalin's death. Angels predominated at the beginning of the period, and crass, if rosy, falsehood marked the peak of zhdanovism (1947–50). The balance shifted at the dawn of the fifties when the regime began to scrutinize mid-range officialdom.[12] Some of the gloss was removed from the literary veneer and, as a side effect, party models became somewhat less unreal. This section shows this unadvertised shift by taking first a seraph and then a more earthy comrade whose type is still prominent today.

As for the seraphim, why was it necessary for the early postwar party models to be so virtuous? Because postwar messages were determined by wartime slippages, and party worship, having slackened at the front, had to be liturgically enforced with the advent of peace. This is the correction that gave birth to the party seraphim. They came in a curious aura of "conflictlessness." The regime, in its mythmaking optimism, ordered its authors to develop conflict not so much between heroes and villains as between heroes and superheroes, between the good and the even better.[13] So, in our first example an enchanting man hurries on his soothing, mediating, healing round. But despite the prescribed soft-pedaling of difficult problems, this miracle man does have a taxing assignment, the taming of tough managers. These men are involved in the detail of power in action, of hiring and firing, of making and breaking lives. Comrade Seraph champions the conservation of the labor force at all cost.

The reader is taken to a Siberian oilpipeline project, huge and very important. The jaded local management fails to produce miracles. Therefore a new managerial group, assembled in Moscow, comes to take over, ruthlessly. But Comrade Seraph, as party organizer, attempts to soften the blow to the old workers.[14] His soft words derive from the traits this kind of person must now have. Simple but not ascetic, he represents both the spirit and the bodily comfort of righteousness. (The revolutionary heroes, one must remember, had only the spirit to fret about.) He is handsome, suntanned, graying at the temples. He smiles irresistibly. He is a happy man; his full, but not ostentatious, family life exudes warmth, hospitality, civility, in short kulturnost at its best. He adores his grown children. Since he clearly knows how to live, he has a five-year-old to fill the house with laughter, and his wife is pregnant. The little girl plays merrily with an abundance of dolls while Comrade Seraph, wearing fur slippers, busies himself setting the table. No male chauvinist, he handles the cheerful teacups adroitly. His obeisance to the current kingdom of God on earth has a hidden purpose, deeply politicized. For he is weirdly deceptive. His main job, the job of every party functionary, is to exercise control. The humanistic verbiage is only a sophisticated means of cutting down the managerial hunger for power. To that effect, he delivers a sermon to an impatient young engineer. Appalled at the apathy of the old staff, this man itches to fire the deadwood he has inherited. Comrade Seraph cautions him with banal, yet pertinent relativism:

"It seems you yourself are not a bad young man, and know how to work. But inevitably some other young man will turn up who will dislike you. In his dogmatic way, he will form a faulty impression of you. Not everyone has the right to judge others. A man is a complex being!"

It is the prerogative of the party and nobody else to give judgment. To make this implication unmistakable, he humbly confesses that he too had massively erred in the past by making snap judgments, and had either sponsored or fired people irresponsibly. "But it's difficult to penetrate a man's soul." This leads to the main point. And the main point is conservation.

"It's silly to be amazed at the sight of other people's shortcomings. Isn't it obvious that even our best people are far from perfect? The birthmarks of capitalism cannot be washed out with water. You and I were taught that under communism man will once and for all free himself of the burden of the past. You are suggesting a new method: to drown the birthmarks in the river. This method is swift but clearly inappropriate. People, you know, may drown along with the birthmarks."

We should not be amazed at the cynicism of this magnanimity. A functional myth is rapidly taking shape here, and that is that the party does not decimate – it saves souls. For all Stalin's savagery, wartime losses had made it uneconomical to drown too many souls, at least in novels. It becomes worthwhile to save souls, and first that of the young efficiency expert himself who is about to drown the slackers. Comrade Seraph persists with the strategy of conservation:

"You are in a great hurry to define people. Photographers have a useful expression: a contrast shot, black and white, without halftones. You are making a mistake in seeing people as black and white. Of course, it is easier and simpler to lump all the questionable and not entirely developed people together as wreckers. But life is not like that. In our country there are few wreckers, but a lot of people whom one may not like because of their many shortcomings. But one can't discard them all!"[15]

God knows, Stalin could. It all depends who does the discarding. Meanwhile, at his own level, Comrade Seraph is entrusted with the new teaching and must stand up to a foil more weighty than the young engineer. He collides with the new manager of the entire project, a very dour man, who ignores the welfare of all his workers, whether in the office or in the ice-cold field. Concentrating on first things first, he means to build a strong administrative core before he worries about anything else. This callousness upsets Comrade Seraph. Jokingly he underscores the difference between party duties and those of a manager: "My business is to chat with people, to amuse them a bit so that they don't get bored." Needless to say, he does more. For one thing, his mellow posture forces the conflict out into the open. The manager attacks:

"You treasure people and you tremble over each one of them. That's good . . . Only aren't you too soft with some of them? I know you keep thinking about those who fell in the war and your care of the living is all the greater. You are right! This or that mediocre worker, untrained or perhaps simply negligent, he is a Soviet man. And one must help him, push him, educate him. But don't you in the process develop a basically dangerous acceptance of people's defects? Aren't you spoiling some of them with your compassion?"   [8, p. 47]

If only this were the substantive dilemma or the real question. But we shall have to wait with our asides. The good comrade, meanwhile, is more than ready with a repartee.

"Now here is my reprimand, friend, so to speak in revenge. Aren't you too severe and hard in your handling of people? Don't you oppress them at times? Shouldn't one be a little more soft, more gentle? I can understand your stern and sometimes cruel demands on management, on the heads of departments. But when you act in the same way with the rank-and-file workers, that's disastrous! At this moment you are not yet in contact with them because you are still sitting in the administration office. But soon and for long stretches of time, you will have to work directly with them. Will you be able to find the key to their hearts? . . . Sometimes I watch you talk to a person and I see him being crushed under the burden of your reprimands. Your purpose and your will are admirable. However, don't oppress people who have not learned yet to work the way you want them to."   [8, p. 48-9]

For the time being, the argument ends in a draw. The oppressive manager admits that some of the criticism is justified and that he is guilty of pressing too hard. Nevertheless, he dismisses the whole thing as a petty issue. "In the important things I am right, in spite of what you say." And that's that. But is he right?

Of course, Comrade Seraph does not let go. He cannot, until he has succeeded in taming this presumptuous manager with the newly formulaic seraphic approach. His real importance is the weight and stature he brings to the problem of undercutting a managerial "Napoleon" without emasculating him; of controlling without shackling. This is the real point. For the smooth working of the new alliance, the inflated self-conception of the potent manager is more of an issue than the way the Seraph himself handles underlings. It takes time to decode the real meaning of the suave flutterings of the party functionary. At last, he gets to the real issue:

"Here is what can happen in our sphere: an admirable and powerful person, enjoying the confidence of the party, becomes a leader. For a period of time everything takes a normal course. But at some point, this comrade ceases to feel the link with the source of his power. He ceases to feel that without the people, without the collective, without the party, he is a total zero. He begins to believe that he himself is the source of his power and the sole cause of his various successes."

[9, p. 50]

The powerful manager, given to self-aggrandizement, must be coaxed back into submission. The theme of partnership now stands out in sharp relief. Comrade Seraph and his manager are partners indeed. They blend the *what* and the *how* of the Big Deal. The forceful manager knows what has to be done, and the seraphic party functionary patiently shows him how to do it.

The didactic nail is driven home with more than one blow. Take the good comrade's domestic bliss and his gentle wisdom. They are paradigmatic, for they help to show in the ever-circular, not to say dialectic, way of middlebrow fiction that the party functionary is right and the promethean manager wrong in every way. Overconfident in his power in the pursuit of his goals, no matter how useful, the manager fails not only the Big Deal but himself as well. He fails to be happy and so to get out of the alliance all that it offers. And this is just as regrettable under the general aspect of well-balanced human conservation and contentment making. Deep underneath, lies the basic sophistry of the Big Deal. In contrast to what Comrade Seraph gets out of it – fur slippers, polka-dotted tea cups, happy children and the warm fun of it all – the big manager suffers from a miserable personal life. A perfect foil, he is glum, to say the least. When first transferred to the Siberian construction project (a camouflaged slave labor site), he had left his wife and his son behind. His son dies shortly after and later his wife refuses to join him and then stops writing altogether. Mellowed and reconstructed by Comrade Seraph, he now gains enough insight to blame himself; and he also understands that he had grievously trespassed against the evolving norms:

"Can I say that I really valued my family? I admit it honestly; I hardly noticed them. At home my wife created an atmosphere of tender worship around me. She didn't even let the flies fly around me when I slept. She didn't let anyone disturb me when I was working or reading. She anticipated all my wishes . . . I keep remembering how frequently we parted and lived away from each other. Let's say that my work demanded it. But now I can see that it could have been different had there been a real will. Too easily sometimes we accept separations and deny ourselves our personal life. I left them in the Crimea. But why couldn't I have brought them with me and arranged for my son's cure here? So here is the result. I didn't treasure my family properly or my love for them. I have learned to do it when it's too late."   [8, p. 51]

But at least he is not too late to prove, at a high price to himself, his party partner right.

Compassionate seraphim made their appearance as a comforting myth for the war-strained populace. Responding to the national emergency, their "humanism" found plenty to do in mediating postwar conflicts, in inviting confessions, in coaxing hidden disgruntlement into the open. But there is another positive type, less busy with consolation. He is the professional efficiency expert, the pure organizer. And if it is hard to say to which the regime is more beholden, both types have superseded the party ideologue.

Comrade Perfect

Comrade Perfect is in his early fifties, gray-haired and wiry. Stalingrad, Kiev, Novosibirsk – he has been to all these places on party business, digging into the local problems. He is now on his way to a strategic northern shipbuilding center, sent by the secretary of the central committee himself, to assist the radical modernization of that enterprise. It is a high-priority assignment.

He is not seraphic. His mind and conduct are pragmatic and streamlined. A model organizer, he is tough in a civilized manner. The comrade travels from Moscow with a well-known academic who has produced the plan for the gigantic reconstruction. The local chief manager, somewhat nervous, meets them both at the station. As they are driven to town, the difference of attitude between the two prestigious guests foreshadows important matters. The professor

here too remained true to himself. He was interested only in figures. He did not look out of the windows of the car. He looked at the back of the manager's large head. Comrade [Perfect] managed to keep up the conversation as well as to examine attentively everything around him.[16]

Well done. This emissary from on high at once becomes absolutely knowledgeable, moving tensely yet quietly from person to person, place to place. crisis to crisis. And at once he begins to be consulted about everything. At all times he speaks the trim expert language of engineers, sometimes with enthusiasm. But his style is always terse.

This style avoids indeterminacy, idle waste of time, masked by external business and feigned preoccupation. You don't have to put on a performance for him. You need not rush from shop to shop with folders under your arm. Neither phoney grandeur nor petty bustle can deceive [him]. He judges you by your actions.

He is

simple in everything and, above all, in his relationships with people. One never heard vague, unclear answers from him: "Let's think it over," "let's discuss it," "let's see." He said only "yes" and "no."

When it is suggested, hesitantly, by the shipyard manager that his way might lead to errors, his answer fits his crisp manner:

"It might. If it happens, one must correct the error. But to drag things out, to twist and turn, to decide nothing – that's the worst of errors. In a war, for instance, that sort of error is frequently irreparable."   [2, pp. 67-68]

He gets cooperation from the regional party power, and he subdues nature's power when the sea threatens to flood the construction docks. He helps a young crash-worker obtain a Stalin prize at the same time as he helps a *louche* playboy to lose his job of running the local club. He resolves old quarrels, looks into family affairs, consoles the young and the old and, above all, encourages everybody's ambitious educational projects. He

walks the thin line between supportiveness and intimidation very adroitly.

The groundwork for all this is laid by his relentless study of people. He
starts from the top. Having grasped the temperament of the chiefs, he
turns to the rank and file. But he avoids flaunting his status. The place is
full of sailors from the ships docked for repair, so he makes himself inconspicuous by donning a kind of naval garb. This helps him keep better
watch over the citizens. At public gatherings and cultural events, he sits in
the back row. Nothing distracts him. At first, he even leaves his family
behind in Moscow. He is dry, one must confess; and he intimidates some
people – not much, but enough. This only enhances his effectiveness.

His genetic lineage is thoroughbred, proletarian. His father, a laborer
in a salt mine, was killed in August 1914, at the front. The adolescent boy
followed in his father's footsteps. Back-breaking work tempered his will
to survive. The revolution and the civil war formed him. After demobilization, he started working in the komsomol. Simultaneously, with relentless energy, he managed to graduate as an engineer. That is a particularly
telling detail. He loves engineering. But the party had marked him out for
rapid promotion. Even before the war, he had been appointed party secretary in a southern shipyard. He fought in the war as regimental commissar. Immediately after the war, he was propelled into the apparatus of
the central committee; so he is a person of considerable interest.

We can observe him as he exercises guidance. For instance, he startles
two young engineers in charge of the technical information office out of
their wits when he moves up on them unheralded. "Why such sorrow on
your faces?" he asked. "I am neither an inspector nor a controller." He
wants to know exactly what they do. He traps them, of course, because he
is so well informed. Since they are not managing well, he first asks
"Who's obstructing you?" Always anticipating obstructionists, and
specializing in unceremonious troubleshooting, he listens with irritation
to the mumbling of the ineffective pair about the vague goals they are
pursuing. The shipyard is being modernized from riveting to automatic
welding, and he asks them what they have specifically undertaken to that
end. Just about nothing, they admit, becoming more and more embarrassed. The very thought that "perhaps he speaks from his office every night
on a direct line to the Kremlin" makes them feel altogether unworthy. He
concurs. But at the same time, he gives first aid on the spot, making them
sit down with him at once and organize their work.

"If you don't have a plan, come closer, please, come closer so that we can discuss
everything right away and jot down together the most important points."

[1, p. 57]

Quod erat demonstrandum – together, right away, competently, professionally. The comrade's success rests largely on his double expertise, organizational and technical. He never stops being an engineer.

Helping his flock receive rewards and affluence, he is frugal himself. His refusal to give up his cramped temporary quarters upsets his closest colleague, the chief manager:

"I don't understand your attitude . ... A man who works as much as you do, a man who works on the assignment of the central committee of the party, does he have the right or doesn't he to demand a good place to live?"

Comrade Perfect's resistance is, of course, strategically motivated:

"I shall accept a new apartment when every single worker has been moved out of the communal housing projects and out of ancient shacks. I must ask you not to bring this matter up again."   [2, p. 67]

This touch of hagiographic atavism is effective. Through his moral superiority, the perfect deputy demonstrates the party's care for its subjects. And his own lean righteousness makes his benediction on material dreams pure and authoritative.

9. Producers

Nomadic management

One special form of unstable management is endemic in the system, tending to affect peripheral enterprises. In the transportation sector of the economy, for instance, one man is

a manager by profession, a man for whom management itself has become a specialty. He had been the chairman of the board of a woodworking shop and he also had been deputy chairman of a district executive committee. Then he had managed the municipal department of supplies and he had also been at one time the manager of both a starch and glue factory and of a liquor and vodka plant. He had also worked in the administration of a regional executive committee. In the end, according to a local expression, he "glued" himself to the automotive transportation center.

This is versatility without substance, the managerial function in pure form. Replaceable wherever he is, this man moves in circles rather than upwards. "Somewhat flabby," always "well dressed," he watches with "alert and shrewd" eyes.

He was not stupid. On the contrary, he was sharp and had managed to learn a thing or two. A certain opinion was formed about him which was expressed in the following way: "Even though he is not a specialist, he is an experienced executive."

He cultivates connections with superiors. His own subordinates mistake his self-protective strategies for competence.

"Ah, he's one of us," "a local man," "a man who grew up under our eyes." For some reason everyone was certain that he would do great things.[1]

Even though he does not, but remains sterile and servile, his local origin works to his advantage. The collective lives in eternal fear of strangers, of emissaries from above, and prefers a parasite of its own, provided he be more or less harmless.[2]

These strange leaders could be called nomads. They have forgotten their original profession and have not acquired a new one. Having become used to living by paperwork, they lose contact with real work. And good relations with highly placed authorities are their ultimate goal.   [1, p. 14]

Servility to those above permits these nomads to remain plausible. For a good long while. They have one principle: "Superiors must be given satisfaction" (p. 14). Nomads suffer from insecurity, engage in elaborate self-protective moves. Backscratching is the least sinister and most functional aspect of stalinist bureaucracy, its most human feature without which the economy could not survive. It is, in fact, a second, albeit illicit, national economy: the Soviet name for it is *blat*. This nomad deals with a number of organizations and holds to the maxim: "Today I help you out, tomorrow you help me out, right?" (p. 15). He is surrounded by people who operate on this mutual understanding. And among them hide thieves. Supply and procurement operations are full of them. But as long as active corruption can be kept covert, it is a blessing, for it gets things done. Its participants, however, can seldom relish it in comfort. The latent danger of corrupt relationships comes from greed. Hungry connivers easily forget to feed on the system and take to eating each other instead.

While this nomad shows servility to those above, he is to some degree a menace to his subordinates. In his plush mahogany office, behind closed venetian blinds, he keeps in private files a record of the errors and failures of his employees. He sees only the defects in people. Through intrigue, he undermines the achievement of the good workers. Pitting man against man keeps him busy. Exceedingly jealous of his "coordinating" prerogatives, he blocks off the organization as a whole from his staff by keeping them from communicating. This is, perhaps, the main feature of his managerial style. For, above all, such a manager fears initiative and, as to himself, he tries to be as inconspicuous as possible.

He feared the wrath of his superiors. But he did not seek their praise. Returning from a stormy meeting of the regional committee, he usually said to his co-workers with satisfaction: "They didn't even remember us." Naturally, he treasured his position: it was a sufficiently solid but, at the same time, secondary organization; it was indispensable, but it was not leading; not everyone was convinced that it was a success, but for all that no one particularly cursed it for being a failure.   [3, p. 84]

A low-profile type, he hides well. It takes a long time to find him out. His new assistant, the muckraking hero of this novel, meditates about the problem with acquiescent understanding:

"The nomad regards himself as the most honest of men. He is fulfilling the plan, he is disciplined, he inspects the operations in the shops – what else do you want! But he gets used to living according to orders. If we are ordered to do something, we do it. We will even kill ourselves in the effort. But if orders are not forthcoming, all the better. He lacks the creative instinct and he does not understand it in others. Life pushes him around and he cannot grasp why. This is the reason for his restlessness . . . He is wholeheartedly for communism. But he understands it

his own way, the [nomad] way. Sometime the day will come and communism will be proclaimed. And that's that. But he does not see communism in our present life."
[1, p. 53]

Suddenly, dangerous winds blow up from opposite directions. In setting subordinates against each other, the nomad provokes them too much and some of his people turn against him. In addition, an important official descends on the enterprise. This time, the nomad fails to camouflage his incompetence and cuts a sorry figure during the inspection, for the reason that he is entirely ignorant of the changes introduced in the shops by his staff. The visitor insultingly ignores him during the tour. But at the end of it, he calls him aside.

"Your people are doing an excellent job," he said without looking at [the nomad], "they should be helped."

"We are doing everything! My administrators are constantly in the shop. We help, we pull, all in all we work away to the best of our ability."

"By the way, comrade [Nomad]," asked [the executive] suddenly, "what is your profession?"

In his embarrassment [the nomad] did not know what to say: "Well you see, I, that is, generally speaking, I am doing leading managerial work, basically – "

"That's much too general. We have to have it stated much more concretely. I suggest you had better think over what kind of work you will be able to assume responsibility for. Real work, according to your own specialty and, most importantly, as you say, according to your ability. Is that clear?"

"It is," the nomad replied in a voice which had suddenly turned hoarse.
[3, p.123]

Had he sat more tightly in his mahogany office, he might have been forgotten. His character and conduct blend well enough with the Big Deal. The system finds him tolerable. But he overplays his hand in intrigue because of his mounting paranoia. This is a built-in feature of stalinist bureaucracy, but its extent had of necessity to be watched, especially in the mid and lower echelons. By being too suspicious, the nomad chokes off the necessary flow of placid, low-grade support. No one can last without local support.

This man falls within the norm. He is not really a scoundrel, or not much of a one. No more harmful than other bureaucratic procrastinators, he does not clown or grovel too much. He attempts to play the game according to the rules, if not too well. The punishment, when it catches up with him, is fairly light, just the amount necessary to hold the standard oscillations of the regime's dealings with postwar managers in check.

Partners are good and bad in various ways. The type dealt with here, while compliant, is unproductive. A contrasting type produces, but in an obstreperous manner. The first is totally dependent. The second craves independence. The sense of the partner's self is very important to the regime, no less than productivity. So, although both parasites and achievers resemble their counterparts elsewhere in the world, the regime reacts to the contrast in its own way, making more allowances for certain transgressions than for others.

The golden calf

Here is a key tale which charts, for the benefit of a novice among working partners, the tricky path between dependence and independence. It shows how problems more weighty than the nomad's must be resolved.

After service at the front, one young manager resembles nothing so much as a frisky colt. Capable and positive, he is appointed manager of the leading state farm, renowned for its pedigree cattle.[3] Now, the pitfalls for an "instant" manager are many. A central problem for this comrade, Comrade Colt, revolves around responsibility. To whom does he owe it? Whom does he represent?

All the necessary difficulties are present. The state farm is in bad shape. War and makeshift management have left their mark. The young man responds to the challenge head-on. In fact he becomes obsessed, and an early alarm is sounded no more than twenty pages into the tale.

District party meetings bore the young man dreadfully. He barely listens to the proceedings and fidgets silently, with his mind on his own pressing affairs. But, at one meeting, several kolkhozes join in a brick-manufacturing project. Since it seems profitable for his own enterprise, he perks up and speaks out forcefully. Seeing this transfiguration, the party secretary steps in, and publicly humiliates the young man by revealing doubts about him. The party secretary's point is that the young man owes everything to the party. He had entered its ranks at the front. He had proved a good organizer; the party trusted him. Yet after demobilization, he has not proved himself at all, and indeed may never succeed, for he does not seem interested, let alone involved, in district affairs. The accused tries to argue that, as a newcomer, his experience is limited. The secretary cuts him off.

"If you take the trouble to look around, you will see that a good half of the people are newcomers. The war has seen to that. Except for your state farm, you don't wish to know anything. The needs of the district do not concern you. The troubles of the district do not concern you. From there it's only a step, and the cares of the state, the cares of the Soviet state stop concerning you . . . If you continue on that path, you will drift down into routine, into narrow pragmatism. You will shortchange our great ideas. You will sleep through the enormous developments which will take place in our country."[4]

The trap which actually brings down the inexperienced manager is sprung by a persuasive young stranger who runs a distant and war-ravaged kolkhoz. This visitor visits Colt in an attempt to purchase two pedigree cows. Comrade Colt rears back in dismay. The sales plan for the current year has been drawn up. The state farm has even oversold its capacity for the year thereafter. Besides, the brash Belorussian should have requisitioned the proper office, the district cattle-breeding administration. The visitor knows that, of course. But he holds a powerful emotional trump. "There are moments when the formalist approach won't do." And he goes on about the unspeakable misery his people have suffered. Every hut had to be rebuilt. There was nothing with which to plow the soil. "And hundreds of eyes look at you, widows' eyes, orphans' eyes: tell us, they say, what's to be done, show the way out."

The thought that to refuse would be petty and senseless flashes through the host's mind. He is convinced that the cattle-breeding manager will turn down an unbudgeted request. He is equally convinced that his own pedantic bookkeeper will not cooperate. Having waited for the tension to grow, the guest now laces his tale of woe with an appeal to the concept of local administrative freedom. He expects it to be plenipotentiary, if within its proper limits. The assumption is important for the story, and effective for his cause.

"Don't tell me you don't have enough power! You are your own boss, aren't you? And what are we arguing about anyway? I don't understand. Two calves."

Comrade Colt, ready to capitulate, reduces the two to one, and gives in. The deal is concluded. He plans simply to confront his sticky bookkeeper with a *fait accompli* by ordering him to adjust the sales operation retroactively. He braces himself with the naive thought:

"After all, I am really my own boss. And this is a political matter. Those kolkhozniks are all heroes. And their chairman is all covered with medals."
[pp. 15-16]

Among many management tales, this one tackles with clarity the dilemma of lateral pressures, of the attempt of peers to join forces, of a horizontal action challenging vertical controls. The two managers make a deal behind the back of their proper party partners. Unfortunately, and to the consternation of everybody, pedantic bookkeeper, stolid party organizer, renowned milkmaid *et alia*, the brash raider absconds with Aspasia, no ordinary creature, but the daughter of their most aristocratic cow. Taken to task at once by the punctilious party organizer of his own enterprise, Comrade Colt attempts to support his daring decision by a question to which he clings, however nervously:

"If the manager has to assume full responsibility for the enterprise, how can he run it if he nowhere and in no matter shows his own will?"

He does not seem ready to grasp that this is not an either/or question. Sometimes the manager is permitted "to show his own will" and sometimes not. The Big Deal does not exist without conflict. It oscillates between changing latitudes of managerial power and these are periodically enlarged and then curtailed. In this fluctuating context, the manager's grasp of his role as deputy – and his comprehension of the correct latitudes of action – matters more than his actions. It is this which Comrade Colt has not quite worked out yet.

Though it takes a long time – for the system is far from efficient and lets the culprit alternate between anxiety and hope that his daring deed had not been detected in higher quarters – retribution is near. He is summoned before the chief of the cattle-breeding administration. The chief, while specifically praising the excellent condition of the state farm, lowers the boom: "There is no extenuation for a crime." Comrade Colt, pale but not yet crushed, insists that he has made a clean breast in a detailed written report. His motives had been pure. This cuts no ice with his superior: "I have gathered that you have a kind heart and that you are not petty. For a manager this does not suffice." Now the beleaguered man violates decorum. He hurls back, and with disdain, something he has found out about the administrator and something that he certainly should have kept to himself. He suggests that, since the administrator had safely weathered the war as a political officer without being anywhere near the front, he lacks understanding of the tragedy of human misery. The administrator blushes, to be sure; but responds that the young man's humanist concern for a remote community is both presumptuous and hypocritical. The state cares. The state cares amply and everywhere, therefore, both he and his co-conspirator should have been kicked out of the party. Shaken to the core, Comrade Colt clutches at the straw in the phrase "should have been." Nothing escapes the boss; he opens a barrage of closely knit questions:

"Didn't you know that the distribution of cattle goes through centralized channels? Didn't you know that you answer with your head for the people's property? Didn't you know that we have a socialist economy and not a private street-corner shop?"

Whatever he knows, it will be of no help to Comrade Colt now. And if the army and the war somehow stand between them, the administrator contributes to the clash:

"Mention is made in your army papers of your good discipline. So you have decided, once the war is over, that you can brush discipline aside?"   [pp. 41-2]

All this bodes ill for Comrade Colt. The bureaucrat plans to fire him. But he must, of course, refer the matter to the party echelon above him. Indeed, a special meeting is convened at which the district party secretary threatens the young man with anathema: "If they expel me, I'll kill myself." (One feels inclined to think the title of this chapter in the tale an understatement: "It Is Hard To Be A Manager.") Let us relax. The final decision is to administer a "severe reprimand," indicative of the party's combined application of distrust and leniency to a productive young partner.

Comrade Colt is both shamed and relieved. The two chiefs chat for a while alone after the meeting. The kinder of the two, obviously the party secretary, drops the conciliatory remark that the young man is crushed by the turn of events. "That's good," replies the cattleman, "now he will think it over twenty times before usurping power."[5]

This last remark fits with Comrade Colt's earlier question about the size of the cage in which the individual must sit. What is and what is not "too much?" And who determines it? The harsh cattleman urges harsh punishment. He regrets that the young man got off so lightly. The party functionary is more thrifty with qualified manpower.

Comrade Colt's mother, a formidable matron in her own right and a renowned overachieving shock-worker, demonstrates minimal motherly emotion by siding with the punitive authorities. According to her, her son needs

"to be beaten hard. Otherwise you will scratch the sore spot and just forget about it. They will beat you very hard all your life. I can see it already."

"Thanks for your kind forecast," he said glumly.   [p. 44]

So, although the roles of manager and deputy conflict, they have to be taken on simultaneously by a novice, and the latter is more important.

While the nomad is an unavoidable byproduct of bureaucratization, he has an unimportant role in the Big Deal. A lightweight in the partnership, he is easily dealt with, easily overlooked and easily replaced. Nor can any producer of consumer goods presume to be among the heavyweights, no matter how thoroughly apprenticed and how successfully molded into a deputy. The main actors on the postwar scene are those men to whom the major enterprises in the military-industrial complex were entrusted, the pride of the alliance between party and managers.

Perfectionism

There is learning enforced by the party and learning that is self-generated. The second is a dangerous kind, especially for the main Big Deal partner in the central arena. This is demonstrated in the novel *Steel and Slag*. Rotov, the manager of a steel combine, has risen high in his own methodical plan for his career; he has been very productive. He commands the respect of the minister of heavy industry himself. This is an exalted relationship. Admiring Rotov's productivity, the minister realizes that the man "is hard and has an iron will"[6] and, for that reason, is not easy to get along with. But since the events happen during the war, his expertise is rewarded, for a while.

Warning signals flash from the start. Rotov's chief assistant who, far off in the Urals, knows more than the almighty minister in Moscow, meditates unhappily. He

could never understand which prevailed in Rotov: will or stubbornness. What had made Rotov so self-confident in such a short time? Could it be the success of the plant in these few months of war? And was it only the plant? For all practical purposes Rotov was also the boss of the city. This was so because absolutely everything that was built in the city belonged to the plant. The plant ran the streetcar system. The plant's community department had surfaced the streets. The plant's recreation department had planted trees along boulevards and in the parks. And the chairman of the city soviet usually came to Rotov not to make demands as a superior. He came to make requests.

In his youth, Rotov had been a rank and file engineer for quite a while.

Having graduated brilliantly from the institute where he had successfully combined his studies with responsible party work, Rotov unexpectedly declared that
he wanted to work in a blast-furnace shop as a forger's assistant.   [p. 68]

The decision perplexed his superiors. One of Rotov's professors was particularly astonished. He had tried to persuade Rotov to become his assistant. Raising the question of narrow specialization as against broad expertise, Rotov replies unequivocally:

"Just because I am an open-hearth man, I must acquire experience with blast
furnaces. I know the steel-smelting process. I know that I can work as a foreman
and start any kind of smelt. But I also want to master all the finesses of the blast-
furnace business."

He prepared his program carefully, setting out to study "all the departments of metallurgy."

He was certain that an important and responsible job awaited him and, like the
captain of a ship, he prepared thoroughly and unhurriedly for the long voyage.
People around him watched with amazement as this young but already heavy
man – created, it seemed, to give orders – carried loads of sand teamed with a
short and puny adolescent.   [p. 69]

As for his personal life:

Young girls were very much drawn to Rotov, although in no way could one have
called him handsome. But in his stride, even and firm, in his manner of speech,
unhurried and self-assured, in his whole appearance there could be felt an inner
strength which was attractive and irresistible. He had amorous involvements, but
they all turned out to be shortlived. Who wanted a young man who allotted his
girl only the evening of his one free day? And they left him for others who were
less busy and more attentive. However, he did find one girl who fell in love with
him and who did not leave him as the others did.

Having taken care of that part of life, his perfectionism becomes more
dogged and streamlined. He begins to cut the underbrush away.

Rotov avoided civic and communal work meticulously. He considered that it took
time of which he did not have enough in the first place. Finally he was summoned
by the party committee and had to give there an account for his behavior. The
party secretary . . . heard him out attentively but did not approve. "You are a
miser. The most authentic Gogolian miser! Your accumulations go into a piggy
bank. But in my opinion you have accumulated enough. You should share your
possessions with others. If you go on, my friend, you will get into the habit of
taking without giving."   [p. 70]

But Rotov is not good at balancing. He is surprisingly stupid in one respect, for he does not seem to grasp how minimal are the new requirements for proper conduct for an achiever in heavy industry: no more than
a few amenities, a modicum of participation in the rituals in which the
system celebrates itself. These rituals *publicly* reassert the primacy and
wisdom of the party. It is as simple as that. But Rotov is stubborn. He

continues self-improvement on his own terms and even thinks of joining the humble maintenance team of the power station.

In his own calculated time and way he succeeds. Promotion follows rapidly: first, head of the blast-furnace shop; then assistant chief engineer; then, in a year's time, chief engineer. And then he sees himself appointed plant manager. When this happened,

he was sorry to leave technical work. And, as a matter of fact, he did not leave it. As before, he had time for everything. He devoted his days to the basic plant shops; his evenings to the remaining ones. Half of the night he invariably spent reading. On Sundays [he] appeared in the shops in order to send home the overly zealous heads of departments. He watched his subordinates closely not only in their work, but in their leisure also.

And as for leisure:

An entire recreational complex was built under him to serve the plant. A rest hostel quickly grew on the shore of a picturesque mountain lake. It had its own theater, movie house, restaurant, boat docks, and beach. Not far away the pioneer camp spread out its tents. To vacation here was obligatory for the senior staff. Only the director could excuse a person from it.   [pp. 73-4]

So far so good. One might even say splendid. Rotov not only has technical expertise, he triumphs, too, in the construction of the affluent dream.

It is evident, however, that Rotov must topple, because he is an over-reacher. It is his rational attempt to chart his own course which finally entraps him by alienating him from everybody.

Rotov measured everybody with his own yardstick and no one measured up. He needed a talented assistant and a docile one. These properties rarely coexist. Docility and compliance characterized only those engineers who were not gifted. The gifted ones invariably turned out to be stubborn and contrary. The conflict was inevitable in both cases: the obedient engineers did not satisfy the manager because they worked poorly, the talented ones because they refused to obey him unconditionally.   [p. 68]

Not only able managers have to cope with this personnel problem. The regime itself is looking all the time for those who are gifted but simultaneously docile. It is a difficult search, as this novel properly points out.

Something begins to be dreadfully amiss in Rotov's kingdom, despite its frantic productivity. Serious trouble surfaces. When the pipeline from the adjoining gas plant fails to deliver sufficient fuel and Rotov curiously pays no attention, his engineers report the bottleneck, not only to Rotov but also to his distant superiors. This initiates his undoing.

Without warning, the minister of heavy industry descends on the plant. He finds Rotov's reception room crowded. He spots the chairman of the city soviet there. This important local personage has been waiting for over two hours. He also finds out from the embarrassed secretary, reduced to instant stuttering, that Rotov is not at that moment in a meeting: indeed he is sitting alone in his office. The minister bursts through the door of the sanctuary, and the "big boss" jumps up sheepishly from behind his desk. The minister proceeds to let all the petitioners in, to settle the city chairman's business "in less than half a minute"; and to expedite the whole crowd "in less than half an hour." Thereupon, he raises the roof. The scandal is grandiose. Leaving Rotov to his alarmed thoughts, the minister hurries about the plant, preparing for the reckoning.

Omniscient and ubiquitous in his own wrong way, Rotov had diligently planted trees, paved roads, and built handsome recreation facilities. Yet it now becomes clear that none of his good works will help him. He should not have presumed. Now even his plausible explanation for delaying the repair of the pipeline is to no avail.

The administration of the entire combine is called by the minister for an open meeting. "For the first time the people assembled there watched the manager in the role of a pupil being taught some basic rules of conduct" (p. 108). A phone call from Beria while the meeting is still in session makes even the minister tremble and, as with Rotov, "large beads of perspiration cover his forehead." The clinching nocturnal sermon, delivered by the minister tête-á-tête, is tantamount to a sentence.

" You don't ask people for advice. You are worried about your prestige. But your prestige is not impressive. Your subordinates execute your orders – yes, they do – but this is the result of discipline and of their sense of responsibility. Real prestige is created only if you know how to combine being helpful with being demanding. And you have forgotten another thing. The head of an organization must be loved. And you, you are not loved in the plant, although you have achieved much here. You have failed to understand that a collective is a large family. And is the head of a family asked to provide only food and clothing? Don't tell me you behave like that at home? You come home, put the money on the table and that's all? It's impossible. You are affectionate with your children and you have a kind word for your wife. The collective also needs a kind word and affection. Does anybody get it from you? You are concerned with everyone in general and with no one in particular . . . We can't now wait while you reform yourself. Characters like yours must be broken."

[pp. 113-114]

Fiat. This man's sins suddenly cumulate. His retail approach to his underlings is not the worst. His methodical career smacks of independence. At the top, he has failed to make a proper show of humility before the party. His perfectionism turns out to be self-defeating, and is not appreciated. The sacrifices he had made to perfect himself are not only not required but make him unfit for Big Deal partnership. What *is* required is balance, simplicity, and bonhomie.

The next tale, about a heavyweight – a man more crude, more arrogant and perhaps even more stubborn than Rotov – shows that the party is not always consistent. Occasionally it tolerates all sorts of transgressions. But it will combat for evermore the presumption of individualism.

My plant

A machine-building plant could not do better and its manager is proud and possessive. He undergoes no "development," nor is he burdened with psychological luggage. His jovial self-confidence combines with condescension toward the less competent folk around. He is on his way up. He has, in fact, arrived. His grip is strong. His name, Potapov, suggests a bear.[7]

Suddenly an unforeseen problem comes up. It results from the collision between the consumer goods industry and heavy industry, between David and Goliath. In a somewhat irregular fashion, the lady manager of a textile plant confronts him in person with a strange request. She asks him to insert at once into his tight, not to say frantic, production schedule an extra item. She wants him to make a textile lathe, designed by her staff. The matter being seemingly of great urgency, she brings the request herself. It has gone through no channels.

One can predict Potapov's reaction. He disdains light industry in general and its textile branch in particular. To him that particular textile plant, staffed largely by women, is nothing but a "cotton republic." Secondly, his competitive zeal allows no remissions. Nothing shall deter him from climbing higher and higher up the "overproduction" ladder. Thirdly, and perhaps most significantly, he cannot bear unchanneled interference with his plans. The request smacks of revolt to him: "I am against anarchy in industry. I stand for the principle of planning."[8] He flatly refuses. When the outraged lady manager retorts that he may be forced by his superiors to accept her order, he silences her:

"Don't worry, they won't force me. I advise you not to waste your time. You should do the proper thing in such cases. I suggest that you push your lathe along the entire bureaucratic merry-go-round."   [p. 111]

When the plot thickens and he is called to justify his crass noncooperation, he retorts:

"Why should the textile plant interfere with the work of my plant? I ask, why? Who gave them the right? . . . I'm not running an experimental shop. I cannot accept an additional order. It is not in the interest of the state to do so." [p. 133]

We must, in this chapter, pay heavy industry its due. What Potapov says here is important. Of all the variants, an industrial manager, and a large-scale one at that, is the regime's most important partner. To get on, he has to be part and parcel of the system. An adventurer or an outsider or a dilettante cannot succeed. To dig himself in, to cling to the core of Soviet economy, the industrialist must be very different from inconsequential nomads who scurry about the noncritical periphery of consumer goods production, agriculture, local commerce, or services. Industrialists are the true servants of the state, not of the people. And like Potapov, they seem to know the interests of the state.

If the nomads suffer from insecurity, the "big shots" exude self-confidence. But they are playing with fire all the same. Their case must not be overstated, and Potapov runs the old risk of overdoing it by challenging the limits of the permissible. In what he has just said he is perfectly right and absolutely wrong – on matters in different categories. But he risks bunching them together. He is right when he invokes procedure. The lady should, indeed, go through the right channels. He is right when he counts on the regime defending the inviolability of heavy industry, its canonization. Where, then, is he wrong? He is wrong in one statement he makes: "Don't worry, they won't force me." He *can* be forced to do *anything*, and not to see this, or to feign not to, is a grievous mistake. If it were only stupidity, it would not be so bad; but the real problem is his arrogance and, in the play, arrogance is treated neither casually nor by implication but as its major theme. This self-assurance is not just a feature of Potapov's public conduct. He shows it at home too, so that his virtuous wife threatens to divorce him, and in doing so clarifies the issue. She is a trade union steward, inconveniently for Potapov, in the bothersome "cotton republic." Torn between husband and colleagues, she reminds him of his earlier characteristic refusal to bail out an agency by manufacturing potato-digging implements. He had been forced from above to accept the order. She rubs it in that he had complied for the wrong reasons, those of fear, vanity, and careerism:

"How stubbornly you refused, how much you kept arguing that they would interfere with your basic plan. How many times you travelled to the district party committee, to the central administration. And you refused even to consider that these two hundred implements were an important matter for the welfare of the workers. I know, I know, even then you ended up by being in the lead . . . and you even received mention in the resolution of the district committee. But I, I would not have honored you. Under no circumstances! Because in the end, you simply understood that you might earn a reprimand. That's one thing. Secondly, that would have tarnished your reputation. Therefore, some time at some formal meeting or other you would not have been elected to the presidium. That's the third reason. It seems to me you started cherishing your seat in the presidium too much."   [p. 117]

Pondering this poor mix of initiative and compliance in him, she comes up with a sharp question which raises a vital point:

"Why do you so often say 'my plant,' 'I am the manager,' 'I am the boss'? You are an executive. And no matter what you say, the boss happens to be the government, the people."   [p. 116]

She is not entirely right there: Stalin is the boss, and no one else. But what she is getting at, and what is actually the hidden trouble here is that stalinist managers did turn out to be bosses at heart. And bossism had somehow to be checked. The stalinist homunculi – an insolent progeny – were useful and irksome, both.

This whole role conflict, between bossism on the one hand and the role of deputy on the other, dominates industrial fiction of the period. The manager has to be firm as a boss; certainly, his subordinates must regard him as generally a firm person. At the same time, *qua* deputy or administrator, his salvation lies in his very elasticity, in his adjustment, in the capacity to change his course, to countermand his own orders without loss of face. And to his own superiors, he must minimize his drive for autonomy or at least camouflage it. A certain kind of personality helps in the more or less smooth execution of these exercises, and Potapov simply does not have it. He does not instinctively grasp the inherent dualism in his managerial role. Thus he can loudly insist to the party secretary:

"I have my own plans. I have my own plant. And I have my own rhythmically scheduled production. I shall not permit any interference. Do you understand?"

Since it is his duty, the party secretary with whom he works in tandem does understand, up to a point. Middlebrow fiction is quite coy about the actual daily implementation of the Big Deal. It is achieved through the partnership of manager and party official. The role of the manager is ambiguous; so, too, are the ways, the manners, the gestures of his partner, the party official. The essence of the partnership lies in the shifting emphasis between a close and clutching relationship and a more relaxed coexistence. This partnership is really like a marriage. When in trouble, the pair attempts to present to the world a happier image than is really warranted. Because of the primacy of his position, the party partner seems to interact with his mate both with greater ruthlessness and with more gallantry. It is he who breaks up the relationship if need be, yet it is also he who can stand up for the manager if he errs, just as a husband might accept responsibility for a delinquent wife.

This dreadful play has its particular use to us in that it sheds some light on this relationship. Potapov, the manager, is "married" to a rather ineffective party mate who has failed to control him, as he publicly admits:

"I feel guilty in the eyes of the party committee for Potapov's conduct. I feel responsible for him even though I do not agree with him on the question under discussion. What does my fault consist of? I shall try to answer. [He turns to Potapov.] We have worked together for two years. We work well together. The production percentages are high. We have gotten used to them, these percentages. And the wider horizon has slipped away from our gaze."

In addition to the short-term commitments, long-range goals must be kept in sight by both pairs of eyes. The party man, continuing his confession, tells of Potapov's earlier error, fortunately averted:

"This was the first bell, the first signal. We managed to persuade you at the time. We managed to convince you. And we forgot about it. But the worm-hole was left in you. I thought you would learn from your own experience. But far from it. As a result, you have now decided to refuse an order without even consulting the party organization. From that moment your own guilt commences. And you yourself must answer for it." [p. 136]

A subtle matter is alluded to here. In certain circumstances, the party partner must be prepared to disavow the manager. Now, if Potapov's immediate party mate is weak, the next in command – the district party secretary – firmly defends for a long while Potapov's right to be boss, postponing reckoning with him. Playing the trump card, the extraordinary success of Potapov's plant, this party official even goes so far as to suggest that Potapov's influence on the local party organization itself is not without virtue (pp. 120-21). Watch out. At just this point, this positive party official runs the risk of exaggerating. Where exactly transgression starts is not easy to determine. The role conflict, at any rate that with which party functionaries must struggle, seems more taxing than that of the managers. They must make it neither too easy nor too difficult for the partners; they must neither displace them nor relinquish their grip on them.

Potapov transgresses, more in manner than in deed. Strife breaks out around him. It spills over into his domestic life. His wife is disaffected. Public opinion is against him. There is, in the end, no choice but to read the riot act to him.

"Now listen, Potapov. You did not grasp the national significance of the invention of the new textile lathe. You did not understand it, Mr. Potapov. What's more, you have ignored the party organization in your plant. You are now given a serious warning. Don't you see, you suffer from a shift in perspective? During the war, light industry lagged behind heavy industry. Your plant became strong during the war and came out of the war prepared for the days of peace. But it seemed to Potapov that it was he alone with a small group of his assistants who had brought the plant out unto the wide road. At some moment, he began to think that the plant's triumph was not the triumph of our party policy but his, Potapov's, personal triumph. From here follows 'my plant,' 'my people,' 'my plan.' Not the State's plan but 'my plan!'"   [p. 137]

The partner should know what to take and what to give. He must give the sweat of his brow. And whatever he takes in return, he must not expect too much "triumph."

One could stop here, with Potapov's capitulation. But it is worth a further glance. As a rule, I have disregarded the response of literary critics to middlebrow fiction. In this case, however, the reception given to the play has a special interest. The playwright clearly intended to make the case against a typical overreaching manager. By the time the play was ready for performance, the balance had tipped away temporarily, at about the time of the nineteenth party congress, from the official campaign against strong managers. The shift in the party line had the effect that the playwright was suddenly found guilty of trespassing.[9] It was revealed that he had ventured into a forbidden territory, namely that of unrealistic problems and that the plot itself was false, since Potapov was absolutely right after all. He was right to defend the inviolability of central planning, and he was right in opposing interference in his own affairs since it was, after all, preposterous that a production order not go through the right channels; which is just what Potapov had thundered in the first place.

Does this reversal of the official view invalidate our decoding? Hardly.[10] The new twist supports the concept of the regime's ambivalence towards its most favored partner. And that is our main theme here. The regime wants the manager to be both effective and unobtrusive, strong and pliable, inventive and docile. In the reappraisal of the play one should see only the continuous cyclical alteration of emphasis, not a change of policy. Potapov, the stubborn overfulfiller of norms, is now upgraded at the expense of the dilettantish "cotton republic" ladies. The foolish person now turns out to be his wife. She should have weathered the storm instead of quarrelling with him. The shift of emphasis, meanwhile, requires the demotion of the impetuous lady manager. She is the real loser. Who said she was the people's friend? Was it not clear to begin with that her initiative could not be trusted because it was unruly and self-generated?

Exegesis on proper interaction

In the huge novel, *Days of Our Life*, packed with factory personnel, one is hard put to pick out the major protagonists. It deals with the production of gigantic power turbines, offering insight into the hectic interaction between management and party.

The tale opens with a high-level conference of industrial managers. They have been summoned by the Leningrad party to the prestigious Smolny Institute. Nemirov, the dapper manager, leaves the awesome gathering,

emphasizing with his altogether informal appearance that he, for one, was young, calm, and healthy and that he could very well run down the steps, regardless of a manager's decorum.

The bigger the industrial potentates, the more severely they had been criticized by the party.

Each had received his due. But he, Nemirov, was neither upset nor vexed. He was sure of his ability. He was sure of being able to make good where he had fallen short.

Why does he seem to enjoy being raked over the coals? Out of perversion? Or does his buoyant pleasure at criticism hint at the institutionally tight interlocking of the Big Deal?

Today's conference had shaken him. It shook him while increasing his thirst for action and success. He loved it when once in a while the party assembled them all together, all the managers of large enterprises. They were old and young, people of different characters and different experience. And each one was used to consider himself a leader, a big boss. And it was, indeed, as bosses that they were summoned here. But here they felt that they were not bosses but communists first of all, members of their party whose word was law. It might have seemed that each was knowledgeable, that he had thought everything through and through and that he could teach others. But here he listened like a pupil. And he began to perceive everything anew. The very essence of his work was laid bare. All one's daily activity was reviewed in the bright light.[11]

These thoughts give a preview of the entire novel.

The trouble which keeps this massive book going issues from on high. An order is handed down to Nemirov to retool the plant from a piecemeal operation to a serial production of infinitely bigger and infinitely better electro-turbines. Furthermore, it is obvious at once – to some if not to others – that the ukaz exceeds even this backbreaking program. It is subliminally understood that the devout collective must offer to accomplish the superproject far in advance of the date prescribed. The entire working force, therefore, shows the mandatory split between resisters and ecstatic pushers. Fear of the seemingly impossible in some members of Nemirov's staff clashes with the yearning for new responsibilities in others.

The reader need not worry that the patterned dialectic will fail. In the end, party wisdom will reestablish order and purpose. Or will it? By 1952, when this book was published, the regime's partnership with managers was so firmly established that the highly placed industrial man was no longer permitted in fiction to live by the production norm alone. The time had come to delve into his psychological problems. They surface as the basis of the plot.

Nemirov's gigantic task entails reassessment of personnel. He is completely dependent on two men under him. One of them, chief engineer of a key shop, is competent, meticulous, cautious – a typical "overinsurer." His foil, a younger subordinate, is fervent, awkward, dishevelled, totally selfless and passionate. The one abhors risk, the other invites it. One wishes to avert chaos by avoiding quixotic overcommitments, the other is quixotic to the bone. One distrusts the workers, the other rhapsodizes about their enthusiasm. One, if not a villain, is altogether problematic. The other is the hero.

This cluttered and clumsy novel is held together by Nemirov's shuffling shift of support from the villain to the hero. In the process, he runs the risk of losing prestige in the eyes of his best subordinates. As an important manager, he must mediate among his key aides. He must be cautious about promotion and demotion of technical leaders. He must protect his authority by maintaining a distance between himself and the rank and file. He cannot have underlings questioning his decisions. Defending the independence of his judgment, he must also be humble and turn for guidance to the party. He must crave chastisement, as he does.

Enter the party partner or, rather, two of them: the organizer of the plant, a most acrimonious comrade, and the less talkative district party secretary. A third man, the city party secretary, is also at hand. Pallid as individuals, the three easily coalesce into one. The party organizer is, of course, constantly present. As the crisis proceeds he tends to do two things. Siding with the "good guys," he reprimands Nemirov in endless tête-à-têtes for not taking drastic measures; yet in front of the collective he engages in masochistic self-blame for all that goes wrong. Actually, however, he cannot help Nemirov, who does not trust him anyway. Mounting pressure triggers signs of paranoia in the manager. He fears that the party partner is undermining his authority. He goes to Moscow explicitly to complain to the minister.

His anxiety is not altogether unfounded. In his absence, the comrades take up the discussion of his problems with the Leningrad party committee. This surprise action behind his back enrages him. The author suggests, in passing, a kind of socio-psychological reason for Nemirov's problem. Having laboriously come up from the lowest ranks of factory work himself, he has fought inch by inch for power. His authority now has great personal importance to him. And he is prone to admire and envy the clarity of the military situation:

"In the army strict discipline is natural and indisputable. The point is that you can't lead without establishing a distance." [p. 530]

He goes to Moscow and sees the minister in great need of reinforcement. But the minister reacts unsympathetically to his anxiety. He gives him promises of lavish economic support and a somewhat sarcastic dressing down. When Nemirov hints to the minister that he feels threatened by his party organizer, the latter says icily:

"Why don't you try to set aside your personal ambition? Why don't you try to look at yourself objectively, with a penetrating gaze, as from the party's point of view? Thank goodness, I have known [the party organizer] for a long time. I remember him when he was still an assembly worker. You want me to believe that [he] is capable of starting trouble, of undermining your authority? Forget it. Errors one must try to correct and sick nerves one must try to cure."

Since this is a pivotal scene, the author provides a striking characterization of the minister.

The minister's glance was piercing and cold. The minister could not abide "psychology." Everybody who worked with him knew it. If you come to him on business, talk business. If you plead for a new machine-tool base, that's business. He understands that you truly need assistance there. The ministry will obtain it for you and will guarantee supplies. If you need funds for retooling shops ahead of schedule, well, that makes sense too. We promise help. But matters of ambition, authority, personnel relations – about such matters you had better talk to your wife, during leisure hours. [p. 527]

Nemirov loses self-control on his return to Leningrad when he finds out that the comrades have, as it seems to him, connived behind his back. When they try to pacify him, he shouts at them that he is not a child and that he understands more than they think. He stares out of the window, as model managers are apt to do, and meditates on the bustling scene of cranes, smokestacks, trucks, and whatnot, a panorama, according to the rules of industrial fiction, "familiar" to the manager "to the last detail and dear to his heart." He gazes, wounded, at the beloved industrial scene.

It seemed that all this belonged to him, was steered by him, all his strength was invested in it. And now, only imagine, they were trying to decide the affairs of this plant, of *his* plant, without him – and, perhaps worse, against him! [p. 540]

When Nemirov continues to bristle with hostility, the big sermon is upon him:

"Of course, you are the only boss. No one is contesting your rights. But what can you do alone, without communists, without the entire collective? You make judgments even about the party organization from the vantage point of your 'I.' They must help *me. My* authority is at stake. You think that communists have nothing else to do but be concerned with you, that their task is to help *you* and not to fulfill the common task *together* with you? Do you want to hear the whole honest truth? Your authority started to shake because you have assessed yourself too highly and have pitched yourself against the collective like some sort of all powerful deity: I can do everything! I can overcome everything! Just obey me and don't interfere with me . . . Remember Stalin's words about Antaeus."[12]

[pp. 541-2]

A transfiguration, obviously, is imminent. Nemirov harnesses his ego, embraces the party, accepts guidance, demotes the resister, commits himself to superhuman deeds, and so on. He also woos his beautiful wife anew, whom he had suspected of infidelity while paranoia held him in its grip. Love emerges refreshed, signifying recovery on all fronts.

The use of this particular novel would be impaired without its surprising sequel on the literary scene. To begin with, it had a mixed reception from orthodox critics. As the dawn of a new era was breaking, its psychological veracity was questioned and some found the tale unconvincing, overpopulated, and undermotivated.[13] The surprise was that a powerful voice, Stalin's proxy among the literati, made himself heard in a letter to the author.

Of course, Alexsandr Fadeev[14] takes the novel as life and not as fiction. Using his own impeccable knowledge of what is what, he tells the author of her errors. She had deviated from reality in the depiction of key characters, not too grossly in Fadeev's judgment but enough to warrant his remedial response. Thereupon he offers advice, precise and specific, for the rewriting of erroneous passages and the rectification of key characters. Predictably, he finds the party organizer flat and disembodied. Unpredictably, he comes out in strong support for the manager! This twist warrants a close look.

Nemirov is the first vital and convincing industrial leader in our literature. He is drawn in the process of his development and the strong characteristics of a leader are explicitly shown in him.

So far so good: the author must have been cheered by this. The construction of an inspiring managerial hero represented the foremost engineering task of the postwar writer. Fadeev goes on:

Nemirov would have been even more lifelike if [the party organizer] had been successful. But the latter happens to fall apart into his component elements and one does not see him in the novel as an integrated character.

From this point praise and criticism join in a microscopic warp and woof.

The culmination of the "clash" between Nemirov and [the party organizer] is located and delineated by you *correctly*. But the image of the party organizer at this juncture would have grown immeasurably (and Nemirov's image would have gained from it also) if *before* the clash the party organizer had been drawn correctly.

Now comes the pièce de résistance, which raises our material on daily managerial problems to the level of policy. Fadeev points, inadvertently perhaps, to the fluctuation of the Big Deal at policy level when the working relationship of the two partners comes under scrutiny and definition of their roles is pressing.

You have committed an error which is committed by many. Wishing to show the primacy of *party* leadership, you have from the start placed [the party organizer] in the immodest position of a man who is "teaching" Nemirov, who is even performing certain functions as an organizer of activities which are, in fact, those tied to production. He performs them *despite* Nemirov *or besides him*. This is an error.

The next passage demonstrates the inexorable dependence of middlebrow fiction on the policy of the Big Deal, despite the difficulty of discovering what that policy is. It is hard to find any exegesis as lucid and at the same time as cryptic as Fadeev's:

With few exceptions, the managers of enterprises are, as leaders, bigger men[15] than party organizers. And it is no accident that in industrial centers such as Zaporozhe, Magnitogorsk, Kuznetzk etc., the managers of combines and plants are, without doubt, members of city party bureaux – not the party organizers. If the party organizer happens to be "stronger" than the manager, it is more profitable for the party to make him manager.

This important point is followed by some pious equivocation, worth attention all the same; elucidation of the proper conduct of Big Deal partners toward each other is not easy to come by.

The function of the party organizer is, as political teacher[16] and organizer of the masses, to *assist* the manager. It is also the function of a party "eye." He controls the enterprise in a broad sense. Therefore, good party organizers are first of all modest and tactful in their relationship with the manager. Can you imagine how much more weighty, and truthful *such* a party organizer would seem if his principled stance, despite everything, led him to a *clash* with the manager? . . . By the way, the secretary of the district committee also speaks . . . with Nemirov in a tone which is wrong and false for a party leader communicating with the manager of the largest kind of plant. He talks "down," as if ordering him about, or lecturing him, or mocking him! This is not the proper style for party leadership.

To pile exegesis on exegesis is cumbersome. Nevertheless, we must emphasize Fadeev's deviousness. His exposition pushes the dialectic into the unknown. He does this by setting minor matters next to major ones. Having undertaken to champion the primacy of the manager in the industrial arena and to defend his rights against interference from the local party organization, and having given weight to the manager's fears of emasculation by the party, Fadeev reduces this lack of coherence in the guidelines to a matter of mere style which he finds improperly assessed in the novel. We still do not know whether the regime was prepared to give proper scope to managerial initiative or not. This reduction of the scope of the argument is clear in the minimal – and eminently feasible – suggestion he bestows on the author.

The very "system"[17] of your novel depicts the role and the place of party leadership quite deeply and correctly. And you would do well to remove the unpleasant small traits of condescension in [the party organizer] and [the district party secretary].[18]

Medals on a broad chest

My crowning story concerns one particular type of manager who makes the Big Deal work and who flourishes with it even though he, too, generates discord. The story is difficult to summarize because its focus splits. Yet this makes the hero more convincing, a truly successful and boisterous Big Deal partner who subdues a foil, a sour resister. And the latter requires as much attention. Since both have been widely discussed, they must keep their Russian names: Listopad, the manager, versus Uzdechkin, the chairman of the trade union committee.

The place is a war plant in the Urals; the time is the adjustment of the plant to peacetime production after the war. The significant theme is the revitalization of heavy industry through optimum management.

Both men give all they have to their work. To say that they are dedicated is an understatement. What rational reason can there be for their not cooperating? Only one, and it cannot be considered rational: Uzdechkin hates Listopad. Listopad is a newcomer, a troubleshooter, a miracle man. He comes of peasant stock, and had a brilliant wartime military career, both good signs. Uzdechkin is of local proletarian origin, a man who has grown up with the town's industrial plant. On his return from the war as a wounded veteran, he finds Listopad solidly enthroned in his managerial glory, running his realm with an iron hand. Medals cover his massive chest. His rank as a general, his abundant privileges and appetite for more underscore the social and ideological incompatibility of the two men. From the first day, Uzdechkin considers this Ukrainian a stranger, a careerist and a usurper who prevents him from building communism on classic ideological terms. But most importantly, he hates him for enjoying his managerial power so much and so visibly.

Both men are introduced at a turbulent party meeting. A major event, it involves the entire local party hierarchy and the representatives of the labor force of several plants. In a long-winded speech, Uzdechkin criticizes Listopad in the presence of other managers.

Uzdechkin's face contorts in a tense grimace. He is pale, haggard, and ugly like all sickly and ill-shaven men. And Listopad, who loved everything beautiful, healthy and cheerful, kept glancing at Uzdechkin with disgust.[19]

Nevertheless Listopad listens patiently and reacts to the accusations internally before he replies. His internal rejoinders show neither too much sarcasm nor defensiveness. Nor does he seem embarrassed. In fact, he concedes some of the criticisms. He has no vindictiveness. His strength seems attractively candid and so, even when attacked, he remains above the battle, looking ahead. His method, a formidable one, is unmethodical, free, generous, spontaneous.

Uzdechkin, armed with a long dossier of facts, rants and raves.

"What did I discover when I returned to the plant? I discovered that the plant manager has no contact with the plant committee and does not seek such contact." [Listopad to himself] "You are a liar. First of all you discovered that the plant is overfulfilling its norm month after month. Under the old manager, you lived in the People's Commissariat where you begged and prayed: please lower our norm by fifteen percent, we can't manage, we have no power." [Uzdechkin] "We have, to tell the truth, absolutely no coordination. What we have is only one-man-bossism, or to be more precise, one-man rule, or to be even more precise, the manager's dictatorship." [Listopad to himself] "Look at that, what marvellous precision."

No one present can remember such things being heard at a party meeting. The party secretary and his deputies sit with their eyes glued on the accuser. He presents evidence that the resolutions of twenty technical meetings in the plant have been totally ignored by the manager. Listopad's musings on that one are especially interesting:

Twenty resolutions – that's quite a number. And some of them are most sensible. Heaven knows why indeed they were not followed up? Well, some were dropped because parallel projects were developed by the chief production engineer. And others he simply forgot because of more urgent matters.

Uzdechkin's diagnosis does not lack logic:

"Here is the only possible conclusion: the manager does not listen to the voice of the masses."
"A sad conclusion," thinks Listopad.
"Instead, every single demand of the chief construction engineer is implemented by him instantly as if this were an order from the People's Commissariat."
"Yes, I do take care of the old man. That is very true and I can't deny it."

The engineer in question is a cantankerous old wizard commanding the manager's admiration. But of all the offenses in Uzdechkin's catalogue, favoritism is the worst. His obsolete proletarian idealism, with its egalitarian overtones, clashes with differentiated incentives. The growth of something like feudalism around the potent figure of the manager offends a purist like Uzdechkin. He finds it unbearable that the manager's protégé has been granted permission to work at home. Even if the old man suffers

from rheumatism, it galls Uzdechkin that the entire engineering staff
must make pilgrimages to his private quarters. For Uzdechkin this stands
for capitalist deviation. But Listopad fears, not deviation, but the old
man's retirement, for no better engineer can be found.

Uzdechkin presses on.

"Or let's take this business with the head of the foundry shop, Grushevoi. Our
committee is opposed to his being given awards. The manager, however, deco-
rates him, so to speak, every Friday. I personally expressed myself against his
being given a medal because the workers have a very clear opinion of him.
Grushevoi thinks only of his own advantage. He only wants to get ahead. But the
manager ignores our opinion."

"I am much too busy to be figuring out what Grushevoi has on his mind. His
shop consistently overfulfills its norm and, therefore, I cite Grushevoi for a decoration. It's as simple as that."

Not quite. Accusing Listopad of dictatorial conduct, Uzdechkin makes
three points. First, Listopad does not listen to the "voice of the masses"; he
consults no one, least of all an old-fashioned trade union representative.
He does not care in the least about the trade union and its dwindling
prestige. Second, he has favorites and gives rewards and privileges according to his whim. Thirdly, and by implication, Uzdechkin raises the
complicated question of the function of these rewards. Does the manager
dispense them as a deputy, expressly charged from above to do so for the
greater glory of the Soviet economy, or does he use them largely to but-
tress his own position as a chieftain, which needs the support of subordinates, or at least of some of them? Does the manager, in other words,
express the system's "love for the people" – as Uzdechkin idealistically
craves – or is he busy building a clique?

There is a vast difference between these two purposes. It resembles the
conceptual and ideological gulf between the bolshevik maxim "to each
according to his needs" as against the stalinist principle of merit. And that
is what Uzdechkin is chafing under. Yet from a vertical vantage point, is
there really a contradiction between a "boss" doling out bonuses, even
arbitrarily, and a "deputy" acting on behalf of a goal which transcends the
consolidation of his own power? If there is no overt contradiction, one can
understand better why the Big Deal works and why managers such as
Listopad happen to be key partners.

Competence alone is not enough. And the mere aloofness of a competent person is downright counterproductive. Listopad, however, is a
magnetic personality, and never stands alone. Simply and naively, it
would seem, he lavishes rewards about him in the exhilaration of power.
Uzdechkin's next outmoded accusation bears this out.

"If we need money for our communal cultural or housing projects, the manager
doles it out unwillingly. We have to beg and make the case in all sorts of ways.
But at the same time, the last time they beat the Moscow team, he gave each of our
soccer players a thousand rubles and two thousand to the goal keeper."

To this piece of information, the manager of the neighboring aircraft plant reacts in an eloquent fashion. He quickly turns to the generous potentate under attack and whispers to him in sheer admiration: "No, really? Oh, you devil!"

But Uzdechkin is still not finished. He finds it scandalous that the manager does not differentiate between people who shed their blood for the fatherland and those who have sat out the war in the rear. Very touchy on this point, he also adds that the manager interferes with the last prerogative of the union committee, that of setting up competitive work projects:

"When it comes to the appraisal of criteria, the manager arrives upon the scene and shoves us aside. And those workers whom we choose, remain in the background. But those who please the manager get pushed forward."

At this one point, Listopad loses his self-control and shouts back for the first time:

"That is because I use a different yardstick than you! It's because I judge a person by his work! It's none of my business how many of your committees he is a member of!"

This provokes a general mêlée, sparked by Uzdechkin's fury: "Did you hear that, comrades! The manager does not care about community work!" As the party secretary calls the meeting to order, Listopad uses the interval before his rejoinder for incisive meditation.

Yes, yes, it was all true. He was tyrannical, destructive, manipulative. This was not because of any desire to reign autocratically. It was rather from an unhappy passion to interfere with everything, to get every single thing going with his own hands, whether it was important or not. This, perhaps, was not very reasonable. In fact, it was probably very unreasonable. But what can you do? That was his nature.

And he says to himself consolingly:

But on the other hand, if his conduct was as antisocial and as antiparty as Uzdechkin made out, was it possible that the very same Riabukhin [the plant's party organizer] and the very same Makarov [the district party secretary] would not have warned him about it? Surely, they would have done so.

Active ties with the party and reliance on its wisdom make up this man's treasure, his safeguard.

Just before rising to speak in self-defense, Listopad makes a mental note of how he is to go about it. He must stress the outstanding productivity of the plant. He must make a joke about the soccer team, and the audience must laugh in response. He must mention the many colleagues who, unlike the bitter and the neurotic ones, have adjusted to his methods. And he must drop a delicate and compassionate hint that Uzdechkin's nerves are not quite what they should be. His physical appearance reinforces the impact of his speech.

He ascended the rostrum – tall, broad, with a collection of bright ribbons on his chest. He wore a resplendent general's uniform which fitted closely to his body and which he donned only for official appearances. He was very strong. In spite of it, the expression of his eyes was that of a child. "Comrades," he began with confidence. The communists, the workers' leaders, people who create public opinion in the plant were going to leave this meeting having forgiven their manager his sins and trusting him as before!   [11, pp. 24-6]

And they do.

For all Listopad's self-will, he has a charismatic appeal. His dictatorial exaggerations only make him more attractive, more human, closer to the ideal Russian authoritarian figure. Wisdom, competence, and fairness are not necessarily the most important attributes. Listopad has two qualities of greater value: strength and simplicity. Deeply embedded in real culture, they gratify the collective's expectations of leadership. And as for his faithful subordinates, his sins are not only forgiven but make him more endearing: for he errs from strength and not from weakness. He makes the Big Deal work for him and for those who depend on him. His soul thrives under the arrangement.

Uzdechkin, on the other hand, gets bogged down whenever he starts anything. So, when entrusted with the decorating of the apprentices' dormitory, instead of getting on with it, he waits for the report of a commission. Omniscient, Listopad descends on him in anger:

"You are waiting for a discussion?! What the hell are you going to discuss?! The degree of participation of each of the commission's members or the color to be chosen to paint the roof? Is this housing fit for human beings? You should be forced to live here yourself, comrade chairman of the union committee! Then, instead of worrying about your prestige and instead of intriguing, you would get on with what the workers expect of you! You publicly beat your chest with your fists and scream that I displace you. But it turns out that if I don't take care of the smallest details myself, nothing is done! Devil take you! Who is supposed to take care of washbasins, you or I? I am asking you: you or I?"   [11, p. 79]

Uzdechkin stands for the vestiges – or revival – of the collective process. He gets nowhere, not only here so much because the process is wrong, as because his personality is defective, pinched, sour. He cannot act, even to save his life, as Listopad can, because the values and ways the two men stand for are contradictions in terms: the old versus the new.

Uzdechkin, holding an elective office of no real importance and lacking professional qualifications, craves communion with the people; Listopad, the expert, reigns over them. By bestowing favors, by circumventing "discussion," and even by pushing the slackers around, he builds support for himself from below. He enjoys his authoritarian role fully. And it keeps him so busy that he does not quite notice the misery of his young wife, for whom he has no time. When she dies in childbirth, leaving a near-suicidal diary behind, Listopad is shocked. But his resilience picks him up soon enough. (Author, reader, critic did not seem too upset either.) And he radiates boisterous self-contentment once more. He knows his work and makes others respect it. Without straining, he accomplishes much. This is the key trait in this key character. He easily establishes a cordial relationship with party officials. He submits candidly to their supervision. In recompense, they give him leeway. Up to a point.

Of course, occasionally the party has to have trouble with such a man. The keepers of his soul have to curb his autocratic inclinations since he refuses to do it himself. Disarmingly, he relies on the party for guidance in the finer points of ethics. Unwilling to be burdened personally with the managerial role conflict, Listopad merely passes it on to the party officials above him. They go through certain motions in that sense. He is repeatedly summoned to the party bureau where he is made to see how wrong his handling of the unhappy trade union chairman is. In fact, he is ordered to pacify his enemy.

"Friends!" said Listopad good-naturedly and helplessly, "suppose I have his office painted like marble. He likes marble. But that won't improve his nerves."

He is rebuked for making inappropriate jokes. And when his mentors enumerate his sins to him once more, he blushes to the roots of his hair and remains in that state throughout the painful visit. It happens to be essential that he blush. This assures his inviolablity. If nowhere else, here in intimate confrontation with the authority of the party, he totally relinquishes his own. He gains his immunity by enacting the alternate role, that of humility.

He can and does listen. Reprimands act as purgatives. He is told that he lives too fast and too gregariously. He enjoys his power to such an extent that he can neither see himself, nor take stock, nor learn to endure criticism. He is admonished that, when the full sweep of postwar economic upsurgence has come about, he will find his own method of wartime one-man-bossism entirely inadequate. Understanding the message, Listopad forcefully interrupts, in spite of his flushed cheeks:

"Well, then, give me people who are a bit stronger! People from whom I could learn something!"

To this his party superiors reply as they must. They stress the difference between plant management and party management. Party management faces a special dilemma. It is occasionally stuck with the thrifty role of a humane society or of a conservation agency. And so they say to him:

"Uzdechkin is an honest and selfless worker. A party organization cannot analyze personality traits and tastes. These materials are tenuous and uncertain. But the party organization can and must protect a comrade. You will have to live in peace with this man who has been placed in your orbit by the will of the workers and who has done no wrong."

"All right," said Listopad dryly, "I shall live with him in peace." [12, pp. 38-9]

When he leaves, the party organizer and the party secretary discuss Listopad's virtues. The party organizer has succumbed to his charm with hardly any reservation. He rhapsodizes about his talents, energy, and enthusiasm. The party secretary, taking the broader view, takes them for granted. Instead, he emphasizes something more important.

"Some people work while sacrificing something of their own, something personal. They perform their duty. They perform it with joy, with readiness, with an understanding of our goals. But nevertheless such a person feels every minute that he is performing his duty. People like Listopad, however, sacrifice nothing. They don't even feel that they owe anything. They don't think of duty. They are organically tied to their work, almost physically. You understand, success in their work is their personal success. Failure in work is their personal failure. And not because of careerist considerations, but because outside of work there is no life for him. You understand: for others there is a five-year plan for the plant. But to him it is a five-year plan of his own life, of his destiny, of his very flesh and blood. That's all his goal, his passion, his scope, his gambling, his sweep – everything."

[12, p. 40]

Curiously, Uzdechkin arrives at the same conclusion. With this in mind, we now turn to a memorable verbal duel. It is clear that Uzdechkin cannot possibly make the first step toward reconciliation. Hatred consumes him. So it is Listopad who acts. With paternalistic grandeur, he sends Uzdechkin a gift, as he does to everybody in his domain on the occasion of an approaching holiday. Lush baskets of fruit, delicacies, and good wine are ferried to the apartments of his subordinates by his personal chauffeur.

Uzdechkin looked at the package as if it were a delayed action bomb and he did not know when it would explode. Through the paper he felt the cans, the fruit, the bottle. And suddenly a feeling of burning insult engulfed him. He grabbed the package and ran after the chauffeur.   [12, p. 32]

As far as Listopad is concerned, the basket is the prelude to a move he is about to make. Late at night he descends on Uzdechkin in his dingy quarters. It must be said here that Uzdechkin's wife was killed as an army nurse; that he himself had served his due at the front; that he is left struggling miserably with the raising of two small children; that his helpless old mother-in-law is an additional burden; that his personal life is grim. When Uzdechkin hears the fatal knock at the door and recognizes the voice, his consternation immobilizes him. Listopad enters with a smile and pushes Uzdechkin slightly aside. He makes himself at home and, in fact, demands tea.

"I could give you some tea," said Uzdechkin, "but it looks as if there is nothing sweet to go with it."
"You know what I think!" said Listopad. "One should live in such a way that there are always sweet things about. Without fail."
"Without fail?" Uzdechkin repeated.

After this pointed reference to the full and beautiful life, so pathetically out of reach for Uzdechkin, Listopad decides to break the ice as rapidly as possible.

"What's happening between us? Can you explain it?"

"It's all very clear," said Uzdechkin, "what is there to explain! You have an account to settle with me and I have an account to settle with you. But I have not presented my bill to you yet."

"I haven't either!"

"But you have. You have no restraint, you can't keep anything secret. I know everything you think about me. You think I give little, to the party, to the people. You think that you give much and I give little. And you consider me small, like an insect. Don't argue, I know."

Listopad, to his credit, does not argue. He sits silently for a while. This lets Uzdechkin take breath and continue more firmly.

"That's where it all comes from. What reason do you have to think that I give little? Just because I work quietly? Without noise? I don't need any noise!"

"What do you need?"

"I need much; but only not noise."

"So you think you give the party much? What do you give?"

"Everything!" answered Uzdechkin. "Everything, absolutely everything I have. Should it be necessary to give my last, I will give it. And you? How much do you give? Three-quarters? Half?"

This kind of mathematics turns from rhetoric to something very important; Uzdechkin is about to point to one of the main springs of the accommodation between the regime and the middle class.

Listopad cannot be bested in anything, and least of all in "givingness." He insists:

"But I give everything I can, it seems to me."

"No. Not everything. Do you give all you have? You have more than that!"

"Thanks for the good word. Allow me to consider it a compliment."

"Perhaps, you do give everything," said Uzdechkin pensively, "but you don't feel it. You get so much pleasure in return. It's a good deal for you." [12, pp. 60-1]

After this moment of communication two things happen. Uzdechkin, somewhat implausibly, mellows, at least to the extent that it becomes possible for the omnipotent Listopad to help him. Second, and more plausibly, the two men stop listening to each other and each goes off on a tangent of his own. This is just as well. What we needed from Uzdechkin was his conclusion, stated loud and clear, that the Big Deal was a good deal for a certain type of partner.

There is not an ounce of self-sacrificial asceticism in Listopad. He gives to the system what he takes from it in terms of deep satisfaction. He submits with pleasure. He does so without the pain of calculating the giving, the taking, and the submitting. In this respect he is a new man.

Part Four

Obstacles and Adaptations

10. Defective Party Partners

Difficulties

Let us say right away that the Big Deal worked because both the regime and the people needed it. Some of them needed it badly. Let us, then, also ask how well did it work?

Granted that party and industrial management personnel are the central, primary, active Big Deal partners, this formidable alliance itself affects Soviet society as a whole, both positively and negatively. Conflicts engendered by the Big Deal inevitably spill out. The best manager, for example, does not always manage to obtain full gratification from his work. The regime does not always succeed in selecting a model partner. Therefore, some difficulties should be seen as institutional, others as generated by the sense of self of the people at work. Some are intrinsic to the Big Deal, others result from pressures on it of the entire social order.

All work always implies the existence of some obstacle, some problem. By its inclination to distrust the working partner, the regime created specifically Soviet problems. Because of the regime's ambivalance toward the producing partner, the recruitment of productive forces, *sine qua non*, found itself in a double bind. Relentless control is not compatible with individual initiative. Docility was a requirement, yet docility inhibits any energetic partner's sense of achievement. Still, the regime wanted the producing partner content. And I contend the human chemistry of postwar reconstruction, obviously more complex than its economic dimension, had induced the regime to recognize that the producing partner had to be granted workable breathing space. If the post war incentives were to be reinforced, recruitment of productive citizens had to be facilitated and opened up. The important question, therefore, is whether the regime's rapprochement with its middleclass ally proved flexible enough to let more people in.

Consummated not on an island and not in mid-air but remedial and interlocked with other social issues, partnership was predicated not only on the choice of individuals and types but on an evolving relationship with the entire population. Some were in, some were out. Some would make it, some never would. Difficult citizens impinged on the Big Deal, for either they did not work out when invited or they did not want to be invited. One way or another, they either made trouble or elicited adaptation.

Several types of citizens were difficult to handle: first, those who had turned into defective partners and, secondly, key spokesmen of those strata of the population, particularly the intelligentsia, which had been excluded from the Big Deal.

Obstacles ranged from fear and fatigue to centrist indifference and to revulsion against manipulation by the regime. There were those who did not help because they confused old beliefs with the regime's new desiderata or failed to rearrange their own priorities. There were those who obstructed by having neither beliefs nor priorities but were merely hangers-on. There were those who championed the cause of intellectual independence. And there were those who hinted at the expansion of the Big Deal on more equitable populist tracks.

It seems the regime responded by distinguishing between obstacles and pressures. The former were pushed out of the way as dead weight. The latter were handled more gingerly. Some adaptations to expanding social goals were not ruled out.

Outdated convictions

At the end of the last chapter, Uzdechkin had accused Listopad of reaping personal benefits from the Big Deal. "It's a good deal for you." Uzdechkin's obsolete idealism makes him angry, not envious. His words are both too sweeping and too helpless when he speaks with fervent yearning: "I want happiness for every man, I want a bright life for everyone."[1] Such a timeless dream surely issues from the stark divide between the haves and the have-nots. In reply, Listopad had simply steered away from the issue of injustice by ridiculing Uzdechkin for his obtuseness about the new life. One should not longer fail to surround oneself with comforts and sweet things, if one can.

A similar counterpositioning occurs in another story, *Great Art*, in which it is shown that an old believer, in a confrontation with the workings of the Big Deal, is bound to lose not only to a model manager like Listopad but even to a scroundrel. This is dramatic evidence of just how outdated the proletarian posture had become. The setting is an automotive plant in the Urals. The brutal manager

bullied, crushed, stamped on everybody under him. He paid no attention to the decisions of the party committee nor to the opinions of the party organizer.[2]

The poor adversary here, the plant's party organizer, resembles Uzdechkin. He, too, is tired and damaged, but considerably more meek. A nervous tic of the eyelid is his special characteristic. Although "of crystalline purity and honesty," he is entirely unsuitable for the job since he

did not possess enough experience as a party organizer to forsee in time an inevitable disaster. In his earlier years he had worked in the komsomol. Later he had
entered the institute where he ended with the title of engineer. Later he had
fought the Nazis before Moscow. He was shellshocked there and the result of that
injury was the tic in his eye.   [p. 16.]

Obviously, of little consequence in fighting the manager, he is thwarted
in every effort, especially those made on behalf of the welfare of the workers. Comrade Meek stakes all he has on a long-awaited housing project for
the workers, for which there is a crying need. The manager crushes the
very idea. Thereupon, at long last, Comrade Meek pens a letter to the
central committee, pushing the tale to its climax. The chief engineer, a
true friend to Comrade Meek, since he suffers equal emasculation by the
manager, shrivels up at the news of the audacious letter.

His whole figure shrank and he said, in a voice which for some strange reason
turned creaky and senile: "You should not have sent it. There will be a scandal
again. And we will not achieve anything anyway. He is powerful. Behind him
stand three thousand eight hundred automobiles beyond and above the norm."

As this fatalistic apprehension is voiced, the phone rings. The regional
party secretary is there in person on his awe-inspiring private line. The
way in which this powerful functionary mediates between the adversaries
is our pièce de résistance. One might well harbor misgivings about his
fairness.

"I have just finished reading the copy of your letter to the central committee. You
state the facts correctly. But you put it badly. This is, of course, a sign of nerves,
to which you and I are not permitted to succumb. I suggest that you think carefully about the following. Once upon a time we had specialists. Some of them
adjusted and even became important people. Others evaporated into nothing.
This manager is a modern specialist."

Comrade Meek, "failing to curb his anger," interjects that this brilliant
modern specialist happens also to be a member of the party and should act
accordingly. This makes no impression on the party secretary, who goes
on:

"Consider that in our country there are different approaches to the working class.
There are some people who have a drooling love-the-workers mania. 'Darlings,
sweethearts!' That's a rat's love!"
  "Why a rat's love?"
  "When a rat gives birth to little rats, it begins to lick them. And sometimes it
licks them with such zeal that they start bleeding. Sensing the smell of the blood,
the rat devours its brood. That's why these people with their drooling love for the
workers remind me of the love of a rat. It's the most nauseating thing in the
world."   [p. 61]

So much for the once-canonized hope of "to each according to his
need." Taken aback by the metaphorical power of this attack, the meek

rat-lover who had merely tried to get houses for his little rats, wants to know where the ruthless manager fits into the sermon.

"I will talk about him later. But there are other people. And they are the majority. They think that the workers, together with the peasants and the Soviet intelligentsia, make up the basis of our society. These people can see not just the predominant, the positive qualities in the working class. They can see the blemishes from the past as well. And they realize that these blemishes must be conscientiously, skillfully, and carefully removed. These blemishes, as you and I should know, are removed not only by pedagogical and propagandist means, but also by creating the material base for a socialist society. It follows, therefore, that a real manager – whether he is producing tanks, lathes, automobiles, sugar or textiles – is the one who is building socialism. Of course, not just by himself, but together with the collective. Inseparable."   [pp. 44-6]

The nail was driven in with a quotation from Stalin.

It all comes down to the following. The blemishes of the past were taken on when the revolution proposed to build the new society primarily by means of an egalitarian ideology, feeding all the little rats pedagogy and propaganda. This is wrong. There can be no socialist society without a material base and no material base without managerial expertise. At this point Comrade Meek is left behind.

Talmudism

Excessively compassionate old believers found themselves out of step with the new ways of doing business. Another type of party functionary, the talmudist, came under more severe attack shortly before Stalin's death. The old believer has too much fervor for equity for the masses, but talmudists have no beliefs at all. They embarrassed the regime because their conduct, rather than their convictions, had become outdated. The pedantry and squeamishness, the rigidity and cowardice characterizing the talmudist were an obstacle which had to be removed.

One such Comrade Talmudist has worked himself up to the position of party secretary in a foundry. He succeeds because of an alliance with the manager who treats him as an underling. Because of his talmudic "accuracy, precision, and above all caution," the manager trusts him and they become inseparable. His career justifies his subservience and strategy.

At one point of his professionless course, he is transferred to this foundry from the "commercial sector," a bad sign. At first he is assigned to the bookkeeping department, another bad sign. Himself ignorant of accounting, the manager relies on this servile clerk. How, then, does the clerk rise to the position of party secretary? How does he come to rule over others? Long ago he had

dreamed of becoming a good party worker. For a long time he had considered himself well prepared for it. For several years he had worked as propagandist in party study groups. And he had accumulated eighty-two notebooks with outlines.

Much of the material and much of what had been said on this or that question on this or that page he knew almost by heart.[3]

In due time he is elected to the party bureau. There was indeed opposition to his candidacy. But the manager's influence overcomes it. And when the party secretary is relocated elsewhere, Comrade Talmudist takes over with "his famous notebooks lying in a neat pile on the desk under his right arm."

He proceeds by making himself indispensable to the manager. Flattering him, he suppresses grumbling from below, by being excessively punitive towards the young party members. He supervises their party studies and fails them whenever he can. In the long run, this is the worst thing he does. It is his very mastery of the marxist-leninist-stalinist scriptures which leads him astray, for he forgets that this had long been superseded by demands for organizational skills, of which of course he has none. He remains in essence a clerk.

Initially, no one feels secure enough to stand up to him. He sports a pince-nez and a military jacket. Entitled to the first as sign of obsolete bookishness, he has no right to the second. Even his patron drops the remark that "everybody knows that he has never been at the front" (p. 134).

Things become difficult when the workers begin to show discontent at the rule of silence imposed on them by the duumvirate. They induce a young worker in charge of the wall newspaper to draw a caricature entitled "the funeral of criticism and self-criticism" in which the pallbearers unmistakably resemble the manager and his henchman. Furious, Comrade Talmudist tears the paper off the wall. The cartoonist bursts into the office. Scolded for "political hooliganism," the young man defends his right to defend the truth. Comrade Talmudist threatens to throw him out of the party. Livid with rage, "his face contorted in a grimace of pain and hopeless despair," the young man pulls his party card out of the breast pocket and flings it on the table in front of "these hateful eyes, these cold eyes behind the pince-nez" (p. 22).

Of course, the fervent young man plays his hand wrongly. The party chastizes him for being reckless with the holy token, especially since the villain capsizes in the faraway last chapter, as he is bound to. At long last, a sound party official prepares to act against him with the following diagnostic thoughts:

"You work, Comrade Talmudist, from nine to five. With precision you use the one-hour rest period to enjoy a tasty lunch and with a smile on your face you repeat what you have learned so well: 'Forward! On to communism!' And you wait for communism. In your opinion, it's about to fall from the skies into your lap. But should one ask you what you need communism for, you couldn't even answer. You are preparing yourself for it in the manner of a person preparing himself in the winter for the summer, a person who does not sow, does not harvest, does not struggle with the snow. He orders himself a summer suit and that's it."   [p. 154]

Retribution is on its way now. Comrade Talmudist is unseated as the plant's party secretary but retains his membership in the bureau. As soon as he gets into trouble, his partner lets him carry the can. This makes the comrade remember with bitterness how during the war he had furnished the managerial table with black-market pork. It transpires, too, that Comrade Talmudist seduces eager office girls galore. In choice restaurants, he laces the girls' wine with tales of his wife's failure to understand him. Unfortunately for him she understands him only too well and denounces him for his adultery. Meshchanstvo turns in on itself.

Party corruption grows into a vast theme[4] – a premature litany for Stalin – in which obsolete propagandists, branded now as talmudists, corrupt and obstruct. Their oratory, the means by which the masses were to be guided, was advocated by Stalin himself. This is the one canon to which the above parasite adheres. He also looks for the protective armor of the enterprise to which he contributes nothing. Ritual is his game.

The bureaucratic cancer began to strangle the entire middle range of the party structure. The talmudists turned out to be deeply systemic and hard to get rid of. This is shown by a regional party secretary commiserating with a functionary under his command who has travelled a long way to complain about an obstructionist at his own lower level. Meaning to console, the important party official observes:

"We too have our babblers. And how! Yours are pygmies compared to ours! Ours are veritable champions of vacuity! Classics!"

And he sketches a vivid portrait of such a champion in action:

"You ask him at a bureau meeting to give his opinion about the personal action of a comrade, let us say. He stands up with thunder and lightning, with fierce intonations, with violent gestures and piercing glances. If you listened to him from a distance, you would think he was uttering a death sentence. But all he is doing is to suggest that the comrade be 'informed.' He has Savonarola's voice, but his tone suggests he is a liberal conniving with degenerates. Or we discuss the question whether we should or should not agree with the ministry in regard to some project . . . And again he will deliver in front of the stenographer an oration which later on, if anything goes wrong, can be interpreted this way or that way. Should we be unable to fulfill in time and they set out to get our scalps, he will say: 'I warned you that we might be accused of irresponsibility! Here it is in the record!' If we are praised for speedy work, he will latch on to that too. He was 'for,' by and large! He will even try to shove his name into the list submitted for decorations. Artists!"

The concluding remarks about the entrenchment of these artists are pessimistic. The system, the source of corruption in the first place, is stuck with them for a good while.

"It's awfully hard to dethrone such artists. They are experienced and they are equipped with an immaculate biography. They have an imposing manner, and they can point to many years of responsible work. And they are well connected. Unfortunately, even in our time, you can't do without protection. Many a one of them has a friend or a brother-in-law sitting in some high-up office. If you touch him – telegrams, telephone calls: 'Submit an explanation! On what grounds?!' If you manage to prove that he is a nonentity, an unprincipled, excuse the expression, snot, and should you be able to get rid of him, you look around and in a short time he emerges in some other region in the very same capacity!"[5]

Requiring ritualistic conduct, the Big Deal begins to attack those who hide behind the ritual. Lip service to the catechism, and piggyback riding on the productivity of others begin to be disclosed, as if for the first time, as reprehensible.

Stalin's homunculi felt threatened by the Big Deal.[6] In office yet insecure, they feared any change. To say that they closed ranks, even figuratively, carries the wrong suggestion. Actively, they did no such thing. How could they have? Passively, by trying to hang on, they became a very great nuisance. They had to be left behind sooner or later; but it was not easy.

11. Professionals Make Trouble

Dr. Ulcer

Others who join in obstructing the Big Deal in their own manner include disgruntled professionals who are either worn out by difficult working conditions or have been damaged by a lack of understanding of their standards. One such doctor wears himself out during the war in sleepless devotion to his patients. He heads a Leningrad front-line hospital. With a Jewish name, the doctor is highly strung, nervous, quarrelsome. The care of wounded pilots is the only goal of his lonely life. Gruff, irritable, difficult, he is totally selfless.

But a proper hero is not now free to let his life become "inseparable from work." Nor does it help him at all that he is a bachelor. This condition shows defectiveness of various categories, private and public, from population depletion to frivolous egotism. None of this fits the good doctor who is rather a Chekhovian vestige. Nonetheless, abdicating his personal needs, this doctor's very humanitarianism, incisive and ulcer ridden, makes the people round him uncomfortable, which is bad. His conscience assumes an independent posture, and that is worse.

Frustrations over difficult working conditions cause him to shout at nurses and subordinate doctors. He thinks particularly poorly of one assistant whom he considers cold and calculating, the very embodiment in fact of that meshchanstvo which he abhors. The feud between the two is long and bitter. The assistant manages to commit two gross misdeeds in one day. Examining a wounded pilot in front of a nurse, he removes the patient's blanket and exposes his nakedness. Then he casually and ruthlessly informs another patient about his hopeless heart condition. Both acts enrage Dr. Ulcer. He doubts the assistant's disinterestedness in studying medicine, writing a dissertation, and becoming a practitioner. He has him on the carpet.

"I want you to tell me what led you to take up the medical profession."

"I refuse to answer such questions."

"I knew you would refuse. You are looking for insults everywhere. You are not a very discerning fellow. Listen, today I found out that you are a doctor's son."[1]

Professionals demand a great deal from each other because their responsibilities intertwine inexorably and the hierarchical rigidity is such that the superior indeed answers for his subordinate in every way. In this instance, it is Dr. Ulcer's own sensitivity that has been exacerbated and he retaliates, unfairly enough, by bringing up guilt by association. The culprit's father had been a family doctor in "the magnificent city of Kursk." Dr. Ulcer deduces he had treated hysterical ladies and merchants with religious manias to make money, to cultivate primordial meshchanstvo, and to feather the nest for his son.

"And so your dear father, an honorable doctor from Kursk, advises his son to study medicine. Do it, he says. You will suffer for four years, but I have planted the garden and you will reap the fruit. Isn't that so? You will enter my business. Did you never have such a conversation? Didn't you?"   [pp. 77-8]

Without waiting for an answer, Dr. Ulcer suggests that he would have done better at building bridges or keeping books in a wholesale grocery. Frightened, the adversary insists that he has managed very well in the past in running his own clinic. For Dr. Ulcer that is the last straw. He now stamps his feet in fury.

"To hell with your clinic and your idiotic prestige! And to hell with the lectures you used to give! I could spit on your smugness! Yes, to hell with it all! We still have altogether too many gentlemen with blown-up scientific titles. And nobody can force me to stand to attention in front of a mere title. Any nurse means more to me than the fact that you are a professor. At some time you have written some rubbish or other. But just the same, sooner or later, life will take away all your documents from you and you will be left standing just as you are. I don't care what kind of clinic you once had! I work with you and I know you are a bad doctor... You and I are no longer members of a physician's guild where one covers up for the other. Will you remember this?"   [p. 79]

The climber from Kursk will remember, if only for purposes of retaliation. Dr. Ulcer threatens to get rid of him. But can he? Who will get whom is the question. In this serialized story the reader is left in suspense at this point.

Actually the trouble with Dr. Ulcer is twofold. First, he is trapped by his own obsolete ascetic style. Second, he copes badly with the transition from war to peace. It is now required that he bow to the prestigious latifundium of a clinic. Carrying on the purist intelligentsia's struggle with meshchanstvo after the war had become a mistake; so, Dr. Ulcer was considered by his critics a neurotic troublemaker and a crank who, hanging on to his hospital as a substitute for happiness, should no longer be permitted to assail prestigious success in others.

It is true that the tale did not quite express all this at the time, for the reason that only the first half of it was published. The conclusion was suppressed. In the next but one issue of the embattled journal *Zvezda*, the author confessed. He had to. He was a member of the journal's editorial board. The rest of the board engaged in public self-castigation separately, but on the same page.

"My story was subjected to just and principled criticism by the readers. It was pointed out that the main hero... lives locked up in his narrow small world, totally submerged in his suffering and that such a person has no right to be called a positive hero."[2]

The trouble that befell the author establishes that disgruntled professionals could cause a great deal of unrest.

Cooled-off engineer

In the midst of a busy crowd laying an oil pipeline through the tundra during the war (with labor not altogether free, one presumes... but the author does not go into that), an engineer of national fame stops functioning. Let us call him Torpor. He is a thorn in the eye of the troubleshooting team flown in from Moscow. Reduced to the rank of assistant to the new chief of construction, he just sits, refusing to cooperate: "Enough! I have done more than my share."[3] Curiously, the spunky young boss protects the "old loafer," as the awesome new chief of the entire enterprise calls Torpor, from being fired. The young man, it turns out, is right. Torpor deserves consideration. The author points out that his greenish mustache is like that of Maxim Gorky. With such an attribute a person cannot be all bad. And, of course, he is not. Heartsearching takes place under his icy surface; the internalized plot is vivid; Torpor's fever, caused by a bad cold, provokes a large-scale confessional dream. In it, according to the pattern for tortured, almost-positive characters, Torpor gives an account of his life to an alter ego. In his militant youth he used to have a militant friend, who later became a famous general and who was killed in the defense of Moscow. It is the cherished spirit of the dead general that sets out to interrogate him:

"Rumors have reached us that you have cooled off... Is it true, Kuzma?... It's hard to believe that you have forgotten the oath which we swore together fifteen years before the revolution... They say that you have grown fat, Kuzma, even though you seem lean."

He accuses the defendant of "philistine contentment," of having become "a clerk whose world has shrunk to the size of a desk and of two filing cabinets."

The answer does not come easily, because an issue is probed which is usually left submerged, that of a revolutionary's devout commitment to the system and the eventual decline of his fervor. Torpor confesses that

having "followed the revolution at her first call," and having worked and
strained selflessly all his life, he does not now, at sixty, understand what
happened to his "faith in high ideals." His mind flails about in an area
which is penumbral to start with:

"Wait, friends. Give me time. Life has gone on at unheard-of speed. The country
compressed entire centuries into several five-year plans. And the torrent was
carrying me too. On the strength of my work, I didn't go under. But is it possible
that I haven't given all I was capable of?"

The general, a simple fellow as alter egos tend to be, pounces on the
perennial "giving" according to the catechism (no longer, incidentally,
entirely satisfactory either to partners or opponents of the Big Deal):
contributing to the glory of Soviet society is synonymous with breathing.
This, alas, does not help Torpor, who continues to grope for the cause of
his backsliding. But at a certain point, he casually juxtaposes two key
pronouns:

"Even in the past it became clear to me at some moment that the actual results do
not correspond with the plans, with the idealism of youth. Almost unconsciously
I wanted a rest, no matter how brief, to collect my thoughts, to readjust fully.
Life did not grant me any respite. I kept on travelling to some new place. And I
was building and building. They spurred me on and I spurred on others. The
tempo became more and more rapid. War brought it to its limit. And suddenly
the test period was there – for me, for the general, for everybody. The general
passed the test. Glory to him. But as for me – "

This lament shows that the forcing of human energy undercuts the sense
of participation in collective goals, and that sooner or later a separation
takes place between "them" and "us," the forcers and the forced.

The general demands that Torpor find a way out. Instead, Torpor
capitulates.

"There is no way out! I gave up! I am no good any more for requests like 'Urgent.
Exceedingly urgent. Immediately. This instant.' I am good for the reserves only.
Or rather, I am good for nothing at all. Old age has come. Do you understand or
don't you? Old age. And I surrender my place in life to a youngster, a representative of the new tribe."   [pp. 109-11]

This author happens to be a scrupulously safe author. But even his
species responds to the mysterious sovereignty of fiction. If a character is
left at night to fend for himself, something worthwhile can come out, and
indeed does here: "It became clear to me that the actual results do not
correspond with the plans." The gap between goals and means is at least
alluded to. And idealists are likely to be devoured by the emphasis on
means.

But Torpor understands more than that. He knows a way out, if not for
him. He knows that one does not have to stumble into this gap between
goal and achievement. At least one obvious alternative offers itself: leave
the problem strictly alone. With its rewards, the Big Deal takes care of the

gap. The chosen partner need not worry. In fact, he *must* not.

Torpor goes on to forecast, perceptively if malevolently, the consequence of this mandatory absolution for the productive citizen from thinking too hard about this, or about any other, gap. Torpor forecasts that that zealous young chief of his will sooner or later be overpowered too by overwork and unmanageable stress. More and more assignments will be hurled at the young man – reports, blueprints, estimates, rush projects, crises. He will be glued to the telephone. He will be forced to make endless pilgrimages to the authorities. He will be pressed to "coordinate" the impossible. He will sit endless hours in conferences, and he will rush about on endless trips. He will always feel as if he was running to put out a fire, and he will always know that he is too late everywhere. Fatigue will overcome him too. Torpor is sure of that. The Young Turk will cool off, in due time. The old man relishes the vindictive thought. He also projects the alternative.

"An indifferent attitude toward work will show itself. He will get used to wine, cards, and empty pastimes. And the trouble, of course, will not be in the pastimes themselves but in that they will give him much more pleasure than work. And he will more willingly give his time to gossip than to ardent and lofty discussions. And maybe he will get married and together with his wife he will start greedily to acquire all sorts of petty belongings: chests of drawers, victrolas, dresses, fur pieces. He will buy a motorcycle in order to rush madly along dusty roads for the sake of vivid sensations. Or else he will acquire a camera to take pictures of photogenic acquaintances, or a shotgun to kill both ducks and time. In other words, he will think of something to amuse himself in his leisure hours. Therefore, from some fateful day onward, he will begin to pile up uncut technical journals behind the stove. And in the end, he will forget to renew the subscription."

In the end also, Torpor predicts, the Young Turk's talent will wilt "like an organism touched by cancer." The capacity to create will be lost. For a disease more serious than cancer will make its inroad, "self-satisfaction and contentment." The Young Turk

"will become insensitive to what might be called the remote perspective. He will be attracted only by the close one. Or, rather, the immediate perspective will cover up the remote one. He will forget the oath of youth, if he ever made it, the oath of constant progress, not to become complacent, to grow, to learn, and to do more and better than yesterday."   [pp. 113-14]

Torpor is not unwise. He knows that the pressures of the system, if they do not kill the citizen, are excessive in two ways. They exhaust the devout builders and make them withdraw. A certain type of builder, less devout, may opt, on the other hand, for a vastly different escape. Unburdened by long-term idealism, and with the permission of the regime, he may escape into the safety of provincial meshchanstvo. So two escapes beckon: the sorry introspection of an idealist gone sour, and the far more cozy corner of the duck-shooting middle magnate. In fact, the regime does not care one way or another about the likes of Torpor, and simply leaves them behind. It is only in particularly compulsive middlebrow fiction that such men are rehabilitated in a trumpet-blaring finale to enjoy a heroic death. Elsewhere, they fall by the wayside through attrition. Although Torpor's prophecy of parasitism should cause concern, it is only in the long run that it can become massively pertinent. Besides, shortly after the war, Torpor's disgruntled vision was related to a vision rather than reality. Ducks, guns, and victrolas were still at that time only a promise for the average citizen.

Melancholic bungler

The next protagonist neither engages in combat like Dr. Ulcer, nor does he have visions. But, in his quiet way, he deserves his pivotal position because of the surprising end to his troubles which shows the kind of flexibility the Big Deal was manifesting.

He is a middle-aged engineer from Leningrad, where the intelligentsia is known to incline toward nonconformism. Having lost his wife during the siege, he has been recently discharged from active military service and evacuated to the hinterland. At first sight, he seems demoralized. On his arrival in a faraway provincial place, Bungler does not report to the shop in which he is demeaningly to work as engineering assistant. Instead, he stays in bed. This irritates the landlady, who notices that his suitcase contains neither underwear nor a spare pair of trousers but is stuffed rather with nuggets of ore and blueprints. The man works in bed from dawn to dawn at mysterious calculations.

When he finally crawls out of bed to assume his duties, he makes the loud and rough manager angry. That young man, for one, knows what is what. He does not care that his strange new underling is not only an engineer but a scientist. He compares him unfavorably with a pushy foreman, "a cheat and a liar" whom he finds "incomparably more useful in the shop." Furthermore, Bungler's appearance violates kulturnost. The manager

could no longer calmly look at this wilted and degraded engineer, at his dirty windjacket, at his trousers which fell accordion fashion over his felt boots, at his fur cap with perpetually unfastened earflaps. He was irritated with the man's slowness. It seemed that all his energy was spent on his personal internal life... that [he] was not giving all of himself to the shop and that his thoughts were preoccupied with something else. [4]

Bungler's thoughts cling to Leningrad, mourning his wife and his work.

Of bygone days there remained only tense meditations about his invention which had already taken so many years of his life. Now these thoughts supported him and gave him a reason for existence. Even before the war, only in work, only in his laboratory, did he have any sense of satisfaction and a feeling of life's fullness. Outside his work everything was unreal to him.   [p. 46]

He is devoted to his own scientific work. The collective, however, cannot accept him because his external appearance lowers the status of a professional. The young manager snaps: "Nothing strange about him. He is a bungler and a melancholic. I can't stand such people."(p. 45). Nor can anybody else.

He needs the assistance of an electrician for his experiments. The latter treats him rudely. Incensed at this, Bungler at last raises his voice in complaint. Authority and status must be upheld. So, the manager does indeed reprimand the electrician on Bungler's behalf. But, alone with Bungler, he sneers:

"Doesn't it ever occur to you to consider what you look like with your stuffed chest? Workers cannot respect you like that. You are sinking lower and lower. Some en-gi-neer!"   [p. 47]

Salvation is on its way, though. The party organizer decides to transfer Bungler from the shop to the more congenial atmosphere of a laboratory. Suddenly fascinated with Bungler's project, which involves research into hard metals, high on any official's list, he is now indignant at the callousness with which the cocky young manager has neglected Bungler in every way. In turn, Bungler regains his voice. And he proves perceptive in the assessment of his adversary:

"He is a natural pragmatist and regards my theoretical research with the greatest skepticism. At first he looked me over, but when I was assigned to his shop and he evidently did not find useful qualities in me from his own point of view, he stopped being interested in me altogether because it was clear that whatever I am doing, he cannot use it this very minute in the fulfillment of his shop's program."
                                                                    [p. 61]

So, at first, the loneliness of a displaced widower generates misgivings in the community, instead of compassion. The damaged individual has a hard time, no matter what the catechism says, and the Big Deal was not designed for the likes of him. But this is not what the tale is really about. Bungler turns out to be a scientist, on a small scale and a loner, but a scientist nonetheless, who sticks to his obsession with research, all alone with no deals, no rewards. When at last the party comes around to recognizing his worth, the adversary snarls sarcastically, feeling threatened by the change of attitude: "Oh, I understand, attention to research, attention to rationalized operations, - politics! I understand" (p. 62). Yes, he understands correctly, almost prophetically. What else would explain the consideration Bungler suddenly gets, along with the acceptance of his eccentricities. Whoever else the regime is willing to shortchange for the sake of the Big Deal, it *is* solicitous about scientists. In the long run, there were to be even more concessions for them. This does not mean, however, that serious issues did not cloud and confuse the relationship between the regime and the academy. Disputes about educational policies and about the price of professionalization and specialization lay just beneath the surface. And the regime's distaste for "internal emigrés" – the puritans, the obsessive, the loners – became part of its huge and insoluble conflict with the intelligentsia.

Something of the intensity of this struggle can be felt, curiously, in a rather casual and relaxed story about a very young man obsessed with what he is doing. He might be thought of as Bungler's younger brother. Yet the difference between the men and their stories is instructive. Because of Bungler's age, achievement and idiosyncrasies, he may be rejected or accepted as he is. The young man in the next story makes trouble, real trouble, for he is not an accident but an obligation. He must first be retrieved from his isolationism, and he must then be properly socialized.

Diesel engine addiction

An ensign enrolls in a naval engineering academy. Combining the stubbornness of an intellectual with a touch of military pride, he makes an interesting hybrid, and commits himself passionately to his specialty. Unlike most freshmen, he adjusts quickly to military discipline. The uniform fits his figure and his sense of self. Against tradition, even the seniors treat him with respect. "Graceful in his movements, meticulous, elegant," he knows how to order champagne in a nightclub. He seems a playboy and yet he is not. Reciting Pushkin's verse, he sometimes makes mistakes, "but in what the ensign called his basic business, he never erred." And that is the study of the diesel engine.

Endowed with an extraordinary memory, he acquires knowledge easily. This arouses envy in his fellow students. Yet, he has friends, at least one or two. And he is downright worshipped by one shy and clumsy young man. But there is no doubt that he causes controversy about his learning habits, which involve the tug-of-war between general and special knowledge. And it grows, by implication, into a debate about self-education. The ensign strives to function effectively. He thinks he knows how to go about it, and he is challenged on precisely that point, on his independence. Acknowledging his ability to grasp every required subject with equal ease, a fellow student accuses him of being narrow in his interests. "Precisely," the ensign replies. "Can everything you study be equally interesting?" This admission turns back on him. The opponent suggests that in discriminating between subjects, the ensign is betraying an interest in an unworthy end, in passing examinations only. The ensign insists that, for a specialist, there is a difference between indispensable and supplementary knowledge, and he must discard the latter when its use, as in passing exams, is exhausted. The fellow student proves obstinate:

"I don't understand such a division of knowledge into the real and formal kind. I don't understand, for instance, how you can know what may be useful to you and what you can throw out."

"My business is to study diesel engines," [the ensign] suddenly becomes heated. "Should I, as you recommend, assimilate everything I learn, my main business would suffer. But I shall never lose interest in it. Isn't that clear?" [5]

The opponent maintains indignantly that the ensign would not have the courage to repeat his views to "anyone else."

"Why?"

"Because what you say is absurd and basically wrong. You are arguing for an artificial distinction between useful and useless knowledge."

"I want you to know that I would certainly have the courage to say it to anyone, no matter who he is. And I shall be able to defend myself."   [p. 88]

When independence collides with authority, the former must lose. Even to argue tentatively on its behalf is imprudent. But prudence cannot always be a panacea either. To keep going, the system must encourage initiative among the young, even if it is clouded by fears of independence. But how? The ensign swims against the stream. Most of his peers do not understand him. The faculty distrusts him. One lieutenant colonel criticizes him with particular energy. He denigrates him by calling his high marks shallow "numerical" achievements. The ensign, in turn, refuses to accept the image of himself as a robot.

"Well, is there a field which absorbs all your attention and all your time?"

"Yes, there is, comrade lieutenant colonel. And I love it very much."

"I know. It's the diesel engine. Have you any love left over for anything else?"

"Of course, I don't have enough of the same kind of love for other things. How could it be otherwise?"

"Don't be a hypocrite. Be honest. For the rest you don't have any love at all. Not a drop."

"But I do all that is demanded of me."

The ensign realizes at once that he has made a strategic mistake and tries to correct himself. But the lieutenant colonel does not let him.

"Don't try to convince me now. You were being frank. That's why you are worried. You do everything, indeed. That cannot be denied. Your marks are excellent. But what's behind them? Only a diesel engine. If your diesel engine bars the world from you, you will soon cease to understand what the diesel engine is for and why we need more of them."   [p. 90]

The diesel engine addict cannot be accused of infatuation with impractical goals. But this makes no difference: he is suspect. The plot demands that eventually he is harmed by his own addiction. But first he falls into the hands of a villain.

The ensign begs his superiors to let him go and visit a diesel engine institute. There he meets a research engineer who is impressed by the young man. The two become fast friends. The flashy expert takes his new protégé to his laboratory and acquaints him with his work. Soon the gullible ensign spends all his leaves in his affluent friend's apartment. Called endearing names, he is driven around in the private car of this man, who is engaged in consultancies all over the country. He offers the ensign a share in the enterprise. The ensign accepts. One lazy Sunday afternoon, reclining in an easy chair, the shady character engages in intimate talk.

"My dear friend, in the course of the week I have so many lectures, so many consultations that all I can do on Sunday is to watch pigeons and play cards. Do you play cards? You should get into the habit. Winter evenings on a ship are long."
     "For long evenings they recommend I do something entirely different."

The authorities recommend that he "enlarge his horizon." This produces merriment in the consulting engineer. He " laughed long and loud."

"So they have caught up with you, young man, have they? So that's what they recommend? And very strongly at that? I can't agree with them at all. Well, how can we, we specialists, become harmonious people? We should rather see to it that we do justice to our expertise. And after that we should be permitted to amuse ourselves, to stretch our bones, to dress up a bit. Who can prove that a diesel engine specialist needs poetry? However, listen, why do they suddenly become so serious? I have noticed this in many of them."

And now he proffers advice, the kind that oils the wheels of any deal. He leans confidently over and whispers:

"You know what? Don't argue against these truths. They say all these things. Well, let them. You should agree with them. It isn't difficult, is it? That way it will be much more peaceful. It's only a conditional agreement. It does not bind you to anything serious."

The suggestion makes the ensign uncomfortable. The other adds soothingly:

"All this concerns, of course, only your most intimate personal life. Some day you will figure it out yourself. What's the point in bruising yourself on sharp corners?"   [p. 92]

     Villains frequently serve to lift the curtain on startling matters. And here it is, the gaping vastness of the no-man's-land. It is populated by shrewd experts, the growing ranks of professional meshchanstvo. They avoid the sharp corners, they master the system's loopholes, the most commodious being the system's inclination to leave them to their cards, cars, and drink. Instead, the regime presses down on the loners, the hedgehogs, who wish to go it alone.
     The surveillance of the ensign tightens. The political department notices his absences. The party organization summons him. He is informed that the "private shopkeeper" he is consorting with cheats "stupid laymen" by making them pay fees for his worthless consultations and that the ensign himself has been exploited by the crook, getting only a pittance from the lucrative racket. He is not told yet the full measure of his punishment. This remains ominously in the air .

"Well, what can they do? What can happen to me now? My dissertation! That's what will get me out of trouble."   [p. 102]

The thought comforts him. He chooses a difficult topic and plunges into it. After a dazzling defense, he earns the final grade of "excellent."

The fictional material pulls one way and the author the other. The ensign does not entirely fit the negative mold, since his resilience is appealing. His ego has not been broken and he continues to think of himself. Instead of grovelling, he concentrates on his work. Moreover, during his training, he is sent to sea to serve as an apprentice engineer. His superiors on shipboard dislike him for his haughtiness. But he gets on well with the men, who treat him with respect. He inspires them to become the best crew in the fleet. For a loner and perfectionist, this is an achievement. Loyalty based on respect lies beyond the easy control of the party.

Punishment, however, catches up with the ensign on the solemn occasion of graduation. With relatives and friends of the cadets holding their breath, the head of the academy slowly reads name after name as he bestows on the class the rank of full lieutenants. But he omits one name. Only when the list is ended, the culprit's name is called out. He is punished by being the only one to graduate as a mere lieutenant junior grade. At the handshaking ceremony, the head of the academy refuses to congratulate him. And at the grand finale, he is made to march alone at the tail of the formation. His comrades turn away from him – in embarrassment, to be sure – but they turn away.

One more test awaits him. He is deliberately posted to the ship on which he had served so well as a student. But he is offered an alternative.

"The sailors remember you well. You will read a serious question in their eyes. They will notice at once that you do not have a second star. This will be additional punishment for you. If you are not strong enough to take it, say so, and you will be sent elsewhere."

"I will cope with it, no matter how difficult it is."   [p. 105]

The title of the tale, "First and Last," means first in grades but last in citizenship. But the design fails to convince. The villain's vulgarity only emphasizes what is attractive in the ensign, his pride and self-reliance. Punished, he does not whine. And that is devotion to his own cause.

The ensign's transgressions are in matters of conduct. He does not play the game right. He does not have the sense of amenities, of ritual, of the demand that can be made on his own time, subtracted from his own pursuits. Mere formal participation in mandatory public activities would have given him much leeway. He knew how to order champagne; but he did not know how easy it would have been to keep the chaplains of cant off his back by going to services . . . and dozing there. Once tempered, however, once buffeted, and having learned the strategy of shielding the private with a minimum of the public, he will be able to succeed with flying colors. For his kind of dogged talent is needed, and allowances are going more and more to be made for it. But he cannot go it alone.

12. Professors Talk Back

After the war, the old and the new *homo academicus* confronted each other on the battlefield of the university. Spokesmen of restored "right-think" attacked the residual vagaries of the purist intelligentsia. The generational collision became standard in novels of student life. The young academics were set up as heroes; the older professors as villains.[1] The conflict centered around the old problem of the intelligentsia's self-image. The righteous young strove selflessly in their pursuit of scholarship as service to the State. The older academics, addicted to opaque meditation, showed that other things than service were on their minds.

The philosophy department of one provincial university is torn by strife, involving a professor in his fifties and a militant representative of the postwar school of philosophy. The positive young man first gets the distinguished professor agitated, then easily defeated, and finally ousted. It is an important detail that the young man makes his career with dizzying swiftness. Because of the depletion of academic ranks by the purges in the thirties, and then the war, university posts were hastily filled with inexperienced people. This pushy young man propels his ascent by attacking "pure" philosophy, one of the zhdanovite synonyms for cosmopolitanism and formalism. On completion of his doctoral dissertation on "Necessity and Freedom in Socialist Society," which blends well with his purposes, he goes to work. Campaigning against science for the sake of science, he works for the purging of the faculty.

The ousted professor shows even in his "esthetic" appearance the required negative signs. A bachelor, he enjoys the comforts of a book-lined apartment and can afford a housekeeper. He dresses impeccably and favors carefully laundered white shirts which he wears with ruby studs. His worldly manners, reddish beard, and piercing eyes earn him the nickname "Old Fox." His shoulders are, of course, sloping; his hands are narrow, long, and well kept. His wit is quick and his tongue sharp. Accusations pile up against Old Fox; one transgression above all is held against him: the dreaded cosmopolitanism. In principle it does not seem substantiated. But that is the point: the mannerisms of erring intellectuals were depicted with greater clarity than their thoughts.

Old Fox has just returned from abroad where he has attended an international conference. He was sent as representative of Soviet philosophy and returns appalled at the "morass" of western thought. He heartily agrees with his vigilant colleagues that western philosophy produces only "clowns like Nietzsche" and that Dostoevsky is distorted in the West because when "a pig digs in dirt it is not interested in gold" and that "since the death of Marx and Engels philosophy has not even stayed overnight in Europe."[2] And yet underneath all this correct armor, something is wrong with Old Fox. His style is that of a cosmopolite: so he must be one.

Under the gathering clouds, he meditates more and more. Self-examination is induced by reading his adversary's opus.

"I too, after all, could have written the same way. Why didn't I? Haven't I spent a long time thinking about man, about his individual freedom? Why didn't I start the same way as he does? Is it possible that I tackled the problem from the wrong end?"   [p. 40]

Once turned fifty, an intellectual tackles practically everything from the wrong end. The present mold for Old Fox gives room for deviousness, and at times he seems to meditate with tongue in cheek. In spite of the author's assurance that he envies his rival, his envy is ambiguous. He implies that he could have stayed on the rails of virtuous stalinism but he did not. And a vindictive note intrudes into his reasoning: "I did not do it like that, and I will not, because my thinking is more original than that."

Beware! Since orginality, individuality, "my thinking" became evil, Old Fox stands accused of moral deficiency. Out of perverse kindness to this negative character, the author insists that he detect the cause of his ailment himself. But it is not easy. Old Fox subscribes to all the verities about the superiority of Soviet society. He knows that the rift between the collective and the individual had been successfully closed. This exact and basic postulate is elucidated by his adversary, and Old Fox approves. What, then, is wrong with him?

The trouble is that he cerebrates too much, using his head instead of his heart. He manages in the end to uncover "a discord between the private and the public," between "I want" and "I must." Therefore, the manner in which he serves society turns out to be forced.

"I knew it was my duty to go to the Urals and to leave the capital with all its spiritual wealth. And I left it, forcing myself to do so. I never bemoaned my decision to do something useful to society. But I did not experience any particular joy over it. Doesn't the author of the dissertation ever feel regrets, even if small ones, unconscious ones?"

It even occurs to him that there exists "a tragic contradiction between himself and his environment." His thoughts press the dialectic into the realm of the emotions; and at its highest point Old Fox rhetorically addresses his adversary in a plea to be saved:

"Teach me how to become one with the social flux without thereby losing my individual features. I am marching in the formation. But I know that I stand out as a general would stand out if he were to march next to a soldier."

According to his dangerous categorization, his adversary is a soldier who accepts "necessity with the same limitations of self with which a soldier accepts the articles of war" (p. 41). At stake here is the sense of self. A soldier accepts the articles of war, but an intellectual has reservations. Old Fox shares the discomforts of self-consciousness with the centrist intelligentsia.[3]

Some orthodox critics praised the novel.[4] Other orthodox critics found it stupid.[5] This discordant reaction to one of the first student tales constructed to fit Zhdanov's specifications emphasizes that the author struck on an important issue, but he overdid it. He too obviously exposed the regime's pressure on equivocating intellectuals. On the other hand, he evoked some sympathy for the intellectual's separatism and loneliness. Old Fox complicates things by being an indecisive nit-picker, self-conscious and complex. All together, his problems make him a problem.

Labels

The beleaguered middle-aged professor multiplied in fiction. For, in the terrible last years of Stalin's life, entirely nonfictional intellectuals swelled the ranks of those behind barbed wires. And fiction, no matter how false, optimistic, and obfuscating, kept pointing by reflex to the victims.

The kinship between Old Fox and our second academic in error stands out clearly. But the second professor does more than meditate: he talks back. The semantic aspect of his name (Kozelsky) suggests a billygoat. An Old Goat, he is treated as such in the novel. A professor of literature, he is in the end fired from Moscow's Pedagogical Institute. According to pattern, he is a distinguished-looking bachelor of fifty. Gray-haired and elegant, he smokes a pipe, collects rare books and drinks fine brandy. He understands ballet and Western art, and has refined tastes.

As we know already, bachelorhood stands for a serious personality defect, either inadequacy or selfishness, both injurious to society. As for oriental rugs, books, cognac – perfectly laudable accoutrements of kulturnost in a safe nonintellectual ambiance – they do this professor no good at all, especially since his father was a prerevolutionary lawyer.

He has a reputation for fierceness. A stickler for facts, he fills his students with fear. Once in a while, he allegedly expresses a condescending attitude toward Soviet literature – a foolish thing to do, considering the atmosphere in the institute, which smacks of corruption. For the students vacillate between slavish submissiveness to faculty members and their punitive urge to denounce them. Old Goat, as befits his "formalist skepticism," stands aloof from the political scene. Of course, this does not help. In the end, he falls to the attack of militant students.

Clouds gather over him early in the story. For one thing, his book on Dostoevsky provokes the wrath of *Pravda* and his enemies take note of that. The activists rise against him, led by a fiery, though not too scholarly, veteran sailor whom Old Goat had imprudently failed. The sailor delivers a heavy indictment against the pedantic approach to teaching which he finds subversive:

"It's a disgrace, don't you understand, when Russian literature is taught by a man with a calculating machine instead of a heart! What? I am not supposed to talk like that? No etiquette? No piety? But what did I come here for? Did I cover seven miles by foot for the sake of a crumb? I came here to learn something. I came here with love for literature, for my own Russian literature. I came to find something new and beautiful in it every day! That's why I came here! And he hits me on the head with dates, dates – as if with an oar!"[6]

After this, dismissal becomes inevitable.

Is there somewhere a commensurate foil, someone more authoritative than a disgruntled student, a noble adversary? Certainly. It happens to be the dean of the faculty. He has known the erring professor for forty years. They were born in the same town and went to the same school. They were students together just before the revolution. And they have met by chance since. The dean's career turned out to be a public one, while Old Goat chose to retreat into scholarship.

The dean never really liked his childhood friend, whose aloofness offended him. When fate brings them together in the same institute, their relationship turns formal. As Old Goat is about to be dismissed, however, the dean expects a call from him, and feels that it will be more than *pro forma*. He hesitates himself. The dismissal documents are still on his desk, although he should have signed them some time ago. Uneasy about the whole thing, he expects an unpleasant confrontation. At last, a secretary announces the professor who "had aged and sagged somewhat." But, impeccable as ever, he maintains decorum. It takes him a long time to light his pipe. Then, he tackles the main point, making it clear that he has not come to beg.

"Strictly speaking, any clarification is useless now. I know it's too late. And I purposely come to you after an interval. There is one thing that interests me. Please give me an answer. I know you must sign the dismissal order. That is obvious. But what I would like to know is, tell me, do you too believe in all these tags and labels?"

The dean wants to know what he means by labels.

"Do I really have to explain to you? All these words: esthete, formalist, cringing before the West. Honestly, I can't remember them all ... These ready-made tags on rubber bands. You stick your neck out and they fix them on you."

Playing for time, the dean asks whether the professor rejects the accusations. Unnervingly, the professor admits a formalist "list" in his thought.

"But what does cosmopolitanism have to do with it? Where is the cringing? Do I cringe when I show how deep Dostoevsky's influence was on world literature? Well? Am I not right? Why don't you say something?"

The model dean has nothing to say, at least nothing to the point. In silence, he prepares to shift his ground.

He stared glumly at his own broad, heavy hands. It was difficult for him to talk to [the professor], very difficult. It was so difficult if only because it was not a young man sitting in front of him but an old one whose life, all in all, was finished. And he had lived it, evidently, not entirely correctly, even, perhaps, entirely incorrectly. And to say this to a man's face directly and without equivocation, oh, that was not easy.

But the professor grows impatient and demands a response. It is the dean's turn to make a startling admission: "Dostoevsky, Dostoevsky has nothing to do with it." Perspiring, he attacks the professor: "If you like you are that very same Chekhovian professor who is not interested in Shakespeare but only in the commentaries." But the professor simply refuses to accept "these childish devices, these empty words, these empty quotations" as he puts it. He presses his demand: "Be so kind as to give me a straight answer – why am I bad?" The dean carries on for a while about the dangers of formalism which lead "to a voluntary and involuntary reduction of content to something insignificant." But the most significant thing is that he does not himself believe in what he is saying and he thinks "with irritation":

"No, that's not it. I am not saying the right thing! What I am saying is flat, dead, trite words, as if someone else were speaking in this disinterested dull voice, not me!"

If he fails to convince himself, he certainly does not impress the professor, who grows more irritable:

"This is some sort of trickery! You can just as easily prove that way that I belong to the black hundred, or that I am a Jesuit, or even a freemason. It is ridiculous that a man who has known me for forty years can obediently repeat after the others all this cheap, prefabricated nonsense! It is ridiculous that he cannot explain to me sensibly what in the world I am guilty of. What's wrong with me? It is ridiculous that he can't find words and just mutters incoherently these phrases out of the official list of charges and accusations."

This is too much for the dean. Suddenly he drums the table with his fists; his face turns a deep purple. The outburst shows the real problem involved in the enigmatic heresy of cosmopolitanism. The dean finds coherent words, but only by changing the subject.

"You want me to talk about all these forty years? Yes? Then, listen! I will say no more about your formalism or your estheticism. These are only the results. The causes are more complicated. And probably no one has ever spoken to you about them. The causes lie in the fact that all these forty years, these stormy, difficult forty years which have roused the whole world, you have not lived correctly. You were concerned with one thing only: how best to protect yourself against being bruised! You chose a style for yourself, that of comfortable skepticism."

The dean wins the argument. The negative professor must be silenced if only because he struggles and talks back. On the surface, the dean accuses him of "formalism" and "cosmopolitanism," the cardinal sins of intellectuals after the war. But because these charges are mainly invective, mainly curse words, they do not lend themselves to logical extension and cannot be discussed in rational terms. Besides, in combating an intellectual, the regime selects as target not the intellectual deviation itself but rather a certain personality with an inherited negative trait, the ability to think for himself. It is specifically this urge that must be punished. (Concentration camps do it in life; the fanciful display of remorse does it in fiction.) The model dean at last levels the accusation:

"In the course of your whole life you have not done anything wholeheartedly, with fire, with your whole conscience. Everything you have done was done with one hand, because with the other you were always holding on to your own welfare."   [11, pp. 89-91]

"Holding on to one's own welfare" points to a badly balanced mixture of the private and the public. Intellectuals, least of all, can afford this transgression. Other social types may even be encouraged to fret about their own welfare, but not a professor.

This running warfare with the intellectuals conscious of their own preferences demonstrates that their rapprochement with the regime was a difficult matter; and that the regime did not try too hard to convince these people of the mutual benefit of their shared goals.

In the next story, an intellectual explains his "own welfare."

The right to err

Our two embattled professors gave some clues about the sense of self which erects a wall between the private and the public. The humanities perhaps induce that introspection which leads astray. Would an exact scientist, a species cosseted by the regime, share the danger?

Our third professor opens up that most important issue, the use of science in Soviet society. His field is useful indeed for industrial development. Yet, as professor of metallurgy, he defends the primacy of pure inquiry and struggles against what he calls the transformation of the university in the antechamber of a steel mill.

The first postwar decade, stringent and punitive, saw a wholesale assault on the intelligentsia, in which even the physical scientists came under attack, however much the country needed them. Although middlebrow fiction glossed over abrasive issues, the varnish was thin, especially in regard to stubborn scientists. In the entire social structure, only these scientists clung, at a terrible price, to a vestige of corporate cohesiveness.

Against this background, the quixotic effort of the third professor looks like heresy. When accusations of "scientific formalism" are hurled at him, he answers by defending scientific principles. He is another villain who steals the show from his righteous opponents. In style of life he follows the pattern of suspect intellectuals. He has no family about him. He dresses neatly, likes his comfort, lives among art objects. He reads Moscow art magazines avidly and drinks only the finest coffee. He has a sharp tongue. But above all, he is an addict of methodology. His enemies call him a coloratura of the scientific experiment.

His colleagues and students lean heavily toward applied science. They are obsessed with day-to-day requirements; they disagree with the professor's methods, and even more with his goals. It is evident from the beginning that he will be challenged for advocating "science for science's sake." This happens soon enough. The trumpets of an open student rebellion start blaring, and a public denunciation of his sins takes place. The party organization acts swiftly against him. Once more, public trial is as inevitable as his expulsion from the university. But where the Old Fox and the Old Goat seem taken aback, Professor Coloratura shows singular preparedness. He is a demanding teacher. But this is not exactly why advanced students treat him with hostility. Brought up on the need for "production," of overfulfillment of tangible norms, they are bound to disagree with his belief that the university should be "a world of science and not a workshop."[7] And the nearer the students move toward the doctorate, the louder the political overtones of their criticism. One of his candidates, a woman, turns out to be especially obstreperous. She begins openly to ridicule the old man's entire theoretical framework. He counters angrily:

"You are forgetting yourself! With your impertinence *here* you hope to earn favors *there*. I am familiar with these intrigues. However, science is governed by other laws. Why don't you go ahead? Why don't you write to the ministry that Yakhontov, doctor of physico-mathematical sciences, is not worth a penny as a scholar?"
[p. 219]

Evidently he had been at one time worth a penny or two. For every effort had been made after the war to give him conditions of work which he was permitted to specify. But this did not mean trust. And it is he who undermines whatever safety he enjoys. For, inadvertently or otherwise, a clue of vast significance emerges at this point. The professor is one of those who know the unutterable, though not subtle, difference between *here* and *there*, between the powerless and the powerful. To voice such knowledge invites disaster. Throughout, the professor seems obsessed with making himself clear. And he proselytizes:

"Science is a love which knows neither unfaithfulness nor indifference. You must learn how to sacrifice yourselves. The reward is so great that I take courage to ask all those who are brave of spirit and of mind to follow me."   [p. 10]

He is, of course, ridiculed for his bombastic rhetorical style too.

The author is no friend of his, but for that matter the professor is no friend of the author's either. For somehow he lives a life of his own. And an articulate awareness of the schisms induced by political power places him not only among the unsuccessful villains but among the unmanageable ones. Even when he teaches trite bits of his credo a strange thing happens.

"You can be a dilettante in music because that is very pleasant in society. You can be a dilettante in painting because it is good for everyday life. You can even be a dilettante in literature because ladies like this very much. But how can you be a dilettante in science!"   [p. 55]

This is not trite, in the face of the damage wrought by the dilettantism of Lysenko during the "science and culture" pogroms. But with the Lysenko-type ideologists still very much in power, our professor has been edging toward a precipice, especially when he takes to obstructing. At one of the numerous meetings between university representatives and chieftains of local industry, the problem of removing metal scraps from one factory yard arises. The professor puts himself on a collision course with the party:

"I beg your pardon, but metal scrap fails to inspire me. I don't feel compelled to puzzle my brain over the manner in which this scrap is to be removed. I would· like to warn my colleagues against being carried away by pedestrian problems. Let us not duplicate the functions of technicians and engineers."   [p. 213]

At this point the pattern demands that an adequate, life-size, fully convincing positive foil appear on the scene. He does; the good Professor Derevyanko (a name suggesting a chunk of wood) thinks in an up-to-date fashion and busies himself zealously as a party activist. A nocturnal confrontation comes about, promising catharsis. The two have been life-long friends. They are alone. The adversary attacks first:

"It's time for you to abandon this shaky position of a man mistreated by God, fate, and by the ministry of education. It's time you said directly and frankly what is your aim when you complain of 'persecution.' I will gladly listen."

This variant of the conflict offers the unusual feature that the culprit is able to counterattack with the help of a principle which proved effective in a later period, and might be called scientific privilege. He begins this prophetic combat by taking a sharp look at his opponent. He sees a brave scholar who has turned into a prudent and willing partner of the regime. He does not approve.

"I remember when you were young as clearly as I remember my own youth. At the time, with all the enthusiasm I was capable of, I applauded your brilliant debut, which testified to your creative courage and to your unusual erudition. You had acquired it as great talents do, almost playfully between childish amusements and adolescent infatuations. You went ahead . . . across swamps and mud. You were ready to tear your heart out in order to light the road."

The opponent interpolates, flattered, that he had not pushed back the darkness for himself alone. The teleological aspect does not seem to interest our professor, who doggedly continues:

"However, you have since then prudently enough taken into consideration that the electric bulb had been already invented, and that highways and steel bridges were also in existence and that, therefore, there was a good way to avoid dangerous swamps without inconveniencing your fiery heart. And most calmly you went from problems to little problems, from science to craft, from passion to a puny enthusiasm, from the unfathomable future to comfortable daily bread. You are now not so much a scholar as a politician. Go ahead, be one, if you please! Be one by all means if it is your true vocation. But don't prevent your fellow man from striving toward those stars of which he dreams at night! Give him a chance to avoid the highways. Let him breathe and err! Yes, even err!"

"Your errors cost the government hundreds of thousands of roubles."

"Granted! Granted! What are millions of roubles in comparison with the truth which will at last be found."   [p. 232]

This suggestion that truth has not been entirely identified under Stalin, fortified by a rejection of the self-serving academic meshchanstvo, causes the opponent to swerve into the budgetary realm. But what Professor Coloratura has to give, the regime needs badly, in the long run. Yet he comes as close to resisting the Big Deal and making serious trouble as is possible in a novel.

The regime's quarrel with the intelligentsia has, obviously, never been an isolated phenomenon. It coincided with the other elements of social change. And the quarrel itself changed. As the Big Deal entrenched itself deeper and won over more young people, it began to stake out longer-term goals and to revise its policy toward science. After Stalin's death there was a shift toward supporting scientists without abrogating the deal with technologists. Under Stalin's successors, theoretical research came into its own, and with it the implicit right to make mistakes in pursuit of knowledge. In this sense, Professor Coloratura's words have had an extended resonance. The academic community in Novosibirsk now enjoys some strange freedoms. But at the same time that does not mean that men like Sakharov are not in constant danger. The peril is great, and they exacerbate it. The wave of the future has brought new complexities. It is not really the formidable issues of academic freedom, the goal of science, or deviation from dogma that enrage the spokesmen of the regime, then as now. It is rather, and simply, the academic's "olympian calm," the steadfastness of the purist intelligentsia, it is above all the refusal to become docile.

13. Women's Liberation Confused

Off the track

After the war, the regime somewhat modified its support of the equality of women in the light of its long-term goals for society as a whole. The two were not in complete accord, and it was women who had to make the adjustment.

Working women had been demanding – and receiving – recognition for their superhuman wartime effort. But this celebration was to turn somewhat sour. In competition with the returning veterans, it became difficult to preserve the thrust of their upward career mobility, still less to increase it. Woman, one might say, was halted. Contradictory demands were now made of her. She was to continue to work and to hymn the glory of her fulfillment in the public arena, but not excessively and not as much as previously. The proper balance was tricky. She was to hold the family together, to comfort her shellshocked husband and to support his aspirations. Nor was she, under any circumstances, to forget the orange lampshade, the geraniums, and the homemade jam.

Neither in theory nor in practice could the regime demobilize the legion of working women, nor could it undercut the main selling point of its new incentives: domestic bliss for its deserving male partners. Some women seemed not to understand this double demand. Some seemed even to resist it. And a subdued, yet enervating, disarray became noticeable in tales about women through the whole social structure. Only the upper-class matron was exempt from confusion, and in a way its beneficiary. Leisure with a large dose of meshchanstvo was granted her, and she did not dream of complaining.

The regime's silent shift from one set of requirements to another showed most clearly in the implied disapproval of "feminist" troublemaking. So, for instance, at the dawn of peace, one shellshocked officer finds his wife and child in a wretched tenement house, in a wretched provincial town, burdened with the hardships of war. He breaks down. His mental recovery proves more difficult than the physical. While in limbo he is supported by his wife, who holds a taxing professional job. He takes to drinking heavily, especially with his regimental friends, romanticizing the war which had given him a "magnificent, dynamic life, life with a capital L, full of adventure and happiness"[1] and, one might add, a pretty nurse to sleep with. As for his wife, she only irritates him for "they had nothing to talk about . . . their paths no longer coincided" (p. 5). One reason for the estrangement is simple enough. Separated during the war, they found it hard to share the advent of peace. He will not look for a job. Plagued by insomnia, he sits in a stupor staring at her while she goes about the household chores after long hours in the office. One of his thoughts becomes obsessive: " . . . a lot she knows about life and death, having sat it out behind the Urals!" (p. 51). Since their mutual suspicion of infidelity, among other things, prevents them from communicating, it is not from her that he learns how she had suffered physical exhaustion during the evacuation, how she had been trucking lumber, how her hands were so frostbitten that amputation had seemed inevitable, and how it was only by a miracle that she had survived typhus. At long last, he does say:

"Your hair is gray" and he regretted the words as soon as they were spoken.
    "Yes, it is," she said calmly. "have you only just noticed?" There was no reproach in her voice, only a touch of sarcasm.   [p. 53]

Frictions turn to hatred.

"What exactly is it that you want from me today?" he said in a piercing whisper which rang unpleasantly in his own ears.
    "I don't want anything from you either today or any other day, except that you should not make life difficult for our child."   [p. 60]

One might expect the author to side with the heroine. There is nothing admirable in the husband's depressing malaise; he feels undermined by her ability to manage on her own; his longing for his wartime mistress does not strengthen his case either. But not so, not at all. One begins to notice some ambivalence toward the abused woman when she becomes harsh in her view of the conflict and begins to suspect that the husband's traumatized state may be malingering. She begins to act accordingly. She sends him off on errands, to shop, to find a plumber, to pay the bills.

And she felt insulted that he should do these things unwillingly and with irritation. After all, shouldn't there be some division of labor? He did not want to surrender. He did not want to find in these errands, in these petty everyday chores the justification for his very existence. But she did not want to understand this. Slowly there grew in her contempt for this unemployed man whom she was forced to support.   [12, pp. 22-3]

All sorts of things come together here, among them a hint of the burden on women harnessed into supporting war casualties. Some women, having proved their courage in survival and in man's work, were not eager to prostrate themselves at the feet of the returning man. Making domestic contentment was not their obvious preference.

Needless to say, the tale ends cheerfully. The husband's rehabilitation in a new job, and their conjugal reconciliation depend on the the now mandatory cutting down of this woman to size. And she comes around, indeed, but only after a seraphic old man, a concerned neighbor speaking opportunely for the ethos of the community, reprimands her. She has failed as a woman by not humbling herself before her husband's suffering. She should not have harped on the "division of labor." Her priorities were wrong. The pressure for equality should have given way to the bolstering of his ego. Remonstrances of this sort became common. Women were asked to accept the Orwellian doctrine that men were more equal.

The next fragment comes from a country story called *Marya*. In the kolkhoz setting, interpersonal and working problems tended to become intertwined. Since members of the same family frequently work together, they either consolidate their effort, which is bad for the system, or break out in internecine warfare, which is bad for them. War had separated a mature couple. Before the war, the wife had not done much. But when she receives notification of her husband's death at the front, she rushes to drown her grief in work. She "finds herself," as the saying is, and the collective finds a great leader in her. She is soon appointed kolkhoz chairman. But the notification was an error and the good man returns. Stunned, he does not know how to adapt to his wife's metamorphosis. He vacillates between admiration, sympathy for her heavy burden, and embarrassment. One malicious old hag hastens to sneer at him as "Marya's husband." There and then he decides that his wife must step down as chairman. She indignantly refuses. Watching her at night pouring over columns of marxism-leninism, he thinks: "Yes, there was nothing to say, Marya was way ahead in the race. He must try to catch up with her, he must try very hard."

His attempt to compete is thwarted because Marya holds power and controls her job. What irritates him most is the challenge to customs he had taken to be unassailable.

He was used to being boss in his house. He used to walk about the village with unhurried step, holding his head high and proud. When he was on his way home from the army, he thought he could move mountains. But there are no mountains. There is nothing to move. And life takes its normal course. And Marya, she moves about, gives orders. And the more she gives orders, the more she grows, even in his eyes. And the more she grows, the smaller he gets. And she, she does not care. She wants to fly on the wings of her thoughts through the whole world. And she flies. She wants to read, and there she sits burning the midnight oil. And it seems she needs her husband and then again it seems she does not.[2]

All sorts of things seethe in this peasant's nocturnal meditation, among them the vestiges of patriarchal masculine rights. But as they dutifully wane, it does not seem right that the man be emasculated. And it is not.

The rancor, the malevolent silence, the estrangement are hard on both of them. As grandparents, they should know better, but do not. They cannot even weep together over the death of their son at the front. It is time for Marya to go to confession. The good-hearted party secretary, appropriately sallow because of heart disease, swiftly coaxes out of her the standard elements of the dispute. She had followed her husband blindly in the prewar past. He had been the ruler of the household, and had shielded her from the world. Now she had succeeded on her own. She wants to keep to her upward road. But he hates it. One might expect the party functionary to deplore the husband's antiquated attitude and to bless her career. But he does not.

"Perhaps you haven't handled him properly. That you want to stay up in front and not fall back, that's good. But why should he be interested in lagging behind?"

While she muses over that one, the functionary asks: "And what is his job under you?" Her reply shows her administrative prowess.

"What do you mean, what's his job? He works in the kolkhoz. I was embarrassed to make him leader of a brigade. All the same, he works. He trucks manure. Well, and whatever else needs to be done."

It is now proper for the party secretary to show dismay. By his up-to-date view, what she has done is even worse than nepotism. She begins to understand, blushing deeply, that "what she considered a petty humdrum problem had grown into a large and serious problem." She is taken to task for having spent a long life with a mate without understanding him:

"You give him any old job? He is supposed to collect pay only? And this now? After the war? No! That's not what your husband lives by! He needs work! Work that will engage all of his soul!" [pp. 23-4]

She is ordered to think hard about that.

Equality and competition conflict when a woman overtakes her mate and rises to a position of authority. Under these circumstances, friction is not uniquely Soviet; nor is it the consequence of the Big Deal alone. We need to discern the tentatively emerging guidelines for resolving the conflict.

In a novel title *Comrade Anna*, the heroine uses her maiden name at work. An attractive woman, she serves as administrative head of a Siberian mining settlement. The traditional range of difficulties, from inadequate supplies to substandard conditions of the native population, seem insurmountable. Comrade Anna has her hands full. Not the least of her problems is that her husband, who happens to be the leading geologist in the area, is under her command. He secures some independence by his fierce absorption in dangerous exploration. But the status rivalry between them at one point becomes a struggle. To force the issue, the author introduces a blonde, overdressed and oversexed, if much needed, lady doctor as "the other woman." And it is hard to say who contributes more to the wreck, the seductress or the stern wife.

At a crucial point, Comrade Anna autocratically exercises her prerogative. Losing faith, for some unspecified reason, in her husband's ability, she arbitrarily cuts off the funds allotted to his geological research. She makes her decision at a bad moment. For he is just about to discover rich deposits of gold. She wounds him deeply, of course, but the injury does not stop there. An old-fashioned heroine, she maintains that her decision has nothing to do with personal animosity. She is solely concerned to save government money. She offers to support his research out of her own savings. He stands up to this castrating assault on his professional ability and rejects her offer. He takes up with the blonde seductress. Comrade Anna turns to despair.

At this point she becomes confused. An old believer, she insists that, among other socialist accomplishments, sex has been sublimated; women have achieved equality; and so-called femininity is merely a regrettable cultural lag. For her, to further one's aims by charm, or what she calls the biological instinct, means to sell out to meshchanstvo. But her position is not up-to-date. Her assistant, a shy and clumsy young engineer, consoles her but also suggests, according to the new pattern, that she is losing her husband because she has stopped being a woman. He holds the view that feminine frailty, even feigned, attracts men. Comrade Anna erupts in anger at such "old stuff." But the engineer stands firm and shows that didactic norms can not only change but turn topsy-turvy. "Old stuff" is no longer "old stuff." And so he concedes:

"Yes, it's old, but that's just why it is so terribly tenacious. It is possible to change a great deal in life, in the relations of man to man as well as in those of an individual to society. But in the domain of relations between man and woman, physiology is all-important. And you cannot change physiology... What happens in life seldom coincides with our best philosophizing."[3]

So much for Comrade Anna. She has failed as a woman by not properly balancing the public and the private, by acting as a purist and an aggressive amazon. After an agonizing transfiguration into a jealous and penitent woman and with the help of a seraphic party secretary as well as of the "people" who prove wiser than she, she gets her husband back. She redeems herself by desperately wanting him back. But some women go off the rails without a desire to get back. They epitomize the obstacle we are here examining.

For instance, a novice reporter is sent on his first assignment to compose a "human interest" story on a famed textile worker. The editor tells him that the woman is not only a crack worker but an inspiring teacher of apprentices, that she has attained the status of VIP and has been sent to the People's Democracies, and that she has been elected deputy to the regional soviet. Expecting to interview a formidable matron, the young man is taken aback and beguiled by the woman's youth, beauty and elegance. She keeps her composure; anticipating his questions and showing some familiarity with interviewers, she gives the essential facts about her life, emphasizing her proletarian origins and rapid achievements. She lets him examine a pile of letters from what she calls foreign friends. She soon ushers him out, for she must be off to the theater. A quiet man, by the way, had let the reporter in and had disappeared into a back room. He had put his head through the door once or twice and had retreated.

Poring over his copious notes later, the reporter realizes that he knows nothing at all about the person. The letters from abroad help least of all. He decides that he must watch her at work. In the factory, looking less festive but just as appealing, she politely shows him her way of speeding production. Going on to the trade union office and the party committee, he collects one favorable opinion about his subject after another. Only later does he remember that the party secretary spoke about the woman somewhat cryptically.

He still cannot, to save his life, begin writing, for he has no personal impression of her. The deadline makes him uneasy. He feels he must see her once more, without an appointment, so as to provoke some spontaneity by surprising her. But she is not home. What is more, the quiet man who again lets him in informs him that she has moved altogether, for she has been rewarded with a brand new apartment. The man invites the youth into the room, which is now desolate. The harsh light hurts the eyes for the lampshade is now gone and melancholy squares on the wall show where photographs had once hung. Apologetically, the man assures the visitor that she did not really want to take anything but that he had insisted, had even packed her belongings. The visitor suddenly feels embarrassed in front of this forlorn, unshaven, hollow-cheeked person. The latter starts talking profusely, sadly, gently.

"It's my own decision not to move. Klasha has become famous. Her interests have changed. Frankly, I have become an uninteresting person to her. Why should I burden someone who is dear to me? At first we though of moving together. Only, I did realize that she sort of does not need me. Just a husband hanging around. Mind you, we have been together almost ten years. And they were good years."

Having on the spot lost interest in the famous lady, the youth asks, as delicately as he can, whether she had stopped loving her husband. The hesitant answer touches on the evolving new mores.

"How should I put it? No, it's not a question of love. I have become an uninteresting person to her" – he repeated what seemed to have become his favorite expression. "She travels abroad, she sits in presidiums, she makes speeches at big meetings. And I, I have remained what I have been before, assistant foreman. Except for my factory shop, I don't know anything... What can I tell her? She knows everything about the factory herself. So I see that she needs another life companion, higher than I am. And here she was offered that apartment."[4]

He goes on speaking lovingly of her and of her career and urges the visitor to do a good story on her, provided he omits the matter of their breaking up. "What happened between us, that concerns only us." The moral of the tale suggests the reverse. It is, indeed, of public concern that this nice and loving man has been discarded by an ambitious wife. The young reporter drops his work on her profile, a step which meets with the approval of an understanding editor. We take from the tale its less obvious messages.

In the past, a "lagging" spouse would have been urged to catch up. By and large, he still is, but not so bluntly. Ample room has been left for other considerations. Here, the woman's drive is uncovered as ruthless. In addition, the tale is significant because one element in the character of this climber distinguishes her from the other confused wives in this chapter. She is neither an awakened peasant woman nor an urban old believer, but a Big Deal creature through and through. In a way, she constitutes an obstacle that the Big Deal has created for itself. Material rewards and prestige have induced her to trample on primary loyalties. She provides no contentment. Absconding with the orange lampshade, she leaves sadness in her wake; and that will not do.

Surtax on equality

People were expected to pay a high price for the benefits offered by the regime. Compared with the male citizen, Soviet woman was taxed at an especially high rate. She had to sustain the Big Deal on two fronts, juggling her commitments at home where it mattered most, and at work, where of course it mattered no less.

Among the masses, poverty pressed on the average woman with particular cruelty. Bereaved, bedraggled, prematurely old, she could not expect any consideration. Like the pauperized village, the average woman's hard lot was never described with honesty in middlebrow fiction. For all its phony sublimation in the glamorized tales, the surtax levied on the professional woman for the better life around the corner is clear; so are the occasional guidelines for her conduct, intended to adapt her to the Big Deal, or vice versa.

Advice about what the new woman was supposed to do, and even more what she was to feel, began to emerge. The new exegesis becomes convincing, of course, when it relates to a model mother and partner. Do you remember the paradigmatic Listopad? A woman who could cope with him without wilting, one who could share his glory on his terms, becomes paradigmatic herself.

Listopad's first wife, a sensitive and fragile child bride, loses all the way. She fights for respect and equality fiercely but unsuccessfully. She wilts under the neglect of her busy tycoon husband. Frustrated, lonely, embittered and, above all, disenchanted with a chauffeured car and a mink coat, she contrives to die in childbirth. His grief is brief, and entirely unaccompanied by self-recrimination. The reader is thus prepared to savor the subsequent arrangement of Listopad's personal life in a way that better suits his indomitable character. Obviously a mature, poised, experienced professional woman is more likely to flourish under Listopad's male chauvinism. He finds just such a woman, who knows what to do and, more significantly, what to want.

She falls seriously ill but it does not cross his mind to cancel his trip to Moscow for that. Just before leaving, he finds time, though, to visit her briefly. Here are her thoughts:

This man will give up nothing for the sake of love. He will not restrict himself. She alone must do the giving up, the sacrificing, the acquiescing, and the waiting. As for him, he will fly to Moscow, go to the ministry, and boast about his new electric saw. He will be talking of the possibilities it opens up for the lumber industry. In the evening he will be having dinner with his friends in a restaurant and again he will boast of his plant, his chief construction engineer, his young people. And everybody will love him. He will remember her and the fact that she is ill and will send a telegram – "wire how you are." She took his big hand resting on her hair and kissed it.[5]

Right-Think: here is the surtax, measured in submissiveness, that the woman now has to pay for equality-cum-happiness. And besides, she must, absolutely must, want personal happiness. This is the new order.

It is served up in another tale as a sermon. The heroine is a metallurgical engineer, mature, handsome, efficient, who lives only for her work. Her husband had been killed early in the war. The formula is brought into play and grief is portrayed as driving her to work harder and engaging her in a research project. Bureaucrats, naturally, oppress her. For help she turns to the party secretary. He treats her a little roughly at first, but deep inside him there throbs benevolent party paternalism. This comrade is a fine comrade: ubiquitous, he knows everything, and he even listens. He becomes involved with her project; in fact, he falls in love with both project and woman. From the rare metamorphosis of a perfect party boss into a lover, one learns much. The startling courtship throws the lady engineer, a purist with a stratum of old beliefs, into a turmoil. Since she has so recently lost her husband, the solitary road of public endeavor seemed the only answer for her. The party secretary's counterargument wins him the lady, and gives us a clear sight of the new ranking of private and public priorities.

"You have no right to live alone just because you once loved a man who is no more, who is completely gone."

As a declaration of principle, the party secretary states that the woman has no right to be unhappy. On this premise he builds the new ethic.

"If he were alive, if there were the slightest hope that he might be alive, you would be right, right entirely. But he is dead. He is no longer living. It's your duty to live by the laws of life. You must not become bitter and you must not cover up your soul. Don't you see that after the war not only are cities being rebuilt, but souls also, those which have been wounded . . . You have wrongly persuaded yourself that now you must live only for others and that you must forget yourself. But who needs sacrificial attitudes? And I will tell you frankly that you won't even manage to live for others that way. You wish to embalm yourself. But by what right? What was it that you struggled for, survived the blockade, and last, and not least, loved your husband?"[6]

The authors, according to pre-Big Deal habits, tended to side with women. One boorish man, for example, simply forbids his wife to get on with her higher education, interrupted by the war: "As for your doctorate, get that nonsense out of your head." When she asks for an explanation, he says:

"Because it has no future. You will have to study for three years and you have fallen behind. You will never catch up. All in all, I won't permit it. And that's that."[7]

The marriage breaks up. Elsewhere, a young engineer becomes increasingly enraged with his wife, just as much of a hardworking engineer, for her neglect of domestic duties:

"No, that's no way to build family life! I am sick and tired of it! Sick and tired, don't you understand! You think neither of me nor of the house! You are up in the clouds somewhere else! I don't exist for you!"[8]

Here, though critical of the man, the author acknowledges that he has a problem. In view of the tradition of defending the woman, the halfheartedness and equivocation of the authors in so doing becomes interesting. They begin to shift the emphasis to primordial feminine submissiveness. And they begin to recommend it in various variants as a key to bliss even to the youngest and most accomplished professional heroines. Bliss was now required. Submissiveness was suggested not only when a woman had to cope with a model big boss as husband. Here are two youngsters, boy and girl, both engineers of equal training and merit. The boy chases off because of a crisis in his shop and leaves the girl languishing at the peak of their courtship. The sense of her personal future is revealed to her:

He will keep forgetting her for the sake of his work. He gives in easily. He is gentle and considerate as long as everything is going well for him. He loves her. And he will gladly, without a murmur, do as she wishes in everything. But should she interfere with his work, he will roll over her like a tank. He will not spare even her. Is this what she was dreaming of? Will she be happy? Will she be able to stand it? Yes, she answered herself.[9]

In the last tale, based on a true story this time, the portrait is drawn of a girl who is an enthusiastic agronomist. Shura, born into a peasant family, graduates from a regional agricultural institute and turns, as she puts it herself, into a new breed, neither fish nor fowl, neither a villager nor a city woman. Earning fame for her record-breaking harvests, she becomes a deputy to the regional soviet, and meanwhile marries a veteran, an officer, who on the standard pattern has much adjusting to do. He first irritates her by not showing sufficient concern for her problems at work. She mutters angrily: "Look at him, the officer! He eats bread but does not want to think about it." When he does become interested in bread, that is in agronomy, it turns out that his training is inadequate. His growth, one might think, takes place under precarious circumstances, for he is given a job as his wife's assistant.

The culminating ingredient needed to conclude this chapter is offered here conveniently. The intervening variables in the other extracts are absent. The husband does not oppress the wife. The wife does not try to crush the husband. The two live and work in harmony. Their modest room is cluttered with agricultural books and journals. And at night, one assumes in a tender manner, she whispers the orders to him that he must carry out on the job as her underling. He must also find time to study. He does all according to conditions she laid down before their wedding:

"At work, I am your chief. Mind you don't resent it. But at home, if you want to, I'll submit to you." But when she thought it over, she refined her statement: "But at home, we'll be equals."[10]

At home she helps him doggedly with his studies. He enrolls for a correspondence course at an institute. She sets up a curious goal for both of them: "In five years or so, I'll be working under his command." He, as a modest person, does not see how this will be possible since by that time she will surely have earned her doctoral degree. He is, by the way, as proud of her dissertation as if it were his own. He does not quite see how he can catch up with her. The writer notices, however, that his tone does not quite harmonize with his words. The perfect wife's interpolation at this point is brief and cogent:

"Come along, help me out, catch up. I can't be the boss for ever. I'll be having children."

There is the key. Equality, priorities, values, goals are all neatly rearranged. The author's brief exegesis of these words helps to keep the private and the public firmly anchored in their crossed-over places:

In her there no longer speaks the stubborn agronomist but a woman's ambition. That ambition consists not of a drive to surpass one's beloved but, rather, in being able to consider him superior to anybody else, including herself. [p. 179]

The simplicity of this desire emphasizes the normalcy of the aims of the Big Deal. They reveal themselves as organic, in more senses than one. Combative equality is reoriented toward the more relaxed task of building the family.

This tale of conflict resolution reminds us that women had been promised equality long before 1917 and that their liberation had remained on the public agenda ever since. The truly ambitious women – the amazons – pushed on with their prestige aspirations and were dismayed indeed over the domestic aspects of the postwar incentives, which seemed to them nothing short of retrogressive. These women have good reason for frustration. They do not hold positions of power and the prospects for change are dim. Madame Furtseva was no Golda Meir, no Indira Gandhi, but rather a rare showpiece. But the special letdown of the amazons – after the era of revolutionary heroics and that of wartime emergency patriotism – is one thing. What the average woman wants is another. How important are the amazons now themselves, with their protests against the world assigned to them, the world filled with geraniums? Seen against the divisiveness of Soviet society, amazons as a species have been waning and their pressure for top equality has been going out of style. The overworked run-of-the-mill professional woman wants something else. And middlebrow fiction does more than just hint at that. She struggles for private comfort at least as much as for public recognition. Equality being a mixed blessing and the double burden of work and family care being heavy, the majority of women crave first of all an easier life. Bypassing the amazons, the Big Deal is adaptable to the average woman's judiciously modified feminist goals.

14. Populist Pressure

Rural quilt

Right after the war, the regime demanded a supply of novels dealing with the rural scene. The legitimacy of collective agriculture was to be reaffirmed. The enemy had discredited it. The Soviet peasant had come in touch with alternatives under occupation or in German forced labor. But this was now of lesser importance than the very rescue of the kolkhoz.

The village was hit by the war so crushingly because, treated as an internal colony, it had been already bled white before the war. During the war it was denuded. Ablebodied men were sent to die and women, children, and the old were simply abandoned. Despite apocalyptic adversity, the peasant community – through its family nexus – somehow held together.[1] All the more tragic, then, stands out the terrible winter of 1946 for the peasant. Total neglect continued as a policy.[2] And the crisis in the village defied description.

Approaching the theme of postwar populism, one must also consider that something happened to the leveling discipline which had been imposed on the peasant in the thirties at such a terrible cost in lives. The war had weakened controls in all of Soviet society. Villages, especially, were left fending for themselves. The party secretary had gone to war, the apparatus was depleted. The village had become a no-man's-land. If the peasant survived, it was because of self-rule and self-help. And just this unruly trend was to be stamped out by edict as soon as peace came. Not programs to assist the peasant but controls were clamped down to force the produce out of his bare hands. Middlebrow fiction does not deal with genocide or concentration camps. But it deals voluminously and deplorably with the peasant and it lies with bucolic monstrosity.[3] To redress any semblance of truth through this source is not possible. But a *sui generis* populism surges in it and this account of the Big Deal cannot be complete without notice of the only *countercurrent* to the alliance with the middle class.

If populism proved something more than a side ornament on official cant, it was stimulated by the war. The peasant army had saved the country. The peasant tragedy impinged on national unity and on all those who had a conscience. Since lying in literature had subsided during the war, the peasant was treated with compassion, sometimes anguished and guilt ridden. But Zhdanov's ukaz stopped the moaning and grieving. Wartime populism was undercut.

The merry shepherds and sherherdesses, welcoming the party officials back from the war, resembled Soviet peasants as much as Watteau's lovers resembled ordinary countryfolk of eighteenth-century France. Still, beneath the overlay of stalinist populism – a stylized falsehood – rural fiction tells us something of the difficulties swamping management, and this is the main concern of this chapter.

Despite the rococo veneer, rural unrest became evident even in these tales. Wartime bribery, speculation, the black market had flourished. Yet, these liberties, granted by default, had worked for the system's advantage. But now the "law" clamped down on all sorts of irregularities as well as on peasant tribalism. The institutional mutations that had helped the peasant to survive were now fiercely investigated. Issues such as the private plot and the private cow came up once more as well as the embattled private life of the peasant. Family loyalty was attacked again, primarily because the problem of consumer versus producer was not decided in favor of the peasant.

The regime undertook no real reordering of priorities. Without support or capital investment, the kolkhoz was simply expected to produce. In an avalanche of folkish ballads, the new management, covered with combat medals, marched home and, after a welcoming binge, began to inspire the people by pushing them around. One such veteran pays what he thinks of as a courtesy call on his predecessor. He finds the ousted chairman prostrate on an unkempt bed. Instead of offering a friendly greeting, the latter snarls:

"Well, so you have pushed me out! Satisfied? And I, I remember very well how I raised you, how I protected you, how I helped you to become a human being."[4]

The submerged theme of the inequity of peasant life became encrusted with the barnacles of repetitive subthemes, especially with the pros and cons of agricultural methods (minus technology), and corruption. Here the issue of the manager as deputy becomes relevant. His responsibility to the peasant community on one hand and his representation of the regime on the other was treated at length, but the rural tales steered clear of the political core of the problem. For neither choice of allegiance nor service to two masters could actually be tolerated. It was the regime the manager served. And since service in agriculture had become more difficult than ever, the manager could only hope to deliver his impossible quotas by keeping up the morale of the serfs, and this was only done by promising pie in the sky.

The relationship with the peasant was colored not by moral considerations but by operational exigencies. These pressed on the entire managerial caste. To satisfy the regime, the rural manager had to try to be accepted by the peasants. His wedged-in posture was uncomfortable but it helped to present him, at least in fiction, in attractive populist guise.

It was he who determined the success or failure of a kolkhoz. What was he to do to increase productivity? The peasant, at least in fiction, refused – because of the lingering touch of unruliness – to exert himself as much as before. Instead, he wanted improvement and recognition. What was the manager to do if conflicting demands were made on him from the bureaucrats above and from the people below?

Power relationships were shaken and dislocated. Resentments had grown between regional party functionaries and kolkhoz chairmen, chairmen and foremen, foremen and the folk. Here is the language of such strife. A fight is caused because a foreman, in charge of the cattle stockmen, attacks a rather sloppy horse groom who happens to be a woman. She also happens to be edgy and loudmouthed and in general an unsatisfactory worker. Having spotted disorder in the stables, the foreman threatens her with a fine. She bristles.

"A fine?" Even in the half-darkness one could see her cheeks turn crimson. She dropped the broom. Her tousled hair covered her face. Her voice sounded harsh. "Hey, there, don't think you have frightened me," she spoke stressing every word. "It seems you are very quick with fines, like the oldtime landlords, I swear! And I am telling you straight out. If I am not good enough for you in the stables, replace me, get somebody better."

"Look how matted and dirty the horses are! Don't you have a brush?"

"Am I supposed to exhibit them?" she snarled. "Perhaps, while you are at it, you will order me to scrub your back in the bathhouse?"[5]

The theme of administrative frictions binds much rural fiction so tightly together that the transition from one tale to another seems imperceptible. This time, a foreman is not bothered by the grooming of horses, since he has none. His kolkhoz is in deep decay. He has to get on with plowing.[6] The peasants flatly refuse to surrender their individual cows (yes, cows) to do the job. The plowing goes undone. Thereupon the perambulating party secretary descends and, angered by what he sees, inquires bitingly whether the foreman had been as lax in the army. The accused barks back and "a fire flickers in his eyes":

"Don't you reproach me with the army Comrade Secretary! That was war. Each one of us knew then how the question stood: either – or. Either the country would live or death for everybody. But now it is not the same. Now some people are trying to take care of themselves."[7]

Accordingly, an obstreperous old woman takes to fending for herself with vengeance. She thunders:

"I won't give my cow! Let them give us tractors! Enough is enough. The war is over. It's high time to treat ourselves to some milk in our tea."

The hard party secretary cannot now treat the peasants as saboteurs. He smiles and murmurs "quite right" instead. The old ways were being amended. Party officials in fiction had to learn to smile. In the past, remembered by some with nostalgia, a party secretary

> used to arrive in some village and one word from him sufficed. People understood him at once and accepted every directive. They were afraid of the authorized agents. "The Soviet power tells you," [he] used to say. But nowadays you can no longer say this.   [p. 116]

The unpleasant party secretary of the preceding tale

> thought he knew the village. But his knowledge was so superficial that he never once considered that collective farmers might have their own opinion based on experience.

And his superiors do not trust him now. His missions become rarer and rarer. Small wonder that, in turn,

> according to his long-ingrained habit, he listened suspiciously to everything that was said here. He did not trust anyone.[8]

And so distrust grows. We close with a fragment in which, most importantly, distrust bubbles up from below, vented by the lowly peasants. As fear of all sorts of outsiders – authorized agents and party officials – somewhat subsides, drowned by unrelieved misery, the peasants begin to take some initiative and ask pertinent questions. They covet self-rule, the bittersweet taste of which they had known in the war. The production plan comes down from the district office to that same lagging kolkhoz in which the individual cows wilfully went on strike. At the board meeting, an agreeable bookkeeper suggests:

> "So, let's accept the plan, yes?"
> "Well, what is there to discuss? A plan is a plan" [somebody] supported him.
> "What do you mean, what is there to discuss? Who is the boss on the kolkhoz? We or the district office?" asked the sturdy... foreman of the gardening team with unexpected sharpness.[9]

Stalinism in populist guise

The populist mood in some quarters of the intelligentsia, among some poets and among a number of professionals, coaxed some response from the regime. Adapted to the new purpose, the official populist doctrine, in full stalinist panoply, could be put to self-serving use.

The myth of love for the peasant veiled operational expediency. While the regime was reestablishing order in the kolkhoz, the time-honored populist formulae helped. They promised a more generous attitude to the peasant problem in the future. This anticipated, in fiction, Khrushchev's forthcoming revisions of Stalin's policy; it facilitated some compromise with the genuine populist element among the restive intelligentsia; and it offered the reader agreeable cathartic fare.

Above all, the populist strategy was useful in coping with the returning veteran. If he had been an officer, he tended to be restless, demanding, even spoiled. Some uprooted party functionaries turned out to be downright troublesome, and the lofty myth that Stalin personally saw fit to send them "into the people" provided an honorific way of wedging some of them into the lower strata of the working force. The honored ethic of populism camouflaged the stinginess with which rewards were doled out, and the harsh fact that, after the war, the regime demanded even more sweat from its citizens. So it came to pass that populism merged with administrative needs. Even more conveniently, the populist trend became a way of controlling cocky bureaucrats. Sending them "into the people" was a way of keeping them in order.

This message was proclaimed by various heroes in populist garb. A stylish example among them is the crippled colonel[10] who insists, on demobilization, on becoming a party worker at the grass roots, to help in the rebuilding of war-ravaged Crimea. He runs into an obtuse regional party secretary. The colonel refuses to be hypnotized by the party bureaucrat's rank and power, and confronts the important civilian with his own evolving philosophy on how most effectively to push on with postwar reconstruction.

"I have a theory – "

"Who doesn't?"

"No, you listen. Now, after this cruel war, we must make such a leap forward that the prewar level must seem insignificant. Right?"

"Let's assume that . . . So?"

"In that case, it seems to me, we must do the following. In the past we used to push people into the city, to Moscow, into the people's commissariats. With the same energy and consistency with which we used to do this, we must now take these very same cadres, trained high up there, and send them back, down."

"Into the people?" [the party secretary] inserted, somewhat sarcastically.

"Yes. Into the people. We must send the commissars down to the regions, their deputies to the districts, colonels to regional defense committees, brigade engineers down to the level of roadworkers."[11]

This massive demotion across the board becomes the colonel's obsession. It blends with his decision to harness himself to an ungrateful, lowly local party job. His brand of populism is functional, organizational, a means to cut the party's surplus fat away. His "radical" position does not readily make friends among the bureaucrats.

The Yalta conference is afoot. Our man is conscripted to help out as guide in the sightseeing offered to foreign dignitaries. He has a surprise encounter with an old army friend. Both had started out as lieutenant colonels. Unlike the hero, the friend has made his way as a career officer. Having reached heights of the general staff, he now struts, resplendent, in a general's uniform. Full of his vulgar self, he deplores the colonel's ineffective destiny.

"Brother, how did you get stuck with the rank of colonel? I have worn my eyes out looking for your name in the High Command lists. I was sure you would be not less than a brigadier-general. Why the devil did you take off to the province? And what about the academy? And don't you remember, you wanted to write? Or was all that just wishful thinking, hm?"   [8, p. 4]

He notes, of course, with a mixture of surprise and disdain, the good colonel's shabby clothes and the crude and creaking artificial limb donated by a kolkhoz. He offers advice as to how his impoverished friend should better himself. He suggests that he somehow reapply for reentry into the military structure. And he even hints at offering him a job under his own command. Our man will not hear of it. Nevertheless, his friend invites him to dine in the resplendent coastal villa which he is using during the Yalta conference. Though aware of being déclassé, the colonel does not resist.

They dined in select company. Four generals and three diplomats. The colonel turned out to be the eighth guest. He was introduced in somewhat vague terms. This made him unpleasantly mysterious, in the manner of a poor relative. Everybody thought that he would at once start begging favors for himself or for local needs. The anticipation embarrassed them.

He does no such thing. On the contrary, he sets out to charm them. With wit and conviction, he unfolds his philosophy to this elite group.

The generals started shouting that he was one hundred percent right and if he had his fill of war combat the best thing to do was to go "into the people." The diplomats joked obscurely. But in a vague way, they sided with him as well.

At this point the author takes over. He speaks for his hero. And the message floats across in rhapsodic overtones:

[He] spoke of country life as if he had spent many years in a village. He did not envy [his friend] who was leaving in a few days for Yugoslavia, nor one of the diplomats who was about to take off for the United States. He knew that all of them would lead a life replete with fascinating experiences, while he would remain in a house... with an unplastered ceiling from which the dust pattered down at night, stirred up by the mice. He knew he would continue to go out in the pouring rain to his lectures, to meeting with people, to sessions of writing letters to the front for those who were illiterate. He had for many years ascended the social ladder. He had become used to the fact that today he occupied a higher position than yesterday and that tomorrow he would rise higher yet. And in that constant upward thrust and growth he had found his happiness. But now his thinking had become very different. He now craved to reverse the direction, to go back down, down to the sources of life and of human strength.

We interrupt him here to emphasize what he has to say next. For his motivation surfaces fleetingly, in passing. Yet the very next statement holds the formula for populism sponsored by stalinism – utilitarian populism. For one thing, the colonel does not intend to settle with the folk on the bottom in perpetuity.

He wanted to descend, however, not because morally he had become impoverished, but because he needed a running start for a high leap. This downward craving was just as strong and as full as the former drive to ascend had
been.   [8, p. 6]

For our purpose this is a seminal passage. The ambiguities in this man's
urges to ascend, descend, and ascend again resolve themselves once his
great leap is understood: it signifies the harnessing of populist sentiment
to the purpose of shaking up and, if possible, rejuvenating the stagnant
stalinist party bureaucracy. In a novel as politically correct as this, one
might expect just this kind of accommodation with the grass roots
philosophy.

The downward-directed colonel's tale culminates in the dizzying scene
where he is summoned by Stalin himself to a private audience, in
Molotov's presence. HE holds the humble colonel's hand for a long time.
HE has been told about what the colonel stands for and is doing.

"I have been told about you and, in my opinion, you have done well," said Stalin
immediately, "in choosing to work at the district level. Regrettably, we still have
many people who prefer being clerks in Moscow rather than their own bosses on
the periphery . . . Such people still exist, but soon their time will run out."
                                                                         [8, p. 9]

HE approves, in homely and unhinging language. The ultimate grace
flows down on the colonel in this beatific scene.

The firm harnessing of populism to stalinist goals undercut and
preempted any genuine surge of populism which concerned itself with the
people, with the neglected, pauperized peasant. This manipulation ex-
pands the Big Deal by taking it into the rural realm and it renders it more
flexible by grafting populist semantics onto it.

Near-populist Hamlet

In the year before Stalin's death, a sketch of sixteen pages, called "District
Doldrums," became an overnight sensation. Two further instalments
were subsequently published in *Pravda*, so becoming matters of state.[12]
The main characters, locked in struggle, gave birth to "isms." The party
functionary Martynov could be identified in the final hour of stalinism as
stalinism with a soul. He undertook to combat his superior, named Borzov, synonymous with unadulterated stalinism. The outcome of the
struggle was to remain uncertain.

Borzov, the party secretary of a rural district, is a negative character
who seems all the more boorish as his administrative methods become
obsolete before the reader's eyes. Martynov, his newly appointed deputy,
the so-called "second," is a good man. But his tentative methods are hard
to label and it is not clear exactly what he stands for. He responds to the
flock more than he guides it. He meditates at length, Hamlet-like. This is
not necessarily good, since he has to do more than brood. His superior,

imprudently, leaves to tend his telltale ulcers in the Crimea and Martynov is saddled with the whole responsibility for the district. Open, flexible, with more heart than ideology, Martynov does not enter the tale ready-made. If the secretary is cast of iron, Martynov develops on the job. He learns to brace himself, to take sides, to use a different kind of control over the sagging rural economy than that imposed by the cocksure Borzov. But Martynov is, finally, ambiguous.

The catalytic agent is the sturdy, overachieving, kolkhoz manager Openkin, who reigns over the richest community for miles round in which he successfully inspires his people to work well, to live well, and so delivers his quota far ahead of time. The only thing he fears is that the destructive bureaucrats will bring him down in one of two ways. First, they may impose a surplus quota retroactively. Second, he may be forced to make grain loans to his lagging neighbors. The loans he has made over many years to his hungry neighbors have never been repaid. Administrators have always protected the slackers. Though neither surplus deliveries nor bad debts can ruin Openkin's sound operation, the stupidity of party administrators still appalls him. He is willing to help out in an emergency, but thinks the principle of patchwork is ruinous to the system. The Openkins know it; the Borzovs do not. The new Martynovs begin to understand.

Borzov, mistrusting Martynov, cuts short his vacation and, immediately on his return, as Openkin had feared, orders Martynov to transfer Openkin's kolkhoz into the higher category of delivery quotas. Martynov refuses to yield. He even defends Openkin from being put into a difficult position in front of his own peasants. This "humanitarian" approach angers Borzov.

"Let him say what he wants to his people. We need bread. What are you worried about him for? He is an old landlord! He'll manage!"[13]

Martynov does not give in.

"I know he will manage to convince his people. They will deliver the grain. But the situation remains unchanged. We take the bread away from them because of those kolkhozes where there is mismanagement and squandering."

He comes up with a novel idea which shows him up as a rather strange populist who sides with the rich, not with the poor:

"Let there be a shortage of bread in some kolkhozes. The people will understand. And they will agree that this is Soviet justice. Our agitators will have something to point to when they say to the people 'You receive in accordance with your work.' And let it happen that the people next door have the right to get three times more bread for their work! That's what our policy should be built on."

Borzov, in oppressing kulaks by stalinist reflex, may do the poor peasants more good than Martynov, overimpressed by the energy of one potent achiever. Borzov, to be sure, pursues only one end: delivery of norms. He does this in disregard of equity. But Martynov disregards equity too, for different purposes. Fretting about the short term, he supports one good manager and sticks by him. He champions productive partnership. But this makes him both a curious elitist and a curious populist at once.

The conflict forces other functionaries to take sides. Those who are for Martynov support his protégé Openkin. One of them chimes in timidly with advice to Borzov:

"Yes, watch out that you don't cut the throat of the goose that lays the golden eggs."

The problem of squeezing without choking leads Borzov to reexamine the option of bringing pressure on the other kolkhozes. But there is not one that is not behind target. And he explodes.

"So why the devil do you preach justice and policy to me! Where is there any bread? Bread right now, this very minute, for loading into trucks and taking to the granaries? Do you think the regional committee will agree to wait until your famous justice is introduced? What will we show in our report? Some policy makers!"

Martynov's retort rings the bell for the last round.

"If deliveries are to be forced without a policy, then no one needs district secretaries. The whole matter could be entrusted to agents."

That does it. Icily, Borzov sums up.

"Now I see that you are the main obstacle in the way of grain delivery, comrade Martynov. You have demobilized yourself and you demoralize the others. You demoralize the party."

For all the exaggeration of the charge, Borzov has a point. The pressure of the entire system comes to bear on him. The party official above him is not likely to settle for any newfangled justice; the man above *him* will not let him. This truth, however, does not subdue Martynov. Meanwhile, in a frenzy, Borzov sends thunderbolt telegrams to every farm and MTS: "fulfill, finish, hurry," all of them spiced with threats of court action. Smouldering with outrage, Martynov counters him with accusations of cowardice, of meaningless "formalist" gestures, of dishonest interference with the hard work of peasants. Borzov stands his ground:

"And doesn't the regional office send us such telegrams? Don't they call us on the phone all the time to ask 'Why aren't you sowing?' when the snow is up to the knees in our fields?"

Martynov replies:

"But we know our situation here at this moment! Do you know what our peasants absolutely cannot stand, [Borzov]? It's stupidity."

Surprisingly, Borzov controls himself, and suggests a solution, both effective and intelligent. He begs Martynov to go away, to ask for a transfer, and he makes the remark for which we have been waiting.

"Please go and talk to them. Whenever you wish. Even today. They will give you a district, maybe next to us. We shall compete. Go ahead, be a leader. You will work with that peasant justice of yours and, me, I shall do it in my proletarian way."   [pp. 211-12]

This is a climactic statement. Proletarian aims were bound to collide with those of the peasant. Openkin derails both comrades, friend and foe, sending them off the tracks of the Big Deal, poorly laid in any case in the rural vastness. While he causes Borzov to constrict him too much, he seduces Martynov into giving him too much latitude.

Borzovism hails from the early proletarian militancy which bureaucrats had taken over, nurturing vindictiveness against the peasant. But Borzov is not altogether a monster, nor is he a thief. Under pressure, he fights as best he can. The country needs bread; the peasants fail to deliver. A vast number of kolkhozes cannot deliver because they are poor. So the struggle goes on, from season to season. The district must produce, for the region squeezes the district as it itself is pressed by the republic. Being the administrator in the middle is Borzov's main predicament. He rules in that vulnerable middle zone, subject to opposite pressures. His loyalty is upward, not downward.

But Martynov is not a genuine populist either. How could he be, as a party functionary? He shows that for a functionary with a new soul, the old problems become more and more difficult. Sensitive to the needs of the new era, he doubts the workings of the Big Deal under Stalin's auspices. His Hamlet-like brooding over rigid controls inhibits him from giving a good stalinist performance. His stance makes him a partner of the regime with a populist twist, anxious for the adaptation of the Big Deal to a wider social band than had been intended. His pragmatic peasant justice might make the recruitment of rural partners easier.[14]

This opaque hero does some good, but blunders as much. His mixed performance signals some mutations in the Big Deal and a need to revitalize it, a difficult task. The tale raises more questions than it answers, but it forecasts change. Stalin had not cared in the least about the peasant. Martynovism marks a shift toward a reexamination of the rural scene, with some amelioration in mind. The regime had to reconsider the peasant question and to respond, to some degree, to the pressure of genuine populism.[15]

The improbable agronomist

Stalinist populism is pseudopopulism. It presses down on the people as does everything else in the dictatorship. The potentates in Moscow did not relish the prospect of lengthy safaris with the plebs in the boondocks. Populism in the form of demotion is no real populism. Still, as an expedient, it helped rationalize the relocation of postwar administrators and invigorate the controlling mechanism of the party bureaucracy.

At some point, however, as Martynov shows, the regime began to notice the new kulaks. It also began to acknowledge peasant poverty, and even to listen to those who advocated the peasant cause. For some people had become its passionate advocates. Authentic populism was becoming a reality in the life of the postwar intelligentsia. As of old, some young professionals found themselves working among the people and liked it "down there." The more they liked what they had undertaken, the more they pressed from below on behalf of the peasant. Once in a while they provoked the powerful. We turn to one such confrontation, a tale published in 1954 and one which could not have appeared earlier. But it was in gestation while Stalin was still alive and was published soon after his death, which shows the contrast and the link between pseudo- and real populism, one responding to the other.

This tale is about the tenacity of real populism which had hung on since the middle of the previous century. It now surfaces rather daringly and relates to the way in which the status quo began, in some permissible areas, to be scrutinized by young people.

The heroine is a bright, well-trained, goal-directed agronomist. Skipants show beneath her old coat. Her high cheekbones give character to her face. A childlike knitted cap perches on her head. She wears pigtails tied with blue ribbons. The descriptive detail is no whim; the author is signalling with both arms. The pigtails stand for innocence. The eyes reinforce it. Openly, eagerly, impatiently, they expect "miracles." The girl has just been sent to join a professional team in a large machine tractor station (MTS). But her reception is cool. The dapper young men, male chauvinists one and all, can hardly conceal their distress at the strange new colleague and nickname her "our improbable agronomist."

Shy and awkward at defending her own interest, this freckled little creature embodies courage. She burns with fervor, and her goal provides the story. Having acquainted herself with the methods of the enterprise, she rebels against its routine. The subservience to pressure from above, in her understanding, precludes a real interest in local problems. Just before seedtime, she decides to revise the crop rotation. Such an unheard-of step sets the entire staff against her. For she is dealing with the most successful MTS in the region. The quotas have always been blindly fulfilled ahead of deadlines. The chief engineer, a cunning careerist, has always seen to that. Hostility against the improbable troublemaker mounts. The staff is now obsessed with getting rid of her. And she keeps sending alarm messages to regional party officials without getting a reply.

What animates her? Unlike the rural functionaries and technicians, she frets over poor farms, for she knows that they are dragged further down by central planning. Animal husbandry sinks lower and lower for lack of fodder. And the plans from above demand crops that will not grow in the local soil. It takes innocence, not indoctrination, to pity the disadvantaged peasants, and you have to be outside all "deals" to start challenging rank and power. The improbable agronomist takes on something more formidable than windmills. The climax deserves unhurried unfolding.

Sowing is in progress. According to his habit, the local potentate, the regional party secretary, visits the renowned MTS on his grand journey through his principality. As the staff conduct the inspection, enthusiastic campaign talk resounds. The improbable agronomist trots along, her eyes glued to the regional secretary. She has never seen such an important man so close. "And she seems to expect from him extraordinarily noble and interesting deeds." Having rapidly inspected everything, he prepared to leave. His last benevolent words are that the harvest promises to be excellent and so do the payments to the peasants.

"No," she cries out, "No, Sergei Sergeevich, that's not true."

Neither the party secretary, who had of course not even noticed her before now and who stares in amazement at the petite figure, nor anyone else present can believe his ears. The chief rivets his eyes on her icily and proffers the following with threatening emphasis:

"It is a bad thing when the chief agronomist works in that defeatist mood. It is bad when such demoralizing words are uttered before sowing."[16]

Rejecting decorum, she blurts out:

"But it's even worse when the first secretary of the regional party committee promises the lagging kolkhozes good pay for three years in a row and then deceives people for three years."

The consternation is unbounded; everybody freezes. And as the narrator, looking back, asks whether it is stupidity or stubborn faith in humanity that impels the rebel on, the corpulent secretary heavily, slowly, and ominously replies:

"The secretary of the regional committee never gives and never promises either harvests or pay. Remember that, comrade chief agronomist. The harvest and its rewards are earned by the labor of peasants under the leadership of specialists. Under your leadership! You must know that, comrade chief agronomist of the MTS. I have been working for eleven years in the regional committee and have never deceived anyone."

The girl presses her fists against her chest and, with pain loud and clear, adds:

"But if the peasants in the lagging kolkhozes again receive nothing for their labor, will you come to them again with your lies?"

No one can guess what the accused boss most feels – outrage, anger, or that same pain that is pushing the improbable agronomist to the brink. His face turns "swollen and dark." And in a dark mood he affirms that next year he will take her on his inspection tour and that it is she who will explain to the peasants why they have earned so little. For he sees their lot as her responsibility. Curiously, she overcomes her embarrassment at this point:

"But I can explain it now. It's because of poor management and wrong rotation of crops. It's because – "

At this point her voice gives out. She starts trembling.

She had been pressing for a change in the rotation without any response from above. No one has so much as recognized the problem. This forces the secretary's hand. He is in a good position to say why her pleas have gone unanswered. And he does. The bureaucrats had vetoed the idea of change at this late hour and had ordered the fixed plans to be enforced. With that clarification given, he wants to leave. His foot is already inside the car. The girl recovers her voice. She implores him to permit changes, however limited. "If only for some kolkhozes! If only for my lagging ones!" The pitiful voice somehow touches him and he asks, not without sarcasm, "So the lagging ones are *yours*. And those which are not lagging, whose are they?" Confused, she cannot answer. At that moment, one person, the only one who can do so, steps in. Of course, it is an old peasant: and therein lies the purpose of the scene.

"How could it be otherwise, Sergei Sergeevich? A sick child is closer to a good mother's heart. And a good agronomist worries most about the poor kolkhozes."

The secretary remains adamant. Yet he indicates that her pleas can be submitted to him next year for discussion. She still follows him "like a sleepwalker." And she speaks to him "as if, apart from the two of them, there is no one else there."

"It cannot be postponed for a year. They have no fodder there at all! Look what I found in one hut. This is what the widow Varvara on the farm 'October' is giving her little girl instead of milk."

She pulls out a baby's bottle filled with a mixture of water and ground sunflower seed. What the secretary says next makes everybody cringe.

"We know all about the existence of lagging kolkhozes. There is no need for this public demonstration."

The tale touches on a covert issue of enormous importance: the system's callousness. Middlebrow fiction requires that such a portentous accusation be placed in the mouth of a child, and sleepwalker at that. But the child succeeds: she manages to delay the departure of the regional secretary. She undermines his hollow euphoria and stops him in his tracks.

As for his face, it had now turned to stone. And his lips turned white. Our improbable agronomist knew how to strike a person's most, most painful spot. Indeed she did! And in her eyes I saw the great grief of a child, the desperate helplessness of a trusting child. She stared at the secretary in such a way, as if that very minute her entire youth were coming to an end. She looked at him in such a way, as if she recognized it and was afraid and still could not believe that such great sorrow was possible on earth.

This populism is convincing, not just in the protagonist but in the folk scene itself, directed against the administration. The secretary would have preferred an office discussion, and cannot conceal his alarm at this public display of self-laceration, at these confessional postures, this babies' bottle passed around accusingly, symbolizing the system's failings. But, even more importantly, there has been a public demonstration of the solidarity of the populist with the people. This embarrasses the bureaucracy, which perpetuates inequity, its hydrocephalic head always tilted upwards.

Who can become one with the people, flesh of their flesh? Ivanushka-Durachok, the pure fool, can. Innocence – foolish and wise, the heart of a child, quivering with old-style Russian compassion. The tale skirts the sentimental, but the tonality is of importance. It takes just this blend – child, folk, sentiment – to place the theme of populism on an effective course, moving toward a vast adaptation of the Big Deal, if not toward an alternative.

The secretary might have left at this point, but he does not. The closing chords herald the party official's salvation. The folk in this heavily populated scene, composed of MTS personnel and the assembled peasants, stand transfixed as they watch him make his decision. Instead of driving away in his chauffeured vehicle, he chooses to atone.

As he stood there with his hand on the door of the car and with his foot on the running board, he suddenly turned toward the girl: "You know what the peasant woman Varvara feeds her child with. That's very good. But do you know how we lived there behind the salt marshes before? No, you don't. I come from there. Not only did we have no milk, but we went without bread."

Reminiscing pointedly and nervously, he recalls the days of revolution and reconstruction, praising Soviet achievements. But what counts is that he opts to bare his soul. Speaking slowly and with difficulty, "as if turning stones over," he concludes by reaching out to the improbable agronomist, by yielding to her. "All right!" he says to her, "Let's go. Let's think your proposals over." He has seen something valuable in the girl's obstinacy. "He felt it, weighed it, and at once forced himself to surmount his own irritation." His image changes in the eyes of his subjects. It matters a great deal that he should appear in a new light, not so much before the peasants as before the pushy group of professionals.[17]

How many times had he visited us before! How many times had we discussed business with him! We respected him, but with some sort of official deference. But at this moment he disarmed us all. Not officially, and not as a tribute to his position and status, but spontaneously and out of deep inner conviction, we acknowledged him as a man stronger and more intelligent than we. [pp. 27-30]

New Tidings

An explorer

My closing vignette needs no explanation. It is enough to see through the Soviet author's eyes, and to stay very close to the text, which is informal enough.

Dozing on a sunny sandy beach one late afternoon, the narrator has been roused several times by a rather shrill female voice admonishing someone: "Komarov, stop it! Komarov, do you hear?" It flashes through the author's mind that this Komarov must be a bothersome person, and that it is hard to tell offhand what he is up to. The voice becomes louder: "Komarov, for the last time, leave Red alone! . . . Get up, Komarov!" This time the accused person replies grudgingly: "But I am not doing anything!"

Curiosity now induces the author to turn around and see what is going on. And he beholds, very close by, a person altogether naked except for a cockily tilted straw hat. The person is about four years old, snub-nosed, freckled, mischievous-looking, with spirited, if unreliable, expression. A fat woman, inappropriately clad in a crackling, stiff, green silk dress, stoops over Komarov. She has her educational hands full: some twenty-five of Komarov's comrades and contemporaries are prostrate nearby on the sand, bellies down and angular shoulder blades sticking out, sunbathing. A compulsive person, the woman wants to know first why Komarov has pushed the aforementioned Red, and second why Komarov has thrown sand about. Komarov answers the first with a cogent counter-question: "Why is he lying there like a dead man?" The second is even more cogent: "Who threw anything? I was just sawing. It's the wind that blew the sand." The narrator suggests that "the shrewd substance" of the answers leads the pedagogue into an impasse and evokes a sigh: "Tiresome boy!" Just then the nurse approaches, pointing to her watch, and the pedagogue waves her stubby arms at her charges like an agitated mother hen. "Get dressed! Get in line!" Everybody busies himself with shorts and sandals, except Komarov. He wishes to know who it is, exactly, who is going to go for a dip in the sea. The pedagogue, with a touch of sarcasm, replies: "Not you, at any rate!" Knowing how hard it is to silence Komarov, she adds that the doctor has forbidden bathing because the water is too cold. With his blend of earnestness and irony, Komarov now asks whether the danger is that "the little children" will catch cold. To this, of course, the pedagogue replies: "Enough talk. Get dressed." Disgusted, Komarov grabs his shorts and runs to take his place in the column. "Off we go!" the pedagogue commands, clapping her hands. The column heaves, starts off, and at once gets ensnarled, with the children piling up on top of each other. From the conglomerate comes much squealing. As it turns out, Komarov had tripped, had pushed over the boy in front, who had produced a chain reaction. The pedagogue manages to sort out the column after much puffing. She gives a new order to depart. Once more, the column instantly collapses. She asks what on earth is the matter, and the children shout ecstatically that Komarov keeps keeling over. She orders the culprit to step forward.

Komarov conscientiously tries to execute the order, makes a strange, foreshortened step, and falls on the sand.

"What's the matter with you, Komarov?" "I'm in a bad way," says Komarov. He gets up, makes one step, and falls down again.

"What's really the matter with him?" – there is despair now in the pedagogue's voice – "Can it be a sunstroke?"

Komarov's comrades are delighted. They roar with laughter as one of them says: "Nina Pavlovna, he has put both legs into one pant leg."

This takes the pedagogue aback. The amused narrator observes that the embattled woman has probably never had children of her own. She stares at Komarov in dejection and her face turns crimson at the clumsy and inexperienced effort to liberate one of his legs.

"Why did you do such a thing?" she asks trying to straighten herself out.

"It's more interesting this way," Komarov explains calmly and benevolently and, suddenly struck by a new idea, he asks "Nina Pavlovna, what is a person?"

"I don't know," she waves him away with irritation, having spontaneously told the truth.[1]

Postscriptum: From Fear to Envy

"Eto u nas tozhe est" or definition of champagne: The favorite drink of the working class, which it drinks through the lips of its finest representatives.

The poet Vladimir Mayakovsky, considered by Pasternak – for a brief moment – the only true citizen of the nascent bolshevik state,[1] long ago warned kindred rebels about the impending takeover of the revolution by Soviet meshchanstvo. In 1921 he saw stagnation spreading over the grandiose social chaos.[2] He saw a grinning meshchanstvo peeking out from behind Lenin's institutions, eager to invade the bureaucratic honeycomb. In meshchanstvo's house, in its private den, he imagined Marx's portrait in an appropriately red frame. Marx gazed out at a kitten snoozing on top of the newspaper *Izvestiya*, while a canary chirped in its hanging cage. This ambience incited Marx to murder. All of a sudden he shouted out that the canary must be beheaded at once lest it defeat communism.[3]

One look today at Soviet citizens in a Rumanian coastal resort, carrying their cameras and their suntan oil, and flashing their eager roubles, suggests that meshchanstvo took over long ago, and that the Big Deal has financed its entrenchment. The street cleaner, the aging faceless woman wrapped in the kerchief of poverty, testifies to the same thing as she picks up cigarette butts from the railings clamped around the treetrunks of Moscow's immaculate Gorky Avenue. So does *Krokodil*, the official satirical weekly, *Pravda's* subsidiary; so does the dissident poet. Any look, at home or abroad, at any group of Soviet citizens suggests the same.

Abrasive disparities separate the haves from the have-nots, inducing cynicism because so much is also shared between the lower and upper social zones. Meshchanstvo has managed to unify Soviet society. The goals at the top and the bottom are the same: acquisitiveness reigns.

If under stalinism it was fear that gripped the whole population (an existential condition as resilient and self-protective as it was aggressive and fratricidal), today the condition which determines the quality of life for Everyman has largely changed into envy. Greed at the top is one thing, while craving at the bottom for minimal material comfort, so long denied, is another. The ponderous deportment of the rulers, surrounded by underlings who await windfall bonuses, patronage, and special privileges should not cloud our effort to understand, from a distance which blurs too many things together, the needs of the people. The envy and the craving of the have-nots for an easier life, so long in coming and as yet so far from realization, is bitter but legitimate. There is, in other words, meshchanstvo and meshchanstvo. It both unites and divides. The need for shoes, the hope of a kitchen not shared with wrangling strangers, the dream of a room other than a cluttered place for beds in which together a family's three generations sleep, this is not the greed for dachas and diamonds. The meaning of the gap between shoes and diamonds may be less obvious to the outsider who is squeamish about philistinism in general and Soviet variants of it in particular.[4]

After Ehrenburg's quasi-prophetic *Thaw* of 1954, Dudintsev's *Not by Bread Alone* of 1956 must be counted among the few pivotal documents, chronicles of transition. Both were fervently discussed by countless citizens at the end of stalinism and in its aftermath. Under his eloquent title, Dudintzev undertook to show that a talented engineer, a creative partner in the Big Deal, requires satisfaction *other* than remuneration and must, therefore, challenge, at great risk for himself, the castrating bureaucrats. At the time the author sounded like the Pied Piper of freedom and was of course mistreated by the authorities as such. Twenty years later, it seems that his plea, important as it was, was of limited social scope and applicability. The author had spoken in appropriately didactic tones for the normative demands of the technical intelligentsia, or rather for a select few among them. The demand for the unshackling of individual creativity differed then as now from the demands of the vast majority. Today, with the waning of cant even in middlebrow fiction, it becomes clearer that for the masses liberation mostly means putting first things first. The people wish to live first by bread alone. "And then we shall see."

Between the greed of the nouveau riche and the hardship of the underprivileged, in the gray intermediary zone, middle-middle meshchanstvo makes its own way. As an example, a fur coat is celebrated for bringing solace to its owner in a compact, compassionate, chiaroscuro ballad, typically small scale and matter-of-fact for a liberal poet of the early sixties. A "superfluous" divorcée is lost in the urban rat race. While her erratic love life brings her nothing but grief, she strains for a little dignity in a world of male supremacy, broken families, the imbalance between the sexes, and the ensuing promiscuity. The poet does not spell all this out, but that backdrop is understood.

> How much noise!
> Oh what a fuss!
> What a lot of fuss!
> A fur coat!

Fur coat.
I hope no harm comes of it.
This fur coat now it's bought
Is not at all bad.
Really quite nice.
Reddish fur glowing,
It hangs over her bed.
Stanislava has turned thirty,
Not some other woman, she herself.
Certainly she has the right·
To wear this coat come winter.

The garment suddenly reveals its Soviet identity because a person must somehow earn a right to its ownership. The poet tells us that this woman could not endure marriage to a philandering boor. Exploitation by lovers makes her suffer even more. But she tries to find herself just the same in the world of men, an effort described as "a raid deep behind enemy lines."

The thirty years have not been easy.
Have seen a lot of bad things!
Even filth.
Stanislava cannot help
Having been born a woman.
Things did not go right for her . . .
She was hungry and she was cold.
But she started to save.
Salesmen were hinting grossly
That times were special now.
In the end, though,
The fur coat came to hang
Over her bed.

As a counter to any glib disdain for meshchanstvo's furs, the poet appeals on the woman's behalf to "Autocrats, Potentates, Judges!" He pleads in the most minor of keys that she be permitted to find family happiness and be given inner peace

To put her thin arms
For the first time,
Holding her breath in her ecstasy
Through these fur sleeves
À trois quart.[5]

A very special warmth is here expected from the fur coat. If exegesis of all the meaning of the overcoat for Gogol's poor clerk Akakii has not yet been exhausted, this coat also tells us something about lost citizens in a society which is simultaneously uniform and atomized. There are, then, fur coats and fur coats.

Meanwhile, with growing self-assurance, the rulers advertise the system's strength. Under their lulling incantations, there emerges a stratified society with its upper and middle ranks committed to the status quo, and with the plebs crowding the entrance hall.

The Big Deal – the ingenuous initial concordat between stalinism and middleclass productivity – worked both because there was no other alternative and because it proved viable, becoming increasingly so during the successive phases of post-stalinism. Its momentum began to sag in the last spasms of stalinism; and Khrushchev's reign, although endeavoring to set it on a sturdier base and to enlarge its constituency, betrayed ambiguities of a residual populist nature; but the Brezhnev regime has embraced it fully and unequivocally. And with it meshchanstvo blossoms. At some point the regime began to respond to the people's need for a better life, the dream which had been shaped long before by middleclass aspirations. Consumer goods became available and improved; Their Excellencies the Refrigerator, the Washing machine, the Television set, the Record player, and, most coveted, the "Volga" made their appearance. More and more people began to worship the goods in showrooms and strained to think them now, perhaps, within their reach. Cookbooks with tempting color plates, featuring jellied sturgeons festooned in radish rosettes and live daisies, were followed by chapters on kulturnost. Lessons in manners, featured in popular magazines and summarized in calendars, go well with recipes for partridges in sour cream. The total style of meshchanstvo's desires has been accepted so thoroughly that it has stimulated the beginnings of a counterculture. This is polarized among the young; between cynics who look for loopholes and shortcuts and, if frustrated, become aggressive; and on the other hand, the genuine dissidents, who have some insight into the system, who are motivated by idealism and revere the handful of martyred leaders. This polarization does not necessarily mean that there are not crosscurrents between the two extremes, but that is another story.

The arrangement by which material benefit is bestowed on chosen citizens is one way in which the Big Deal pacifies meshchanstvo. But since Stalin it has offered more than that, facilitating the upward mobility of more and more people, a way out of the peasant or worker milieu and into the establishment. It gives thousands of citizens status, the most savory ingredient of the good life. Under Brezhnev, stability is maintained by engaging younger partners to perform in the economy while keeping their role marginally insignificant in the political system. The present regime also seems to bank successfully on the hostility of these junior partners to those who challenge the politics of the Big Deal. The former, as they acquire more goods and more liberties, are viscerally threatened by critics who seem to be rocking the boat. What is being continuously renegotiated by the regime with the droves of the newly inducted is not the norm but the rate of exchange.

The broad question of whether the Big Deal achieved its economic goals is overshadowed by the social response. It was this response which finally turned out to be more significant than the mere modernization of national productivity. It was this response which has released the aspirations of the common citizens in a less fettered fashion than before. The life of some is now embellished by scalloped doilies, orange lampshades, and petunias. These may become accessible to all who crave them.

The attempt made in this study to document Stalin's reaching out to his own middle class helps us to understand the conduct and preferences of many citizens two decades after his death. To restate a premise, Stalin was not interested in his subjects' souls but in their bodies, not in what they were thinking but in what they were saying and doing. Pragmatist that he was, consequences mattered to him, not causes. His concern was not thought reform among his subjects, but reform of their reflexes, their actions, and their reactions. In other words, he was not trying to shape a new man. He was molding, lethally and furiously, the stalinist social order. Therefore he had to build on something already existing, natural and well rooted in the social structure. Meshchanstvo gave him that foundation. The men of power under Stalin were meshchane, one and all, brought up from the bottom: the stakhanovite, the officer, the manager, the scientist. This number was impressive. But at the same time, because of the terror, the upward movement was erratic and subject to cancellation.[6] Although meshchanstvo was gaining strength under Stalin's auspices, it could not come to full fruition, since nothing else could either. But after Stalin, when large-scale terror subsided and was removed from the daily fears of the vast majority, meshchanstvo truly enmeshed with the heralded long-range purposes of the current regime. It began to carry on its crest the hope of most Soviet citizens for the good life. Nor should it be forgotten that, apart from terror, stalinism meant revolution from above or the terrible and dreaded hammering in of new social forms such as collectivization, industrialization, the forced resettlement of the population beyond the Urals, not to speak of concentration camps. If Lenin was stopped in some of his cataclysmic projects, nothing stopped Stalin. And his remodeling was successful. This is one more reason why meshchanstvo is bursting out in full bloom under Brezhnev. For revolutions have been put to rest. Since there is no need for further reshaping, Soviet society sits firmly in its mold; its leaders merely maintain it; their goals are principally the reproduction and perpetuation of the status quo.

Meshchanstvo today is canonized, its spirit enshrined. It could, therefore, even be said that Stalin's successors are currently in a mood to conclude a deal with the whole of Soviet society. Whatever the sources of resistance, they seem negligible compared with the mainstream of Soviet youth, of middleclass youth, pushy, cynical, careerist as it now is. In Soviet materialist society the have-nots strain for that which those on top have won and hold on to. Meshchanstvo welds the clerk with the professor, the stenographer with the cosmonaut. As for leadership, it has itself become the incarnation of the Big Deal. Up there they all engage in the same activity: they do business. During the times examined in this study, the difficulties of partnership were revealed, and specifically the frictions between party officials and managers; but something important has now started to erode. It is the difference in role and function, in accountability and initiative, between managers and party bosses. The partners have become more easily interchangeable. The military brass and industrial potentates as well as scientists sit down together and simply wheel and deal. From within Soviet society, no visible danger, for the moment, seems likely to threaten the Big Deal, which is growing bigger and bigger. This does not mean that one can predict lasting stability. Bad harvests have their way. There may be surprises in store. Curiously, meshchanstvo at the top is not altogether relaxed, and stability under the Brezhnevs at times gives the impression of brittle narrowness. Official cant is still blared loudly without completely drowning out the heretics. The incantational shrillness suggests that the regime does not take anything for granted. The common citizen is not yet trusted, still less the purist intelligentsia which stubbornly manages to think for itself. The regime seems incapable of handling dissent without the use of punitive martyrdom which boomerangs. Given some possible economic reverse or some rift at the summit, a push toward anarchy in the populace cannot summarily be ruled out. Even without large reverses, discontent may significantly increase among minorities, as well as among workers and, not least, the peasantry. The chances cannot be calculated.

Meanwhile, current domestic circumstances are propitious in themselves. But global contacts seem to be even more beneficial for the Big Deal. Stimulating a two-way exchange, the social impact of détente on the Soviet Union may be more important than economic agreements. Catherine the Great did as much damage as good when she imposed foreign potatoes, among other more monumental borrowings, on the populace. The scope of post-stalinist borrowing from the West would dazzle the eighteenth-century Romanovs and so would the posture that goes with it. The bourgeois West, with its artifacts and mores, has in fact become the measure of Soviet achievements. Both the leadership and the run-of-the-mill engineer sent abroad to supervise deliveries of capitalist gadgetry engage in comparisons obsessively. While he eats steak or buys purses or underwear that his wife has asked him to bring back, the emissary's facial muscles betray invidious admiration for American goods and food, shifting instantly to a mandatory kind of put-down. *I khochetsya i koletsya.* The formulaic equivocation before Western wealth signals more clearly than parochial bedazzlement how firmly national self-assessment has been put on a foreign platform. Like strange peeping Toms, Soviet officials look in on their own world from the outside. What is learned from the West, massively borrowed, or dearly purchased, increases the force of Soviet meshchanstvo. The knowhow of General Motors business techniques, coveted bureaucratic efficiency, empirical industrial sociology, even the braggadoccio of the military-industrial mystique, all these wonders of advanced civilization abroad can uphold Soviet goals. In this way the promulgated traffic with the West underpins meshchanstvo, strong enough on its domestic foundation. Kulturnost is acquiring a foreign cachet. As for the Soviet contribution to the global deal, history has contrived to overturn the Russian revolutionary impetus with amazing ease. The détente does not stir up any untoward feelings in Moscow or Novosibirsk, and by affirming the status quo it upholds Western conservatism as well in perfect two-part harmony.

Soviet experience has offered foreign admirers various lures at various times. The powerful attraction of the leninist utopia was exhilarating, intoxicating, cathartic. For a different set of aficionados and in a different mode, less exuberant and very costly, Stalin's excessively concrete realization of utopia was also attractive. From the sidelines, it was not difficult to convince oneself that the stalinist price paid by the indigenes was paid not altogether in vain and that something intrinsically grandiose was involved in the changing of a social order. So stalinist dynamism was found fetching in its time too. The paradox today is that the Brezhnev regime currently presides over a huge realm of stability. Becalmed and Victorian to the bone, Soviet philistines emphasize the sturdy nature of Soviet conservatism, making it attractive to philistines everywhere, and especially to those who hold power. Those in the West who crave safety from adventures, who seek assurances against the unfathomable, and who fear unrest above all have begun to admire the bulwark of Soviet ruling meshchanstvo.

Meanwhile the Soviet bosses have been enjoying life, and so have their retinues for quite some time.

> I like everything in this house: the stately rustle of
> the silk worn by the hostess and her dusky shawl.
> But, most of all, I like my sleeping princess –
> the crystal – held captive in a glass vitrine.
>
> In its transparent coffin, the rosy spectrum, composed
> of seven blushing hues, is dead and charming.
> But I have sprung to life. The ritual of welcome,
> as in opera, is finished, danced and sung . . .
>
> One of the guests, her glass extended,
> herself as hazy as the ceiling's gesso dove,
> puts to me a question, capricious and unkind:
> "Tell me, is it true your husband is a wealthy man?"[7]

This fragment is taken from a ballad inspired, not by a museum nor an accurately restored private mansion, but by an ambiguous reception in the Kremlin for various troublemakers among the younger poets while Khrushchev was master. The silks rustle on Nina Petrovna, or Madame Furtseva. The entire poem is ironical and even angry, the work of an obstreperous and moody intellectual. But we see that the irony is directed more against the clumsy inhabitants than against the style of life they try to adopt. Even sophisticated individualists press for privacy by honoring objects, possessions, artifacts – the curious attributes of the desired freedom. And the older the objects, the better. Libertarians have turned antiquarians. Some have even become connoisseurs.[8]

And what of the actual style of life at the bottom? All sorts of feelings on the subject began to be expressed, on the left and on the right, from power and from impotence. It is an interesting thought that not everybody should be scrambling upwards and that there is virtue in remaining settled in one's own social niche, however lowly. Khrushchev, revivalist that he was at times, reminded the populace that not every little girl could or ought to become a ballerina.[9] If they had a sincere ring, what would such feelings sound like when expressed by a champion of common citizens?

> Neither overpraised
> Nor maligned,
> I am simply a rank-and-file
> Hardworking man,
> Drawn to the vacant lots
> On the city's outskirts,
> To their inconspicuous grass.
> For good reason
> I dream more and more
> Of the courtyards
> Of my lost childhood
> While light blue laundry
> Still hangs on the line,
> Forgotten for a while.
> Outskirts! At early dawn
> I stand by the window.
> Women in aprons,
> I recognize the music
> Of your wrangles,
> I hear the clatter of your plates
> And pots,
> I hear the shuffle of old slippers.
> Gas burners in these kitchens
> Are holy to me. They mean shelter.
> Housepainters,
> Metalworkers,
> Tailors,
> Sales clerks,
> Teachers –
> So earthy, one and all,
> That Earth does not remember them –
> Chauffeurs and waiters.
> For good reason
> I feel akin
> To their inconspicuous talents,
> Their simple kindness.
> I am serene,
> At ease,

At home
Among the modest
Hardworking side streets,
Bereft of glamor.
The judges whom I accept must
Not intrude from the outside.
They are the destinies alone
Of the people right here,
The destinies whose reflection
I carry.[10]

A miniature like this genre picture, poignantly typical of the post-stalinist mood in somewhat disaffected circles, deserves a longer look than, off hand, one might think warranted. The poem's function and intention ask for a special clarity of vision in the reader. Somewhat muted and doleful, the confessional elements here can be easily twisted. The classic stalinist middlebrow output presented no such problem. Whatever cause these gray foreshortened lines may promote, they give the feel of a lowerclass suburb. The poet superimposes his own feelings on the description, even more, his judgment, which is not entirely aligned with poststalinist editorials. One must, therefore, ask how such mildly contrary verses found their way into a leading journal for komsomol readers. Were they written to order? Not in the same way as stalinist literature was ordered, invoiced, and stamped "received." Did this poem, so bleak and lacking in adroitness, slip by the multipronged mechanism of censorship? No, of course not. More commodious – but in their way no less vigilant – controls passed this, like scores of similar quietist miniatures, because there was no longer any compelling reason *not* to publish it. This kind of poetic, slightly devious muttering enjoyed in the sixties its own rather special audience, also tolerated because there was no reason not to. The exploratory function of literature – within well-determined limits – was permitted to emerge, along with the declining need for the new regime to exploit didacticism alone. The frenzied struggle against the independent drive of writers changed into a partial tolerance and partial indifference towards mild forms of self-expression. In this transition, Khrushchev even declared with remarkable absence of cant that writers henceforth were to act like grown-ups, that they were not to look to the party for constant guidance because the party had more important things to do than to watch over their internecine bickering.[11] Once a modicum of realism was permitted, and once publishable poets began to speak not just for the regime (another sign of embourgeoisement), it became a condition of the decoding of the messages to grasp who spoke for whom, a question which had had no meaning under stalinism. As a consequence of this new use of literature, a policy largely designed to release some steam from the pressure cooker, writers rapidly and openly splintered into the orthodox, the centrists, and the liberals – though they also divided into generations, regions and so on. The fragment above is the sottovoce of a quiet liberal with populist overtones. And it is, perhaps, one other indicator of the final embourgeoisement of Soviet society that it is hard to say whether the scene he paints is praised for being proletarian or middleclass. Certainly it is one in which the canary overpowered the militant collective myth a long, long time ago. Unlike Mayakovsky, the oracle of the twenties who had inveighed against meshchanstvo of any kind, the poet of the sixties murmurs a quietist Hosannah to domesticity, no matter how unprepossessing, to the canary no matter how archaic, to the private worlds of small citizens.

The rhapsodizing of folk meshchanstvo, struggling along on the humble outskirts of the metropolis, does not contest upperclass embourgeoisement, it blends with it by default or, perhaps, even by design. "To each his own" is the liberal message, scarcely susceptible of alternative interpretation. It is far less clear how such a separatist wish comes about, such a heralding of private corners. If the liberal poet does not now readily extoll public myths of large purpose – neither the worn-out official ones nor the emerging dissident ones – he does take a stand. In this instance, he pledges loyalty to his modest social provenance, and shows reluctance, at least poetically, to leave his tenement. Obviously, in a society as complex as Soviet society today, the massive drive of urban middleclass youth to rise into the establishment is accentuated by the reluctance of some of them to do so. Smaller in numbers, adhering to the style of the purist intelligentsia, some offer the populist reason for not wishing to climb. The quoted poet is obstinate. He will not be judged by standards other than those of his own social milieu; so he sounds like a genuine populist. He champions in the liberal, if not radical, manner, the inviolability of "separation," of one's own private realm. This gives him scope to transfigure Everyman's family kitchen stove into a spiritual good. In turn, this strangely minimal fervor may well mean acceptance of the status quo as much as the manuals on protocol for Kremlin banquets.

From the right and from the left, it would seem, from the top and from the bottom, private acquisitiveness is celebrated – cut-crystal goblets for the rich, clattering pots and pans for Ivan Ivanovich – so marking the triumph of the canary.

Postscript II

The motto I had chosen in 1976 – "Soviet novels explain both Soviet life and Soviet novels" – still stands. It helped me at the time to try to decipher gosizdat literature of the Stalinist postwar period in regard to both its function and its contents. Clearly enough, its function was to transmit to the reader the regime's value preferences. They in turn revealed strange shifts within the Marxist–Leninist–Stalinist canon which permitted what I had called the "Big Deal" to be concluded, i.e., the regime's alliance with the needs and aspirations of the growing middleclass.

With the advent of glasnost – whatever it may untranslatably mean – Soviet novels, curiously enough, have become less revelatory in a certain sense than they had been under strict controls. From the point of view of the writer, pre-glasnost revelation originated either out of unplanned and unpredictable illuminations or – less miraculously but truly honorably – out of the need and courage to say the truth and thereby take risks, God knows. Today's enforced de-Stalinization in poems, novels, and plays is, indeed, mandatory. But no matter how goal-directed and fervent the posthumous condemnations and accusations, the Soviet social fabric has become so torn and people so angry both diachronically and synchronically – divided by age, by place, by nationality, by class, by profession, and not least by sex – that the very revelatory effort has become splintered. The reader, especially the non-native reader, is lost.

The avalanche of published literature has also become an obstacle for an outside observer trying to understand what on earth is going on. Therefore, one is required to gather detail, for this self-made mini-avalanche requires looking back to what was occurring in Stalin's time. Without the memory of Stalinism and the inexhaustible attempt to understand it over and over, neither outsiders nor insiders will understand anything at all about the crushing problems of Soviet life as it approaches the new millennium.

My long-term observations of a process I had called "pronouns in transition" helped me in my attempt to understand the changing mode and contents of the making of myths in Soviet society. I understood then as I understand now that poems, plays, and tales contain and transmit myths and reflect the evasive matter of reality. Thus, it turned out that the waning and wilting of the exuberant, ecstatic, fortissimo revolutionary first pronoun plural – the proletarian WE in proletarian revolutionary odes and hymns – marked the passage from the revolutionary Bolshevik period to the Stalinist period. It had stood in dramatic, loud, repetitive abbreviation for Vladimir Kirillov's reigning phrase "collective breast." Stalin's absolutist third pronoun singular HE crushed both the myth and reality of the collective. And it took thereafter the advent of the Second World War, with its unspeakable loss of human life, to resurrect de profundis the private, personal, lyrical, doleful, and solacing singular pronouns *ty da ia* – you and me.

Thinking in long continuities, in long historical sequences, is both mandatory and dangerous. Nevertheless, it does not take too much research, documentation, or hairsplitting to realize that today's promised reforms need solid domestic support across the entire class structure. At the present time, evidence of its emergence is scanty and uncertain. What would the leadership of perestroika give for the first pronoun plural – the WE of Soviet youth today, especially from the underprivileged masses – to stand behind them firmly and united among themselves! Perestroika needs a community, a collective, even if only to express the hopes and aspirations of a civic society beyond, and especially above, the divisive self-interests of cliques. Cliquishness is not solidarity. Where are the agglutinate forces in the Soviet Union today? Where is brotherhood? Where is the legacy of *sobornost?*

I would like to close with two poems that embrace seventy-three Soviet years, 1917–1990. To do so, I repeat in its entirety Vladimir Kirillov's canonized hymn to the Bolshevik revolution with its "cosmic messianism," as it was called, and with its ardent hope for the proletarian world revolution.

We

We, innumerable dread legions of labor,
We have conquered spaces of sea, ocean, and land.
We have kindled cities with the light of artificial suns.
Our proud souls burn with the conflagration of revolts.
We are gripped by mutinous, passionate intoxication.
Let them shout at us: "You are executioners of beauty!"
In the name of our Tomorrow we shall burn Raphael,
Shall demolish museums, trample on flowers of art.
We have thrown off the load of oppressive heritage,
We have rejected the chimeras of wisdom bled white –
Our girls in the radiant kingdom of the future
Shall be more beautiful than the Venus of Milo.

Our eyes are drained by tears, our tenderness killed.
We have forgotten the odor of grass and blossoms of spring.
We have fallen in love with the might of steam and power of dynamite,
With the song of the siren, the motion of shafts and wheels.
We have become kindred with metal, have merged our souls with machines,
We have unlearned to sigh and pine for heaven.
We want everyone on earth to have enough to eat,
No groans and wails for bread shall be heard.

You poet-aesthetes, go on cursing Great Ham,
Kiss the fragments of the past beneath our heels,
Water with your tears the ruins of the broken temple:
We are free, we are bold, we breathe a different beauty.
The muscles of our arms thirst for gigantic labor,
Our collective breast burns with a creative pang.
With marvelous honey we shall fill the comb to its brim.
We will find a new and dazzling road for our planet.

We love life, its intoxicating furious rapture.
Our spirit has been toughened by stormy struggle, by suffering.
We are everybody. We are in everything. We are a light-dimming flame,
We are our own Deity and Judge and Law.

(trans. A. Kaun)

Robert Rozhdestvensky's recent poem speaks about pain, fear, and lost-ness even if or, perhaps, because meshchanstvo's orange lampshade, the foreign TV set, and the caged chirping canary have endured. Whatever else the pronoun in this long statement represents, it certainly speaks for the enormous Soviet professionalized middleclass which seems to both crave and fear perestroika.

Insomnia

We
   who fear the hole in the ozone,
      AIDS and co-op managers,
we
   who are stuffed since childhood
      with drugs, rumors, nitrates,
we who pray, curse,
   age, and grow,
we – the KGB interrogators and the interrogated,
   at work and on strike,
we who argue how to build a house –
   foundation first or first the roof,
we who crave
   instant democracy
      or blood,
we – uniform, typical,

seemingly untypical,
suddenly grown smart
  to create "consensus"
    "conversion," and "impeachment,"
waiting for instructions
  what to do
    and what not to do,
we who adore either Schnittke's music
  or tug-o'-war,
we who speak three languages
  and don't know our own,
ready to join a group of five
  provided the five
    attack one someone,
we – standing watch, beholden and indebted,
  superactive and on the sick list,
    boasting of a piece of sausage or of a foreign TV set,
by habit reporting to the authorities
  about early spring sowing,
some of us departing West for freedom
  others going North for money,
we who live in dormitories,
  mansions, basements, flats
demanding "bread and condoms"
  instead of "bread and circuses,"
united, divided,
  – phobes – addicts – philes,
we who favor jogging
  and detective films,
we – who crawl inside our shell,
  familiar with the Hermitage
    and the Butyrki prison,
dealing cards and dealing with exams,
  rotating guards
    and turning in empty bottles,
choking from smog,
  from happiness,
    and from insults,
making discoveries,
  pompous faces,
    dirty tricks,
we – gazing with fear at our
  feverish villages and towns,
dreaming of a bright future
  and of lasting till payday,
we – moral and immoral,
  looking ahead and backward,
incessantly in search of enemies
  and finding them always,

bursting with health,
    coughing up nicotine slime,
reliable and perplexed,
    beggars and grabbers,
we – wearing furs and quilted jackets,
    bathing suits and bulletproof vests,
lovers of flox and of dominoes,
    steam baths and operettas,
marching to work early along a frosty side street,
cursing sciatica and the State Planning Commission,
    holding faith in Kashpirovsky, the psychic,
screaming at our children, roaming about stores,
squeezed into subway cars,
    listening but not hearing,
we – who line up under the red,
    black,
        or white banner,
we ask ourselves
    what will become
        of us all?

(*Ogonyok*, No. 1, 1990; trans. VSD)

VERA S. DUNHAM

Notes

CHAPTER 1 THE BIG DEAL

The Front

1   A. Werth, *Russia At War* (New York, 1964), p. 423.
2   A. Korneichuk, *Front* (The Front) (1942), Sobranie sochinenii (Moscow, 1956), vol. 1, p. 134.
3   The need for military professionals was so pressing that it refracted in war fiction in the astonishing subtheme of military caste apartheid. In A. Kron's play *Ofitser flota* (Naval Officer) (1944), the hero – a trim, brisk, laconic cadre officer – defends the honor of the newly gold-braided épaulettes as if he were a runaway of the Pushkinian era. With elitist pride, he runs grave personal risks; bruises himself on sharp corners; attacks careerists and obstructionists (the luxuriating military meshchanstvo); keeps referring to *"My* Baltic Sea," *"My* Navy"; advocates duelling among officers; and, in the end, brings an aging rear admiral around to his side. Professionalism, caste pride, and initiative triumph over submissiveness. What happened when peace came? Though uniforms retained their separatist splendor, the political chiefs returned. Privileges granted were now revised, some revoked. The hedgehogs in uniform were ordered back into harsh training. The concentration camps overflowed. And the toll of the military was tragic. But despite the last spasms of stalinism, the worth of military expertise could not be questioned. It assured the country's safety. Military professionals remained *special* partners in the national renaissance. With ambivalence, the Big Deal keeps accommodating to the uniform.
4   K. Simonov, "Ty pomnish, Alyosha" ("You remember, Alyosha"), *Voina* (War) (Moscow, 1944), p. 44.
5   K. Simonov, "Vozvrashchenie v gorod" (Return to the Town) (1943), *Tri tetradi* (Three Notebooks) (Moscow, 1964), p. 263.
6   A. Tvardovsky, *Vasilii Tyorkin* (Moscow, 1946), pp. 6-8.
7   Y. Yakovlev, "Frontovaya shapka" (Battle Headgear), *Znamya*, No. 6, 1947, p. 80.
8   V. Turkin, "V okope" (In the Trench), *Oktyabr*, Nos. 3-4, 1946, p. 163.
9   L. Khaustov, "Sukho i krepko" (Dry and Strong), *Zvezda*, No. 5, 1948, p. 63.
10 O. Berggolts, "Tvoi put" (Your Road) (1945), *Izbrannye proizvedeniya*, vol. 1 (Leningrad, 1967), p. 202.

11   N. Gribachev, "Rodina" (Motherland), *Znamya*, No. 4, 1944, p. 63.
12   A. Surkov, "Stalinskie soldaty" (Stalinist Soldiers), *Pesni groznogo serdtsa* (Songs of a Stern Heart) (Yaroslavl, 1944), p. 26.
13   A. Zhdanov (1896–1948), Stalin's deputy on the cultural front, master-minded and enforced the theory of socialist realism. From 1946 until his death he was the power behind the purges of the "cosmopolites," "formalists" and other ideological victims. Beyond his own death, in memoriam as it were, he is the father of zhdanovism, synonymous with the repression of creativity and thought.
14   P. Pavlenko, "Schaste" (Happiness), *Znamya*, No. 7, 1947, pp. 40-1.
15   L. Leonov, *Vzyatie Velikoshumska* (The Taking of Velikoshumsk) (Moscow, 1944), pp. 64-6.

Postwar challenge

16   The party admitted 1,845,000 servicemen between 1941 and 1943. See Chapter 7, "World War II: Party and Army," in T. H. Rigby, *Communist Party Membership in the USSR, 1917–1967* (Princeton, 1968), pp. 236-72. Further, "Only one third of the party's 6 million full and candidate members in January 1946 had been in the party before the German invasion, and of these at least half had less than three years' previous experience of party membership under peace conditions," pp. 275-6.
17   Guard regiments were formed in the spring of 1942; the orders of Suvorov, Kutuzov, and Nevsky were founded, among others, by the Presidium of the Supreme Soviet soon thereafter; épaulettes were restored early in 1943, together with officers' privileges.

Conversion of public values

18   In comparison with this understanding, special transactions with parts of the population in the past were less happy. In the twenties and thirties, for instance, the confrontation with the peasantry, tacit victim of centralized administration, led to tragic consequences. So, too, did the collision with the higher echelons of the intellectuals, that extraordinarily cohesive and articulate center of at least potential dissent. And so did the fratricidal encounter of rival groups within the party itself.

Meshchanstvo and intelligentsia with a note on kulturnost

19   "Meshchanin, meshchane (from West Slavic *Mesto* – city or town). In the Grand Duchy of Lithuania, townspeople; in general, the burghers, who in most of the cities enjoyed self-government on the basis of the Magdeburg Law. The term meshchane came into eastern Russia in the 17th century, after several Ukrainian provinces had been united with Russia as a result of the Pereiaslavl' Treaty of 1654 and the Russo-Polish War of 1654–57. In the 18th century the term meshchane was used in two senses; either it meant the entire commercial-artisan class in the towns and the cities (like the Moscow term Posadskie Liudi); or, in a limited sense, petty tradesmen, craftsmen, and the like. In the 19th century it had only the latter meaning. According to imperial legislation the meshchane were a particular legal

class (Soslovie) which constituted in each city a *meshchanskoe obshchestvo*, headed by an elected *meshchanskii starosta*, with an executive board called *meshchanskaia uprava*," *Dictionary of Russian Historical Terms from the Eleventh Century to 1917*, compiled by Sergei G. Pushkarev (New Haven, 1970). pp. 59-60.

20 Ivanov-Razumnik (pseudonym of R. V. Ivanov, 1878–1946), a social philosopher and literary critic close to the Socialist Revolutionary Party, published in 1906 *A History of Russian Social Thought*, and subtitled it, tellingly, *Individualism and Meshchanstvo in Russian 19th Century Literature and Life*. The theme is individualism of the intelligentsia *versus* meshchanstvo. He saw Russia's spiritual life, and hence its social thought, originating in the ethos of the intelligentsia, not a class, not a caste, but a group characterized by creative individualism, engaged in liberating and safeguarding the vital forces of the people. He saw meshchanstvo as the intelligentsia's antipode and its archenemy: "narrowness, flatness and lack of individuality" (3rd definitive edition, St. Petersburg, 1911; also Russian Reprint Series, The Hague, 1969, p. 17). Meshchanstvo to him was not a class but the intelligentsia's fearsome and stubborn counterforce. "Meshchanstvo's negative definition as a group is the fact that the intelligentsia does not enter it; therefore, intelligentsia and meshchanstvo are concepts which limit each other and are mutually contradictory" (p. 16). For an especially harsh characterization of meshchanstvo see N. Berdyaev's chapter "The Lure of the Bourgeois Spirit. Slavery to Property and Money" (pp. 181-9) in *Slavery and Freedom*, Charles Scribner's Sons (New York, 1944).

21 *The Russian Intelligentsia*, ed. R. Pipes (New York, 1960), helps with this complicated subject. The compendium is broadly gauged and undogmatic. Its tone is set by Pipes: "What is the 'Russian intelligentsia,' or, for that matter, an 'intellectual' or *intelligent* anywhere? . . . These terms can mean all sorts of things to all sorts of people. Some use the term intelligentsia to refer to anyone engaged in non-physical labor, whether he be a lyric poet or a veterinarian (such, for example, is the official Soviet definition); others apply it to a person with a liberal education regardless of the nature of his employment; yet others confine it to persons critically disposed to the existing economic and political order, and ready to sacrifice themselves in order to change it fundamentally in accord with some higher (but secular) ideal" (p. 2, Foreword). See L. Labedz, "The Structure of the Soviet Intelligentsia" (pp. 63-80) and M. Malia, "What is the Intelligentsia?" (pp. 1-19).

22 L. G. Churchward in *The Soviet Intelligentsia: an essay on the social structure and roles of the Soviet intellectuals during the 1960s*, (London, 1973), defines his subject, admittedly under the influence of Soviet definitions, as "persons with a tertiary education (whether employed or not), tertiary students, and persons lacking formal tertiary qualification but who are professionally employed in jobs which normally require a tertiary qualification" (p. 6), and gives a thorough account of the growth and differentiation of a new hybrid class.

23 "When closely peering at the character of an average Russian *intelligent*, a typical trait strikes one at once. He is, above all, a person who from his youth lives *outside of himself*, in the strict sense of the word. He acknow-

ledges as the only worthy object of his interest and concern something that lies outside of his person: the people, society, the state." Mikhail Gershenzon, *Istoricheskie zapiski* (Historical Notes, 1910, Russian Reprint Series, The Hague, 1965), pp. 153-4. When closely peering at themselves: "the self-image of the Russian intelligentsia was originally shaped as a counterpoint to the *meshchanstvo*, to the servile yet complacent philistinism to be discerned in existing privileged society. This self-image underwent many variations and transformations in the course of the history of the intelligentsia, but most of its guardians never really wavered from the view that they were distinct from the stagnant and undifferentiated world at large, in a position of intellectual and moral autonomy which made them the chosen carriers for the creation and implementation of new ideas, new values, new truths," Leopold H. Haimson, "The Solitary Hero" in *The Russian Intelligentsia*, op. cit., pp. 103-4.

CHAPTER 2 THE USES OF LITERATURE

Literature and society

1 Alexander Gerschenkron turned to postwar fiction for just this kind of "recurring fragments of information, all pointing in the same direction." ("Neglected Source of Economic Information on the Soviet Union," *Economic Backwardness in Historical Perspective* (Cambridge, Mass., 1966), p. 317). This essay, and several similar ones which followed, are classics of their kind, perceptive about the nature of mass literature under Stalin as well as inventive in the culling of sober economic intelligence. The pioneer in reading Soviet fiction with the same purpose of extricating kernels of *Wahrheit* from the avalanche of *Dichtung* was Vera Alexandrova. A posthumous volume of her prewar essays, *Literatura i zhizn* (Literature and Life), 1969, is especially valuable for her insight into the Soviet class structure in general and the problems of the peasantry in particular.

2 Unquestionably, not all the letters are spontaneous. Many, no doubt, are ghost written; many might well be editorial fabrications. Some have an authentic ring, signed by one person and dealing with some small matter. In economic life, letters from people provide the system with corrective checks. They are supposed to function similarly in literature. And even when forced or faked, they give the reader who would not dream of voicing his opinion the impression of a lively commotion and a means to identify with, or reject, the view of a participant other than the writer and critic.

3 The excesses of zhdanovism induced this kind of feedback. For instance, the reader stood the sermon on its head by ridiculing the cardboard party hero in K. Simonov's *Dym otechestva* (Smoke of the Fatherland) of 1947 and by opting for the far more credible "villain," an energetic, unorthodox achiever.

4 In the abundance of memoirs, the apocalyptic truth of Nadezhda Mandelstam's recollections is not the only one to render the feel of what Stalin did. I. Ehrenburg's near-confessions also recreate the postwar nightmare on the cultural scene. As to the meaning of Stalin's constant personal interference, A. Gerschenkron stresses its systemic nature: "When Stalin, during his night vigils in the Kremlin, used to telephone – in the small hours of the

morning – factory managers and party bureaucrats throughout the huge country, inquiring, commanding, and threatening, he knew well that incessant and arbitrary intervention of dictatorial power is one of the conditions of its stability." "On Dictatorship," *The New York Review of Books*, June 19, 1969.

5   For instance, I. Sadofev's "Terpkoe vino" (Tart Wine), *Zvezda*, No. 1, 1946, pp. 75-6. See also A. A. Zhdanov, *Literature, Philosophy, and Music* (New York, 1950), p. 28.

6   The importance of the belief that the word is equivalent to action can be seen in the punishment meted out for errors made inadvertently in the press or in those instances when the regime seems to revert to primitive magic by enacting the physical destruction of the wordd. It attempts to obliterate its referent with all the complex reality clinging to it. One need only consider the implications behind the incisive request that went out to subscribers of the *Bolshaya sovetskaya entsyklopediya* to arm themselves with a razor blade and to excise the entry Beria, leaving the Bering Strait to reign supreme on that one page. See Basil Dmytryshyn, *USSR: A Concise History* (New York, 1965), p. 266. Dissidents, one might add, share this belief in the potency of the word.

7   B. Moore, Jr., *Political Power and Social Theory* (Harper Torch Books, 1965), p. 10 and p. 27.

8   An evaluation of present-day Soviet writing along these lines, however, would not make as much sense. From the standpoint both of the present regime and of the people, comparable materials have undergone some change in their mediating function. Even if the regime's view of the printed word as "creative" or "administrative" remains the same, there have been fluctuations in the use of controls since Stalin's death. The readership of middlebrow fiction is likely to have diminished. Soviet society has changed from being impoverished to being semiaffluent. Leisure has taken other forms, more satisfactory for the average literate person. A new divide has been erected between middlebrow and highbrow literature and writers have splintered more than before, as have the readers, into feuding groups. And in some quarters the need for truth now seems to outbid the craving for hope.

Middlebrow fiction

9   Speculate, for example, on Khrushchev's posthumous tenacity. His whim-sicality – if one might call it that – embodied in the mass of his published speeches, still holds a place on bookshelves across the country. The Russian intellectual today veritably trembles over those sacrosanct possessions, books, especially if they are foreign, or of emigré provenance, or old. The love poured out on the books one owns seems incomprehensible in its fervor to outsiders.

10 The expression is attributed to Stalin, as is the basic engineering job on the foundations of socialist realism.

11 The untranslatable term in *syuzhetnost:* being well plotted and full of relevant, gripping subject matter.

12 A. Fadeev, a stalinist *par excellence*, offered the following bludgeoning exegesis: "One may ask, is it possible to depict a living human character 'as

he is' and at the same time 'as he ought to be'? Of course, it is possible. This not only does not counteract realism but is true realism. Life must be dealt with in its revolutionary development. I shall give an example from the world of nature. An apple, as it is in nature, is a rather sour wild fruit. An apple, raised in a garden, especially in a garden such as Michurin's, is an apple 'as it is' and at the same time 'as it ought to be.' Such an apple expresses the essence of an apple more fully than the wild forest fruit. The same is true of socialist realism." "Zadacha literaturnoi kritiki" (The Task of Literary Criticism), *Oktyabr*, No. 7, 1947, p. 150. In turn, Fadeev's futuristic apple is taken up penetratingly by Alexander Solzhenitsyn. He reveals its poison in the blabber of a stalinoid meshchanka. Presuming familiarity with belles-lettres, she holds forth: "Sincerity can in no way be the main criterion of a book. Wrong thoughts and alien tendencies only increase the harmful impact of a literary work. Sincerity is harmful! Subjective sincerity may thwart the truthful representation of life." *Rakovyi korpus* (Cancer Ward) (Paris, 1968), p. 246. She goes on: "To describe that which is is considerably easier than to describe that which is not but ought to be, which will be tomorrow. Therefore, one should describe our miraculous 'tomorrow'!" (p. 248).

13 In B. Polevoi's *Povest o nastoyashchem cheloveke* (The Tale of a Real Man) (1946), based on the life of a Soviet military pilot, the hero or rather superhero, with both legs shattered in a crash, manages to crawl out of the enemy zone. After prolonged hospitalization, he doggedly returns to active duty. This promethean performance is accompanied throughout by lofty and orthodox ideological meditation. The actual deed, however, was in all likelihood motivated by the stark circumstance of the moment. It was not a good idea for a Soviet pilot to be caught by the Germans.

14 The notion of the Thaw, meaning a modicum of liberalization, originated with I. Ehrenburg, who had the ingenuity to title a didactic novel *The Thaw* (1954). Thereupon, discussion swept the land. The title alone encapsulated an issue impinging on everyone. It is no exaggeration to say that the book was scrutinized and debated in every party cell. For many bureaucrats it must have been pleasant reading. Brutal dilemmas of conscience, bequeathed by Stalin, were ever so cleverly resolved, and ever so tidily.

15 "Verisimilitude" approximates the commodious Russian children's word *vsamdelishnost* which combines "reality," "in fact," "embodiment," and which evokes an altogether overdone and unrealistic realism, that of, say, an American toy such as the Barbie doll.

16 The press in all of its branches, from the Moscow satirical *Krokodil* to the bulletins of Arctic whale oil refineries is replete with "live material," with human interest stories denouncing the lower bureaucracy.

17 The security of Western societies permits the reader the inclination toward the reverse procedure. In pursuit of individual experience, especially if well off and intellectually sophisticated, he is likely to metamorphosize the general, typical, social elements in fiction into private, personal, secret images.

Looking for clues

18 As a literary style, at least in the textbooks, this realism distinguishes Ibsen from Ionesco, Goncharov from Sologub.

19 The relativism and sloppiness in the use of the term realism, which confuses an author's intention with the reader's judgment about it, as well as the cumulative formation of the nineteenth-century realistic tradition, was brilliantly treated by Roman Jakobson as far back as in 1921 in "O khudozhestvennon realizme" (About Realism in Art), *Cerven*, 4 (1921), pp. 300-4, only recently rediscovered and republished.

20 Unrealistic reality in fiction need not be less real than the realistic. The difference between real and realistic is crucial to the principle here proposed. One is an existential term, the other a literary one. But they blend. Beautification, simplification, and the downright violence done to life in stalinist fiction undeniably represent a reality. But it is of a special order. It is primarily that of the writer's own compliance and of the dictatorship's need to obtain it from him. However, middlebrow fiction contains not only the reality of a static ideology but also clues pointing to palpable social issues which induced shifts in value preferences. Fiction both propagated and reflected these shifts. The analyst profits from this multifunction.

21 A. Sinyavsky's essay on socialist realism ironically champions surrealistic distortion: *On Socialist Realism* (New York, 1960). Helpful for the understanding of its origin and strategies are chapters 6, 7, and 8 in H. Ermolaev's *Soviet Literary Theories, 1917–1934* (Berkeley, 1963).

22 Among the descriptions of this literary method, L. Rzhevsky's seems especially apt: 'A method of 'realistic' depiction of unrealistic phenomena, absent in reality," *Materialy* (Materials), Institute for the Study of the History and Institutions of the USSR (Munich, 1951), p. 45. Alexander Solzhenitsyn concurs: "Having barely entered the world of literature, all of them – social novelists as well as lofty playwrights, public poets and especially the publicists and critics – all of them agreed not to say the main truth about any subject or issue, the truth that, without literature, is instantly apparent to people. This vow to abstain from truth was called socialist realism." *Bodalsya Telyonok s Dubom*, YMCA Press (Paris, 1975), p. 13.

23 A. Nedogonov, "Flag nad selsovetom" (Flag over the Village Soviet), *Novyi mir*, No. 1, 1947, p. 21.

24 Nothing is quite so appalling in retrospect as the callous falsehood of the bliss portrayed in kolkhoz fiction about the ravaged, starving, and forgotten villages in the last period of stalinism.

25 The very notion of pattern raises problems of the size of the sample, of intervening variables and the like. However, since stalinist literature is entirely subservient, it is hard to see where intervening variables could come from. As for "How many times?", the uniformity of that literature was solidly underpinned by its mandatory redundancy. Kolkhoz novels pitting the old management against the new were ordered and delivered. Plays attacking cosmopolitanism were ordered and delivered. If a tale bore a resemblance to one which was awarded a Stalin prize, a pattern thereby had already been formed. In such tightly prefigured straits, details could not help being "typical." So, two examples do as well as twenty-two. This is not to say that details are not more valuable for social analysis than the crest of generalizing didacticism. They are more revelatory than central themes because of their less dogmatic function. The author was free to bring them into the story or omit them. And in their flickering eidetic

character lies their worth. Each detail is typical because issuing from a prepatterned matrix, and revelatory because it has surfaced instead of having been omitted. Inductively, perhaps, the size of the sample matters, but not deductively.

26   A. Koptyaeva, *Tovarishch Anna* (1946).

27   V. Kaverin, *Doctor Vlasenkova* (1951).

28   This last hint comes up more clearly in another pattern, that of the marital collision. In juxtaposing the filial subtheme with the depiction of the marital problem, one can see that the former was treated more stiffly than the latter.

29   The spirit of party officialdom, for example, in the nasty Skorobogatov in A. Koptyaeva's *Ivan Ivanovich* (1949) and in Sukhov in S. Antonov's "Novyi sotrudnik" (New Colleague) (1953) is here contrasted with that of the humbly repentant Pashkov in Yu. Kapusto's *V srednem rayone* (1950) and the disarmingly last-name-less secretary Ivan Ilich with his "yellow sickly face and penetrating gleam in his eyes" in G. Medynsky's monumental *Marya* (1949).

30   This keeps Zalkind, one of the last positive party Jews, especially busy in V. Azhaev's *Daleko ot Moskvy* (1948).

31   An example of the first is Dr. Levin at Yu. German's *Podpolkovnik meditsinskoi sluzhby* (1949) and of the second, the long suffering trade union representative Uzdechkin in V. Panova's *Kruzhilikha* (1947).

32   The hysterical Korytov in P. Pavlenko's *Schaste* (1947) and V. Ovechkin's Borzov in *Rayonnye budni* (1952).

33   V. Kochetov, *Zhurbiny* (1952).

Artifacts

1   To show this change, fictional fragments from two periods will be compared, separated by a considerable timespan. The twenties and early thirties will be projected against the first postwar decade. Two reasons justify the jump. First, this study is not a chronological survey of Soviet fiction. The focus is on the postwar period and comparisons are culled out of earlier literature only for the sake of perspective. Secondly, the thirties represent in middlebrow fiction a period of lingering (on revolutionary mythology), of confusion (about the permissible limits of its cognitive function), and of escape (into the safety of the nationalistic historical past). It is a much muddled period of transition from bolshevism to stalinism.

2   V. Dobrovolsky, "Troe v serykh shinelyakh" (Three Men in Gray Uniforms), *Novyi mir*, No. 1, 1948, p. 41.

3   Zh. Gausner, "Vot my i doma" (Home Again), *Zvezda*, No. 11, 1947, p. 8.

4   V. Panova, "Sputniki" (Companions), *Znamya*, Nos. 2–3, 1946, pp. 36-7.

5   Yu. Trifonov, "Studenty" (Students), *Novyi mir*, Nos. 10–11, 1950, pp. 71-3.

6   V. Kochetov, "Zhurbiny" (The Zhurbin Family), *Zvezda*, No. 1, 1952, p. 83.

7   P. Shebunin, "Stakhanovtsy" (Stakhanovites), *Novyi mir*, No. 7, 1950, p. 182.

8 A. Sofronov, "Karera Beketova" (Beketov's Career), *Novyi mir*, No. 4, 1949, p. 66.
9 Under Khrushchev this very undercutting was reversed. The middle class was invited to rub shoulders much more freely with the elite.
10 A. Surov, "Zelenaya ulitsa" (The Green Street), *Novyi mir*, No. 5, 1949, pp. 104-5.
11 V. Vassilevskaya, "Kogda zagoritsya svet" (When There Will be Light), *Zvezda*, No. 11, 1946, pp. 8-9.
12 A. Surov, "Rassvet nad Moskvoi" (Dawn over Moscow), *Oktyabr*, No. 1, 1951, p. 129.

Who wins what

13 V. Ketlinskaya, "Nastya," (1945), *Den prozhityi dvazhdy* (A Day Lived Twice) (Moscow, 1964), pp. 372-3.

CHAPTER 4 NEW PROTAGONISTS

Road to life

1 N. Ostrovsky, *Kak zakalyalas stal* (The Tempering of Steel) (1934) (Moscow, 1947), p. 189.
2 *Road to Life* is the English title of a film made by N. Ekk, based on a work on education, *Pedagogical Poem* by A. Makarenko, a voluminous account, fictional only in form, of Makarenko's experiences with and efforts on behalf of the *besprizornye*, literally the "uncared for," lost and abandoned children whom the revolution and civil war had tossed into the vortex of destruction and survival. Many had become criminals. Makarenko, it seems, was successful in rehabilitating some. The commune in which he worked was under the patronage, *mirabile dictu*, of the Cheka. With collectivist fervor, Makarenko rhapsodizes in conclusion: "And on healthy soil, surrounded by Cheka men, supported every day by their energy, education, and talent, the commune grew into a collective of dazzling beauty, of genuine constructive richness, of lofty socialist culture" (Moscow, 1947), p. 637.
3 Yu. German, "Aleksei Zhmakin," *Literaturnyi sovremennik*, No. 10, 1937, p. 119.
4 I. Ehrenburg, *Zhizn I Gibel Nikolaya Kurbova* (Life and Death of Nikolai Kurbov) (Berlin, 1923), p. 21.
5 *Besprizornik*, see note 2.
6 N. Ostrovsky, op. cit., p. 77.
7 A. Fadeev, *Razgrom* (The Route) (1925) (Moscow, 1947), p. 113-14.
8 N. Ostrovsky, op. cit., p. 137. The message of this massively propagated work belongs to the romantic twenties. The book of a true believer, it was used through the thirties as a catechism for the young. One can assume, as the regime's needs were changing, this Sunday school text was offered for edification in the expectation that as the young reader matured, confrontation with life would bring the necessary adjustments.
9 F. Gladkov, *Tsement* (Cement) (1925) (Moscow, 1931), p. 45. There are three versions of this work, as important as it is artistically faulty, over

which the author fussed a lot: 1925, 1930, and 1944. The most accomplished is the middle version, cited here. The last is an example of self-inflicted disfigurement. Whatever spark, however primitive, the earlier style possessed was extinguished and all "naturalistic" detail removed to comply with the heavy prudishness of socialist realism.

10 See N. S. Timasheff's durable *The Great Retreat* (1946); M. Fainsod's *How Russia is Ruled* (second edition), pp. 104-8; and especially B. Moore Jr.'s *Soviet Politics – The Dilemma of Power* (second edition, 1965), chapter 8. "The Mythology of Status and the New Bureaucracy." pp. 159-88.

11 N. I. Ezhov (1895–1940), one of Stalin's most sinister henchmen, Commissar of Internal Affairs from 1936 to 1938, succeeded by Beria. His name engenders "ezhovshchina," the synonym for the bloodiest of purges.

Pronouns in transition

12 V. Mayakovsky, "Pyatyi internatsional" (Fifth International), *Sobranie sochinenii*, vol. 3 (Moscow, 1968), p. 72.

13 V. Kirillov, "My" (We) (1917), *Izbrannye stikhotvoreniya* 1917–32 (Moscow, 1933), pp. 15-17.

14 M. Isakovsky, "Pesnya o Staline" (1936) (Song about Stalin), *Izbrannye stikhotvoreniya* (Moscow, 1941), pp. 157-8.

15 Or worse. Foreshadowing what the collective was to run into during the thirties, N. Tikhonov in his "Ballada o gvozdyakh" (Ballad about Nails) (1919) sang the iron discipline of a crew of prerevolutionary sailors off on a suicide mission. The praise resounds in the laconic requiem: "One should make nails out of these people. There would be no tougher nails on earth." *Stikhi i proza* (Verses and Prose) (Moscow, 1945), p. 94. Stalin took his advice.

16 A militant communist, the playwright V. Kirshon perished in the purges of 1938. In the mid fifties he was "rehabilitated."

17 V. Kirshon, "Khleb" (Bread), *Izbrannoe*, (Moscow, 1958), pp. 192-3.

18 "No fully developed despot, it may be surmised, can content himself with compelling his subjects' assent to policies exclusively rational. Only then may he regard his people as fully subject to his will when he can compel their assent to procedures palpably outrageous and absurd": Ronald Hingley, *The Russian Secret Police* (London, 1970), p. 152.

19 K. Simonov, "Zhdi menya" (Wait for Me), *Voina* (War) (Moscow, 1944), pp. 54-5.

20 S. Shchipachev, untitled, *Den poezii* (Day of Poetry) (Moscow, 1956), p. 38.

21 No less didactic than "We" poetry, the postwar odes to Soviet valor could not do without the "We" posture either. But in the emerging pronominal promiscuity, the first pronoun singular had long ceased to be an obscenity.

22 M. Lukonin, "Pridu k tebe" (I Shall Come to You) (1944), *Antologiya russkoi sovetskoi poezii*, 1917–57, vol. 2 (Moscow, 1957), pp. 443-4.

23 M. Lukonin, "Prishedshim s voiny" (To Those Who Have Returned from War), ibid., pp. 444-5.

24 A. Tvardovsky said this, without dodging responsibility, in a requiem for the darkest times and a tainted generation:

Just try to find the man who
Did not praise and glorify him.

Just try and find him!
Probably not in vain
The son of the East
To the very end
Fulfilled the traits
Of his hard,
Of his cruel,
Wrongness
And rightness.
But who of us is fit to be a judge,
To decide who is right, who is wrong?
We speak of people. And people
Do they not create gods themselves?

"Za dalyu dal," (Horizon Beyond Horizon), *Sobranie sochinenii*, vol. 3 (Moscow, 1962), p. 341. Not only did these reminiscences in verse receive the 1961 Lenin prize but the confessional portion containing this extract was, unhingingly to some, first published in *Pravda*.

25 A. Kron, "Kandidat partii" (Party Candidate), *Novyi mir*, No. 10, 1950, p. 19.
26 The death scene of the party organizer Zernov in A. Gribachev's "Vesna v 'Pobeda'" (Spring in 'Pobeda'), *Znamya*, No. 12, 1948, p. 48. In a visionary revelation, shared by author and hero, Stalin speaks thus:

"You have struggled not in vain.
You have labored not in vain.
Your last day is your first step into the
    commune.
Here comes its dawn."
Thus, at dawn
    in 'Pobeda'
Zernov, the party organizer,
    died.

Truth in trouble

27 Skeptics are advised to consult A. G. Preobrazhensky, *Etimologichskii slovar russkogo yazyka* (Moscow, 1910), vol. 2, p. 121.
28 M. Aliger, "Zoya," *Stikhi i poemy* (Moscow, 1944), p. 129.
29 A. Tvardovsky, "Dom u dorogi" (1942–1946) (House by the Road), *Sobranie sochinenii*, vol. 3 (Moscow, 1967), pp. 12-14.
30 A. Mezhirov, "Stikhi o malchike" (Verses about a Boy) (1945), *Antologiya russkoi sovetskoi poezii*, 1917–57, vol. 2 (Moscow, 1957), pp. 572-3.
31 A. Surkov, untitled (1941), *Pesni groznogo serdtsa* (Songs of a Wrathful Heart) (Yaroslavl, 1944), p. 38.
32 A. Krongauz, "Minuta" (A Minute) (1946), *Antologiya russkoi sovetskoi poezii*, 1917–57, vol. 2 (Moscow, 1957), pp. 621-2.
33 Accused of defeatism by Zhddanov's people, the poetess was defended by K. Simonov, editor of *Novyi mir* at the time. Attacks: S. Tregub, "Novye stikhi Margarity Aliger," *Literaturnaya gazeta*, October 26, 1946, and V. Ermilov, "O partiinosti v literature i ob otvetstvennosti kritiki," *Literatur-

naya gazeta, April 19, 1947. Defense: K. Simonov, "Zametki pisatelya," *Novyi mir*, No. 1, 1947.

34 M. Aliger, untitled, *Novye stikhi* (New Poems), as quoted by K. Simonov in "Zametki pisatelya," *Novyi mir*, No. 1, 1947, pp. 167-8.

35 L. Oshanin, "Nachalnik rayona proshchaetsa s nami" (The District Boss Bids Us Farewell), *Antologiya russkoi sovetskoi poezii*, 1917–57, vol. 2 (Moscow, 1957), pp. 273-6.

Young people quarrel

36 Yu. Trifonov, "Studenty" (Students), *Novyi mir*, No. 10, 1950, p. 157.
37 A. Chakovsky, "Mirnye dni" (Days of Peace), *Zvezda*, No. 10, 1947, p. 22.
38 E. Malzev, "Ot vsego serdtsa" (From the Heart), *Oktyabr*, No. 9, 1948, p. 22.
39 This novel received the Stalin Prize for 1948. The heroine was at the moment proclaimed impeccable. When zhdanovism came out of joint ahead of Stalin's death, the novel was harshly reevaluated by critics and the heroine was now ranked by some among the most wooden and implausible. The erring husband's assets went up on the fickle market of Soviet morality. We do not care one way or another. In this particular instance, regardless of the reversal of critics, the gap between his and her proclivities marks one kind of oscillation in the constantly shifting adjustments of the Big Deal.

Jaded people adjust

40 S. Antonov, "Novyi sotrudnik" (New Colleague), *Novyi mir*, No. 3, 1954, p. 51

CHAPTER 5 STATUS

The ways of a scoundrel

1 Yu. Trifonov, "Studenty" (Students), *Novyi mir*, No. 11, 1950, pp. 151-2.
2 probivatsya v lyudi
3 There is a difficulty in using negative characters as spokesmen for the regime's desiderata. But there is also a difficulty in relegating the sorting out of the negatives and the positives to official literary criticism. The frequent reliance on negative characters in this study and the decision, by and large, to omit references to literary criticism both derive from the need to come to grips with the pervasive yet oblique manner in which middle-class themes are treated in middlebrow fiction. To be specific, the feel and flavor of middleclass culture one gets from that fiction provides one also with an insight into conflicts which that spreading culture produced among fictional citizens. Some of its manifestations, such as flagrant meshchanstvo, were frequently deplored by authors and the regime certainly gave lip service to such self-righteousness. But that is just the point. What was cover-up and cant on one hand and the real shift in objectives on the other? In the obscure and transitional period dealt with here, does the

very dichotomy of positive and negative characters illuminate the conflict itself? Does this didactic dichotomy, a carryover from earlier periods of greater ideological clarity, impinge on the reading of source materials underlying this study? It is too risky to enlist characters, designated as negative by the authors, as spokesmen of the regime's position? To do so is to ignore the avalanche of official literary criticism charged with preventing the shadow of negative characters from falling across the regime's official proclamations. I feel that the risk is minimal. Official criticism in the early postwar period is of little help in this or any other analytical effort. In fact, it impedes it because of special systemic obtuseness. (At no time, for that matter, was the dogma of socialist realism sophisticated enough to obliterate successfully real social issues.) Since the regime now no longer easily betrayed where it really stood on a number of social issues, it provoked controversies between critics in the period of zhdanovism. The orthodox were no longer fully trusted in their role of jobbers between the establishment and the writers. Their judgments were reversed from above while the writers they maligned were on occasion vindicated there and then. The vortex of questions of literary policy is not central to the issues of this book. And on the thematic and substantive side, the stability of the positive-negative polarization itself became questionable. Because of the ambiguity in which the regime couched its rapprochement with the middle class, it obscured the formerly rigid line-up of villains and heroes. The authorial gradations between both categories became all the more informative. And some sprightly "negatives" acted as better carriers of the regime's changing long-term options than the forever stilted "positives."

New child rearing

4   V. Panova, "Yasnyi bereg" (Clear Shore), *Zvezda*, No. 9, 1949, pp. 66-7.
5   Pasha Angelina, "Lyudi kolkhoznykh polei" (The People of Kolkhoz Fields), *Oktyabr*, No. 6, 1948, p. 125.
6   A. Makarenko, *Kniga dlya roditelei* (A Book for Parents) (Moscow, 1937).
7   Andrei Platonov was a real writer and I apologize to his memory – as well as to one or two other authors – for having used his story and theirs. In this instance, his talent and taste transformed a genre piece about a family torn by the war into a classless revelation of basic relationships and compassion for the vulnerability of Everyman. Since under zhdanovism a direct correlation existed between good literature and assault on it, one can find a devastating attack on the "un-Soviet," i.e. human, framework of this story in L. Subotskii, "Zamechaniya o proze 1946 goda" (Remarks on the Prose of 1946), *Novyi mir*, No. 3, 1947, pp. 151-2.
8   A. Platonov, "Semya Ivanova," *Novyi mir*, Nos. 10-11, 1946, p. 100.
9   G. Berezko, "Noch polkovodtsa" (The Night of the Commander), *Znamya*, Nos. 11-12, p. 26.
10 "Uchis'," yes, "uchis'" the mother says. One must lament the loss in translation of the reflexive suffix in the mother's helpless imperative, a tiny matter, perhaps, in the enormity of the social panorama but not so small in the context. Purely morphemic, with a dimmed, subdued significance, the particle signals: "school *yourself* to become somebody." The implicit limita-

tions of this reflexive particle, one should imagine, were also firmly recognized.

11   T. Leonteva, "Vospitanie chuvstv" (The Education of Feelings), *Novyi mir*, No. 6, 1946, pp. 65-6.
12   Remeslenniki
13   Kulturnaya mamasha
14   E. Nagaeva, "U nas v shkole" (In Our School), *Novyi mir*, No. 5, 1950, pp. 176-7.
15   *The Tale of a Real Man* is the title of B. Polevoi's famous war book (see note 13 on p. 256). What marks Meresev's kind of heroism, as against that of the bolshevik collectivist version, is the power of his own rather simple joy of life, his masculine individuality, his professional expertise, all of which amount to individual glory.

Status and love

16   A. Korneichuk, "Kalinovaya roshcha" (A White Grove), *Novyi mir*, No. 6, 1950, pp. 115-16.
17   A. Geveling, "Tanya," *Oktyabr*, No. 3, 1950, p. 72.
18   Both the horrendous comedy and this kind of narrative versification came closest to Zhdanov's idea of the postwar literary renaissance. Other genres, the sketch and short story, for instance, fared less well.
19   A. Sofronov, "Moskovskii kharakter" (A Moscow Type), *Oktyabr*, No. 1, 1949, p. 108.
20   P. Shebunin, "Stakhanovtsy" (Stakhanovites), *Novyi mir*, No. 7, p. 114.
21   Yu. Trifonov, "Studenty," *Novyi mir*, No. 10, 1950, p. 60.
22   For her melancholy undertone, muted polarization of good and bad, and allegedly for falling into the trap of being untypical, the author got into trouble with orthodox critics. This indicated at the time that the reverse of the last accusation may have prevailed at large. See, for instance, sermon plus equivocation by B. Brainina, "Tretya deistvitelnost" (Third Reality), *Novyi mir*, No. 5, 1948.
23   Zh. Gausner, "Vot my i doma" (Home Again), *Zvezda*, No. 11, 1947, p. 8.

What became of the simple worker?

24   Zh. Gausner, "Vot my i doma" (Home Again), *Zvezda*, No. 11, 1947, p. 28.
25   During the NEP, the exploration of the underworld – a complex and vitally marginal territory – became an important literary theme. It lingered through part of the thirties. After the war, however, the regime did not welcome the opening up of that aspect. The underworld was placed off-limits as "untypical."
26   A. Kron, "Kandidat partii" (Party Candidate), *Novyi mir*, No. 10, 1950, p. 13.
27   Who wrote courageously at the time.
28   Iz prostykh rabochikh v lyudi vyshel.
29   V. Kochetov, "Zhurbiny" (The Zhurbin Family), *Zvezda*, No. 1, 1952, p. 55.

CHAPTER 6 PARASITES AND BUILDERS

Untouched

1 A. Cherkasov, "Den nachinaetsya na vostoke" (The Day Starts in the East), *Oktyabr*, No. 5, 1946, pp. 31-2.

2 I remember being told in my Moscow childhood that in remote Siberian villages peasants had sung "God Save the Tsar" throughout the early twenties.

3 V. Popov, "Stal i shlak" (Steel and Slag), *Znamya*, No. 1, 1949, pp. 113-14.

4 V. Lifshits, "Petrogradskaya storona" (The Petrograd District), *Novyi mir*, Nos. 10-11, 1946, p. 165. The fascination with Priestley and Hemingway over native reading matter signals sophistication on one hand and the grievous error of cosmopolitanism that fanned Zhdanov's anger on the other.

5 Official criticism had attempted to explain the little hyena away as an atavism somehow overlooked in a Leningrad closet. See, for instance, L. Subotsky, "Zametki o proze 1946 goda" (Notes on the Prose of 1946), *Novyi mir*, No. 3, 1947, p. 142.

6 A. Koptyaeva, "Ivan Ivanovich," *Oktyabr*, No. 5, 1949, p. 79. The novel deals with the time shortly before the attack on the Soviet Union, with references made to the possibility of a Nazi attack on England. Significantly, through, this story of meshchanstvo, despite its prewar setting, was written after the war.

Reluctant bricklayers

7 The stylized combination of the foreign name Nelly with the archly domestic patronymic prefigures the final victory of the character's patriotic self over vainglory.

8 A. Minchkovsky, "My eshche vstretimsya" (We Shall Meet Again), *Zvezda* Nos. 5-6, 1948, p. 16.

9 O. Dzhigurda, "Teplokhod Kakhetiya" (The Ship Kakhetiya), *Znamya*, No. 1, 1948, p. 4.

10 V. Dobrovolsky, "Zhenya Maslova," *Novyi mir*, No. 1, 1950, pp. 14-15.

A residue to reckon with

11 His name is here preserved in the Russian original because he made such a commotion in the literary townhall, creating a concept.

12 K. Simonov, "Dym otechestva" (The Smoke of the Fatherland), *Novyi mir*, 11, 1947, pp. 26-7.

13 During the controversy over this tale, orthodox critics complained that this villain manqué negated his flat and rigid opponent's chance to win the reader over to his side. A decade or so later, official tolerance increased considerably toward the multiplying Kondrashovs. His kind of drive and competence became acceptable in the poststalinist era.

Fighting achievers

14 "Negative" women are more numerous in urban novels than in rural. As

one reason, one might suggest that the nineteenth-century literary tradition of respect for peasant womanhood had been revived.

15 The predecessors of this type in the thirties were squarely considered villains. By now, their heirs have been entirely rehabilitated. In the transitional postwar period this type hovered in limbo between the war and poststalinist reforms.

16 G. Nikolaeva, "Zhatva" (Harvest), *Znamya*, No. 6, 1950, p. 68.

17 Despite the regime's brutal disregard for peasant poverty, one learns something about side issues from these false and merry books. The private marketing of individual produce had turned into almost the only effective means of economic advance for the peasant. Whether acknowledged or not, commerce proved desirable.

18 The cohesiveness of the small rural team was, off and on, fiercely attacked under the sobriquet of *semeistvennost* (familiness). The attack, for instance, on the solidarity of composers, under the guise of an attack on formalism among intellectuals, was no different in nature.

19 V. Pomerantsev, "Ob iskrennosti v literature" (Sincerity in Literature), *Novyi mir*, No. 2, 1953, p. 225.

CHAPTER 7 TWIN ROOTS OF MESHCHANSTVO

1 1913 census 139.3 million; 1926 census 159.2 million.

2 For a concise and lucid account of what happened to the idea of equality, see B. Moore, Jr., *Soviet Politics – The Dilemma of Power*, Harper Torchbooks (1965), pp. 182-8.

3 "Above all, the basic improvement in the material conditions of workers has served as the foundation for the stakhanovite movement. Life has become better, comrades, life has become more merry. And when life is merry, work goes well." Speech at the first All-Union conference of stakhanovites, 17 November, 1935, I. V. Stalin, *Sochineniya* (Words), vol. I [XIV], 1934–40, The Hoover Institution, 1967 [reprint], p. 89.

CHAPTER 8 COMRADE CHAMELEON

Comrades Wholesale and Retail

1 Attacks on bureaucracy began to mount at Stalin's death and, naturally, reached a peak thereafter. The fairly early date of this story (1947) and the authority of the orthodox author show how urgent it was to get rigid middle-rank party functionaries to understand the implications of the Big Deal.

2 P. Pavlenko, "Schaste" (Happiness), *Znamya*, No. 7, 1947, p. 17.

3 A. Koptyaeva, "Ivan Ivanovich," *Oktyabr*, No. 5, 1949, p. 91.

4 Intelligentskie shtuchki

Myopia

5 N. Virta, "Khleb nash nasushchnyi," (Our Daily Bread) *Zvezda*, No. 6, 1947, p. 22.

6 Bditelnost and blat.

Learning is forever

7 M. Asanov, "Sekretar partburo" (Secretary of the Party Bureau), *Zvezda*, No. 10, 1949, pp. 42-3.

8 Surfacing occasionally before Stalin's death, the theme of apprenticeship frequently appeared in bitter variants after his death, marking the open overhauling of the local party. A pattern emerged in which fossilized officials were made accountable for malfeasance throughout and specifically for oppressing novices and choking organic Big Deal energy.

9 G. Nikolaeva, "Zhatva" (Harvest), *Znamya*, No. 5, 1950, p. 21.

10 Y. Kapusto, *V srednem rayone* (In an Average District) (Moscow, 1950), p. 166.

11 Stalin edited the *History of the Communist Party of the Soviet Union (Bolsheviks)*, *Short Course* (Moscow, 1939), and is credited with writing every word of the key fourth chapter.

The seraphic comrade

12 The publication of V. Ovechkin's sketches, dealing with the ruthlessness of rural party bosses, in *Pravda* of July 20 and 23, 1953, cannot be otherwise understood, particularly since his even more sensational sketch, the "Rayonnye budni" (District Doldrums) had been published in 1952 and had blended with the heretical notes of alarm over rural pauperization in his wartime "S frontovym privetom" (Greetings from the Front). Middlebrow fiction illuminates the situation in the recent past more than the present because it lags behind political decisions. Since the response in the overall output of fiction is not always neat and uniform, there ensues an overlap of thematic patterns.

13 The interpenetration of the good with the best produced in V. Kozhevnikov's play "Ognennaya reka" (Fiery River), *Novyi mir*, No. 3, 1949, such insufferable deposits of saccharine that the playwright was taken to task by those whom he tried to please. His effort deserves mention, if only for fashioning the busiest of all seraphims. A young foreman invents a daring method for the pouring of steel, fantastically profitable. His purpose is thwarted in three ways. First, a prestigious professor – the industrial sites were replete with renowned academics in overalls crawling all over the forges – fails to support the invention, for it conflicts with his own. Second, a no-less-renowned foreman, for intertwined reasons of pedagogy, prestige, and envy, fails to support the young man as well. Thirdly, the young man's own ego – pinched, insecure, arrogant at once – prevents him from seeking help effectively. Thereupon, the seraphic party secretary goes to work. He is an expert at reconciling everybody. He incessantly implores the citizens to assist each other. Properly imbued with the principle of the Big Deal, he firstly initiates the metamorphosis of private values into the public. Under seraphic tutelage, the inventor's ardent heart learns to blend love of material reward with the proper socio-political convictions. In this way, the inventor is granted the joy of aggrandizement, at the expense of the collective. Once the seraphic comrade makes it perfectly clear that it is for the public good that the productive citizen be privately assisted, everybody comes around. And the marriage of "creative labor" with "our great Soviet science" is consummated.

14   Named Zalkind, he carries the special responsibility of being one of the last positive party Jews.

15   V. Azhaev, "Daleko ot Moskvy" (Far from Moscow), *Novyi mir*, No. 8, 1948, p. 22.

Comrade Perfect

16   V. Kochetov, "Zhurbiny" (The Zhurbin Family), *Zvezda*, No. 1, 1952, p. 43.

CHAPTER 9 PRODUCERS

Nomadic management

1   A. Rybakov, "Voditeli" (Chauffeurs), *Oktyabr*, No. 1, 1950, p. 14.

2   The heady stuff of the grotesque is not what compliant writers produce. All the more remarkable is G. Troepolsky's tale "Prokhor Semnadtsatyi, Korol zhestyanshchikov" (Prokhor XVII, King of Tinsmiths). It deals with the mercurial activities of an imbecile nomad who ruins and robs many a nook and cranny of the peripheral economy. The fact that this stonily grinning caricature of a petty bureaucrat ends up heading a kolkhoz implies that the martyred village offers the last refuge to a wrecker, rejected everywhere else. The pertinent twist of the tale, however, is that it happens to be about partnership. The nomad alone does nowhere near the harm that he does together with his sponsor, an aging party functionary. Fired in one spot, Prokhor is swiftly reassigned to another. Each investiture is assisted by his sponsor. Managerial parasitism is revealed in its linked, locked, indivisible partnership with the party. Each time the nomad is about to be sent to jail, he beats his chest in a paroxysm of self-denigration, sometimes offering to kill himself. And each time the sponsor has the power to bail him out. "Already old, bald, toothless, [he] stood up for him and did not permit any harm to be done to him." "*Iz zapisok agronoma*" (From the Notes of an Agronomist), *Novyi mir*, No. 8, 1952, p. 61. Of course retribution at last catches up with both. The protégé sits there "bulky and broad but understanding nothing, emptied from within" awaiting a one-year sentence of corrective labor while his sponsor allows: "Well, you had to be fired under all circumstances, I foresaw that. But why am I fired? Why was I chased out of the party? Why was I maligned?" (p. 75). A good question. These two are bound inseparably. The nature of their partnership says a great deal about the system. The question is why both are tolerated for so long. The low-grade party functionary, of venerable age, has been ensconced in the bureaucracy. He is well known and no one needs to fear him. The nomad, his factotum, lends him the semblance of potency. The need for a docile drinking companion is real. And both – and that is the inadvertent point of the tale – are tolerated because of systemic lethargy and inefficiency.

The golden calf

3   The setting is not a rural collective economy, but a state enterprise which is important to the homogeneity of this chapter.

4   V. Panova, "Yasnyi bereg" (Bright Shore), *Zvezda*, No. 9, 1949, p. 11.

5   This key sentence, germane to our reading, was added by the author to the
    version in book form (Moscow, 1950), p. 86.

Perfectionism

6   V. Popov, "Stal i shlak" (Steel and Slag), *Znamya*, No. 2, 1949, p. 33.

My Plant

7   Though a multitude of Russian names is confusing and English nicknames
    have been substituted wherever possible, it seems best to leave the names of
    the four industrial managers in this chapter as they are – Nemirov,
    Potapov, Rotov, Listopad – because of their crucial position in this study.
8   A. Sofronov, "Moskovskii kharakter" (Moscow Type), *Oktyabr*, No. 1,
    1949, p. 134
9   A. Sofronov had got into worse trouble with his play *Karera Beketova*
    (Beketov's Career), which was touched upon in Part II, chapter 3.
10 See editorial in *Literaturnaya gazeta*, No. 7, 1950, and Konstantin Simonov,
    "Za bolshevitskuyu partiinost" (For the Bolshevik Party Spirit) in the
    canonical *Bolshevik*, No. 3, February 1950, pp. 43-5.

Exegesis on proper interaction

11 V. Ketlinskaya, *Dni nashei zhizni* (Days of Our Life) (1952) (Leningrad,
    1958), p. 4.
12 Much could be conjectured from Stalin's choice of model in Greek mythol-
    ogy. The giant Antaeus, son of Poseidon and of Earth, maintains his
    invincibility as long as he remains in bodily contact with Mother Earth,
    enacting his nationalist pledge and, one might suspect, the populist and
    chauvinist vows as well.
13 For instance, A. Kondratovich, "Zavod i lyudi" (The Factory and the
    People), *Novyi mir*, No. 12, 1952, pp. 245-9.
14 Alexander Fadeev, 1900–56, author of the revolutionary short novel *The
    Rout* (1924) and the wartime best seller *The Young Guard* (1945), long-time
    secretary and chairman of the Union of Soviet Writers, Stalin's fervent
    servant, well knew how to rewrite fiction since that is what he had to do to
    his own wartime saga. On Khrushchev's advent to power he committed
    suicide.
15 The adjective *krupnyi* is used, connoting institutional prominence, high
    place, merit, honor.
16 *vospitatel* – guru rather than mere teacher.
17 He means intrinsic structure. The italics and curious quotation marks are
    Fadeev's.
18 A. Fadeev, *Za tridtsat let* (In the Course of Thirty Years) (1952) (Moscow,
    1959), pp. 790-1.

Medals on a broad chest

19 V. Panova, "Kruzhilikha" (The Plant Kruzhilikha), *Znamya*, No. 11, 1947,
    p. 22.

CHAPTER 10 DEFECTIVE PARTY PARTNERS

Outdated convictions

1 V. Panova, "Kruzhilikha," (The Plant Krushilikha) *Znamya*, No. 12, 1947, p. 62.
2 F. Panfyorov, "Bolshoe iskusstvo" (Great Art), *Oktyabr*, No. 11, 1949, p. 52.

Talmudism

3 V. Ocheretin, *Pervoe derzanie* (First Daring) (Moscow, 1953), p. 19.
4 The subject of party villainy entered fiction in irregular sequence. In the early postwar years it surfaced gingerly, erupting vigorously at the time of Stalin's death. The corrupt local official turned into a cliché. As to the development beyond that, the following might be considered. The Big Deal spans the Stalin and the Khrushchev eras. Stalin's death is no real turning point. Grumbling about inky souls, talmudists, and local tyrants preceded his death. Discontent with the party's sergeants, as Stalin had called them, signaled something important, an alarm about the weakening of the Big Deal and about the diminished vigor with which reconstruction proceeded. The effort to reinforce the Big Deal falls, then, to Khrushchev.
5 V. Ovechkin, "V tom zhe rayone" (In the Same District), *Novyi mir*, No. 3, 1954, p. 47.
6 In a paradigmatic play, right after Stalin's death, a stalinist homunculus personifies the Big Deal's prime obstacle. Comrade Stone, a party functionary, drinks and plays cards excessively with his cronies, exercises the so-called cult of personality, oppresses peasants, engages in bribery or denunciation, and obstructs any change. Since his days on the job are numbered, he fights by appealing to classic stalinist party mores. Aghast at the reformist new party boss who introduces open debate in party meetings. Comrade Stone asks ominously: "What will the rank and file say should the generals start thrashing each other?" (A. Korneichuk, "Krylya" (Wings), *Novyi mir*, No. 11, 1954, p. 25) and he is bewildered by the hero's opinion that "in the party there are no generals," an opinion at odds with Stalin's own views: "In our party, if we have in mind its leading strata, there are about 3,000 to 4,000 first rank leaders whom I could call our Party's corps of generals. Then there are about 30,000 to 40,000 middle rank leaders who are our Party corps of officers. Then there are about 100,000 to 150,000 of the lower rank Party command staff who are, so to speak, our Party's non-commissioned officers." (I.V. Stalin, report to the Central Committee on March 3, 1937 (New York, 1946), pp. 27-8.)

CHAPTER 11 PROFESSIONALS MAKE TROUBLE

Dr. Ulcer

1 Yu. German, "Podpolkovnik meditsinskoi sluzhby" (Lieutenant Colonel of the Medical Corps), *Zvezda*, No. 1, 1949, p. 77.
2 *Zvezda*, No. 3, 1949, p. 108. In the so-called year of protest, 1956, this work was finally reworked and published.

Cooled-off engineer

3 V. Azhaev, "Daleko ot Moskvy" (Far from Moscow), *Novyi mir*, No. 8, 1948, p. 109.

Melancholic bungler

4 I. Druts, "U staroi plotiny" (By the Old Dam), *Zvezda*, No. 4, 1948, p. 22.

Diesel engine addiction

5 S. Marvich, "Pervyi i poslednii" (First and Last), *Zvezda*, No. 7, 1949, p. 87.

CHAPTER 12 PROFESSORS TALK BACK

Old Fox

1 If the young intellectual – as portrayed in our sedate fiction – seemed rather tame and proper through most of this period, he suddenly turned into a nuisance by the mid-fifties. In life, he engaged the regime as a real problem. This is true to this day. And fiction, both controlled and underground, began after Stalin's death to record voluminously the complex and variously shaded disaffection of distinct groups of educated youth.
2 G. Konovalov, "Universitet" (University), *Oktyabr*, No. 6, 1947, p. 27.
3 Fellow travellers had undertaken incessantly, and by definition, to plead. They pleaded with themselves, with the Zeitgeist, with the "general course." Mayakovsky and Esenin did, and so did Bagritsky, Martynov, Selvinsky. A vivid example is Selvinsky's synthesizing "Our Biography" of 1934, in which the poet expresses the dread of remaining an outsider in the new order.
4 See A. Fadeev's supportive letter to the author of May 11, 1955 in *Za tridzat let* (In the Course of Thirty Years) (Moscow, 1959), p. 803 and, for instance, V. Ivanov, "Filosofiya i zhizn" (Philosophy and Life), *Oktyabr*, No. 6, 1948, pp. 184-91.
5 B. Runin, "Belletrizatsiya tezisov" (Theses Turned into Fiction), *Znamya*, No. 7, 1948, pp. 173-8 or S. Golubov, "Razdumie"(Meditation),*Novyi mir*, No. 1, 1948, pp. 285-6.

Labels

6 Yu. Trifonov, "Studenty" (Students), *Novyi mir*, No. 10, 1950, p. 130.

The right to err

7 V. Dobrovolsky, "Zhenya Maslova," *Novyi mir*, No. 1, 1950, p. 281.

CHAPTER 13 WOMENS LIBERATION CONFUSED

Off the track

1 V. Vasilevskaya, "Kogda zagoritsya svet" (When There Will be Light), *Zvezda*, No. 11, 1946, p.7.

2 G. Medynsky, "Marya," *Zvezda*, No. 4, 1949, p. 17. (First part, not serialized, Moscow, 1947.)
3 A. Koptyaeva, "Tovarishch Anna," *Oktyabr*, Nos. 3-4, 1946, p. 54.
4 P. Shebunin, "Neinteresnyi chelovek" (An Uninteresting Person), *Ogonek*, No. 19, 1953, pp. 19-20. The tale was considered important enough to be included in the prestigious yearly anthology of best short stories, *Rasskazy 1953 goda* (Moscow, 1954).

Surtax on equality

5 V. Panova, "Kruzhilikha" (The Plant Kruzhilikha), *Znamya*, No. 12, 1947, p. 70.
6 A. Chakovsky, "Mirnye dni" (Days of Peace), *Zvezda*, No. 9, 1947, pp. 34-5.
7 V. Dobrovolsky, "Zhenya Maslova," *Novyi mir*, No. 1, 1950, p. 14.
8 Yu. Bondarev, "Inzhenery" (Engineers), *Oktyabr*, No. 3, 1953, p. 22.
9 D. Granin, "Iskateli" (Explorers) (1951–53) (Moscow, 1960), p. 424.
10 Yu. Kapusto, "Khleboroby" (Agricultural Workers), *Novyi mir*, No. 4, 1950, p. 178.

CHAPTER 14 POPULIST PRESSURE

Rural quilt

1 Alexander Solzhenitsyn's prisoner Ivan Denisovich is so devoted to his family that he refuses to make demands on them. He does not ask them for food packages.
2 In 1953, in a speech on agriculture, Khrushchev made reference to the fact that ninety percent of kolkhozes after the war had received no pay and no support. The chapter in his taped memoirs which deals with the Ukraine in 1946 and 1947 and mentions starvation, cannibalism, and Stalin's refusal to help makes hair-raising reading. Even so, the picture is fleeting and partial; just a hint. *Khrushchev Remembers* (Boston, 1970), pp. 227-45.
3 The ballads "Kolkhoz 'Bolshevik'," in 1947 and "Spring in 'Pobeda'," by N. Gribachev as well as "Banner Over a Village Soviet" (1957), by A. Nedogonov remain unmatched. In prose, S. Babaevsky holds his own with a renowned conflictless novel *Cavalier of the Golden Star*, 1947–48. A cogent statement of disgust by the "unwashed cosmopolite" critic A. Schtein over similar saccharine prevarications is angrily quoted by K. Simonov in *Novyi mir*, No. 3, 1949, p. 191.
4 S. Krushinsky, "Altaiskii khleb" (Altai Bread), *Novyi mir*, No. 9, 1947, pp. 95-6.
5 A Subbotin, *Prostye lyudi* (Simple People) (Moscow, 1948), p. 8.
6 The use of the MTS had to be paid for by the kolkhoz at a high price.
7 I. Ryaboklyach, *Zolototysyachnik* (Moscow, 1949), p. 112.
8 A. Subbotin, op. cit., p. 64.
9 I. Ryaboklyach, op, cit., p. 64.

Stalinism in populist guise

10 The colonel, one of the few successful heroes, is a good guide through the maze of early postwar themes. He, therefore, surfaces in Part I, Chapter 1, and in Part III, Chapter 1.

11 P. Pavlenko, "Schaste" (Happiness), *Znamya*, No. 7, 1947, p. 112.

Near-populist Hamlet

12 *Pravda*, July 20 and 23, 1953.
13 V. Ovechkin, "Rayonnye budni" (District Doldrums), *Novyi mir*, No. 9, 1952, p. 210.
14 Who listens to whom, and in what direction the administrator's ear was to be turned, up or down, was debated far more openly after Stalin's death. Writers leaning toward populism felt safe enough to say this in 1956, though not before:

A good leader listens on both sides. The bad one is hard of hearing in one ear. What they order him from above, that he catches. But what is suggested to him from below, it doesn't even reach him. [V. Tendryakov, "Sasha otpravlyaetsya v put" (Sasha Sets Out), *Novyi mir*, No. 2, 1956, p. 39.]

15 Ovechkin continued his tales about Martynov in several installments after Stalin's death. At one point in his reformist zeal, Martynov fails. It was predictable that he would. It turns out that he exaggerates his conflict with Borzov, by the same token overdoing his commitment to the one kolkhoz manager, Openkin. The latter, meanwhile, ends up as not quite suitable for Big Deal partnership, for all his energy and know-how. The trouble lies, somewhat perversely, in the legacy he carries. His peasant roots are too strong. He is not flexible enough, and loyalty to his own community pulls him outside the power field of mutual accommodation with the regime. Martynov in the end loses his grip on operational strategy. As organizer, he fails to pay attention to the local cadres. Furthermore, he is in the end upstaged by a real populist, a formidable iconoclast and renowned Moscow scholar who renounces academic glory and wealth and glides down, of his own free will, into the people. He seeks the lowly post of MTS manager and salvages that ailing enterprise. Martynov has nothing as dramatic up his sleeve. V. Ovechkin, "V tom-zhe raione." (In the Same District), *Novyi mir*, No. 3, 1954.

The improbable agronomist

16 G. Nikolaeva, "Povest o direktore MTS i o glavnom agronome" (Tale About an MTS Manager and the Chief Agronomist), *Znamya*, No. 9, 1954, p. 15.
17 It was not until later that the ample unfolding of the theme of populism came. In a typical story of the interesting mid-sixties (Ya. Ilichev, "Zhivoe delo" (Vital Enterprise), *Zvezda*, No. 5, 1956), a distinguished professor of agriculture assumes the Tolstoyan legacy at the apex of his career. Revolted by the stupidity of central planning, he takes effective pity on a pauperized kolkhoz. At the loss of personal privileges and comforts, he leaves Moscow for good to become manager of that humble peasant community. He succeeds in helping them but only by violating party orders and by using his own unfettered initiative. The professor's courage and competence triumph to the cheer of the people and to the consternation of local functionaries. The author makes it clear upon whom destiny now smiled.

NEW TIDINGS

1   Yu. Nagibin, "Komarov," *Ogonyok*, No. 38, 1953, pp. 30-2.

POSTCRIPTUM: FROM FEAR TO ENVY

1   "It occurred to me that this man was, perhaps, in essence, the only true citizen of the state. It was precisely through his blood that the newness of the times flowed. He was strange through and through, with the strangeness of the epoch which was only half-realized as yet." Boris Pasternak, *Okhrannaya gramota* (Safe Conduct) (Leningrad, 1931), p. 128.

2   Mayakovsky's combat with meshchanstvo is one of the main themes in E. J. Brown's superb *Mayakovsky; A Poet in the Revolution* (Princeton, 1973).

3   V. Mayakovsky, "O dryani" (About Trash) *Biblioteka poeta*, vol. I (Moscow-Leningrad, 1963), p. 289. "Skoree/golovy kanareikam svernite/ chtob kommunizm/kanareikami ne byl pobit."

4   If a Western observer treats meshchanstvo with condescension, he should at least attempt to distinguish the different kinds of revulsion. Aesthetic intolerance, laced with snobbism, is one thing. Mourning over shattered hopes for a revolution that had promised to be just and liberating is another. In either case, the positive side of meshchanstvo should not be minimized. It manages to shelter the citizen somewhat even under catastrophic circumstances. For it strengthens the family nexus under all circumstances. It brings comfort. Even from the position that judges the Soviet system against its own ideals and myths, one can say that meshchanstvo, in the long run, is coupled with a war on poverty and with some effort to equalize wages.

5   A. Mezhirov, "Stanislava," *Den poezii* (Moscow, 1962), pp. 188-9.

6   One thinks of Solzhenitsyn's *Gulag Archipelago*, a book both revelatory and déjà vu, the latter characteristic being a summons to the reader to face what he has so long chosen only to half-know.

7   B. Akhmadulina, "Dozhd" (Rain), *Literaturnaya Gruziya*, No. 12, 1963, pp. 9-11.

8   A young poet pays sophisticated tribute to the eighteenth century's intellectual clarities by bowing to Derzhavin's saltcellar, "Friend of mushrooms and soups," sapphire blue, embraced by the finest filigree silver. A. Kushner, "Solonka" (Saltcellar), *Den poezii* (Leningrad, 1962), p. 127.

9   *Pravda*, September 21, 1958.

10 V. Lugovoi, "Okrainy" (Outskirts), *Molodaya gvardiya*, No. 4, 1964, p. 96.

11 Speech delivered on May 12, 1959 to the Writers Congress, *Tretii sezd pisatelei SSSR, Stenograficheskii otchot* (Moscow, 1959), p. 98.

Bibliographical Note

There is not much Western, still less Soviet, scholarship directly relevant to the subject of this book: values of Soviet society during the Stalin era. The major thrust of social science research has been directed toward the exploration of the twenties or the post-Stalin period. Writings on the Stalin era tend to be either general histories or biographies of Stalin. (Conquest, Tucker, Ulam, Hingley, Adams.) Although there is little that treats stalinist society from a vantage point comparable to that of this study, there is a vast literature on Soviet society, dealing mostly with poststalinism. On the other hand, a number of books and articles help with the background on which I have not dwelt in detail. It seems appropriate to point to focused, specialized books dealing with party apparatchiks and managers (in periods following the timespan of this book): Azrael, J. R. *Managerial Power and Soviet Politics* (Cambridge, Mass.: Harvard University Press, 1966); Granick, D. *The Red Executive, A Study of the Organization Man in Russian Industry* (New York: A Doubleday Anchor Book, 1961); Berliner, J. S. *Factory and Manager in the USSR* (Cambridge, Mass: Harvard University Press, 1957); Hough, J. F. *The Soviet Prefects, The Local Party Organs in Industrial Decision-Making* (Cambridge, Mass.: Harvard University Press, 1969); and to one general study which is lucid and durable, a classic published first in 1950 and reprinted with a new epilogue fifteen years later: Moore, B. Jr. *Soviet Politics – The Dilemma of Power, The Role of Ideas in Social Change* (New York: Harper Torch Books, 1965).

Aitov, N. A. "An Analysis of the Objective Prerequisites for Eliminating the Distinctions between the Working Class and the Peasantry" in G. V. Osipov (ed.) *Town, Country and People* (London: Tavistock Publications, 1969), pp. 120-39. (Soviet view.)

Alexandrov, G. F. "Bourgeois Theories of the 'Middle Class,'" in P. Hollander (ed.), *American and Soviet Society* (Englewood Cliffs, N.J.: Prentice-Hall, 1969), pp. 137-9. (Soviet view.)

Aleksandrova, V. *Literatura i zhizn, ocherki sovetskovo obshchestvennovo razvitiya* (Literature and Life, Essays on Soviet Social Development), sponsored by the Russian Institute of Columbia University (New York, 1969).

Aron, R. *Dix-huit Leçons sur la Société Industrielle* (Leçon XII, "Le Modèle Soviétique," pp. 234-52) (Paris: Gallimard, 1962).

Bialer, S. "... But Some Are More Equal Than Others," *Problems of Communism*, 9, No. 2 (March–April 1960), 40-50.

Bilinsky, J. "The Rulers and the Ruled," *Problems of Communism*, 16, No. 5, (September–October, 1967), 16-26.

Bottomore, T. B. *Classes in Modern Society* (New York: Pantheon Books, 1966).

Bullitt, M. M. "Toward a Marxist Theory of Aesthetics: The Development of Socialist Realism in the Soviet Union," *Russian Review*, 35, No. 1 (January 1976), 53-77.

Churchward, L. G. *The Soviet Intelligentsia, An Essay on the Social Structure and Roles of the Soviet Intelligentsia during the 1960's* (London: Routledge and Kegan Paul, 1973).

De George, R. T. *Soviet Ethics and Morality*. Chapter 6, "Moral Inculcation and Social Control," pp. 105-22, (Ann Arbor Paperbacks, 1969).

Djilas, M. *The New Class, An Analysis of the Communist System* (London: Allen and Unwin, 1966).

Dodge, N. T. *Women in the Soviet Economy* (Baltimore: Johns Hopkins University Press, 1966).

Feldmesser, R. A. "Social Status and Access to Higher Education," *Harvard Educational Review*, 27, No. 2 (Spring 1957), 92-106.

"Towards the Classless Society?" in R. Bendix and S. M. Lipset (eds.), *Class, Status, and Power* (London: Routledge and Kegan Paul, 1966), pp. 527-33.

"Function and Ideology in Soviet Social Stratification" in K. London (ed.), *The Soviet Union: A Half-Century of Communism* (Baltimore: Johns Hopkins University Press, 1968), pp. 183-222.

Field, M. G. "Workers (and Mothers): Soviet Women Today" in D. R. Brown (ed.), *Women in the Soviet Union* (New York: Teachers College Press, Columbia University, 1968), pp. 7-50.

Fischer, G. *The Soviet System and Modern Society* (Chapter 3, "The Social Origin of Executives," pp. 65-92) (New York: Atherton Press, 1968).

Gasiorowska, X. *Women in Soviet Fiction, 1917–1964* (Madison: Wisconsin University Press, 1968).

Gecys, C. "Social Stratification of Soviet Citizens," *Ukrainian Quarterly*, 27, No. 1 (Spring 1971), 69-76.

Giddens, A. *The Class Structure of Advanced Societies* (New York: Harper & Row, 1973).

Goldthorpe, J. H. "Social Stratification in Industrial Society," in Bendix and Lipset, pp. 648-59.

H. H., "Education and Social Mobility in the USSR," *Soviet Studies* 18, No. 1 (July 1966), 57-65.

Hollander, P. *Soviet and American Society, A Comparison*, Chapter 6, "Stratification and Styles of Life," pp. 202-37 (New York: Oxford University Press, 1973).

Inkeles, A. "Myth and Reality of Social Classes," in A. Inkeles and K. Geiger (eds.), *Soviet Society* (Boston: Houghton Mifflin, 1961), pp. 558-73.

Social Change in Soviet Russia, especially Part III, "Social Stratification," pp. 133-210 (Cambridge, Mass.: Harvard University Press, 1968).

Lane, D. *The End of Inequality? Stratification under State Socialism* (Baltimore: Penguin, 1971).

282   Bibliographical note

Madison, B. Q. *Social Welfare in the Soviet Union* (Stanford University Press, 1963).

Marshall, T. H. *Class, Citizenship, and Social Development*, part 2, "Social Class," pp. 71-257 (Garden City: Anchor Books, 1965).

Matthews, M. *Class and Society in Soviet Russia* (New York: Walker and Company, 1972).

Mehnert, K. *Der Sowjet-Mensch, 1929–1957* (Stuttgart: Deutsche Verlags-Anstalt, 1958).

Meissner, B. "The Power Elite and Intelligentsia in Soviet Society," in K. London, pp. 153-82.

Meissner, B. (ed.), *Social Change in the Soviet Union, Russia's Path Toward an Industrial Society* (University of Notre Dame Press, 1972).

Miller, S. M. "Comparative Social Mobility," *Current Sociology*, 9, No. 1 (1960), 1-62.

Miller, W. W. *Russians as People* (New York: E. P. Dutton and Co., 1961).

Newth, J. A. "Income Distribution in the USSR," *Soviet Studies*, 12, No. 2 (October 1960), 193-6.

Nogee, J. (ed.), *Man, State, and Society in the Soviet Union* (New York: Praeger, 1972).

Ossowski, S. *Class Structure in the Social Consciousness* (New York: Free Press, 1963).

Parkin, F. "Class Stratification in Socialist Societies," *British Journal of Sociology*, 20, No. 4 (December 1969), 355-74.

Class Inequality and Political Order, Social Stratification in Capitalist and Communist Societies (New York: Praeger, 1971).

van het Reve, K. *Het Geloof der Kameraden*, Chapter 6, "Klassen en Klassenstrijd," pp. 103-18 (Amsterdam: G. A. van Oorschot, 1970).

Shubkin, V. N. "Social Mobility and Choice of Occupation," in G. V. Osipov (ed.), *Industry and Labor in the USSR* (London: Tavistock Publications, 1966), pp. 86-98. (Soviet view.)

Simirenko, A. (ed.), *Soviet Sociology, Historical Antecedents and Current Appraisals* (Chicago: Quadrangle Books, 1960).

Skharatan, O. I. "The Social Structure of the Soviet Working Class," in P. Hollander (ed.), *American and Soviet Society*, pp. 144-50. (Soviet view.)

Vladimirov, L. *The Russians* (New York: Praeger, 1968).

Wädekin, K. E. "Zur Sozialschichtung der Sowjetgesellschaft," *Ost-Europa*, No. 5 (May 1965), 321-9.

"Soviet Rural Society, A Descriptive Stratification Analysis," *Soviet Studies*, 22, No. 4 (April 1971), 512-38.

Weselowski, W. "The Notions of Strata and Class in Socialist Society," in A. Beteille (ed.), *Social Inequality* (Baltimore: Penguin, 1969).

Yanowitch, M. "The Soviet Income Revolution," *Slavic Review*, 22, No. 4 (December 1963), 683-97.

Yanowitch, M. and N. T. Dodge, "The Social Evaluation of Occupations in the Soviet Union," *Slavic Review*, 28, No. 4 (December 1969), 619-44.

Yanowitch, M. and W. A. Fisher (eds.), *Social Stratification and Mobility in the USSR*, (New York: International Arts and Sciences Press, 1973).

Turning now to a stringently limited list of works on the development and politics of Soviet literature, in periods close to ours, it might similarly be best to point to those most germane to the themes of this study first: Brown, E. J. *The Proletarian Episode in Russian Literature, 1928–32*, (New York: Octagon Books, 1971); Ermolaev, H. *Soviet Literary Theories, 1917–1934, The Genesis of Socialist Realism* (Berkeley: University of California Press, 1963); Mathewson, R. *The Positive Hero in Russian Literature* (New York: Columbia University Press, 1958); Tertz, A. *On Socialist Realism* (New York: Pantheon Books, 1969); and Vaughn, J. C. *Soviet Socialist Realism, Origins and Theory* (New York: St. Martin's Press, 1973).

Brown, E. J. *Russian Literature since the Revolution* (New York: Collier Books, 1969).

Farrell, R. (ed.), *The Soviet Censorship* (Munich: Institute for the Study of the USSR, 1971).

Gibian, G. *Interval of Freedom, Soviet Literature during the Thaw, 1954–1957* (Minneapolis: University of Minnesota Press, 1960).

Hayward, M. "The Struggle Goes On," in Brumberg, A. (ed.), *Russia Under Khrushchev*, pp. 375-407 (New York: Praeger Paperbacks, 1963).

"The Decline of Socialist Realism," *Survey*, 18, No. 1 (1972), 73-97.

and L. Labedz (eds.), *Literature and Revolution in Soviet Russia, 1917–62* (London: Oxford University Press, 1963).

Maguire, R. *Red Virgin Soil, Soviet Literature in the 1920's* Princeton University Press, 1968).

Rogers, T. F. *Superfluous Men and the Post-Stalin 'Thaw': the Alienated Hero in Soviet Prose During the Decade 1953–1963* (The Hague and Paris: Mouton, 1972).

Steininger, A. *Literatur und Politik in der Sowjetunion nach Stalins Tod* (Wiesbaden: Otto Harrasowitz, 1965).

Struve, G. *Russian Literature under Lenin and Stalin, 1917–1953* (Norman: University of Oklahoma Press, 1971).

Swayze, H. *Political Control of Literature in the USSR, 1946–1959* (Cambridge, Mass.: Harvard University Press, 1962).

Twarog, L. "Literary Censorship in Russia and the Soviet Union," in L. B. Blair (ed.), *Essays on Russian Intellectual History*, pp. 98-123 (Austin: University of Texas Press, 1971).

Vickery, W. N. *The Cult of Optimism, Political and Ideological Problems of Recent Soviet Literature* (Bloomington: Indiana University Press, 1963).

For the understanding of general ideas underlying the comparative study of high and low culture, the following books are helpful:

Duncan, H. *Language and Literature in Society* (University of Chicago Press, 1953).

Gans, H. *Popular Culture and High Culture, An Analysis and Evaluation of Taste* (New York: Basic Books, 1974).

Klapp, O. E. *Heroes, Villains, and Fools. The Changing American Character* (Englewood Cliffs, N.J.: Prentice-Hall, 1962).

Lowenthal, L. *Literature, Popular Culture, and Society* (Englewood Cliffs, N.J.: Prentice-Hall, 1961).

Index

The Author

Vera Sandomirsky Dunham, Professor of Russian Literature, Emerita, was born in Moscow, educated in Europe, and in 1940 came to the United States. She worked for the Office of Strategic Services (OSS) during World War II and thereafter taught at Wayne State University, the University of Michigan, the City University of New York, and Columbia University. She is now Adjunct Professor and an Associate of the Harriman Institute for Advanced Study of the Soviet Union at Columbia University.

Library of Congress Cataloging-in-Publication Data
Dunham, Vera Sandomirsky, 1912–
In Stalin's time : middleclass values in Soviet fiction / Vera S. Dunham ;
with new introduction by Richard Sheldon. – Enl. and updated ed.
p. cm. – (Studies of the Harriman Institute, Columbia University)
Includes bibliographical references and index.
ISBN 0–8223–1085–6
1. Soviet fiction – History and criticism. 2. Russian fiction –
20th century – History and criticism. 3. Literature and state –
Soviet Union. 4. Communism and literature. 5. Middle classes –
Soviet Union. 6. Soviet Union – Politics and government – 1936–1953.
7. Social values in literature. I. Title. II. Series: Studies of the
Harriman Institute.
PG3095.D8 1990
891.73'4209355 – dc20   90–42414   CIP

Soviet studies/Literary studies

This new edition of *In Stalin's Time* brings back into print Vera S. Dunham's 1976 landmark study of popular fiction in the Soviet Union during the Stalinist regime. It is updated with a new introduction by Richard Sheldon, professor of Russian language and literature at Dartmouth College. Both descriptive and analytical, Dunham's complex picture of "high totalitarianism" both reveals insights into the details of Soviet life and illuminates important theoretical questions about the role of literature in the political structure of Soviet society.

In praise of the first edition

"No one could have predicted that a book which investigates in scholarly detail the official literary product of Stalin's time would turn out to be—as this work is—a literary gem. . . . The book is a *tour de force* of delightful complexity."—*Russian Review*

"This stunning book, by a literary scholar, is surely one of the finest studies of Soviet Russian society ever to appear. . . . [Dunham's] work is first-class literary sociology. What is simply breathtaking about the book is Dunham's picture of Soviet culture-in-becoming during the late Stalin years."—*American Journal of Sociology*

"Professor Dunham is not the first to use Soviet literature for insights into *la vie Sovietique*. . . . Yet no one else . . . has done it with as much sagacity, humor, and verve as Dunham. Nor, to my knowledge, has anyone dealt so perceptively with the function of popular literature in the USSR."—*Dissent*

Vera S. Dunham is Professor of Soviet Literature Emerita at Columbia University, and Adjunct Professor and Associate of the Harriman Institute for the Advanced Study of the Soviet Union.

Studies of the Harriman Institute
Duke University Press
6697 College Station
Durham, North Carolina 27708
ISBN 0-8223-1085-6

36   324TF   BRP   4621
08/92   24-950-00